The Best

Pub Quiz

Book EVER!

First published in 1996 by
Carlton Books Limited
20 Mortimer Street
London W1T 3JW
Second edition published in 2006

Copyright © 1996, 2006 Carlton Books Limited

All rights reserved. No part of this publication may be reproduced,
stored in a retrieval system, or transmitted, in any form, or by any
means, electronic, mechanical, photocopying, recording or otherwise,
without the prior permission of the publishers.

This book is sold subject to the condition that it shall not, by way of
trade or otherwise, be lent, resold, hired out or otherwise circulated
without the publisher's prior written consent in any form of cover
or binding other than that in which it is published and without a
similar condition including this condition being imposed upon the
subsequent purchaser.

ISBN (13): 978-184442-180-0
ISBN (10): 1-84442-180-5

Printed and bound in Great Britain

Questions set by The Puzzle House

The Best Pub Quiz Book EVER!

SECOND EDITION

CARLTON
BOOKS

Contents

Introduction

Over the past decade snugs and lounges in pubs the length and breadth of the country have become, if not seats of learning at least seats of intellect. Which makes a change from seats of worn leatherette (although these still prevail in some areas). The pub quiz has transformed the bar into an arena of knowledge where beery brethren battle to the final bell. The format is simple: some friends, acquaintances, even complete strangers, will do, a questioner, some paper, a collection of ragged Biros and a surfeit of beer and questions are all that is needed to create the perfect evening's entertainment. Wits are challenged, heads are huddled and patience is tested as teams attempt to outdo each other in their show of trivia retention. At these events you will learn that no fact is too small, no sport star too obscure and no war too insignificant to test the pub crowd's grey matter. In fact, the more obscure and wide-ranging the questions the greater the chance of involving the entire barroom – nothing will gain the pub idiot greater respect than showing that they have the entire cast, storyline and signature tune of "Emergency Ward 10" lodged in their head, except perhaps their switching from slip-ons to lace-ups. So take heart, and a copy of *The Best Pub Quiz Book Ever!* to the boozer and have a few warm up sessions and see if you can't organize your own pub quiz. You know it makes sense; it's the only way you'll know all the answers.

The main aim of *The Best Pub Quiz Book Ever!* is to entertain, so it is important that you retain a sense of humour and good sportsmanship as you play along, whether you are testing friends at home or setting a quiz for your local hostelry. That aside, you also have to ensure that you are fully in control of your questions and players: remain calm, speak in a steady voice and be constantly unflapped when challenged by any of the more heavily imbibed, as indeed you will be.

If the locals do get testy your best bet is to head for the door while throwing beer nuts in the air to confuse them, though this should happen in only the roughest pubs or on outings with the extended family – in which case you should attempt to rescue your spouse, if you can do so without spilling your drink and it isn't them causing the trouble.

The Best Pub Quiz Book Ever! is divided into three sections of Easy, Medium and Hard questions, which are all subdivided by specialist and pot-luck rounds. The former can be chosen either to help or hinder your players; giving Easy sports questions to the literature fanatics is bound to reveal some interesting answers but it is possibly more challenging to tailor your questions so that the experts receive the brain-wracking Hard questions and the novice the stupefyingly simple Easy questions. Nothing hurts a fanatic more than being beaten on their specialist subject and the division of questions gives you the chance to employ a handicap system. Other handicap systems will also become apparent as you continue as quiz master. The team that wins the Sunday-afternoon quiz will doubtless fail when it comes to Sunday night, although if you want to set a quiz on Friday night you should check pupil dilation first, as on that evening of great relaxation you may find your teams asleep or brawling before calling the whole thing quits and joining them in a drink ... or three.

In the interest of further clarification there follows a brief run-down of each section:

Easy

In this primary round the main objective is to keep breathing, these questions are so easy that even the most docile pub idiot could gurgle his way through them in the time it takes to down a pint and still have time left to knock over the stack of pennies on the bar.

Medium

On your toes people, things are getting tricky. By now even the ringers on the out-of-towners' team will be sweating. These questions make for a challenge, but you are bound to get the odd smug bar steward who will fancy his chances, for which you should continue on to section three.

Hard

Ask a full thirty of these questions and only the shrill wail of the pub cat fighting in the yard will be heard, brows will be furrowed, glances exchanged and beer stared into. To set an entire quiz using just these questions is a form of evil so dark-hearted Fu Manchu would blanch.

All that is left to say is good luck with your testing and if you can't keep your spirits up at least try to keep them down.

The Easy Questions

If you think that Louis Armstrong was the first man on the moon or that Uri Geller was the first man in space then you will no doubt struggle through the next few questions terribly. For the rest of us though these are the EASY questions, so called because if the quizzee falters on these they are either three sheets to the wind or far too young to be in the pub – either state rendering them toddling buffoons whose social graces will equal their breadth of knowledge. So beware their flailing arms as you attempt to collect the answers.

These questions are perfect when used in the first round of an open entry quiz as they lull everyone into a false sense of security, although you must ensure that contestants don't shout answers out, which creates a problematic precedent for the later, harder questions. Another way of placing these questions is to dot them about throughout the quiz, thus making sure that on every team everyone should know the answer to at least one question despite their age.

If you are running a league quiz then some of your team members may heap derision on such obvious questions, but don't worry: even the cleverest quiz team member can come a cropper, as was noted in a championship final when a contestant was asked to name the continents. He deliberated before eventually beaming out the answer, "A, E, I, O, U!"

Quiz 1 | Pot-Luck 1

Answers – page 11

1 What is the highest number used in a Sudoku puzzle?
2 What is the term for a positive electrode?
3 In "Last of the Summer Wine" what was Nora's husband called?
4 Which swimming stroke is named after an insect?
5 Which English queen has the same name as a type of plum?
6 Which Rovers does veteran cartoon character Roy play for?
7 How many dots are used in each letter in the Braille system?
8 Who won the Oscar for best actor in both 1993 and 1994?
9 What is a female deer called?
10 What does the letter B stand for in an ASBO?
11 What can be an island, a sweater or a potato?
12 What unit is used to measure horses?
13 Who is Reg Dwight better known as?
14 Who provided Aslan's voice in the 2005 movie of "The Lion, the Witch and the Wardrobe"?
15 Which Eamonn left the GMTV sofa in the summer of 2005?
16 How many tenpin bowling skittles need knocking down for a strike?
17 How is 77 represented in Roman numerals?
18 Who is the patron saint of music?
19 What are birds of a feather said to do?
20 "Kiss Me Kate" is a musical version of which play by Shakespeare?
21 The single "Papa Don't Preach" came from which Madonna album?
22 Betz cells are found in which part of the body?
23 What is the only bird that can hover in the air and also fly backwards?
24 Who earned the nickname "Slow-hand"?
25 In the Bible who goes after Mark and before John?
26 Which country does opera singer Pavarotti come from?
27 Which is the third largest of the Channel Islands?
28 Who was Liverpool's skipper in the 2005 European Champions League triumph?
29 In which Puccini opera does Mimi appear?
30 How many sides has an octagon?

Answers | Pot-Luck 2 (see Quiz 3)

1 Gregorian. 2 Guitar. 3 Portsmouth. 4 Katrina. 5 Seven. 6 Rome. 7 Goat. 8 25. 9 John Sullivan. 10 Four. 11 Australia. 12 Cher. 13 Waterloo. 14 The Diddymen. 15 Thursday. 16 Kevin Pietersen. 17 Lilliput. 18 Dish. 19 Aardvark. 20 Seven. 21 Dirty. 22 George Best. 23 Siesta. 24 Edgar Allan Poe. 25 One minute. 26 Harrow. 27 M. 28 Badger. 29 Madonna. 30 Fernando Alonso.

Quiz 2 Sport: David Beckham Answers – page 12

1 Which shirt number was linked with David Beckham at Man Utd?

2 In which area of London was David born?

3 Who was Man Utd boss when Beckham broke into Man Utd's team?

4 Beckham was first sent off for England in 1998, against which country?

5 What was wife Victoria's nickname in the Spice Girls?

6 Is Beckham's middle name Alex, Edward or Joseph?

7 The Beckham's first son was named after an area of which American city?

8 David's autobiography was called "My..." what?

9 Which Beckham baby shares a name with a Shakespeare character?

10 What was the second country in which Beckham played domestic football?

11 How many players before Beckham had been sent off twice playing for England?

12 What was Mrs Beckham's original surname?

13 Which TV soccer pundit Alan got it hopelessly wrong about Man Utd "kids" not winning anything?

14 What was the usual colour of the shorts during Beckham's Man Utd days?

15 Who are Ted and Sandra in relation to David?

16 Which country beginning with a "C" did Becks score against in France '98?

17 Victoria and David married at a castle in which country?

18 Which England soccer boss gave Beckham the captaincy?

19 Young Beckham was part of a side known as Fergie's what?

20 What was the nickname of the Beckhams' palatial home in Hertfordshire?

21 Beckham was sent off a second time for England against which country?

22 What was David's squad number at Real Madrid – 13, 23 or 43?

23 Against which Premiership side did David score from the half-way line in the 1996/7 season?

24 In which major 2002 sporting opening ceremony was David involved?

25 Beckham's transfer fee moving to Real Madrid – £10m, £15m or £25m?

26 Which team ended Beckham's and England's World Cup hopes in 2002?

27 Why was the game against Getafe on 3 December 2005 significant for Beckham?

28 Which English international Michael was with Becks at Real Madrid?

29 Which Englishman was England boss when Becks was first capped?

30 Who is the older – David or Victoria Beckham?

Answers | I'm a Celebrity ... *(see Quiz 4)*

1 Carol Thatcher. 2 Will Young. 3 Girls Aloud. 4 Strictly Come Dancing. 5 Aled Jones. 6 Hear'Say. 7 David Dickinson. 8 Chicago. 9 Nell McAndrew. 10 Sugar. 11 Australia. 12 Prince William's. 13 Louis Walsh. 14 Dragon's Den. 15 Will Young. 16 Pasquale. 17 Llewelyn Bowen. 18 Properties. 19 Hancock. 20 The Sun. 21 Jill Halfpenny. 22 Big Brother. 23 Sharon Osbourne. 24 Overhaul your wardrobe. 25 Kidman. 26 Ali G. 27 The Pussycat Dolls. 28 Hurley. 29 Colin Jackson. 30 Ant & Dec.

1 Which type of calendar is used today in the western world?

2 What instrument can be bass, electric or Spanish?

3 Think about this – which club did Harry Redknapp manage first – Portsmouth or Southampton?

4 Which female-named hurricane devastated New Orleans in September 2005?

5 What do the numbers add up to on the opposite sides of a dice?

6 Which city is said to have been founded by Romulus and Remus?

7 In the zodiac, which animal is linked with Capricorn?

8 How many years are involved in a silver anniversary?

9 Who scripted "Only Fools and Horses"?

10 In music, how many quavers equal a minim?

11 Which country originated the term "plonk" for wine?

12 How did Cherilyn Sarkasian LaPierre become better known?

13 What was the final battle that Napoleon fought in?

14 Which men used to perform with Ken Dodd?

15 On which day are British elections held?

16 Which member of the 2005 Ashes-winning side sported a diamond earring and a two-colour hairstyle?

17 What was the name of the land where Gulliver met the Little People?

18 In the nursery rhyme, who ran away with the spoon?

19 Which animal's name comes first in the dictionary?

20 How many sides has a 20-pence piece?

21 What is Den's nickname in "EastEnders"?

22 In the 1960s which footballer was called "The Fifth Beatle"?

23 In Spain what is the word for an afternoon nap?

24 Who wrote "The Pit and the Pendulum"?

25 How long is there between rounds in boxing?

26 Which public school did Sir Winston Churchill go to?

27 What is the thirteenth letter of the English alphabet?

28 Which is the largest land carnivore in Britain?

29 Who made the album "Confessions on a Dance Floor"?

30 Which Fernando became the youngest F1 World Champion in 2005?

Answers | Pot-Luck 1 *(see Quiz 1)*

1 9. 2 Anode. 3 Wally. 4 Butterfly. 5 Victoria. 6 Melchester. 7 Six. 8 Tom Hanks. 9 Doe. 10 Behaviour. 11 Jersey. 12 Hands. 13 Elton John. 14 Liam Neeson. 15 Eamonn Holmes. 16 Ten. 17 LXXVII. 18 St Cecilia. 19 Flock together. 20 The Taming of the Shrew. 21 True Blue. 22 The brain. 23 Hummingbird. 24 Eric Clapton. 25 Luke. 26 Italy. 27 Alderney. 28 Steven Gerrard. 29 La Bohème. 30 Eight.

1 Which PM's daughter won the 2005 "I'm a Celebrity ... Get Me Out of Here"?
2 Who beat Gareth Gates to win "Pop Idol"?
3 Who were "Popstars: The Rivals" winners, Girls Aloud or Atomic Kitten?
4 It "Takes Two" is the follow-up programme about which show?
5 Which Welsh singer, famous for "Walking in the Air" appeared on "Strictly Come Dancing"?
6 Myleene Klass was part of which band?
7 Which antiques celebrity coined the phrase "cheap as chips" on TV?
8 Which musical about gangsters did Pop Idol's Darius Danesh join in 2005?
9 How is model Tracey Jane McAndrew better known?
10 Which entrepreneur Alan appeared in "The Apprentice"?
11 In which country was the third series of "I'm a Celebrity" held?
12 Kate Middleton was whose girlfriend when they graduated from St Andrews University in 2005?
13 Which juror walked out of "The X Factor" in autumn 2005?
14 Which was the reality TV show, "Dragon's Den" or "Lion's Den"?
15 Which "Pop Idol" winner appeared with Judi Dench in "Mrs Henderson Presents"?
16 Which comedian Joe has been voted King of the Jungle?
17 Which Lawrence was a star of "Changing Rooms"?
18 Does Sarah Beeny present programmes on properties or food?
19 Which Sheila, widow of John Thaw, appeared in "Grumpy Old Women"?
20 Rebekah Wade, Mrs Ross Kemp, edited which paper when they made front-page news concerning assault allegations?
21 Which Jill won "Strictly Come Dancing" in December 2004?
22 Which reality TV series had a family member's name in its title?
23 Which "X Factor" celebrity is married to Ozzy Osbourne?
24 Do Trinny and Susannah overhaul your wardrobe or clean your house?
25 Which actress Nicole advertised Omega watches?
26 Which Ali was created by Sacha Baron Cohen?
27 Which girl band is fronted by Carmen Electra?
28 Which Elizabeth did Gwyneth Paltrow replace as the face of Estee Lauder?
29 Which sprint hurdler was a 2005 "Strictly Come Dancing" contestant?
30 Which duo were booked to interview Princes Charles, William and Harry to mark the 30th anniversary of the Prince's Trust?

Answers | David Beckham *(see Quiz 2)*

1 No 7. 2 Leytonstone. 3 Alex Ferguson. 4 Argentina. 5 Posh Spice. 6 Joseph. 7 New York (Brooklyn). 8 My Side. 9 Romeo. 10 Spain. 11 None. 12 Adams. 13 Hansen. 14 White. 15 Parents. 16 Colombia. 17 Ireland. 18 Sven Goran Eriksson. 19 Fledglings. 20 Beckingham Palace. 21 Austria. 22 No 23. 23 Wimbledon. 24 Commonwealth Games. 25 £25m. 26 Brazil. 27 He was sent off. 28 Michael Owen. 29 Glenn Hoddle. 30 Victoria.

1 In "EastEnders" what is the name of Den Watts' widow?
2 How many children were there in Enid Blyton's Famous Five?
3 Kerry Katona found fame in which all-girl band?
4 What kind of animal was Phillip Schofield's puppet pal Gordon?
5 What is the stage name of Harry Webb?
6 Which Sadie was married to Jude Law?
7 Which film gave Jack Nicholson his first Oscar?
8 Which season do Americans call the Fall?
9 The fabled bird the griffin had the head of which real bird?
10 On which Common would you find the Wombles?
11 Whose catchphrase is, "Nice to see, to see you nice"?
12 Who was the first Labour MP?
13 Whom did Boris Yeltsin make his Prime Minister in 1999?
14 Which country does Bryan Adams come from?
15 Who was known as the lady with the lamp?
16 What is the plural of the word sheep?
17 In golf, who won the British Open in 2005?
18 What is the symbol for the Gemini sign of the zodiac?
19 Where in a horse is the coffin joint?
20 What word can go before cheese, plant and roll?
21 Which Simon and Garfunkel song features the words "Jesus loves you more than you can say"?
22 Which "famous first" is attributed to asparagus in Britain?
23 Which substance is most used for pencil lead?
24 To ten years either way, in which year did Charles Dickens die?
25 Which long-running radio programme was devised by Roy Plomley?
26 Which Lloyd Webber musical does the song "Memory" come from?
27 What drink does pear juice make?
28 What name can be a lettuce or a mass of floating frozen water?
29 Which vegetable did Sir Walter Raleigh bring to England?
30 In the strip cartoon, what is the name of Snoopy's brother?

Answers | Pot-Luck 4 *(see Quiz 7)*

1 Kipps. 2 Michael Vaughan. 3 Union. 4 Condoleezza Rice. 5 Gilbert and Sullivan. 6 Lucy Locket. 7 Edward Fox. 8 Blue. 9 Right. 10 Bruno Tonioli. 11 The General Lee. 12 Desdemona. 13 15. 14 Motor racing. 15 Japan. 16 Turkey. 17 The Doors. 18 12. 19 France. 20 Maria Callas. 21 Quarto. 22 Even numbers. 23 Two. 24 Hangman. 25 Kidneys. 26 Knot garden. 27 Billy J. Kramer. 28 17th. 29 Greta Garbo. 30 None.

1 What was the name of Bill Haley's backing group?
2 Which shoes did Elvis warn you not to step on in 1956?
3 What kind of doll was Cliff Richard's first No 1?
4 Which blonde film star sang about her Secret Love?
5 Where was the Doggie when Lita Roza asked how much it was?
6 What relation to each other were Don and Phil Everly?
7 Where were the tulips from, which Max Bygraves sang about?
8 According to Connie Francis where did she find lipstick?
9 Whom did the Beverley Sisters see kissing Santa Claus?
10 How were the Balls of Fire described by Jerry Lee Lewis?
11 According to Frank Sinatra how do Love and Marriage go together?
12 Which Buddy was killed in a plane crash?
13 What did Perry Como ask you to catch and put in your pocket?
14 Which Biblical Garden did Frankie Vaughan sing about?
15 Who sang "Oh Carol" about fellow singer/songwriter Carole King?
16 Who's Boy Child did Harry Belafonte sing about in 1958?
17 Which line follows "Be Bop A Lula" at the start of the Gene Vincent hit?
18 Which 1950s pop star is Kim Wilde's father?
19 Who had hits with "When I Fall In Love" and "Stardust"?
20 Where did the Lace which the Big Bopper sang about come from?
21 Who asked "What do you want, if you don't want money"?
22 Where did Pat Boone write his Love Letters?
23 Which late soul singer had a hit with "Reet Petite" in 1957?
24 How many steps are there to heaven?
25 What Blues ain't there no cure for, according to Eddie Cochran?
26 In the song title, what did Shirley Bassey ask her Honey Honey to do?
27 Which record machine appeared in coffee bars in the 1950s?
28 According to Lonnie Donegan what might lose its flavour on the bedpost overnight?
29 How many tons did Tennessee Ernie Ford sing about?
30 According to the Platters what gets in your eyes?

Answers   The Royal Family *(see Quiz 8)*

1 One. 2 Prince Charles. 3 Duchess. 4 France. 5 Army. 6 Balmoral. 7 Philip. 8 Andrew. 9 Princess Anne. 10 Two. 11 Eton. 12 Corgi. 13 Mrs Wallis Simpson. 14 Victoria. 15 Buckingham Palace. 16 Six. 17 Saturday. 18 Mark Phillips. 19 Prince Andrew, Duke of York. 20 Prince Edward. 21 Golden Jubilee. 22 Her sister (Princess Margaret). 23 Windsor. 24 Henry. 25 Princess Anne. 26 Prince Edward. 27 Cornwall. 28 Duke of Windsor. 29 Sandringham. 30 Horsewoman.

Quiz 7 Pot-Luck 4

Answers – page 13

1 "Half a Sixpence" is based on which story by H. G. Wells?
2 Who captained England to their Ashes win in 2005?
3 Soyuz was the name of a Russian spacecraft, but what does the name mean?
4 Which lady became George W. Bush's Secretary of State in his second term of office?
5 Who wrote the Savoy operas?
6 Who lost her pocket?
7 In the film "The Day of the Jackal", who played the Jackal?
8 What colour is a sapphire?
9 Does Elizabeth II face to the left or right on a British coin?
10 Which Bruno is on the "Strictly Come Dancing" panel of judges?
11 What did Bo and Luke Duke call their car?
12 In Shakespeare's "Othello", who is the female lead?
13 In the pirate song, how many men were on the dead man's chest?
14 Mike Hawthorne was the first Briton to win the World Championship in which sport?
15 Venetian blinds originated in which country?
16 A poult is the young of which creature?
17 Which group recorded the original of "Light My Fire"?
18 In an English trial, how many people sit on the jury?
19 Marcel Desailly was a World Cup winner playing for which country?
20 Which great soprano earned the name of "La Divina"?
21 What measure of paper is 8 by 10 inches?
22 On a standard roulette wheel which numbers appear on the black?
23 What number is dos in Spanish?
24 In which game do you draw part of a gallows for every wrong answer?
25 Bright's disease affects which organs of the body?
26 What name is given to a garden with geometrically arranged beds and small hedges?
27 Who sang with the Dakotas?
28 In which century was 1658?
29 Which actress said, "I want to be alone"?
30 How many kings of England have been called Philip?

| **Answers** | Pot-Luck 3 *(see Quiz 5)* |

1 Chrissie. 2 Four – one was a dog. 3 Atomic Kitten. 4 Gopher. 5 Cliff Richard. 6 Frost. 7 One Flew Over the Cuckoo's Nest. 8 Autumn. 9 Eagle. 10 Wimbledon. 11 Bruce Forsyth. 12 Keir Hardie. 13 Vladimir Putin. 14 Canada. 15 Florence Nightingale. 16 Sheep. 17 Tiger Woods. 18 Twins. 19 Foot. 20 Swiss. 21 Mrs Robinson. 22 First frozen food. 23 Graphite. 24 1870. 25 Desert Island Discs. 26 Cats. 27 Perry. 28 Iceberg. 29 Potato. 30 Spike.

1 How many daughters does Queen Elizabeth II have?
2 Who is the father of Princes William and Harry?
3 Did Camilla Parker Bowles use the title Duchess or Princess after she married Prince Charles?
4 In which country did Princess Diana tragically meet her death?
5 Did Prince Harry join the Navy or the Army after his gap year?
6 What is the Queen's residence in Scotland called?
7 Which Prince is Duke of Edinburgh?
8 Which Prince was a helicopter pilot in the Falklands War?
9 Who is the Princess Royal?
10 How many children does the Duchess of Cornwall have?
11 Which school did Prince William start at in 1995?
12 What is the Queen's favourite breed of dog?
13 What was the name of the woman for whom Edward VIII abdicated?
14 Which Queen was married to Prince Albert?
15 What is the name of the Queen's London residence?
16 How many English kings have been called George?
17 On what day of the week did Charles and Camilla marry?
18 What was Princess Anne's first husband called?
19 Who is the father of Princesses Beatrice and Eugenie?
20 Who is Queen Elizabeth II's youngest son?
21 Which Jubilee did the Queen celebrate in 2002?
22 In 2002, the Queen lost her mother and which other close relative?
23 Which castle was badly damaged by fire in 1992?
24 What is Prince Harry's proper first name?
25 Which Royal survived a kidnap attempt in 1974?
26 Which son of the Queen has a daughter called Louise?
27 Prince Charles is Duke of which county of southwest England?
28 Which title did Edward VIII take after he abdicated?
29 What is the name of the Queen's residence in Norfolk?
30 Is the Queen's granddaughter Zara Phillips an accomplished horsewoman or a top tennis player?

Answers | Pop: Sounds Of The 50s *(see Quiz 6)*

1 The Comets. 2 Blue Suede. 2 Livin'. 4 Doris Day. 5 In the Window. 6 Brothers. 7 Amsterdam. 8 On Your Collar. 9 Mommy. 10 Great. 11 Like a Horse and Carriage. 12 Holly. 12 A Falling Star. 14 Eden. 15 Neil Sedaka. 16 Mary's. 17 She's My Baby. 18 Marty Wilde. 19 Nat King Cole. 20 Chantilly. 21 Adam Faith. 22 In the Sand. 23 Jackie Wilson. 24 Three. 25 Summertime. 26 Kiss Me. 27 Jukebox. 28 Chewing Gum. 29 16. 30 Smoke.

1 Which cabinet minister resigned following visa allegations in 2004?

2 How many stomachs has a cow?

3 With which swimming stroke do races begin in the water?

4 What have you been doing if you finish by casting off?

5 How is the Roman city of Verulamium known today?

6 Roy Jenkins was a founder of which political party?

7 What does Susan Hampshire suffer from?

8 In which sport did Michael Phelps win gold at the Athens Olympics in 2004?

9 Which city in the world has the largest population?

10 Whose ship was the first to sail round the world?

11 In music hall, who was the "Prime Minister of Mirth"?

12 Who composed "The Flight of the Bumble Bee"?

13 "Freedom" was the first UK top ten hit for which Robbie?

14 What is the full name of BBC Radio 5?

15 What was invented by Lewis Waterman in the 1880s?

16 Which illustrator was famous for detailed drawings of weird and wonderful mechanical inventions?

17 Which US President was nicknamed "The Comeback Kid"?

18 Following the 1963 Peerage Act, who was the first peer to disclaim his title?

19 What was "Prisoner: Cell Block H" originally called?

20 Which instrument usually has 47 strings?

21 What is the name of Dennis the Menace's dog?

22 For over 30 years, which tobacco company gave its name to a football yearbook?

23 Who wrote "Help Me Make It Through the Night"?

24 Moving anti-clockwise on a dartboard what is the number next to 4?

25 Who created the detective Paul Temple?

26 Who pricked her finger on a spinning wheel and slept for 100 years?

27 Who became Earl of Stockton on his 90th birthday?

28 Which traffic light follows green?

29 In "My Friend Flicka" who or what was Flicka?

30 Which is the first month of the year to have exactly 30 days?

Answers | Pot-Luck 6 *(see Quiz 11)*

1 Angela Merkel. 2 Two. 24 Greek, 26 English. 3 Pancakes. 4 Leaves. 5 Perseus. 6 Noah. 7 John Peel. 8 John Curry. 9 1986. 10 Eight. 11 First test tube baby. 12 Excalibur (also referred to as Caliburn). 13 Russell Harty. 14 Desert island. 15 Tongue. 16 Richard Nixon. 17 Quentin Crisp. 18 Bob Hope. 19 Harry Palmer. 20 Private Eye. 21 Celine Dion. 22 Roker Park. 23 West Germany. 24 88. 25 Eight. 26 Pavement. 27 Crocodile. 28 Harold Pinter. 29 Fifty years. 30 Three.

1 The Severn, the Trent and the Ouse are all what?
2 In which county are all ten of England's highest peaks?
3 Which is the second largest city in England?
4 Which London station was named after a long-reigning Queen?
5 In which county are the seaside resorts of Clacton and Southend?
6 Leeds Castle is in Kent. Where is Leeds?
7 Which seaside resort is famous for its Tower and its Golden Mile?
8 What might you see at Regent's Park, Chester and Whipsnade?
9 What is the name of the famous cathedral in York?
10 Which is the largest island in England?
11 What did Sunderland become in 1992 which Manchester, Liverpool and Birmingham became in the 19th century?
12 Which river runs through London?
13 Which is further north, Southport or Northampton?
14 Which stretch of water divides England and France?
15 What do the letters NEC stand for?
16 What is the area around Stoke-on-Trent known as?
17 Which northern city is served by Ringway airport?
18 Which motorway starts south of Birmingham and goes northwest towards Scotland?
19 Which part of the country would a Geordie come from?
20 Near which large city would you find the Wirral?
21 Which two cities are the home of England's two oldest universities?
22 Which range of northern hills is called the backbone of England?
23 Which moorland area of southwest Devon is the site of a high-security prison?
24 What were Dagenham, Luton and Cowley famous for producing?
25 Where would a Manx person come from?
26 Which famous stones can be seen on Salisbury Plain?
27 Whose birthplace might you be visiting in Stratford-on-Avon?
28 In which county is the English terminal of the Channel Tunnel?
29 How many square miles is the City of London?
30 Which was England's smallest county before the 1974 changes?

Answers | 40s and 50s Films *(see Quiz 12)*

1 Bambi. 2 80 days. 3 Over the River Kwai. 4 White Christmas. 5 Tramp. 6 Ben Hur. 7 Fantasia. 8 Gone with the Wind. 9 Bob Hope. 10 Casablanca. 11 Laurence Olivier. 12 Brief Encounter. 13 Hitchcock. 14 Welles. 15 Alec Guinness. 16 Ealing Comedies. 17 In the Rain. 18 Hot. 19 Genevieve. 20 James Dean. 21 Grace Kelly. 22 Brigitte Bardot. 23 Ten. 24 At the Top. 25 Elizabeth Taylor. 26 Rogers. 27 Brando. 28 Arsenic. 29 Love. 30 Eternity.

1 Which lady replaced Gerhard Schroeder as German Chancellor?
2 How many more letters are there in the English than the Greek alphabet?
3 Which food item is used in an annual race at Olney?
4 Which part of the mint plant is used to make mint sauce?
5 In legend, who slew the gorgon Medusa?
6 Who had sons called Ham, Shem and Japheth?
7 Which former Radio 1 DJ had a commemorative day on 12th October 2005?
8 Which British Olympic gold ice skating medallist died in 1995?
9 When did Halley's Comet last appear?
10 How many legs has a lobster?
11 Louise Brown will always hold which famous first?
12 What was the name of King Arthur's sword?
13 Who on TV often used the phrase "you are, are you not..."?
14 On the radio where are you sent with eight records of your choice?
15 Which part of its body does a snake use to detect noise?
16 Who was the first American president to resign from office?
17 In "The Naked Civil Servant" whom did John Hurt portray?
18 "Thanks for the Memory" was the theme song of which comedian?
19 Whom did Michael Caine play in "The Ipcress File"?
20 Which magazine has been edited by Richard Ingrams and Ian Hislop?
21 Who topped the US and UK charts with "My Heart Will Go On?"
22 Which soccer ground did Sunderland move from in 1997?
23 In which country was Checkpoint Charlie located?
24 What number in bingo is two fat ladies?
25 How many notes are there in an octave?
26 What is it that Americans call the sidewalk?
27 Which creature links Jimmy Nail's Shoes and Elton John's Rock?
28 Which Harold won the Nobel Prize for Literature in 2005?
29 How many years are involved in a golden celebration?
30 How many faults are incurred for a refusal in showjumping?

Answers	Pot-Luck 5 *(see Quiz 9)*

1 David Blunkett. 2 Four. 3 Backstroke. 4 Knitting. 5 St Albans. 6 Social Democrat Party. 7 Dyslexia. 8 Swimming. 9 Tokyo. 10 Ferdinand Magellan. 11 George Robey. 12 Rimsky-Korsakov. 13 Robbie Williams. 14 Radio Five Live. 15 Fountain pen. 16 Heath Robinson. 17 Bill Clinton. 18 Tony Benn. 19 Prisoner. 20 Harp. 21 Gnasher. 22 Rothmans. 23 Kris Kristofferson. 24 18. 25 Francis Durbridge. 26 Sleeping Beauty. 27 Harold Macmillan. 28 Amber. 29 Horse. 30 April.

1 Which Disney film released in 1942 was about a little fawn?
2 How many days did it take David Niven to go Around the World?
3 In the 1957 film about Japanese prisoners of war, where was the Bridge?
4 Which yuletide classic was first sung by Bing Crosby in "Holiday Inn"?
5 If Lady is a pedigree spaniel what is the name of the mongrel?
6 Which Ben won 11 Oscars in 1959?
7 In which 1940 film did Mickey Mouse conduct the orchestra?
8 In which film did Vivien Leigh play Scarlett O'Hara?
9 Who starred in the Road films with Dorothy Lamour and Bing Crosby?
10 Which film set in Rick's Café starred Humphrey Bogart and Ingrid Bergman?
11 Which distinguished actor, later a Lord, played the lead in "Henry V"?
12 Which film starred Celia Johnson, Trevor Howard and a train station?
13 Which Alfred directed the thrillers "Rebecca" and "Notorious"?
14 Which actor Orson starred in "Citizen Kane" and "The Third Man"?
15 Who played eight different characters in "Kind Hearts and Coronets"?
16 What was the series of comedies made in West London studios called?
17 Where was Gene Kelly Singin' in 1952?
18 How did Some Like It in the film with Jack Lemmon, Tony Curtis and Marilyn Monroe?
19 What was the name of the car that involved Kenneth More and Dinah Sheridan in the London to Brighton road run?
20 Which young star of "East of Eden" died in a car crash aged 24?
21 Which actress married Prince Rainier of Monaco?
22 Which French "sex kitten" starred with Dirk Bogarde in "Doctor at Sea"?
23 In the Charlton Heston film how many commandments were there?
24 Where was there Room in the film starring Laurence Harvey?
25 Who was the young star of "National Velvet" in 1945?
26 Which dancer/actress Ginger won an Oscar in 1940?
27 Which actor Marlon starred in "On the Waterfront"?
28 What goes with Old Lace in the title of the Cary Grant film?
29 What is A Many Splendored Thing in the film about the Korean War?
30 From Here to where is the Oscar-winning movie with Deborah Kerr, Burt Lancaster and Frank Sinatra?

Answers | Around England *(see Quiz 10)*

1 Rivers. 2 Cumbria. 3 Birmingham. 4 Victoria. 5 Essex. 6 Yorkshire. 7 Blackpool. 8 Zoo. 9 The Minster. 10 Isle of Wight. 11 A city. 12 Thames. 13 Southport. 14 English Channel. 15 National Exhibition Centre. 16 The Potteries. 17 Manchester. 18 M6. 19 Northeast. 20 Liverpool. 21 Oxford. Cambridge. 22 Pennines. 23 Dartmoor. 24 Cars. 25 Isle of Man. 26 Stonehenge. 27 Shakespeare's. 28 Kent. 29 One. 30 Rutland.

1 What does an arctophile collect?
2 Which of Verdi's operas is set in Ancient Egypt?
3 What gives red blood cells their colour?
4 What was the name of Nintendo's 2005 canine computer game?
5 On TV, what kind of creature was Flipper?
6 Which animals took Hannibal over the Alps?
7 How is the auracaria tree more commonly known?
8 In which team game do you try to move backwards all the time?
9 Which country did the British and Irish Lions tour in 2005?
10 Who was the first British monarch to visit New Zealand?
11 Who recorded the albums "John Wesley Harding" and "Nashville Skyline"?
12 Who does the Beast fall in love with?
13 What is the main ingredient in a brick?
14 What hangs down from the roof of cave – a stalagmite or a stalactite?
15 What is the body of a penguin covered with?
16 How does Saturday's child work for a living?
17 Who presented the first series of "Big Brother"?
18 Which musical direction means at ease, at a slow comfortable pace?
19 Which bell said, "You owe me five farthings"?
20 Which king is said to have burnt the cakes?
21 Which British national daily newspaper ceased publication in 1995?
22 Which girl shares her name with a Christmas song?
23 How many edges in a cube?
24 Which dance comes from "Orpheus in the Underworld"?
25 At what age does a filly become classified as mare?
26 What type of creature is a Pacific sea wasp?
27 Who had a No 1 in 1995 with "You are Not Alone"?
28 How many are there in a baker's dozen?
29 Who is the eldest of the Corrs?
30 Is the South Pole at the Arctic or the Antarctic?

Answers | Pot-Luck 8 *(see Quiz 15)*

1 Rugby. 2 Mongoose in a Rudyard Kipling story. 3 Three. 4 Bedrock. 5 Australia. 6 Mrs Emery. 7 Richard Adams. 8 The giant tortoise. 9 Joseph. 10 Epidermis. 11 Sausages. 12 Robbie. 12 A backbone. 14 Little John. 15 Germaine Greer. 16 Nine. 17 Asia. 18 Perry Mason. 19 Istanbul. 20 Tottenham Hotspur. 21 Irving Berlin. 22 Taurus. 23 Windsor. 24 7-0. 25 Sandie Shaw. 26 Stamps. 27 Spandau. 28 Benjamin Britten. 29 Pay As You Earn. 30 Richard Beckinsale.

Answers – page 24

LEVEL 1

1 Who plays home games at Ewood Park?
2 Which team are known as the Gunners?
3 What colour are Manchester United's home shirts?
4 Which European country was drawn in the group with England in the 2006 World Cup in Germany?
5 Wayne Rooney joined Man Utd from which club?
6 Which city has teams called Wednesday and United?
7 Jose Mourinho joined Chelsea from which club in Portugal?
8 Who plays against Rangers in an Auld Firm derby match?
9 How many minutes in the second half of a Premier League match?
10 What name is shared by Birmingham, Coventry and Leicester?
11 Which colour card is used to send a player off?
12 Which German city hosted the final of the 2006 World Cup?
13 Which country does Ryan Giggs play for?
14 Which Graeme has managed Blackburn, Liverpool, Newcastle and Rangers?
15 Which East Anglian team is nicknamed the Canaries?
16 How many players should be on the pitch at the start of a game?
17 Who won the World Cup in 1958, 1962, 1970 and 1990?
18 Which team plays home games at Villa Park?
19 Raphael Benitez managed which British club to win the 2005 Champions League?
20 Hearts and Hibs come from which Scottish city?
21 What number is traditionally worn on the goalie's shirt?
22 Which England keeper Paul moved from Leeds to Spurs?
23 Which country does Freddie Ljunberg play for?
24 If you were at Goodison Park who would be playing at home?
25 Martin O'Neill managed which club to the Scottish title?
26 Which Nottingham club was managed by Brian Clough?
27 What is the colour of the home strip of both Everton and Chelsea?
28 Who managed England during the 2002 World Cup campaign?
29 Can a goalkeeper score a goal for his own team?
30 At which Lane do Spurs play when at home?

Answers	Soups (see Quiz 16)

1 Queen Victoria. 2 Dingle. 3 The patio. 4 Ramsay. 5 Brown. 6 Emmerdale. 7 Frankie. 8 Falcon. 9 Ric Griffin. 10 Home and Away. 11 H. 12 Peyton. 13 Crossroads. 14 Fowler. 15 The Colbys. 16 Knot's. 17 Brookside. 18 Jason Donovan. 19 Jack and Vera Duckworth. 20 Angie Watts. 21 J.R. 22 Sadie. 23 Girl. 24 Emmerdale. 25 Melbourne. 26 The Bill. 27 Rita Sullivan. 28 Ena. 29 America. 20 Barbara Windsor.

1 Thomas Arnold was headmaster of which public school?
2 What kind of creature was Rikki-Tikki-Tavi?
3 In the story, how many men were in Jerome K. Jerome's boat?
4 In which town do the Flintstones live?
5 In 1930, which country did Amy Johnson fly to from England?
6 What is the name of the incontinent character in "Little Britain"?
7 Who wrote "Watership Down"?
8 Which animal is regarded as the one with the longest life span?
9 Who in the Bible had a coat of many colours?
10 What is the outer layer of skin called?
11 What meat appears in a Punch and Judy show?
12 Who left "Take That" in July 1995?
13 What does an invertebrate not have?
14 Who was the tallest of Robin Hood's Men?
15 Who wrote "The Female Eunuch"?
16 In "Countdown" how many letters are selected for the letters game?
17 Which continent suffered a devastating earthquake in October 2005?
18 Della Street was secretary to which famous legal character?
19 What did Constantinople become known as in March 1930?
20 Sol Campbell joined Arsenal from which club?
21 Who wrote the song "White Christmas"?
22 Which star sign has the bull as its symbol?
23 In which English town did Charles and Camilla marry?
24 In a tennis tie-break, what is the largest winning margin?
25 Who won the Eurovision Song Contest in bare feet?
26 What do philatelists collect?
27 Rudolf Hess was the last prisoner in which jail?
28 Who composed "Peter Grimes"?
29 What does PAYE stand for?
30 Who played student Alan Moore in "Rising Damp"?

Answers | Pot-Luck 7 (see Quiz 13)

1 Teddy bears. 2 Aida. 3 Haemoglobin. 4 Nintendogs. 5 Dolphin. 6 Elephants. 7 Monkey puzzle. 8 Tug of War. 9 New Zealand. 10 Elizabeth II. 11 Bob Dylan. 12 Beauty. 13 Clay. 14 Stalactite. 15 Feathers. 16 Hard. 17 Davina McCall. 18 Adagio. 19 St Martins. 20 Alfred. 21 Today. 22 Carol. 23 12. 24 The can-can. 25 Five. 26 Jellyfish. 27 Michael Jackson. 28 13. 29 Jim. 30 Antarctic.

Quiz 16 | TV: Soaps

Answers – page 22

1 What is the name of the pub in Albert Square?
2 Which "Emmerdale" family's members include Sam and Delilah?
3 What was Trevor Jordache buried under in "Brookside"?
4 In which street is "Neighbours" set?
5 What was Cilla's surname before she married "Coronation Street"s Les Battersby?
6 In which soap is there a pub called the Woolpack?
7 Who was Danny Baldwin's wife when they first moved into Coronation Street?
8 Which bird added to a Crest completes a soap series?
9 Who was Jess Griffin's dad in "Holby City"?
10 Which Australian soap is set in Summer Bay?
11 On which Cell Block might there be a Prisoner in an Australian soap?
12 Which Place was the the name of the first major US soap?
13 Which British soap was set in a motel?
14 In "EastEnders" what was Sonia's surname when she married Martin?
15 Which soap was a spin-off of "Dynasty"?
16 In which Landing did some members of Dallas's Ewing family settle?
17 Which soap has featured the Corkhills, the Grants and the Dixons?
18 Who left his role as Scott Robinson and became a West End Joseph?
19 Which couple took over the Rovers' Return after Bet Gilroy left?
20 Who was Sharon's mum in "EastEnders"?
21 By what initials was actor Larry Hagman known as in "Dallas"?
22 Which character in "Emmerdale" was played by Patsy Kensit?
23 In "Home and Away" was Bobby Simpson a boy or a girl?
24 Where was there a horrific air crash in December 1993?
25 In which Australian city is "Neighbours" set?
26 Which police series is based at Sun Hill police station?
27 In "Coronation Street" who owns the Kabin?
28 What was the first name of legendary Street character Mrs Sharples?
29 Which country did Michelle go to when she left Albert Square?
30 Which Carry On star became Phil and Grant's mum in "EastEnders"?

Answers	Sport: Football (see Quiz 14)

1 Blackburn Rovers. 2 Arsenal. 3 Red. 4 Sweden. 5 Everton. 6 Sheffield. 7 FC Porto. 8 Celtic. 9 45. 10 City. 11 Red. 12 Berlin. 13 Wales. 14 Souness. 15 Norwich City. 16 22. 17 Brazil. 18 Aston Villa. 19 Liverpool. 20 Edinburgh. 21 1. 22 Robinson. 23 Sweden. 24 Everton. 25 Celtic. 26 Forest. 27 Blue. 28 Sven Goran Eriksson. 29 Yes. 30 White Hart.

Quiz 17 | Pot-Luck 9

Answers – page 27

1 Which Girls took "Sound of the Underground" to No 1?
2 What is the zodiac sign of Pisces?
3 What is the fruity name of Gwyneth Paltrow's daughter?
4 Who had a No 1 hit with the song "Wuthering Heights"?
5 With which branch of medicine is Mesmer associated?
6 In recent years, which politician John punched an assailant in North Wales who threw an egg an him?
7 In the nursery rhyme, what did Tom, Tom the piper's son steal?
8 Who wrote "Where Have All the Flowers Gone"?
9 In "HMS Pinafore" whom did Sir Joseph Porter bring on boat along with his sisters?
10 According to the proverb, what begins at home?
11 Which birds are traditionally used by Japanese fishermen to help them catch fish?
12 Who played TV's Inspector Morse?
13 Called chequers in America, what's the name of this game in Britain?
14 Who was the last queen of England by succession before Elizabeth II?
15 What is the term for fear of enclosed spaces?
16 Name the consortium that runs the National Lottery?
17 What was the name of the Big River sung about by Jimmy Nail?
18 What is the name of the person who delivers the mail in Greendale?
19 Which city is the setting for "Saturday Night Fever"?
20 What was the No 1 recording made by Matthews Southern Comfort?
21 Which food item is most consumed by humans throughout the world?
22 Which boxer said, "Know what I mean, 'Arry"?
23 Which day of the week is named after the god Thor?
24 Who first recorded "A Whiter Shade of Pale"?
25 What is Sweden's national flower?
26 What do entomologists study?
27 What tree does a date grow on?
28 In the song, what did my true love send to me on the seventh day of Christmas?
29 Who was the famous son of Uther Pendragon?
30 How many goals did France score in the 1998 World Cup final?

| **Answers** | Pot-Luck 10 *(see Quiz 19)* |

1 Westlife. 2 The Rolling Stones. 3 Dennis Rickman. 4 Dire Straits. 5 Tennis. 6 Ethelred. 7 Phil. 8 Australia. 9 Abraham Lincoln. 10 Davy Crockett. 11 India. 12 New York. 13 Home on the Range. 14 Mars. 15 Wins. 16 Four. 17 Rin Tin Tin. 18 Toytown. 19 India. 20 Female. 21 Argentina. 22 Male. 23 Gordon Richards. 24 Saffron. 25 Chest. 26 American. 27 Blessed. 28 The Saint. 29 Honey bees. 30 Women's Royal Air Force.

1 Michael Crawford starred in the musical about "The Woman" in which colour?
2 Who wrote the long-running play "The Mousetrap"?
3 Complete the title of the comedy: "No Sex Please _____"
4 In "Starlight Express" what do the performers wear on their feet?
5 What was Jesus Christ according to Tim Rice and Andrew Lloyd Webber?
6 According to the comedy, There's a what in My Soup?
7 Where is the Fiddler in the musical which starred Topol?
8 Which London theatre's motto was, "We never closed"?
9 Which New York street is famous for its theatres?
10 Which musical about Professor Higgins and Eliza Doolittle is based on "Pygmalion"?
11 Who wrote the music in the comic operas for which Gilbert wrote the words?
12 What do the initials RSC stand for?
13 Which musical is based on T. S. Eliot's poems?
14 Who first played the title role in "Evita" in the West End?
15 Which musical is the name of a US state?
16 Which show includes "Climb Ev'ry Mountain"?
17 Which musical is the name of a fairground ride?
18 Which musical is about a circus impresario?
19 In which musical does Fagin appear?
20 Which Boulevard is the title of a musical?
21 Which part of the Pacific is the setting for a popular musical?
22 Which class of Society is a musical based on "The Philadelphia Story"?
23 Which Arthur wrote "Death of a Salesman", a play revived in the West End in 2005?
24 The Importance of Being what is the name of an Oscar Wilde play?
25 Who are with the Guys in the show about gangsters?
26 Which girl is the lecturer Educating in the play by Willy Russell?
27 Which Miss is a musical set in Vietnam?
28 What is the full name of the show often just referred to as Les Mis?
29 What do you say to Dolly in the title of the show?
30 Aspects of what are the theme of which Lloyd Webber musical?

| **Answers** | 40s and 50s Newsround *(see Quiz 20)* |

1 Churchill. 2 Hitler. 3 The Blitz. 4 Prisoner of war. 5 Vera Lynn. 6 Dad's Army. 7 USSR. 8 Africa. 9 France. 10 Europe. 11 1945. 12 Princess Elizabeth. 13 Israel. 14 Miss World. 15 Jeans. 16 John F. Kennedy. 17 USSR. 18 Everest. 19 Hovercraft. 20 Premium Bonds. 21 Hula hoop. 22 Mini. 23 M1. 24 Teenagers. 25 Coffee. 26 Holiday camps. 27 Meters. 28 USSR. 29 Skiffle. 30 The Bomb.

1 Which boy band had a 2003 No 1 with "Mandy"?
2 What was the most famous group managed by Andrew Loog Oldham?
3 Who was Dirty Den's son as played by Nigel Harman?
4 Who recorded the album "Brothers in Arms"?
5 In which sport is the Davis Cup played for?
6 Which English king was said to be Unready?
7 Which of the Neville brothers was first to leave Man Utd?
8 Which team did England beat in the 2003 rugby World Cup final?
9 Which US president was assassinated in a Washington theatre?
10 Who had a rifle called "Old Betsy"?
11 David Lean's film was about a passage to which country?
12 Which city was "so good they named it twice"?
13 In song, where do the deer and the antelope play?
14 Which planet is fourth from the sun?
15 According to a Nick Berry song title every loser does what?
16 How many sides has a parallelogram?
17 Which film star dog had three names each containing three letters?
18 Where did Larry the Lamb live?
19 In which country did the Thuggee – from which we derive the word thug – operate?
20 Is Mickie a male or female character in Holby City?
21 Which country did Juan Perón rule?
22 Is it the male or female cuckoo that makes the "cuck-oo" call?
23 Which jockey was knighted in 1953?
24 On TV, what's the name of Edina's daughter?
25 What can be a box or part of the body?
26 What nationality was the notorious murderer Dr Crippen?
27 Which Brian appeared in "Z Cars" and "Cats" and is an authority on Mount Everest?
28 Which holy-sounding character was created by Leslie Charteris?
29 Which insects live in apiaries?
30 What does WRAF stand for?

Answers | Pot-Luck 9 *(see Quiz 17)*

1 Girls Aloud. 2 Fish. 3 Apple. 4 Kate Bush. 5 Hypnotism. 6 John Prescott. 7 A pig. 8 Pete Seeger. 9 His cousins and his aunts. 10 Charity. 11 Cormorants. 12 John Thaw. 13 Draughts. 14 Queen Victoria. 15 Claustrophobia. 16 Camelot. 17 Tyne. 18 Postman Pat. 19 New York. 20 Woodstock. 21 Rice. 22 Frank Bruno. 23 Thursday. 24 Procol Harum. 25 Lily of the valley. 26 Insects. 27 Palm. 28 Seven swans a-swimming. 29 King Arthur. 30 Three.

1 Which Winston took over as prime minister in 1940?
2 Who was the German leader throughout World War II?
3 What name was given to the persistent air attack on London?
4 What does POW stand for?
5 Who was known as the Forces' Sweetheart?
6 What was the popular name for the Home Guard?
7 Which country was Stalin leader of?
8 Which continent was El Alamein in?
9 In which country did the D Day landings take place?
10 V-E Day commemorated victory on which continent?
11 World War II ended in which year?
12 Whose engagement to Philip Mountbatten was announced in 1947?
13 Which Jewish state was founded in 1948?
14 Which competition did Miss Sweden win the first of in 1951?
15 Which type of denim trousers took Britain by storm in 1955?
16 Which future US president did Jacqueline Bouvier marry in 1953?
17 Which country launched the first satellite – Sputnik 1 – in space?
18 What was climbed by Edmund Hillary and Tensing in 1953?
19 Which craft which floats on an air cushion was invented in 1958?
20 What type of prize-winning Bonds were introduced?
21 Which large plastic hoop became a sports craze in the 1950s?
22 Which small car did Austin and Morris launch in 1959?
23 What was the name of the London to Birmingham motorway?
24 Which word for 13- to 19-year-olds was first coined in the 1950s?
25 A frothy version of which non-alcoholic drink became popular in this era?
26 What did Billy Butlin found in the 1950s?
27 What type of parking payment machine was introduced in London?
28 Where did spies Burgess, Maclean and Philby defect to?
29 Which type of 1950s music used a washboard?
30 What did CND marchers on the way to Aldermaston want to ban?

Answers	Theatre and Musicals *(see Quiz 18)*

1 White. 2 Agatha Christie. 3 We're British. 4 Skates. 5 Superstar. 6 Girl. 7 On the Roof. 8 The Windmill. 9 Broadway. 10 My Fair Lady. 11 Sullivan. 12 Royal Shakespeare Company. 13 Cats. 14 Elaine Paige. 15 Oklahoma! 16 The Sound of Music. 17 Carousel. 18 Barnum. 19 Oliver! 20 Sunset. 21 South. 22 High. 23 Miller. 24 Earnest. 25 Dolls. 26 Rita. 27 Saigon. 28 Les Misérables. 29 Hello. 30 Love.

1 What type of singing voice does Russell Watson have?
2 In which TV programme do Patsy and Edina appear?
3 Which band had a chart hit with "Speed of Sound"?
4 In which month does the grouse shooting season start in Britain?
5 What type of racing has only two cars competing on the track at the same time?
6 How many years are celebrated by a platinum anniversary?
7 What is an oblong bar of gold called?
8 Harry Kewell is a football international for which country?
9 Which European soccer trophy did Spurs become the first British team to win?
10 In the Paul McCartney/Stevie Wonder hit what went with ebony?
11 In which month is Twelfth Night?
12 In which city is the Whitney art gallery?
13 In which soap do the Sugdens appear?
14 What are the initials of thriller writer James?
15 Who recorded the album "The Immaculate Collection"?
16 In the book title, whom did writer Laurie Lee have cider with?
17 Which musical does "I Know Him So Well" come from?
18 Which fictional Scottish doctor kept a casebook?
19 Who made up Abba with Benny, Bjorn and Annifrid?
20 Which traveller had the unusual first name of Lemuel?
21 Who wrote the words to "The Boxer"?
22 In which country is Hampden Park Stadium?
23 What can be upside down, ginger or Dundee?
24 What was the name of the musical show about Frank Sinatra, Sammy Davis and Dean Martin?
25 Who was the lead singer with Culture Club?
26 What do the French words au revoir mean ?
27 Who said, "Am I dying beyond my means?"?
28 Who played the character of Mrs Fawlty?
29 Which Marie is supposed to have said, "Let them eat cake"?
30 What do the initials TB stand for?

Answers | Pot-Luck 12 *(see Quiz 23)*

1 Andrew. 2 300. 3 Spain. 4 Edward VIII. 5 Dido. 6 Valhalla. 7 Iron. 8 Rommel. 9 Mrs Dale's Diary. 10 January. 11 Queen Vic. 12 Piano. 13 Mick McCarthy. 14 Haddock. 15 Avocado. 16 Austria. 17 Plimsoll Line. 18 Soup. 19 Lorna Doone. 20 Vivaldi. 21 Dublin. 22 Richmal Crompton. 23 XIV. 24 Chair. 25 Alexander the Great. 26 Karen. 27 Intelligence. 28 Spencer. 29 Jerusalem. 30 Bonsai.

1 Is Australia in the northern or the southern hemisphere?
2 What does each star on the flag of the United States stand for?
3 Which country does the holiday island of Ibiza belong to?
4 Which island would you visit to kiss the Blarney Stone?
5 In which country would you be if you were visiting the Taj Mahal?
6 The south of which continent is closest to the Falkland Islands?
7 In which mountain range would you find Mount Everest?
8 Which country is Luxembourg the capital of?
9 What colour is the spot in the middle of the Japanese flag?
10 The island of Sicily is at the toe of which country?
11 Which country is also known as the Netherlands?
12 In which country are Maoris the indigenous population?
13 In which Scandinavian country would you find fjords?
14 Which country's languages include English, Zulu and Afrikaans?
15 Which country's name could be part of a Christmas dinner?
16 In which city is the Vatican City?
17 What is K2?
18 In which country is the Yellow River, also known as Huang He?
19 Which country has four letters, the last one q?
20 Which country, capital Bangkok, used to be called Siam?
21 Which ocean lies between Europe and America?
22 Which European country has an area called Flanders?
23 Which stretch of water separates Anglesey and Wales?
24 Which Rock is on the south coast of Spain?
25 Which isle lies between England and Northern Ireland?
26 Which island to the south of India used to be called Ceylon?
27 Which sea separates Europe and Africa?
28 In which ocean is Fiji?
29 Which island, in the Arctic Ocean, is the largest in the world?
30 In which continent is the world's longest river, the Nile?

Answers	Sounds of the 60s *(see Quiz 24)*

1 Happiness. 2 Blue Jeans. 3 Dustman. 4 Downtown. 5 Congratulations. 6 Sonny. 7 Diana Ross. 8 Pins. 9 Whiter. 10 The Pacemakers. 11 24. 12 Freddie. 13 Herman. 14 Roy Orbison. 15 Go. 16 Lollipop. 17 Fashion. 18 Billy J. Kramer. 19 The Rising Sun. 20 Lulu. 21 Four. 22 Cilla Black. 23 The Monkees. 24 Nights. 25 Dusty Springfield. 26 The Who. 27 Yellow. 28 The Shadows. 29 The Beach Boys. 30 Papas.

1 At the end of 2005, which was the only son of the Queen who was unmarried?

2 How many minutes in five hours?

3 A car with the international registration letter E comes from where?

4 Who came first, King Edward VIII or George VI?

5 Who recorded the million-selling album "Life for Rent"?

6 Where were Norse gods said to live?

7 Fe is the symbol of which chemical element?

8 Which army commander was known as "The Desert Fox"?

9 In which early radio soap was Mary worried about Jim?

10 What is the first month of the year to have exactly 31 days?

11 Under the floor of which building did Chrissie bury Dirty Den's body?

12 Which musical instrument has dampers, hammers and strings?

13 Who was the Republic of Ireland's World Cup manager in 2002?

14 Which fish is smoked and cured and called "finnan"?

15 Which pear-shaped tropical fruit has given its name to a bathroom suite colouring?

16 The Spanish Riding School is in which country?

17 What was the original name of the line on a ship showing the level to which it could be loaded?

18 Bouillabaisse is what kind of fish dish?

19 John Ridd is the male lead in which book with a girl's name as its title?

20 Who wrote the music "The Four Seasons"?

21 In which city in 1916 was the Easter Rising?

22 Who wrote the stories about a schoolboy named William Brown?

23 Which King Louis built the palace at Versailles?

24 Sedan, arm and high are all types of what?

25 Who had a horse called Bucephalus?

26 What was the first name of the female singer in the Carpenters?

27 In the USA what does the I stand for in CIA?

28 What was the surname of Frank in "Some Mothers Do 'Ave 'Em"?

29 "Walk upon England's mountains green" is the second line of which rousing song?

30 What name is given to the Japanese skill of growing miniature trees?

Answers | Pot-Luck 11 *(see Quiz 21)*

1 Tenor. 2 Absolutely Fabulous. 3 Coldplay. 4 August. 5 Drag Racing. 6 70. 7 Ingot. 8 Australia. 9 European Cup Winners' Cup. 10 Ivory. 11 January. 12 New York. 13 Emmerdale. 14 P. D. 15 Madonna. 16 Rosie. 17 Chess. 18 Doctor Finlay. 19 Agnetha. 20 Gulliver. 21 Paul Simon. 22 Scotland. 23 Cake. 24 The Rat Pack. 25 Boy George. 26 Until we meet again. 27 Oscar Wilde. 28 Prunella Scales. 29 Antoinette. 30 Tuberculosis.

1 What was Helen Shapiro Walking Back to in 1961?
2 What was Venus wearing in 1962 according to Mark Wynter?
3 What was the occupation of Lonnie Donegan's old man?
4 In which part of town was Petula Clark in the 1960s?
5 What was the title of Cliff Richard's 1968 Eurovision song?
6 Who was Cher's first singing partner with a hit song?
7 Who was lead singer with the Supremes?
8 What did the Searchers sing about along with Needles?
9 What shade of Pale did Procol Harum sing about?
10 Who was Gerry's backing group?
11 How many Hours was Gene Pitney from Tulsa?
12 Who sang with the Dreamers?
13 Who had Hermits?
14 Who was known as "The Big O"?
15 What followed Ready, Steady in the title of the pop show?
16 My Boy, according to Millie, is called what?
17 What were the Kinks Dedicated Followers of in 1966?
18 Who sang with the Dakotas?
19 According to the Animals, what was the name of The House in New Orleans?
20 Who was heard to "Shout" in 1964?
21 How many were there in the Tops, Pennies and Seasons?
22 Which Liverpool lady took "Anyone Who Had a Heart" to No 1?
23 Which US band "aped" the Beatles and sang "Daydream Believer"?
24 What was in White Satin according to the Moody Blues?
25 Who left her two group members and sang "I Only Want to be with You"?
26 Which group wrote the rock opera "Tommy"?
27 What colour was the Beatles' Submarine?
28 Who was Cliff Richard's backing group?
29 Who felt "Good Vibrations" in 1966?
30 Who sang with the Mamas?

Answers | Geography (see Quiz 22)

1 Southern. 2 A state. 3 Spain. 4 Ireland. 5 India. 6 South America. 7 Himalayas. 8 Luxembourg. 9 Red. 10 Italy. 11 Holland. 12 New Zealand. 13 Norway. 14 South Africa. 15 Turkey. 16 Rome. 17 Mountain. 18 China. 19 Iraq. 20 Thailand. 21 Atlantic. 22 Belgium. 23 Menai Strait. 24 Gibraltar. 25 Isle of Man. 26 Sri Lanka. 27 Mediterranean. 28 Pacific. 29 Greenland. 30 Africa.

1 Who was the only woman on the "Strictly Come Dancing" panel of judges for 2005?

2 Which country was the first to win the World Cup five times?

3 Which former British Prime Minister who died in 2005 was a keen yachtsman?

4 Who had a No 1 hit with the song "I Just Called to Say I Love You"?

5 Who wrote "The Owl and the Pussycat"?

6 What are beds of snooker tables traditionally made of?

7 By what name was travelling show tap dancer Luther Robinson known?

8 What was the name of the "Neighbours" character played by Kylie Minogue?

9 What word describes the permanent disappearance of a species?

10 The Star of Africa is what type of gem?

11 In education, what does BA stand for?

12 In the human body, what has four chambers?

13 Which creature can turn its stomach inside out?

14 There are 78 cards in which type of pack?

15 What is arachnophobia the fear of?

16 Which two writers created "Auf Wiedersehen, Pet"?

17 How many cards of the same suit are needed for a flush in poker?

18 What name is given to an athletics event such as running or hurdling?

19 Which war in Europe took place between 1936–9?

20 Under what name did Samuel Clemens write?

21 Who recorded the album "Tubular Bells"?

22 In which city is the Obelisk of Luxor?

23 Which day of the week is named after the moon?

24 In the USA what is a greenback?

25 October 2005 witnessed events to mark the bicentenary of which admiral's death?

26 Which Charles wrote "The Origin of Species"?

27 Donnerstag is German for which day?

28 Jennyanydots was what kind of cat?

29 What is the federal republic of Switzerland divided into?

30 Who wrote "Rebecca"?

Answers | Pot-Luck 14 *(see Quiz 27)*

1 Confessions on a Dance Floor. 2 Schilling. 3 Measles. 4 Oasis. 5 Bob Geldof. 6 Cabriolet. 7 Clock. 8 Cilla Black. 9 Scott Joplin. 10 Bell. 11 Enya. 12 1931. 13 Bread. 14 Cabbage. 15 Derby County. 16 Three. 17 Radioactivity. 18 Larry Grayson. 19 Tyne. 20 Anthony Quinn. 21 Sex change. 22 Blue. 23 Lawson. 24 Cruet. 25 Nap. 26 The Blue Angel. 27 Prince Charles. 28 Captain W. E. Johns. 29 Fifty. 30 World Boxing Association.

1 In which Italian city were the 1960 Olympic Games held?
2 What nationality were 1961 Wimbledon finalists Christine Trueman and Angela Mortimer?
3 What was the first name of heavyweight boxing champion Liston?
4 Who won the FA Cup for the first time, under Bill Shankly?
5 What was the surname of cricketer Fiery Fred who retired in 1968?
6 What nationality was 1962 Wimbledon champion Rod Laver?
7 In what kind of racing was Jim Clark world champion?
8 Which Stanley retired from playing football aged 50?
9 Who won the World Cup in 1966?
10 Which Glasgow soccer team were the first British side to win the European Cup?
11 In 1969 Tony Jacklin was US Open Champion in which sport?
12 What was the surname of boxer Cassius?
13 What was the first name of British Wimbledon champion Mrs Jones?
14 What was the first name of US golfer Palmer?
15 Which Henry was British heavyweight champion in 1963?
16 Which father of Damon won the World Drivers championship in 1962?
17 What was the surname of Wimbledon singles champion Billie-Jean?
18 Which country does 1969 motor racing champion Jackie Stewart come from?
19 What was the surname of former Manchester United legend George?
20 How did Anita Lonsborough win an Olympic gold medal in 1960?
21 Which country was banned from the Olympics because of apartheid?
22 Which jump won Mary Rand a gold medal at the 1964 Olympics?
23 What was the surname of international footballers Jackie and Bobby?
24 Which international football trophy was stolen in 1966?
25 At which sport were Margaret Court and Maria Bueno champions?
26 Who were the runners-up in the 1966 World Cup?
27 What sport was Jack Brabham famous for?
28 Which England manager Alf received a knighthood?
29 Which UK tennis championship was the first to be seen on TV in colour in 1967?
30 Sir Matt Busby retired as manager of which football club?

Answers	The 60s *(see Quiz 28)*

1 Coronation Street. 2 Z Cars. 3 Forsyte Saga. 4 University Challenge. 5 Your Lucky Stars. 6 Dr Who. 7 Dr Finlay. 8 Flintstones. 9 Liver Birds. 10 Magic Roundabout. 11 Man from UNCLE. 12 Match of the Day. 13 Horse. 14 Adam. 15 The Avengers. 16 Home. 17 That was the Week That was. 18 Mason. 19 Peyton Place. 20 The Saint. 21 Songs of Praise 22 Star Trek. 23 Till Death Us Do Part. 24 Tomorrow's. 25 Top of the Pops. 26 Williams. 27 England, West Germany. 28 Dudley Moore. 29 Winters. 30 The Beatles.

1 "Hung Up" was a track featured on which Madonna album?
2 What is the currency of Austria?
3 Which childhood disease is also known as rubella?
4 Who recorded the album "Definitely, Maybe"?
5 Who was presented a 2005 MTV award, for organizing the Live8 concert?
6 Cab is a shortening of which word?
7 In rhyming slang what is meant by dickory dock?
8 How is Priscilla White better known?
9 Who wrote "Maple Leaf Rag"?
10 The Tsar Kolokol is the biggest what in the world?
11 In November 2005, which Irish singer released her album "Amarantine"?
12 To five years either way, when was the Empire State Building finished?
13 Which comedy series featured the Boswell family?
14 Brassica oleracea is better known as what?
15 Which club once played soccer home games at the Baseball Ground?
16 How many sides has an isosceles triangle?
17 What does a Geiger counter detect?
18 Whose catchphrase was, "Shut that door!"?
19 Which major river flows through Newcastle?
20 Who was the star of "Zorba the Greek"?
21 Which much-publicized operation did Doctor Richard Raskind undergo?
22 In the song, what colour are Crystal Gale's brown eyes made?
23 Which Nigel is a former Chancellor of the Exchequer?
24 What is the word for a condiment container?
25 What can be a sleep or how fabric lies?
26 In which film did Dietrich sing "Falling in Love Again"?
27 Which Prince visited Ground Zero with his wife in the autumn of 2005?
28 Who created Biggles?
29 According to Paul Simon, how many ways are there to leave your lover?
30 In boxing, what does WBA stand for?

Answers | Pot-Luck 13 (see Quiz 25)

1 Arlene Phillips. 2 Brazil. 3 Edward Heath. 4 Stevie Wonder. 5 Edward Lear. 6 Slate. 7 Bojangles. 8 Charlene. 9 Extinction. 10 Diamond. 11 Bachelor of Arts. 12 The heart. 13 Starfish. 14 Tarot. 15 Spiders. 16 Clement and La Frenais. 17 Five. 18 Track. 19 Spanish Civil War. 20 Mark Twain. 21 Mike Oldfield. 22 Paris. 23 Monday. 24 A dollar bill. 25 Nelson. 26 Darwin. 27 Thursday. 28 Gumbie Cat. 29 Cantons. 30 Daphne du Maurier.

1 Which soap, which started in 1960, tells of life in Weatherfield?
2 Which Cars were at the heart of a long-running police drama series?
3 Which family Saga spanned the Victorian and Edwardian eras?
4 Which university quiz was hosted by Bamber Gascoigne?
5 What did you Thank in the ITV Saturday-evening pop show?
6 Which Doctor arrived on our screens in the Tardis in 1963?
7 Whose Casebook was based in a Scottish village surgery?
8 Which cartoon series had a Stone Age setting with Fred and Wilma?
9 Which Birds were flatmates in Liverpool?
10 Which Roundabout was about Dougal, Florence and Zebedee?
11 How was the the Man from the United Network Command for Law and Enforcement better known?
12 Which show began broadcasting highlights of the day's football?
13 What kind of animal was Mr Ed who was able to talk?
14 What was the first name of sci-fi adventurer Adamant?
15 Which series included Emma Peel and Steed?
16 Where was Cathy told to Come in the 1966 play about homelessness?
17 Which satirical programme was abbreviated to TW3?
18 What was the surname of Los Angeles defence lawyer Perry?
19 Which Place was the setting for the early soap with Mia Farrow and Ryan O'Neal?
20 What was the nickname of amateur sleuth Simon Templar?
21 Which long-running hymn singing programme began in 1961?
22 Which programme saw the first adventures of the starship Enterprise?
23 Which series starred the controversial Alf Garnett?
24 Which World about new inventions and discoveries began in 1965?
25 Which chart music show started in 1964?
26 Which American Andy hosted a long-running easy music show?
27 Who played in the football match watched by 32 million in 1966?
28 Who starred with Peter Cook in "Not Only... But Also"?
29 What was the surname of comedy duo Mike and Bernie?
30 In 1963 which Fab Four were all four panellists on "Juke Box Jury"?

Answers	Sport: The 60s *(see Quiz 26)*

1 Rome. 2 British. 3 Sonny. 4 Liverpool. 5 Trueman. 6 Australian.
7 Motor. 8 Matthews. 9 England. 10 Celtic. 11 Golf. 12 Clay. 13 Ann. 14 Arnold.
15 Cooper. 16 Graham Hill. 17 King. 18 Scotland. 19 Best. 20 Swimming. 21
South Africa. 22 Long. 23 Charlton. 24 World Cup. 25 Tennis. 26 West Germany. 27
Motor racing. 28 Ramsey. 29 Wimbledon. 30 Manchester United.

1 Red, yellow and blue are what type of colour?
2 Which Sharon was voted best expert at the 2005 National TV awards?
3 Which John was Labour leader before Tony Blair?
4 Which soccer side has Alexandra in its name?
5 The Acol system is used in which game?
6 How many years are celebrated by a ruby anniversary?
7 What three colours are in the flag of Belgium?
8 Whom did Ashley Peacock marry after Maxine's death in "Coronation Street"?
9 What number does the Roman numeral C stand for?
10 What was the name of Miss Rigby in the song by the Beatles?
11 In which month is Valentine's Day?
12 Which Ron played Fagin on film?
13 Roberta Flack had a No 1 with a song about the First Time I Saw Your what?
14 What are the initials of the poet Eliot?
15 What did Polly Flinders do?
16 Which Frederick wrote "The Day of the Jackal"?
17 Which term means related to the moon?
18 Which star actor links "Ocean's Eleven" and "The Brothers Grimm"?
19 Olympiakos have won the soccer league most times in which country?
20 On what part of your body would you wear a muff?
21 Which Wendy starred in "Butterflies"?
22 In which city is the Oval cricket ground?
23 Which Florence was known as the lady with the lamp?
24 What is a young fox called?
25 On which course is the Derby run?
26 Which special name is given to a group of ravens?
27 Who recorded the album "Thriller"?
28 On TV, is "Brookside" a close, an avenue or a drive?
29 Grandfather, cuckoo and carriage are types of what?
30 RoSPA is the Royal Society for the Prevention of what?

Answers | Pot-Luck 16 *(see Quiz 31)*

1 Flying. 2 Florence Nightingale. 3 Germany. 4 Dr Doolittle. 5 Tony Blair. 6 HMV – His Master's Voice. 7 Carbon. 8 Popeye. 9 Red and white. 10 November. 11 Martin Bashir. 12 Arnold Layne. 13 Poker. 14 Geometry. 15 Simple Minds. 16 13. 17 Five. 18 Limbo. 19 Eight. 20 Grimm. 21 Heidi. 22 Temple. 23 Heifer. 24 Natalie. 25 Godiva. 26 Midas. 27 Domesday. 28 Paris. 29 Eye. 30 Briers.

Quiz 30 | 60s Films

Answers – page 40

1 On which Side of New York was the musical Story about rival gangs?
2 Who starred as Cleopatra and married co-star Richard Burton?
3 With which country is Lawrence associated in the film with Peter O'Toole?
4 Which role did Warren Beatty play to Faye Dunaway's Bonnie?
5 What type of Cowboy was Jon Voight in the 1969 film?
6 Who was The Graduate in the film of the same name?
7 Who won an Oscar as Professor Higgins in "My Fair Lady"?
8 Which musical by Lionel Bart was based on a Dickens novel?
9 Which western actor won his only Oscar for "True Grit"?
10 Which actress Mia starred in the controversial "Rosemary's Baby"?
11 What were the hills alive with in the musical set in Austria?
12 What was the nationality of Zorba in the film with Anthony Quinn?
13 Guess Who's Coming to which meal in the Katharine Hepburn film?
14 Which nanny did Julie Andrews win an Oscar for playing?
15 Who played Alfie?
16 Which blonde Julie was a Darling?
17 Who played Fanny Brice in "Funny Girl"?
18 Which Doctor did Omar Sharif play in the film set in the USSR?
19 Which Gregory won an Oscar for "To Kill a Mockingbird"?
20 Which Miss was Maggie Smith whose Prime won an Oscar in '69?
21 Which actor Paul played Thomas More in "A Man for All Seasons"?
22 How many Dalmatians starred in the 1961 Disney film?
23 Who was Butch Cassidy's partner?
24 In the 1968 film when was "The Space Odyssey"?
25 Which 1960 Hitchcock film has the most famous shower scene ever?
26 Which meal was taken at Tiffany's in the film with Audrey Hepburn?
27 Who played James Bond in "Dr No"?
28 What accompanied the Bad and the Ugly in the Clint Eastwood film?
29 Which Sweet girl was played by Shirley Maclaine in the 1968 musical?
30 Which film with Vanessa Redgrave was about King Arthur's court?

Answers	Transport *(see Quiz 32)*

1 M1. 2 Right. 3 Essex. 4 Ford. 5 Hot-air balloon. 6 Wright. 7 Queen Elizabeth II. 8 France. 9 Rolls Royce. 10 Atlantic. 11 Train. 12 English Channel. 13 Jet. 14 Concorde. 15 Black. 16 M25. 17 Manchester. 18 Jaguar. 19 Queen Mary. 20 M11. 21 Waterloo. 22 Germany. 23 Underground. 24 Paris. 25 Lorry. 26 Railway. 27 Folkestone. 28 London. 29 Moscow. 30 Dartford.

Quiz 31 | Pot-Luck 16 | Answers – page 37

1 Dennis Bergkamp has a phobia about which form of travel?
2 In 1907, who was the first woman to receive the Order of Merit?
3 Which country does a car come from if it has the international registration letter D?
4 Which doctor had a pet chimp called Chee Chee?
5 Who was the youngest British PM of the 20th century?
6 Which company had Nipper the dog as its trademark?
7 C is the symbol of which chemical element ?
8 Which cartoon character has Bluto as his arch rival?
9 Which two colours appear on the flag of Denmark?
10 What is the last month of the year to have exactly 30 days?
11 The "Living with Michael Jackson" documentary was made by which British journalist?
12 In a Pink Floyd song who had the strange hobby of collecting clothes?
13 If you are playing Southern Cross you are playing a form of which game?
14 Euclid is associated with which branch of mathematics?
15 Which group had a No 1 with "Belfast Child"?
16 How many players are in a Rugby League team?
17 In the UK what is the maximum number of years between General Elections?
18 What type of dance involves moving under a low horizontal pole?
19 How many pints in a gallon?
20 Which brothers, Jacob and Wilhelm, wrote fairy tales?
21 Johanna Spyri created which little girl?
22 Which child star Shirley won an Oscar at the age of six?
23 What name is given to a cow that has not had a calf?
24 What is the first name of Nat King Cole's singing daughter?
25 Which Lady rode naked through the streets of Coventry?
26 In legend, which king turned everything he touched into gold?
27 William the Conqueror ordered which Book to be compiled?
28 Which Hilton heiress is named after a European capital city?
29 REM stands for rapid movement of what?
30 Which Richard starred in "Ever Decreasing Circles"?

Answers | Pot-Luck 15 *(see Quiz 29)*

1 Primary. 2 Sharon Osbourne. 3 Smith. 4 Crewe. 5 Bridge. 6 40. 7 Black, red and yellow. 8 Claire. 9 100. 10 Eleanor. 11 February. 12 Moody. 13 Face. 14 T. S. 15 Sat among the cinders. 16 Forsyth. 17 Lunar. 18 Matt Damon. 19 Greece. 20 Hands. 21 Craig. 22 London. 23 Nightingale. 24 Cub. 25 Epsom. 26 Unkindness. 27 Michael Jackson. 28 Close. 29 Clock. 30 Accidents.

1 Which motorway runs from London to Leeds?
2 Do more countries drive on the left or on the right?
3 In which county is Stansted airport?
4 Which company made the first production-line car, the Model T?
5 What did the Mongolfier brothers fly in in 1783?
6 What was the surname of aviation pioneers Orville and Wilbur?
7 What is the full name of the QE2?
8 Which country do Renault cars come from?
9 Who produced the luxury Silver Ghost?
10 Over which ocean did Alcock and Brown fly in 1919?
11 What would you be travelling in if you were in a Pullman?
12 Under which stretch of water would you be if you were on Le Shuttle?
13 Which engine for aircraft was patented by Frank Whittle in 1930?
14 Which Anglo-French supersonic aircraft made its first flight in 1969?
15 What is the traditional colour for a London taxi?
16 Which motorway circles London?
17 Which city is served by Ringway airport?
18 Which type of sports car is also the name of a big cat?
19 What was the Queen Elizabeth's luxury sister ship?
20 Which motorway runs from London to Cambridge?
21 Which London railway station is named after a battle with Napoleon?
22 Which country do Volkswagen cars originate in?
23 How would you be travelling if you were taking the Jubilee line?
24 In which city is Charles de Gaulle airport?
25 What type of vehicle is a juggernaut?
26 Which type of transport is George Stephenson famous for?
27 Near which Kent port is the English opening of the Channel Tunnel?
28 In which English city was the traffic system virtually shut down following terrorist bombs in 2005?
29 The Trans-Siberian railway runs from Vladivostock to which Russian city?
30 At which Thames crossing is there a tunnel and the Queen Elizabeth Bridge?

Answers | 60s Films *(see Quiz 30)*

1 West. 2 Elizabeth Taylor. 3 Arabia. 4 Clyde. 5 Midnight. 6 Dustin Hoffman. 7 Rex Harrison. 8 Oliver! 9 John Wayne. 10 Farrow. 11 The Sound of Music. 12 Greek. 13 Dinner. 14 Mary Poppins. 15 Michael Caine. 16 Christie. 17 Barbra Streisand. 18 Zhivago. 19 Peck. 20 Jean Brodie. 21 Scofield. 22 101. 23 The Sundance Kid. 24 2001. 25 Psycho. 26 Breakfast. 27 Sean Connery. 28 The Good. 29 Charity. 30 Camelot.

1 2005 marked which anniversary of the Gunpowder Plot?
2 What is the zodiac sign of the Bull?
3 On a dart board, which number is bottom centre?
4 Who had a No 1 hit with the song "Dancing Queen"?
5 Born Arthur Jefferson in 1890, what was this comic better known as?
6 What profession did Hillary Clinton previously practise?
7 Who partnered Robbie Williams on the hit single "Kids"?
8 In which sport are there madisons and pursuits?
9 Who is the only singer to have No 1 hits in the 50s, 60s, 70s, 80s and 90s?
10 According to proverb, what does the hand that rocks the cradle do?
11 What was founded in 859 at Fez, Morocco, that is reckoned to be the oldest of its type in the world?
12 Which writer established the Three Laws of Robotics?
13 Called hood in America, what's this part of the car called in the UK?
14 Titan is a moon of which planet?
15 What is hydrophobia the fear of?
16 How many furlongs in a mile?
17 Which Terry created the 2005 movie "The Brothers Grimm"?
18 Which annual race was first held in 1829?
19 What type of animal is a Lhasa Apso?
20 Garibaldi, Nice and Ginger Nut are all types of what?
21 In the USA, which are the two main political parties?
22 Which Noel said, "Television is something you appear on: you don't watch it"?
23 What was the trade of Thomas Wolsey's father?
24 What did Siam change its name to?
25 Which Colin played the title role in Oliver Stone's movie "Alexander"?
26 Which Bay housed the island prison Alcatraz?
27 What colours are on the flag of Argentina?
28 In which town did Jesus grow up?
29 Who set up Biba?
30 If a triangle has an angle of 58 degrees and an angle of 77 degrees, what is the third angle?

Answers | Pot-Luck 18 (see Quiz 35)

1 Captain Jack Sparrow. 2 Katherine Jenkins. 3 Altimeter. 4 George Michael. 5 Burt Reynolds. 6 Edward VIII. 7 Talk. 8 Fred Astaire. 9 Six. 10 Leviticus. 11 Housemaid's knee. 12 Milan. 13 Captain. 14 Black. 15 The Kabin. 16 Seven. 17 Fish. 18 On the face. It's a nose. 19 Mersey. 20 Dana. 21 Osama Bin Laden. 22 Hillary Clinton. 23 Prue. 24 Thompson Twins. 25 School. 26 Cairo. 27 Porridge. 28 Cricket. 29 Aubergine. 30 Ronald Reagan.

1 Which tough guy star of "Casablanca" married Lauren Bacall?
2 Who co-starred with Bob Hope in the Road films and died playing golf?
3 Which actress was shunned by Hollywood when she left her husband and children for director Roberto Rossellini?
4 What is the first name of actor Curtis, father of Jamie Lee?
5 Which Officer and a Gentleman married supermodel Cindy Crawford?
6 How was Ruth Elizabeth Davis better known?
7 Which director Cecil B. was famous for epic movies?
8 Which Kops were the creation of director Mack Sennett?
9 Which daughter of Judy Garland won an Oscar for "Cabaret"?
10 Who is Kirk Douglas's famous son?
11 Which actress Ava was Frank Sinatra's second wife?
12 What relation is Shirley Maclaine to fellow star Warren Beatty?
13 Which Katharine had a long relationship with Spencer Tracy?
14 Which actress Grace became Princess of Monaco?
15 Which British suspense film director worked in Hollywood from 1939?
16 Which actress daughter of Henry was known as Hanoi Jane because of her anti-Vietnam War activities in the 1970s?
17 Who co-starred with Vivien Leigh in "Gone with the Wind"?
18 How is Jack Lemmon's co-star in "The Odd Couple", Walter Matasschanskavasky better known?
19 Who was Fred Astaire's most frequent dancing partner?
20 Which child star Shirley went on to be a US Ambassador?
21 Which silent movie star Rudolph died at an early age?
22 Hollywood legends Lionel, Ethel and John share what surname?
23 Which actor Paul is the husband of actress Joanne Woodward?
24 Who was married to Sean Penn and was chosen for the role of Evita?
25 Who was born Doris Kappelhoff and co-starred with Rock Hudson?
26 Which star of "Top Gun" married Nicole Kidman?
27 Which actor James, famous for gangster roles, is credited with the catchphrase "You dirty rat!"?
28 Why was Jimmy Durante nicknamed Schnozzle?
29 Who married Richard Burton twice?
30 Which actress Demi married Bruce Willis?

Answers | **Around Scotland** (see Quiz 36)

1 East. 2 John o' Groat's. 3 Edinburgh. 4 Yes. 5 Hadrian. 6 St Andrews. 7 Whisky. 8 Balmoral. 9 Highland Games. 10 Skiing. 11 Mountains. 12 Aberdeen. 13 Shetland. 14 Ness. 15 Skye. 16 Kintyre. 17 Clyde. 18 Edinburgh. 19 Haggis. 20 Gretna Green. 21 Lake. 22 Ben Nevis. 23 Dundee. 24 Perth. 25 Tweed. 26 North Sea. 27 Valley. 28 Glasgow. 29 Dundee. 30 St Andrew.

1 Which character did Johnny Depp play in the movie "Pirates of the Caribbean"?
2 Which classical singer's second album was called "Second Nature"?
3 Which instrument measures a plane's height above sea level?
4 Who recorded the album "Listen without Prejudice"?
5 Who played the Bandit in "Smokey and the Bandit"?
6 Which king of England abdicated and was succeeded by his younger brother?
7 In rhyming slang what is meant by rabbit and pork?
8 How was Frederick Austerlitz better known?
9 How many players are there in a volleyball team?
10 What is the third book of the Old Testament?
11 What is the common name for the complaint bursitis?
12 In which city is La Scala opera house?
13 In the British army which rank comes between Lieutenant and Major?
14 What colour is the gem jet?
15 What is the name of the newsagent's in "Coronation Street"?
16 How many sides has a heptagon?
17 What type of creature is used for the dish Bombay duck?
18 Where on your body is your olfactory organ?
19 Which major river flows through Liverpool?
20 Which singer had a No 1 with "All Kinds of Everything"?
21 Who founded Al Qaeda in the 1980s?
22 Who was the first wife of a President in office to appear before a Grand Jury?
23 What is the first name of TV cook Leith?
24 Which trio took their name from characters in the Tintin cartoons?
25 What can be a group of fish or a place of education?
26 What is the capital of Egypt?
27 Which Ronnie Barker comedy was set inside a prison?
28 In which sport might you see a Chinaman and a maiden?
29 Which vegetable is also known as the egg plant?
30 Jane Wyman was the first wife of which famous American?

Answers | Pot-Luck 17 *(see Quiz 33)*

1 400th. 2 Taurus. 3 3. 4 Abba. 5 Stan Laurel. 6 Lawyer. 7 Kylie Minogue. 8 Cycling. 9 Cliff Richard. 10 Rule the world. 11 University. 12 Isaac Asimov. 13 Bonnet. 14 Saturn. 15 Water. 16 Eight. 17 Terry Gilliam. 18 Oxford and Cambridge boat race. 19 Dog. 20 Biscuit. 21 Democrats and Republicans. 22 Coward. 23 Butcher. 24 Thailand. 25 Colin Farrell. 26 San Francisco. 27 Blue and white. 28 Nazareth. 29 Barbara Hulanicki. 30 45 degrees.

1 Is Dundee on the east or west coast of Scotland?
2 Which is the most northerly point on the British mainland?
3 Which city is Scotland's capital?
4 Are Scottish banknotes legal tender in England?
5 Who built a wall to divide Scotland from England?
6 Where is the Royal and Ancient Golf Club?
7 The name of which Scottish product means "water of life"?
8 Where is the Queen's Scottish residence?
9 What is the name of the Games held at Braemar?
10 Which sport is Aviemore particularly famous for?
11 What are the Cairngorms?
12 Which east coast port is known as the Granite City?
13 Which islands give their name to ponies and wool?
14 In which Loch is there said to be a monster?
15 Which Isle was linked to the mainland by a bridge in 1995?
16 Which Mull was the title of a song by Paul McCartney?
17 Which river flows through Glasgow?
18 Which city holds an annual Arts Festival?
19 Which speciality's ingredients include sheep's stomach and oatmeal?
20 Which village was a popular destination for runaway couples?
21 What does the word "loch" mean?
22 What is Scotland's highest mountain?
23 Which city gives its name to a rich fruit cake?
24 Which city shares its name with a city in Australia?
25 Which river in the Borders gives its name to a woollen fabric?
26 Which sea is to the east of the Scottish mainland?
27 What is a glen?
28 In which city is Hampden Park Stadium?
29 Which is further north, Edinburgh or Dundee?
30 Who is Scotland's patron saint?

| **Answers** | Hollywood *(see Quiz 34)* |

1 Humphrey Bogart. 2 Bing Crosby. 3 Ingrid Bergman. 4 Tony. 5 Richard Gere. 6 Bette. 7 De Mille. 8 Keystone. 9 Liza Minnelli. 10 Michael Douglas. 11 Gardner. 12 Sister. 13 Hepburn. 14 Kelly. 15 Alfred Hitchcock. 16 Jane Fonda. 17 Clark Gable. 18 Walter Matthau. 19 Ginger Rogers. 20 Temple. 21 Valentino. 22 Barrymore. 23 Newman. 24 Madonna. 25 Doris Day. 26 Tom Cruise. 27 Cagney. 28 Nose. 29 Elizabeth Taylor. 30 Moore.

1 Dr John Pemberton invented which drink in 1886?
2 Which Harry Potter film was released in November 2005?
3 What was the surname of the 41st and 43rd Presidents of the USA?
4 Victor Barna was five times world champion in which sport?
5 What is the Welsh name for Wales?
6 How many years are celebrated by an emerald anniversary?
7 In which village is "Emmerdale" set?
8 What three colours are on the flag of Australia?
9 What number does the Roman numeral L stand for?
10 Who recorded the album "Everything Changes"?
11 In cartoons, who "kept on walking"?
12 What do you suffer from if you have coryza?
13 What is the first name of TV cook Tovey?
14 What are the initials of comic writer Wodehouse?
15 Who directed the film "Tommy"?
16 The Haka is a dance performed by which rugby union team?
17 Which George wrote "Porgy and Bess"?
18 Snooker's Eddie Charlton comes from which country?
19 In which year were women first given the vote?
20 On what part of your body would you wear espadrilles?
21 Which of the following can vote in a general election: the mentally ill, criminals, people under 18?
22 In which country is the Curragh racecourse?
23 Which element is used in computer chips?
24 To five years either way, when was the GLC formed?
25 Which planet is 4,500 million years old?
26 What does the French word "pomme" mean?
27 What trees belong to the genus Quercus?
28 What was the last movie that Marlon Brando ever made?
29 Who wrote the poem "Anthem for Doomed Youth"?
30 The musical "The Woman in White" was based on a novel by which writer?

Answers | Pot-Luck 20 *(see Quiz 39)*

1 Darkness. 2 David Dimbleby. 3 John Joseph. 4 Bryan Robson. 5 Macmillan. 6 Devil Woman. 7 Bram Stoker. 8 Forget-me-not. 9 Cancer. 10 1855. 11 Nell Gwyn. 12 Enya. 13 Pack. 14 Orienteering. 15 Lee Marvin. 16 8. 17 Stave. 18 Robert Frost. 19 Peer Gynt. 20 General Custer. 21 Power boat racing. 22 Le Métro. 23 Gorilla. 24 Des O'Connor. 25 Wainwright. 26 St Francis. 27 John Prescott. 28 Krypton. 29 Toto. 30 Bull.

Quiz 38 Nature: Animals

Answers – page 48

LEVEL 1

1 Where does a kangaroo keep its young?
2 Which black and white mammal lives in China's bamboo forests?
3 Where do koalas live?
4 How many legs does an adult insect have?
5 What type of creature is a black widow?
6 Which animal's nickname is "ship of the desert"?
7 Which breed of spaniel shares its name with a king?
8 Which sea creature is known as a Portuguese man-of-war?
9 What is a female sheep called?
10 What do carnivorous animals live on?
11 Which animals are described as canine?
12 What is a fox's tail called?
13 Which saint is the heaviest breed of dog named after?
14 What is special about a guinea pig's tail?
15 What are pigs' feet called?
16 Which elephants have the smaller ears, African or Indian?
17 What are edible sturgeon eggs called?
18 What name is given to the period of winter sleep by some animals?
19 What is Britain's hardiest and shaggiest bovine breed?
20 What would a billy and a nanny produce?
21 Which black and white mammal sprays a foul smelling liquid when attacked?
22 How does a boa constrictor kill its prey?
23 Why does a fish need gills?
24 What does a scorpion have at the end of its tail?
25 What does a chameleon change to camouflage itself?
26 What does an Isle of Man Manx cat not have?
27 What type of insect is a Red Admiral?
28 What is another name for an Alsatian dog?
29 What kind of animal is a Suffolk Punch?
30 A lynx is a member of which family group?

Answers | Sport: Cricket *(see Quiz 40)*

1 Australia and England. 2 Manchester. 3 Before. 4 Cork. 5 Andrew Flintoff. 6 Jack Russell. 7 Lord's. 8 Randall. 9 Jerusalem. 10 England. 11 Two. 12 Yorkshire. 13 Wicket keeper. 14 Nottingham. 15 None. 16 India. 17 W. G. 18 Yorkshire. 19 Stewart. 20 Caught and bowled. 21 Left. 22 Lancashire. 23 Sunday. 24 Six. 25 Brian Johnson. 26 Terence. 27 Australia. 28 Six. 29 Middlesex. 30 None.

1 Which band's first album was called "Permission to Land"?
2 Who has presented the BBC's "Question Time" since 1994?
3 What are the real first names of racehorse trainer Jonjo O'Neill?
4 Which England soccer skipper was injured in both the 1986 and 1990 World Cup final stages?
5 Which Harold said, "Most of our people have never had it so good."
6 Cliff Richard and Marty Robbins had different songs that shared which title?
7 Which writer featured Jonathan Harker in his most famous novel?
8 Myosotis is more commonly known as which flower?
9 Which Tropic is further north, Capricorn or Cancer?
10 To ten years either way, when did Thomas Cook organize his first continental holiday?
11 Which orange seller became mistress of Charles II?
12 Who recorded the album "Shepherd Moons"?
13 What is the word for a group of hounds?
14 Which sport is a mixture of map reading and cross-country running?
15 Which actor recorded that he "was born under a wand'rin' star"?
16 How many legs has a spider?
17 In music, name the horizontal lines around which notes are written.
18 Which New England poet had "miles to go before I sleep"?
19 Which work does Anitra's Dance come from?
20 Who made his last stand at Little Bighorn?
21 Which sport awards the Harmsworth Trophy?
22 What is the Paris underground called?
23 Which is the largest of the apes?
24 Who did Morecambe and Wise not want to sing on their show?
25 Which Alfred mapped out moorland routes in northern England?
26 Which Italian saint was born at the town of Assisi?
27 Who became Deputy Prime Minister after Labour's election victory of 1997?
28 Which planet does Superman come from?
29 Who took "Africa" into the record charts?
30 What name is given to an adult male seal?

Answers | Pot-Luck 19 *(see Quiz 37)*

1 Coca Cola. 2 Harry Potter and the Goblet of Fire. 3 Bush. 4 Table tennis. 5 Cymru. 6 55. 7 Beckindale. 8 Blue, red and white. 9 50. 10 Take That. 11 Felix the Cat. 12 Common cold. 13 John. 14 P. G. 15 Ken Russell. 16 All Blacks. 17 Gershwin. 18 Australia. 19 1918. 20 Feet. 21 None. 22 Ireland. 23 Silicon. 24 1965. 25 Earth. 26 Apple. 27 Oaks. 28 The Brave. 29 Wilfred Owen. 30 Wilkie Collins.

Quiz 40 | Sport: Cricket

1 Which international teams contest the Ashes?

2 In which city is the ground Old Trafford?

3 In LBW what does the B stand for?

4 Which bowler Dominic took a Test hat-trick in 1995?

5 Which cricketer was voted BBC Sports Personality for 2005?

6 Which English wicket keeper shares his name with a breed of dog?

7 The Nursery End, the Pavilion End and St John's Wood Road are all linked with which ground?

8 Which former England batsman Derek was known as "Rags"?

9 Which patriotic song was adopted by England in the 2005 Ashes?

10 Robin Smith is an international for which country?

11 How many bails are there on a set of wickets?

12 Which county does Geoff Boycott come from?

13 What was the specialist position of Australia's Rodney Marsh?

14 Trent Bridge is in which English city?

15 How many runs are scored in a maiden over?

16 Which country was captained by Kapil Dev?

17 What were the initials of legendary Victorian cricketer Dr Grace?

18 Which county does Michael Vaughan play for?

19 In the 1990s, which Alec has opened and kept wicket for England?

20 In scoring, what does c & b stand for?

21 Was David Gower a left- or right-handed batsman?

22 Which English county did West Indies skipper Clive Lloyd play for?

23 On which day of the week were John Player League games played?

24 How many valid deliveries are sent down in a Test cricket over?

25 Which cricket commentator on radio was known as "Johnners"?

26 What does the initial T stand for in I. T. Botham's name?

27 In which country do Sheffield Shield games take place?

28 What does the batsman score for a shot that sends the ball over the boundary without touching the ground?

29 England skippers Brearley and Gatting have both captained which county?

30 How many Tests did England win on the tour of Pakistan late in 2005?

Answers	**Nature: Animals** *(see Quiz 38)*

1 In a pouch. 2 Panda. 3 Australia. 4 Six. 5 Spider. 6 Camel. 7 King Charles. 8 Jellyfish. 9 Ewe. 10 Meat. 11 Dogs. 12 Brush. 13 St Bernard. 14 It doesn't have one. 15 Trotters. 16 Indian. 17 Caviar. 18 Hibernation. 19 Highland cattle. 20 Kids. 21 Skunk. 22 Squeezing. 23 To breathe. 24 Sting. 25 Colour. 26 A tail. 27 Butterfly. 28 German Shepherd. 29 Horse. 30 Cat.

the big **+** plus
READING WRITING NUMBERS

$20 - 27 - 26$

$25(26-1)$

$27 - 7$

-26

$2 \times 4 - 120$

$112 \quad 130$

$4 \quad 65$

$5 \quad 65$

$6 - 5 - 260$

$11 \quad 112 - 130 -$

$13 - 16 - 260$

$260 \times 6 - 156$

$y \, 7/9 - 13$

1 What is the name of the computer game hedgehog?
2 What is the zodiac sign of the Crab?
3 Which gardener Alan wrote the novels "Mr MacGregor" and "Only Dad"?
4 Who had a No 1 hit with the song "Maggie May"?
5 In golf what is the term for two over par?
6 The initials TC stand for which cartoon character?
7 What were followers of John Wycliffe called?
8 Which country's national flag is a green rectangle?
9 Which subject does Simon Schama specialize in when making television programmes?
10 Who said – though not in English – "I think therefore I am"?
11 In education, what does GCSE stand for?
12 Which rock superstar is a former chairman of Watford football club?
13 Called a trailer in America, what's the name of this vehicle in the UK?
14 In which month is Royal Ascot horse-racing season?
15 What is agoraphobia a fear of?
16 What do the initials RAM stand for in computing?
17 Which village does Jane Marple live in?
18 How many kilogrammes make one metric ton?
19 Which comedian used the catchphrase, "Rock on, Tommy"?
20 What type of food is dill?
21 Which Scottish soccer team are known as "The Dons"?
22 Whom was Michael Schumacher driving for when he won his first Grand Prix?
23 Which day of the week is named after the Anglo-Saxon god Tiw?
24 On what date is American Independence Day?
25 What kind of animal is a seahorse?
26 The failure to produce enough insulin leads to which medical condition?
27 Which soccer side play at a Cottage?
28 Which insect transmits malaria?
29 In the fable, what did the boy cry to trick the villagers?
30 Which Colin was appointed George W. Bush's Secretary of State in 2001?

Answers | Pot-Luck 22 *(see Quiz 43)*

1 Germany. 2 Roman Abramovich. 3 Mother of pearl. 4 Simply Red. 5 The Corpse Bride. 6 O. 7 Eyes. 8 Judy Garland. 9 Terms at Oxford. 10 Samson. 11 Music. 12 Zither. 13 Blue whale. 14 Red. 15 Brian Jones. 16 Ten. 17 Numbers. 18 Walpurgis. 19 Peter Wright. 20 Swan. 21 Interpol. 22 Milligan. 23 Black Beauty. 24 Sturgeon. 25 Desmond Lynam. 26 Brussels. 27 Blue. 28 Olympus. 29 Squash. 30 Very High Frequency.

1 What is the first name of Mrs Bucket of "Keeping Up Appearances"?

2 Which actress Joanna played Patsy in "Absolutely Fabulous"?

3 Who was the café owner, played by Gorden Kaye, in "Allo Allo"?

4 In which sitcom does grumpy Victor Meldrew appear?

5 What is the surname of Del Boy and Rodney of "Only Fools and Horses"?

6 Was Ally McBeal a lawyer or an advertising executive?

7 What kind of Life did Jerry and Margo's neighbours Tom and Barbara lead?

8 What was the profession of Steptoe and Son?

9 In the sitcom title how many Children did Bill and Ben Porter have?

10 Which of Nora Batty's wrinkled garments turned on Compo?

11 Which two characters were "Just Good Friends"?

12 During which war was "Dad's Army" set?

13 Which senior political position did James Hacker MP reach?

14 In what type of establishment was "Are You Being Served?" set?

15 In which northeast city was "Auf Wiedersehen Pet" set?

16 Who is Tracey's sister in "Birds of a Feather"?

17 Whose servant was Baldrick?

18 Which sitcom was about the Boswell family from Liverpool?

19 At which hotel was Manuel the waiter?

20 In which series would you meet the Yellowcoats from Maplin's?

21 How were the Lads Terry Collier and Bob Ferris known?

22 Who shares an apartment with Grace?

23 Which clerical caper was set on Craggy Island?

24 How were the Men Behaving in the series about Gary and Tony ?

25 Which sitcom was set in a bar in Boston?

26 Who were Tom and Diana Waiting for at the Bayview Retirement Home?

27 What sort of Statesman was Alan B'Stard MP?

28 Where were the characters in "Porridge"?

29 Which Ricky created and starred in "The Office"?

30 Which series gave us the catchprase, "I don't believe it!"?

Answers	60s Newsround *(see Quiz 44)*

1 John F. Kennedy. 2 6. 3 Berlin. 4 Eichmann. 5 Marilyn Monroe. 6 Wilson. 7 Beeching. 8 Martin Luther King. 9 Harold Macmillan. 10 Shrimpton. 11 Eagle. 12 India. 13 Moors. 14 Smith. 15 Wight. 16 USSR. 17 Manson. 18 West Germany. 19 Garland. 20 Edward. 21 Prince Charles. 22 The Moon. 23 Kray. 24 Israel. 25 Economics. 26 Flower. 27 Campbell. 28 Mini. 29 Czechoslovakia. 30 Brian Epstein.

1 Which country is Lufthansa from?
2 Who was the owner of Chelsea FC when they won the 2005 Championship?
3 What is another word for nacre?
4 Who recorded the album "Stars"?
5 In 2005 Tim Burton's directed a movie based on folk tale about what type of "Bride"?
6 In Morse Code what letter is represented by three dashes?
7 In rhyming slang what are mince pies?
8 How is Frances Gumm better known?
9 What are Trinity and Hilary?
10 In the Bible, who was betrayed by Delilah?
11 In which branch of the arts is the metronome used?
12 Which musical instrument featured in the theme of "The Third Man"?
13 What type of whale is the largest?
14 What colour is vermilion?
15 Which member of the Rolling Stones is the movie "Stoned" about?
16 How many sides has a decagon?
17 What is the fourth book of the Old Testament ?
18 Which night is April 30th?
19 "Spycatcher" was the controversial memoirs of which former intelligence officer?
20 A cob is a male of which creature?
21 Hello, hello, hello, what was founded in Vienna in 1923?
22 Which Spike said, "Money can't buy friends, but you can get a better class of enemy"?
23 What was the horse in the title of Anna Sewell's novel?
24 From which fish is caviar obtained?
25 Who took over from Richard Whiteley as the host of "Countdown"?
26 What is the capital of Belgium?
27 What colour is the dye obtained from the plant woad?
28 Which mountain was said to be home of the Greek gods?
29 Which game is played in an enclosed space with both players hitting the ball in the same direction?
30 What does VHF stand for?

Answers | **Pot-Luck 21** *(see Quiz 41)*

1 Sonic. 2 Cancer. 3 Alan Titchmarsh. 4 Rod Stewart. 5 Double bogey. 6 Top Cat. 7 Lollards. 8 Libya. 9 History. 10 René Descartes. 11 General Certificate of Secondary Education. 12 Elton John. 13 Caravan. 14 June. 15 Open spaces. 16 Random Access Memory. 17 St Mary Mead. 18 One thousand. 19 Bobby Ball. 20 Herb. 21 Aberdeen. 22 Benetton. 23 Tuesday. 24 4th July. 25 Fish. 26 Diabetes. 27 Fulham. 28 Mosquito. 29 Wolf. 30 Colin Powell.

1 Who defeated Richard Nixon to become US president in 1960?
2 James Hanratty was charged with a murder on which A road?
3 Which European city was divided into East and West by a Wall?
4 Which Adolf was executed in May 1962 for his part in the Holocaust?
5 Which screen sex symbol was found dead in a bungalow near Hollywood in August 1962?
6 Which Harold became leader of the Labour Party in 1963?
7 Which Doctor wielded his axe on the railway network?
8 Who made a speech proclaiming, "I have a dream"?
9 Which Conservative resigned as prime minister in 1963?
10 Which model Jean was known as "The Shrimp"?
11 What type of creature was Goldie who made the headlines by escaping from London Zoo?
12 Mrs Indira Gandhi was appointed prime minister of which country?
13 Which notorious Murders involved Myra Hindley and Ian Brady?
14 Which Ian declared independence for Rhodesia?
15 On which Isle was there a 1969 rock festival featuring Bob Dylan?
16 Leonid Brezhnev became leader of which country?
17 Which Charles led "The Family" in the Sharon Tate murder?
18 Willi Brandt became chancellor of which country?
19 In 1969 which actress and singer Judy died at the age of 47?
20 Which Kennedy was involved in the car accident at Chappaquiddick?
21 Which member of the royal family was invested as Prince of Wales?
22 Neil Armstrong became the first man to set foot where?
23 Which gangland twins Ronald and Reginald were jailed?
24 Golda Meir became the first woman prime minister of which country?
25 LSE, the scene of student protest, was the London School of what?
26 What type of Power symbolized the 1967 peace and love festivals?
27 Which Donald was killed trying to break the world water speed record?
28 Which type of skirt was the main fashion of the 1960s?
29 Soviet tanks moved to crush the Dubcek reforms in which country?
30 Who was manager of the Beatles by the time they made the charts?

| **Answers** | TV: Sitcoms (see Quiz 42) |

1 Hyacinth. 2 Lumley. 3 René. 4 One Foot in the Grave. 5 Trotter. 6 Lawyer. 7 The Good Life. 8 Rag and bone men. 9 2 Point 4. 10 Stockings. 11 Vince and Penny. 12 Second World War. 13 Prime Minister. 14 Department store. 15 Newcastle. 16 Sharon. 17 Blackadder. 18 Bread. 19 Fawlty Towers. 20 Hi de Hi! 21 Likely Lads. 22 Will. 23 Father Ted. 24 Badly. 25 Cheers. 26 God. 27 New. 28 Prison. 29 Gervais. 30 One Foot in the Grave.

1 If it rains on St Swithin's Day, how many more days is it supposed to rain?
2 By which name of one word is Katie Price better known?
3 Released in 2005, the album "Tissues and Issues" was a success for which star?
4 Which composer wrote "The Marriage of Figaro"?
5 What is a low, shallow basket used by gardeners called?
6 How many years are celebrated by a golden anniversary?
7 In "David Copperfield" what was the surname of Uriah?
8 What is the first name of the main detective in "A Touch of Frost"?
9 What number does the Roman numeral M stand for?
10 What sort of creature is a capercaillie?
11 In which month is Remembrance Day?
12 Which TV drama was set in the delightfully named Glenbogle?
13 How many faces has an icosahedron?
14 What are the initials of "Lady Chatterley" author Lawrence?
15 What name is given to a litter of piglets?
16 What type of dancing is associated with Margot Fonteyn?
17 Which soap pub sells Churchill Strong?
18 Who recorded the album "Both Sides"?
19 How many children did Queen Victoria have?
20 Who is the resident Lord in "Private Eye"?
21 What are paper measures called equal to 500 sheets?
22 In which country is Flushing Meadow tennis stadium?
23 What is the domed recess at the east end of a church called?
24 What is a young goat called?
25 How did master escapologist Harry Houdini die?
26 After which George was the American state of Georgia named?
27 Which viral disease is also called grippe?
28 Who said, "Anyone can get old. All you have to do is live long enough"?
29 In what game do you peg, and score for pairs and fifteens?
30 What does PYO stand for?

Answers	Pot-Luck 24 *(see Quiz 47)*

1 Scapegoat. 2 300. 3 Norah Jones. 4 France. 5 Warhol. 6 Seven. 7 Lead. 8 Slade. 9 Intestate. 10 A pig. 11 Annie Oakley. 12 Meatloaf. 13 Swarm. 14 Clarinet. 15 Coyote. 16 Seven. 17 Natural. 18 Susan. 19 72. 20 Grape. 21 2 Point 4 Children. 22 Liverpool. 23 Will Young. 24 Flute. 25 Mrs Hudson. 26 Beaufort. 27 Paris. 28 Pictionary. 29 The Red Crescent. 30 Six.

1 In which Swiss mountain range is the Jungfrau?
2 Which is the next largest island in the world after Australia?
3 Which seaside resort is Super-Mare?
4 On which continent is the Kariba Dam?
5 What are Lakes Michigan, Superior, Huron, Erie and Ontario known as collectively?
6 If the southern limit of the tropics is Capricorn what is the northern limit called?
7 Which island is to the south of Australia?
8 In the south of which country was Saigon?
9 If you were in Benidorm in which country would you be?
10 Which London palace has a maze?
11 Which isle off the west coast of England has three legs as its symbol?
12 Which country is connected to Wales by the Severn Bridge?
13 Which US state is a collection of islands in the Pacific?
14 Which language do natives of Hamburg speak?
15 Which county has a red rose as its symbol?
16 Which Queen gave her name to the capital of Hong Kong?
17 Which Bank is made of sand in the North Sea?
18 In which county is Penzance?
19 Which islands are Sark and Alderney part of?
20 Greece is in which continent?
21 What are the counties of Essex, Suffolk, Norfolk and Cambridgeshire collectively known as?
22 Is Japan in the northern or the southern hemisphere?
23 What is the name of the biggest Canyon in Arizona?
24 The London Eye was built by which river?
25 Is the Arctic Circle near the north or the south pole?
26 On the south of which continent are the Andes?
27 If you were looking at the Ganges which country would you be in?
28 Which country do the Scilly Isles belong to?
29 Which country originally produced Fiat cars?
30 What is the most westerly point of England?

| **Answers** | Pop: Sounds of the 70s *(see Quiz 48)* |

1 The Brotherhood of Man. 2 Lee. 3 Glitter. 4 Bay. 5 Sweet. 6 Tyrannosaurus. 7 Slade. 8 Rod Stewart. 9 Kiki Dee. 10 Queen. 11 The Pips. 12 The Rubettes. 13 10 cc 14 5. 15 Sing. 16 Blondie. 17 Survive. 18 Nilsson. 19 Abba. 20 Genesis. 21 Electric Light Orchestra. 22 Fire. 23 Eagles. 24 Tiger. 25 Love. 26 Garfunkel. 27 Soul. 28 The Bee Gees. 29 Mungo Jerry. 30 Mondays.

Quiz 47 | Pot-Luck 24

1 What animal-linked name describes someone who always gets blamed?
2 How many seconds in five minutes?
3 "Come Away with Me" was the first No 1 album for which female artist?
4 Which country hosted the last World Cup of the 20th century?
5 Which Andy said, "In the future everyone will be famous for 15 minutes?"
6 In snooker what is the score for potting a black?
7 Pb is the symbol of which chemical element?
8 Who recorded the seasonal song "Merry Xmas Everybody"?
9 Which term means dying without having made a will?
10 Who or what was the Empress of Blandings?
11 Who was Little Sure Shot according to Sitting Bull?
12 Who recorded the album "Bat Out of Hell"?
13 What is the word for a group of bees?
14 Which musical instrument is played by Acker Bilk?
15 What is another name for the prairie wolf?
16 How many colours are there in the rainbow?
17 In music, what is a note if it is neither sharp nor flat?
18 Whom was Madonna desperately seeking in her first feature film?
19 How many inches in two yards?
20 What type of fruit is dried to produce a sultana?
21 Apart from "The Flowerpot Men" in which show do Bill and Ben appear?
22 Robbie Fowler started his career with which club?
23 Which Will advised "Leave Right Now" in 2003?
24 What instrument does James Galway play?
25 What is the name of Sherlock Holmes's housekeeper?
26 Which Admiral gave his name to a weather measurement scale?
27 Where was Glenn Miller flying to when his plane disappeared?
28 In which game do players have to guess a word from a drawing?
29 What is the Muslim equivalent of the Red Cross?
30 How many squares on a Rubik Cube never move?

Answers | Pot-Luck 23 *(see Quiz 45)*

1 40. 2 Jordan. 3 Charlotte Church. 4 Mozart. 5 Trug. 6 50. 7 Heap. 8 Jack. 9 1,000. 10 A bird. 11 November. 12 Monarch of the Glen. 13 20. 14 D. H. 15 A farrow. 16 Ballet. 17 Queen Vic (EastEnders). 18 Phil Collins. 19 Nine. 20 Lord Gnome. 21 Ream. 22 USA. 23 Apse. 24 Kid. 25 A blow to his stomach. 26 King George II. 27 Influenza. 28 Groucho Marx. 29 Cribbage. 30 Pick Your Own.

1 Which Brotherhood had a Eurovision winner in 1976?
2 Peters and who said "Welcome Home" in 1973?
3 Which Gary was Leader of the Gang?
4 Which City Rollers had a hit with "Bye Bye Baby"?
5 A "Ballroom Blitz" came from which sugary-sounding group?
6 What had the T originally stood for in T Rex?
7 Which group led by Noddy Holder sang "Weer All Crazee Now"?
8 Who sang "Do Ya Think I'm Sexy"?
9 Who sang with Elton John on "Don't Go Breaking My Heart"?
10 "Bohemian Rhapsody" was recorded by which group?
11 Who helped Gladys Knight "make it through the night" in 1972?
12 "Sugar Baby Love" and "Jukebox Jive" were hits for which group?
13 What was the capacity of the group who said "I'm Not in Love"?
14 How many Jacksons were there when they sang "I Want You Back"?
15 What did the New Seekers say they would like to teach the world to do?
16 Fair-haired Debbie Harry sang with which group?
17 What did Gloria Gaynor say she would do in 1979?
18 Which Harry was "Without You" in 1972?
19 Which Swedish group met their Waterloo in 1974?
20 Which band has the same name as the first book in the Bible?
21 What does ELO stand for?
22 What joins Earth and Wind in a group's name?
23 Which birds of prey sang about the Hotel California?
24 What sort of feet did Mud sing about?
25 Showaddywaddy were Under the Moon of what in 1976?
26 Which singer Art had a solo No 1 after duo success with Paul Simon?
27 Which David of "Starsky & Hutch" fame charted with his ballads?
28 Who were "Stayin' Alive" with "Night Fever" in 1978?
29 Which Jerry sang "In the Summertime"?
30 What day did the Boomtown Rats not like?

| **Answers** | Geography *(see Quiz 46)* |

1 Alps. 2 Greenland. 3 Weston. 4 Africa. 5 Great Lakes. 6 Tropic of Cancer. 7 Tasmania. 8 Vietnam. 9 Spain. 10 Hampton Court. 11 Isle of Man. 12 England. 13 Hawaii. 14 German. 15 Lancashire. 16 Victoria. 17 Dogger Bank. 18 Cornwall. 19 Channel Islands. 20 Europe. 21 East Anglia. 22 Northern. 23 Grand Canyon. 24 River Thames. 25 North. 26 America. 27 India. 28 United Kingdom. 29 Italy. 30 Land's End.

1 What colour is a peridot stone?
2 What is the zodiac sign of the Twins?
3 In which part of the body is the patella?
4 Who had a No 1 hit with the song "Bachelor Boy"?
5 What is the second letter of the Greek alphabet?
6 What is the nest of an eagle called?
7 Which film star has a statue in Leicester Square?
8 Who wrote the screenplay and starred in the movie "Nanny McPhee"?
9 What was the name of David and Victoria Beckham's first child born in Spain?
10 What did the Rochdale Pioneers pioneer?
11 Which 1995 movie starred a wet Kevin Costner?
12 Which board game involves moving through rooms to solve a murder?
13 Called a tuxedo in America, what's this garment called in the UK?
14 What type of jewels are traditionally associated with Amsterdam?
15 What is zoophobia a fear of?
16 Which Irish boy band took their first seven singles to No 1?
17 What was Charon's job?
18 Which Edith sang "Je ne regrette rien" (No Regrets)?
19 What colour is the Central Line on a London Underground map?
20 What type of food is a bagel?
21 What sits on a dolly in a television studio?
22 Who says, "You'll like this – not a lot!"?
23 Which day of the week is named after the god Woden?
24 Who recorded the album "From the Cradle"?
25 Which "Coronation Street" supermarket employed Reg and Vera?
26 What is the claw of a bird of prey called?
27 Which colour features on the kit of both Blackburn Rovers and Newcastle United?
28 Dr Stephen Hawking wrote a brief history of what?
29 Which Club is concerned with pedigree in the dog world?
30 Which English king was painted by Hans Holbein?

Answers	Pot-Luck 26 *(see Quiz 51)*

1 Dan Brown. 2 Rupee. 3 Mark, Martin. 4 64. 5 Stuarts. 6 Eight. 7 Joey. 8 Sting. 9 Bush. 10 Solomon. 11 Gestapo. 12 Netherlands. 13 Holland. 14 Mauve. 15 Acer. 16 12. 17 St Valentine's Day. 18 Lodge. 19 John Keats. 20 Apron. 21 Israel. 22 Madness. 23 Jack Russell. 24 Cabbage. 25 Christina Aguilera. 26 Hydrogen. 27 Alan. 28 Ngaio Marsh. 29 Six. 30 Visual Display Unit.

1 Bobby Moore captained which country in the 1970 World Cup?
2 Which British golfer Tony won the US Open Championship?
3 In 1970 Margaret Court won four major tournaments in which sport?
4 Which horse-riding princess was voted Sportswoman of the Year?
5 At which Scottish stadium was there a crowd disaster in 1971?
6 Which Sebastian completed a hat-trick of running records in 1979?
7 John Conteh became a champion in which sport?
8 Which London team won the League and FA Cup double in 1971?
9 What was the sport of Britain's David Wilkie?
10 In 1976 which cricketer Viv hit 291 runs in an innings against England?
11 Which 19-year-old Evonne triumphed at Wimbledon in 1971?
12 Which Ray was the most successful snooker player of the 70s?
13 Which soccer team won the Scottish League every season from 1970 to 1974?
14 Which horse won the Grand National three times?
15 Who was manager of Nottingham Forest when they won the European Cup?
16 Which Brendan won the only British track and field medal of the 1976 Olympic Games?
17 Bjorn Borg comes from which country?
18 Which Barry became world 500cc motor-cycling champion?
19 Which Daley became the youngest ever athlete to represent Britain in the decathlon?
20 Which British player won the 1977 women's singles at Wimbledon?
21 Which English soccer side twice won the European Cup?
22 In which sport was Mike Brearley an England captain?
23 Which country outside the UK won the Grand Slam in 1977?
24 Which Suffolk soccer side won the FA Cup in 1978?
25 Which team won the 1978 soccer World Cup staged in Argentina?
26 In 1978–9 Hull Kingston Rovers were champions in which sport?
27 Which Niki was badly burnt in the 1976 German Grand Prix?
28 Which TV mogul started his own cricket unofficial Test series?
29 Which Jackie was world champion motor racing driver in 1971 and 1973?
30 Ally MacLeod was manager of which national soccer side?

Answers	70s Films *(see Quiz 52)*

1 Star Wars. 2 The Godfather. 3 A car. 4 A shark. 5 Saturday. 6 Kramer. 7 Superman. 8 Cuckoo's. 9 Grease. 10 Third. 11 Nile. 12 Rocky. 13 Kermit. 14 Eagle. 15 King Kong. 16 Towering Inferno. 17 M*A*S*H. 18 Orange. 19 Jackal. 20 Bugsy. 21 Clint Eastwood. 22 Diamonds. 23 Deer. 24 Beverly Hills. 25 Dog. 26 Robert Redford. 27 Great and Small. 28 Now. 29 Moon. 30 Poseidon.

Quiz 51 | Pot-Luck 26 | Answers – page 57

1 Who wrote the mega-selling book "The Da Vinci Code"?
2 What is the currency of India?
3 On TV, what are the names of Pauline Fowler's two sons?
4 How many squares are there on a chess board?
5 James I and Charles I were members of which royal dynasty?
6 How many lanes are there in an Olympic swimming pool?
7 What was the name of the "Friends" spin-off starring Matt LeBlanc?
8 How is Gordon Sumner better known?
9 What name links singer Kate and former USA President George?
10 In the Bible, who was famous for his wisdom?
11 What was the secret state police of Nazi Germany called?
12 In which country is Schiphol airport?
13 Which Republic of Ireland player Matt shares his surname with a country?
14 What colour is heliotrope?
15 Which tree family includes the sycamore and maple?
16 How many sides has a dodecagon?
17 Which event did the first popular greeting card celebrate?
18 What is the home of a beaver called?
19 Who wrote of "Season of mists and mellow fruitfulness"?
20 What name is given to an extension of a stage in front of a curtain?
21 Of which country was Golda Meir prime minister?
22 Who recorded the album "Divine Madness"?
23 Which short-legged dog is named after the 18th-century parson who bred them?
24 Which vegetable is the main ingredient in coleslaw?
25 Who had a US and UK No 1 with "Genie in a Bottle"?
26 Which element has the atomic number 1 in the periodic table?
27 What is the first name of gardener and presenter Titchmarsh?
28 Who created Chief Inspector Alleyn?
29 How many legs has a daddy-long-legs?
30 What does VDU stand for?

Answers | Pot-Luck 25 *(see Quiz 49)*

1 Green. 2 Gemini. 3 Knee. 4 Cliff Richard. 5 Beta. 6 Eyrie. 7 Charlie Chaplin.
8 Emma Thompson. 9 Cruz. 10 The Co-op. 11 Waterworld. 12 Cluedo. 13 Dinner
jacket. 14 Diamonds. 15 Animals. 16 Westlife. 17 Ferryman who, in Greek mythology,
takes the dead to the underworld. 18 Piaf. 19 Red. 20 Bread roll. 21 A camera. 22
Paul Daniels. 23 Wednesday. 24 Eric Clapton. 25 Bettabuys. 26 Talon. 27 White. 28
Time. 29 Kennel. 30 Henry VIII.

Quiz 52 | 70s Films

Answers – page 58

1 Which Wars were there in 1977?
2 Which 1972 film, with Marlon Brando, was about the Mafia?
3 What was Herbie?
4 Which creature took a starring role in "Jaws"?
5 What Night was there Fever in the movie with John Travolta?
6 Who was versus Kramer in the Dustin Hoffman film?
7 Who is Clark Kent better known as?
8 Which bird's Nest did One fly over in 1975?
9 In which film did John Travolta and Olivia Newton-John sing "You're the One That I Want"?
10 What Kind of Close Encounters were there in 1977?
11 On which Egyptian river was there Death in the Agatha Christie film?
12 Which boxer did Sylvester Stallone play?
13 Name the frog in "The Muppet Movie".
14 Which bird of prey Landed in the war movie based on Jack Higgins' novel?
15 Which 1970s film about a giant ape was a remake of a 1933 movie?
16 Which disaster movie was about a fire in the world's tallest building?
17 Which film told of a mobile hospital in the Korean War?
18 Which fruit was Clockwork in the Stanley Kubrick film?
19 Which animal's Day was it in the film about an assassin based on the Frederick Forsyth novel?
20 What was the first name of gangster Malone?
21 Who starred in the western "Every Which Way but Loose"?
22 What were Forever in the James Bond movie?
23 What sort of Hunter was Robert de Niro in the film with Meryl Streep?
24 Where was Eddie Murphy a Cop in the film series?
25 Digby was the biggest what in the world?
26 Who starred with Paul Newman in "The Sting"?
27 How were All Creatures described in the 1974 film about a vet?
28 When was Apocalypse in the 1979 film?
29 Which planet features in the title of a 1979 Bond movie?
30 Which Adventure was about a disaster on a luxury liner?

Answers	Sport: The 70s (see Quiz 50)

1 England. 2 Jacklin. 3 Tennis. 4 Princess Anne. 5 Ibrox Park. 6 Coe. 7 Boxing.
8 Arsenal. 9 Swimming. 10 Richards. 11 Goolagong. 12 Reardon. 13 Celtic. 14 Red Rum. 15 Brian Clough. 16 Foster. 17 Sweden. 18 Sheene. 19 Thompson. 20 Virginia Wade. 21 Liverpool. 22 Cricket. 23 France. 24 Ipswich. 25 Argentina. 26 Rugby League. 27 Lauda. 28 Kerry Packer. 29 Stewart. 30 Scotland.

Quiz 53 | Pot-Luck 27 | Answers – page 63

1 Catherine Parr survived which royal husband?
2 Whom did Roger Federer beat in the final of the 2005 US Open?
3 What is meant by the Latin phrase caveat emptor?
4 Which English club did soccer TV pundit Alan Hansen play for?
5 What spirit is made from fermented sugar cane?
6 How many years are celebrated by a silver anniversary?
7 Which actress played opposite Jim Carrey in "Eternal Sunshine Of The Spotless Mind"?
8 What is the capital of the Isle of Man?
9 How did Yetta Feldman die in "So Haunt Me"?
10 Which Tom starred in "Magnum"?
11 Which word meaning letter is in titles of books of the Bible?
12 Who recorded the album "Simply the Best"?
13 What paper is used to test acid and alkali?
14 What are the initials of English writer Priestley?
15 Who presented the first ever edition of "Mastermind"?
16 How many seconds in quarter of an hour?
17 Which special day follows Shrove Tuesday?
18 Who came first as US President, Washington or Lincoln?
19 Diana Ross, Florence Ballard and Mary Wilson formed what?
20 How is the UK golfing term albatross known in America?
21 Which social security benefit was introduced in 1909?
22 What name is adopted by Don Diego de la Vega?
23 What were the first three Eddystone lighthouses lit by?
24 What is a young hare called?
25 At what degree celsius does water freeze?
26 Which animal's name means river horse?
27 What is the first name of TV cook Carrier?
28 Which day of the week is dimanche in French?
29 Which actor George directed the movie "Good Night and Good Luck"?
30 Which actress does Orlando Bloom try to save in the movie "Pirates of the Caribbean"?

Answers	Food and Drink *(see Quiz 55)*

1 Eggs. 2 Deer. 3 Mint. 4 France. 5 Pancakes. 6 Chips. 7 Rasher. 8 Honey. 9 Smoked. 10 Potato. 11 Holland. 12 Oats. 13 Soup. 14 Ketchup. 15 Colourless. 16 Spain. 17 Apples. 18 Almonds. 19 Hot. 20 Sausage. 21 Yorkshire. 22 Beans. 23 Yellow. 24 Fish. 25 Brown. 26 Cheese. 27 Peas. 28 Italy. 29 Beer and lemonade. 30 Isle of Islay.

1 Which soap has the pub the Malt Shovel?
2 How many minutes in two and a half hours?
3 Which country is a car from if it has the international registration letters CH?
4 Who created and starred in the TV series "Extras"?
5 Which actor played Legolas Greenleaf in the "Lord of the Rings" trilogy?
6 In darts, what is the lowest score for three trebles?
7 N is the symbol of which chemical element ?
8 Who recorded the album "Parklife"?
9 Which member of the famous Arquette family was married to Nicolas Cage?
10 What is the last month of the year to have exactly 31 days?
11 Which Australian bird does not fly?
12 Which veteran DJ Tony was the first voice on Radio 1?
13 In geometry, how many minutes are there in a degree?
14 What is a segment of garlic called?
15 Which Barbra sang "A Woman in Love"?
16 What is the first letter on the bottom line of a keyboard?
17 Where is the veterinary surgery of Alistair Hebden Lloyd?
18 What is "black gold"?
19 How many feet are there in ten yards?
20 What is Edward Woodward's only hit single?
21 Which Henry started the Promenade Concerts?
22 Which composer wrote the Water Music?
23 What word means dry on a bottle of Italian wine?
24 Which garden shrub is known as the butterfly bush?
25 Whom is Debbie McGee married to?
26 Which types of programme does Hazel Irvine most usually present?
27 Which Dustin starred in "The Graduate"?
28 In the 1850s a Singer sewing machine became the first item to be sold under which trading terms?
29 Starting in March, in which month does the coarse fishing close season end in British rivers?
30 Which word can be someone in an army or a piece of toast?

Answers	Pot-Luck 29 *(see Quiz 56)*

1 John Peel. 2 Leo. 3 Chris de Burgh. 4 Marks and Gran. 5 Head. 6 Harry Enfield. 7 The Goon Show. 8 Ronnie Barker, Ronnie Corbett. 9 Baldrick. 10 Deep. 11 Independent Television News. 12 Flamingo. 13 Music hall. 14 Edward. 15 Horses. 16 Sweet Charity. 17 Dane. 18 Ruth. 19 Family Affairs. 20 Loaf of bread. 21 Polo. 22 Michael Barrymore. 23 Friday. 24 Frank. 25 Sri Lanka. 26 Tim Burton. 27 Spector. 28 Japanese flower arranging. 29 Andrew Flintoff. 30 London.

Quiz 55 | Food and Drink | Answers – page 61

1 What is the main ingredient in an omelette?
2 Which animal does venison come from?
3 Which garden herb is made into a sauce often eaten with lamb?
4 In which country did the word biscuit originate?
5 What is traditionally eaten on Shrove Tuesday?
6 What is another name for French fries?
7 What is a slice of bacon called?
8 Which edible sugary substance do bees make?
9 What is done to a herring to make it into a kipper?
10 Which vegetable can be King Edward or Desirée?
11 Which country does Edam cheese originate from?
12 What do you add to milk to make porridge?
13 What is minestrone?
14 What is bottled tomato sauce called?
15 What colour is vodka?
16 Where did the dish paella originate?
17 Which fruit is covered with toffee at a fairground?
18 Which nuts are used to make marzipan?
19 Is a Spotted Dick usually eaten hot or cold?
20 What meat dish is Cumberland famous for?
21 Which pudding is eaten with roast beef?
22 Which vegetables can be French, runner or baked?
23 What colour is piccalilli?
24 What sort of food is a rollmop?
25 Is wholemeal bread brown or white?
26 If something is cooked "au gratin" what must it contain?
27 Petits pois are small what?
28 In which country is Peroni beer bottled?
29 What are the two main ingredients of a shandy?
30 Which Scottish island has seven working whisky distilleries on it?

Answers | Pot-Luck 27 *(see Quiz 53)*

1 Henry VIII. 2 Andre Agassi. 3 Buyer beware. 4 Liverpool. 5 Rum. 6 25. 7 Kate Winslet. 8 Douglas. 9 Choked on a chicken bone. 10 Selleck. 11 Epistle. 12 Tina Turner. 13 Litmus. 14 J. B. 15 Magnus Magnusson. 16 900. 17 Ash Wednesday. 18 Washington. 19 The Supremes. 20 Double eagle. 21 Old age pension. 22 Zorro. 23 Candles. 24 Leveret. 25 0. 26 Hippopotamus. 27 Robert. 28 Sunday. 29 George Clooney. 30 Keira Knightley.

Quiz 56 | Pot-Luck 29 | Answers – page 62

1 "Margrave of the Marshes" is a memoir to which late DJ?

2 What is the zodiac sign of the Lion?

3 Who recorded the album "Spark to a Flame"?

4 Which duo created "Birds of a Feather"?

5 In the Bible, what part of John the Baptist's anatomy did Salome demand as a reward for her dancing?

6 Which comedian talked about "Loadsamoney"?

7 Which radio show was originally called "Crazy People"?

8 Which two TV comedians say "It's goodnight from me..." "...And it's goodnight from him"?

9 Who did Tony Robinson play in the "Blackadder" series?

10 According to proverb, how do still waters run?

11 In the broadcasting sector, what does ITN stand for?

12 Which exotic bird stands on one leg?

13 The Americans call it vaudeville, what is it called in Britain?

14 At the beginning of 2005 which was the only son of the Queen who was married?

15 What is hippophobia a fear of?

16 Which musical does "Hey Big Spender" come from?

17 Which Great breed of dog sounds as if it comes from Scandinavia?

18 What is the first name of TV cook Mott?

19 In which soap was Gary Costello played by Gary Webster?

20 What type of food is a bloomer?

21 Chukkas are the playing periods in which sport?

22 Who says, "All wight?"?

23 Which day of the week is named after the goddess Frigg?

24 Which Anne kept a diary while in hiding during the Second World War?

25 What was Ceylon renamed as?

26 Which Tim was director of the 2005 version of "Charlie and the Chocolate Factory"?

27 Which record producer Phil produced a "wall of sound" in the 1960s?

28 What is ikebana?

29 Which sportsman wrote an autobiography called "Being Freddie"?

30 Where will the 2012 Olympics be held?

Answers	Pot-Luck 28 *(see Quiz 54)*

1 Emmerdale. 2 150. 3 Switzerland. 4 Ricky Gervais. 5 Orlando Bloom. 6 Nine. 7 Nitrogen. 8 Blur. 9 Patricia. 10 December. 11 Emu. 12 Tony Blackburn. 13 60. 14 Clove. 15 Streisand. 16 Z. 17 Ambridge (in the Archers). 18 Oil. 19 30. 20 The Way You Look Tonight. 21 Wood. 22 Handel. 23 Secco. 24 Buddleia. 25 Paul Daniels. 26 Sport. 27 Hoffman. 28 Hire Purchase. 29 June. 30 Soldier.

1 Which Irish comedian held a cigarette, sat on a bar stool and chatted?
2 What was the profession of the Angels?
3 Which poetess Pam won "Opportunity Knocks" in 1975?
4 What made up the Bouquet in the series with Susan Penhaligon?
5 Whose Angels were undercover detectives?
6 The Duchess of which street was part of a 1970s drama series?
7 Which king and son of Queen Victoria was the subject of a TV serial?
8 Which Tudor queen was played by Glenda Jackson?
9 The Fall and Rise of which Perrin was played by Leonard Rossiter?
10 What was the first name of Basil Fawlty's wife?
11 How were Bill Oddie, Tim Brooke-Taylor and Graeme Garden known?
12 Which children's series told of life in a London comprehensive?
13 In which series did The Fonz appear?
14 Who was told It Ain't Half Hot in the sit com set in India?
15 When will it be Alright in the Denis Norden series begun in 1977?
16 Which Jim fixed it?
17 Which series about three delinquent OAPs began in the 1970s?
18 Whose Flying Circus was a big 1970s hit?
19 Which early-evening news magazine was transmitted throughout the country?
20 Which series about sheep dog trials began in the 1970s?
21 What was the nationality of detective Van Der Valk?
22 Which Liverpool shipping Line was an extremely popular long-running series?
23 In which part of the country was the Poldark series set?
24 Which building moisture problem was the title of the series about Rigsby and Miss Jones?
25 Who was Starsky's police partner?
26 Who started presenting "That's Life" in 1974?
27 Who starred in their Christmas Show watched by 28 million in 1977?
28 To what was Audrey Fforbes-Hamilton born?
29 If Lord Bellamy was Upstairs, where were Hudson and Mrs Bridges?
30 In which part of England was "When the Boat Comes In" set?

Answers	Literature *(see Quiz 59)*

1 Harry Potter novels. 2 Agatha Christie. 3 Brontë. 4 Wodehouse. 5 Adrian Mole. 6 Vet. 7 Cartland. 8 Rumpole. 9 Lady Chatterley. 10 Horse racing. 11 Archer. 12 Collins. 13 Rendell. 14 Peace. 15 Treasure. 16 Twist. 17 Pan. 18 Eagle. 19 Catherine. 20 James. 21 Alice. 22 Three. 23 Crusoe. 24 The Willows. 25 Scrooge. 26 Da Vinci. 27 Daffodils. 28 Poetry. 29 Belgian. 30 Monk.

Quiz 58 | Pot-Luck 30

Answers – page 68

1 Who wrote the travel book "Himalaya" and starred in the TV series with the same name?
2 What is the currency of the Netherlands?
3 What is the first name of TV cook Dimbleby?
4 Which birds congregate in a gaggle?
5 Who recorded the million-selling album "Be Here Now"?
6 Which veteran cricket commentator retired after the 2005 Ashes series?
7 In rhyming slang what is the Sweeney Todd?
8 How is Robert Zimmermann better known?
9 Which university did Prince William graduate from in 2005?
10 In the Bible, what was the name of the first garden?
11 How many minutes in four and three quarter hours?
12 What is the name of "She Who Must be Obeyed"?
13 Which cartoon character says, "Smarter than the average bear"?
14 What colour do you get if you mix red and yellow?
15 Which sport does Sam Torrance play?
16 How many sides has a rhombus?
17 In which children's TV show did Bungle, George and Zippy appear?
18 What colour was the Pimpernel in Baroness Orczy's novel?
19 Which major river flows through Vienna?
20 Which song was a hit for both Buddy Holly and Mud?
21 What can dogs do that wolves cannot?
22 In the film "Free Willy" what was Willy?
23 Where in the body is the cranium?
24 Which rock guitarist had a band called the Experience?
25 What can be planes or sprays of water?
26 What is the capital of Norway?
27 Grant and Truman have been presidents of which country?
28 Which name is shared by model Cindy and actor/singer Michael?
29 Who recorded the album "A Night at the Opera"?
30 What does VCR stand for?

Answers | Pot-Luck 31 *(see Quiz 60)*

1 Tuesday. 2 Sharon Osbourne. 3 Paddington. 4 Gary Rhodes. 5 Alaska. 6 30.
7 Endive. 8 Tank. 9 Simon Preston. 10 Tracy. 11 December. 12 Madness. 13
Badminton. 14 1878. 15 Wizzard. 16 Puffin. 17 Lenin. 18 Seafood/Fish. 19 T. Rex.
20 By sense of smell. 21 Suez. (The opera was Aida.) 22 Chestnut. 23 Kissin' Cousins.
24 Foal. 25 Jimmy Nail. 26 The Queen Mother. 27 Roger Federer. 28 Pepys. 29
Fish. 30 Open University.

1 Which best-selling novels centre round Hogwarts School?
2 Who created the character of Miss Marple?
3 Which Emily wrote "Wuthering Heights"?
4 Which creator of Jeeves and Wooster is known by his initials P. G.?
5 Whose first Secret Diary was written when he was 13 3/4?
6 What was the profession of James Herriot?
7 What was the surname of romantic novelist Dame Barbara?
8 Which London barrister was created by John Mortimer?
9 Whose Lover was the subject of a book by D. H. Lawrence?
10 Which sport are Dick Francis' novels about?
11 Which politician Jeffrey wrote "Kane and Abel"?
12 Which novelist Jackie has an actress sister called Joan?
13 Which Ruth created Inspector Wexford?
14 What did Tolstoy write about together with War?
15 What was on the Island Robert Louis Stevenson wrote about?
16 What was the surname of the Dickens character Oliver?
17 Which Peter took the Darling children to Never Never Land?
18 Which bird of prey Has Landed, in the book by Jack Higgins?
19 What was the first name of novelist Miss Cookson?
20 Which detective novelist is known by her initials P. D.?
21 Which little girl had Adventures Through the Looking Glass?
22 How many Musketeers were there in the title of the book by Dumas?
23 Which Robinson was shipwrecked on a desert island?
24 Where is the Wind in the story about Toad and Badger?
25 What was the surname of Ebenezer in "A Christmas Carol"?
26 Which artist's name features in the title of Dan Brown's best-selling book?
27 Which popular yellow spring flower did Wordsworth write about?
28 What type of writing is John Betjeman famous for?
29 What is the nationality of Agatha Christie's detective Poirot?
30 What is the religious occupation of medieval detective Cadfael?

Answers | TV: The 70s *(see Quiz 57)*

1 Dave Allen. 2 Nurses. 3 Ayres. 4 Barbed Wire. 5 Charlie's. 6 Duke Street. 7 Edward VII. 8 Elizabeth I. 9 Reginald. 10 Sybil. 11 The Goodies. 12 Grange Hill. 13 Happy Days. 14 Mum. 15 On the Night. 16 Savile. 17 Last of the Summer Wine. 18 Monty Python's. 19 Nationwide. 20 One Man and His Dog. 21 Dutch. 22 Onedin Line. 23 Cornwall. 24 Rising Damp. 25 Hutch. 26 Esther Rantzen. 27 Morecambe and Wise. 28 The Manor. 29 Downstairs. 30 North East.

1 On which day of the week is the Budget usually presented?

2 Which feisty female's autobiography was called "Extreme"?

3 Which fictional bear is named after a London station?

4 Who wrote a cookery book called "Keeping It Simple"?

5 What is the largest state of the USA?

6 How many years are celebrated by a pearl anniversary?

7 Which curly-leaved salad plant is a member of the chicory family?

8 Which armoured combat vehicle was first used in World War I?

9 Which doctor did Simon Shepherd play in "Peak Practice"?

10 In "Coronation Street" what is the name of Deirdre's daughter?

11 In which month is the shortest day?

12 Who recorded "Michael Caine"?

13 In which sport is the Thomas Cup awarded?

14 To ten years either way, when were women first allowed to take degrees at British universities?

15 Which group had a No 1 with "See My Baby Jive"?

16 Which bird is associated with Lundy Island?

17 How is Russian revolutionary Vladimir Ilyich Ulyanov better known?

18 Rick Stein's Cornish restaurant specializes in what type of food?

19 What were Marc Bolan and Micky Finn better known as?

20 How do male moths find female moths in the dark?

21 Which canal had an opera written especially for its opening?

22 What type of nut is a marron glacé?

23 In which film did Elvis Presley play a double role?

24 What is a young horse called?

25 Who recorded the album "Crocodile Shoes"?

26 Who became Lord Warden of the Cinque ports in 1978?

27 Who beat Andrew Murray in the final of the 2005 Thai Open?

28 Which Samuel kept a famous diary in the seventeenth century?

29 What is a coley?

30 In education, what does OU stand for?

Answers	Pot-Luck 30 *(see Quiz 58)*

1 Michael Palin. 2 Guilder. 3 Josceline. 4 Geese. 5 Oasis. 6 Richie Benaud. 7 Flying Squad. 8 Bob Dylan. 9 St Andrews. 10 Eden. 11 285. 12 Hilda Rumpole. 13 Yogi Bear. 14 Orange. 15 Golf. 16 Four. 17 Rainbow. 18 Scarlet. 19 Danube. 20 Oh Boy. 21 Bark. 22 A whale. 23 The head. 24 Jimi Hendrix. 25 Jets. 26 Oslo. 27 USA. 28 Crawford. 29 Queen. 30 Video Cassette Recorder.

1 What is Wales' highest mountain?
2 Which Welshman wrote "Portrait of the Artist as a Young Dog"?
3 Which Sea is to the north of Wales?
4 What are the Brecon Beacons?
5 Which island lies off the north west coast of Wales?
6 Which spring flower is a Welsh emblem?
7 What is the capital of Wales?
8 Which Channel is to the south of Wales?
9 Is Caernarvon Castle in the north or south of Wales?
10 Caerphilly is a town and also what type of food?
11 Which creature of legend is seen on the Welsh flag?
12 Which city in the south of the country is its second largest?
13 Which sport is played at Cardiff Arms Park?
14 Which wild cat gives its name to a Bay on Cardiff's quayside?
15 The production of which fuel affected the Welsh landscape until its decline in recent years?
16 Who was invested as Prince of Wales in 1969 at Caernarvon Castle?
17 Which vegetable is a Welsh emblem?
18 Which country lies to the east of Wales?
19 Who is the patron saint of Wales?
20 What is the mountainous area around Snowdon called?
21 Which Welsh Bay shares its name with a woollen jacket?
22 Which is the only Welsh county to have a first-class cricket team?
23 What is the currency of Wales?
24 Wales has the highest density in the world of which farm animal?
25 Which Welsh Secretary challenged John Major for the Tory Party leadership in the summer of 1995?
26 Which county is further north, Clwyd or Gwent?
27 Which Strait separates Anglesey from the mainland?
28 Which North Wales university town shares its name with a resort of Northern Ireland?
29 The UK's longest river rises in Wales. What is it called?
30 Which town is further south, Aberystwyth or Swansea?

Answers | Sport: Football *(see Quiz 63)*

1 Newcastle. 2 Vieira. 3 Blue and white. 4 Houllier. 5 USA. 6 Bristol. 7 Goal. 8 Newcastle. 9 Cole. 10 Blackpool. 11 Schmeichel. 12 Spain. 13 Rangers. 14 Manchester United. 15 Northern Ireland. 16 Red. 17 France. 18 Tottenham. 19 Bolton. 20 As hosts they automatically qualified. 21 Pleat. 22 Own goal. 23 2005. 24 Keegan. 25 Bramall. 26 Liverpool. 27 3.00pm. 28 Man Utd. 29 Everton. 30 Chelsea.

Quiz 62 Pot-Luck 32

Answers – page 72

1 How did Van Gogh commit suicide?
2 What is the upper age limit for being an MP in the UK?
3 Who recorded the album "Time to Grow"?
4 Who was the first reigning British monarch to visit a Communist country?
5 Which opera features the song "Take a Pair of Sparkling Eyes"?
6 In snooker, how many points are scored for potting the green ball?
7 S is the symbol of which chemical element?
8 Who recorded the album "Music Box"?
9 Which card game is another name for a prison van?
10 What is the second month of the year to have exactly 31 days?
11 In the Bible, who led the children of Israel to the Promised Land?
12 What goes before "mantle", "slipper" and "smock" in flower names?
13 Which famous Welsh opera star celebrated his 40th birthday in 2005?
14 Which movie started out as a TV series about good ol' boys Bo and Luke Duke?
15 Which horse won the English Triple Crown in 1970?
16 Timperley Early and Cawood Castle are types of what?
17 In the solar system which is the third planet from the sun?
18 What has subdivisions comprising 12, 52 and 365 units?
19 How many sides in four oblongs?
20 According to proverb, a little what is a dangerous thing?
21 What would you be playing if you were talking about spares and strikes?
22 In rugby, what name is given to a forward on either end of the front row of a scrum?
23 Whose catchphrase was, "Heavens to Murgatroyd"?
24 What is the first name of TV cook Harriott?
25 What is the least valuable piece on a chessboard?
26 What was the name of Barnum's famous giant elephant?
27 Which Mr Clarkson wrote "The World According to Clarkson"?
28 How many pieces of silver did Judas get for betraying Christ?
29 Which food is made from the lining of a cow's stomach?
30 What collective name is used for items made from precious gems?

Answers | Pot-Luck 33 *(see Quiz 64)*

1 Two. 2 Virgo. 3 Han Solo. 4 Clog. 5 Microsoft. 6 Kent. 7 Table Mountain. 8 Willy Wonka. 9 Holby City. 10 Simple Minds. 11 Robert Kennedy. 12 Scotland. 13 Monaco. 14 Ocean's Twelve. 15 Vodka and tomato juice. 16 Sparrow. 17 Squash. 18 Celine Dion. 19 Billy Joe McAllister. 20 Soup. 21 Rolls Royce. 22 Michael Caine. 23 Saturday. 24 As Time Goes By. 25 Outside. 26 Marilyn Monroe. 27 Blue. 28 Light flyweight. 29 500. 30 Cher.

1 Which team is known as the Magpies?
2 Which Patrick was Arsenal skipper when they went a season unbeaten in the Premiership?
3 What two colours are in Blackburn's home strip?
4 Which Gerard was the first Frenchman to manage Liverpool?
5 In which country were the 1994 World Cup finals held?
6 Which city has teams called Rovers and City?
7 What position did Peter Shilton play?
8 At which club did Shearer and Owen line up in the same side?
9 Which surname is shared by England players Ashley and Joe?
10 Which club is linked with the playing career of Jimmy Armfield?
11 Which Peter kept goal for both Man Utd and Man City?
12 Which country do Real Madrid come from?
13 In QPR what does the letter R stand for?
14 Which club did Steve Bruce play for in a Premiership-winning season?
15 Which country did George Best play for?
16 What is the home colour of Nottingham Forest?
17 Which country does David Ginola come from?
18 At which club did Terry Venables and Alan Sugar clash?
19 Which club appointed former player Sam Allardyce as manager in October 1999?
20 Why did France not play in qualifying games for the '98 World Cup?
21 Which David has managed Spurs, Luton and Sheffield Wednesday?
22 What do the letters o.g. stand for?
23 In which year did Roy Keane end his playing days with Man Utd?
24 Which Kevin has managed Newcastle, Fulham, Man City and England?
25 Which Lane do Sheffield United play at?
26 Which club is associated with the song "You'll Never Walk Alone"?
27 What is the traditional kick-off time for Saturday League games?
28 Edwin Van der Sar left Fulham to join which other Premiership club?
29 David Moyes first managed in the Premiership at which club?
30 Which London side did Ruud Gullit join in 1995?

Answers	**Around Wales** *(see Quiz 61)*

1 Snowdon. 2 Dylan Thomas. 3 Irish Sea. 4 Mountains. 5 Anglesey. 6 Daffodil. 7 Cardiff. 8 Bristol Channel. 9 North. 10 Cheese. 11 Dragon. 12 Swansea. 13 Rugby. 14 Tiger. 15 Coal. 16 Prince Charles. 17 Leek. 18 England. 19 St David. 20 Snowdonia. 21 Cardigan. 22 Glamorgan. 23 Pound sterling. 24 Sheep. 25 John Redwood. 26 Clwyd. 27 Menai Strait. 28 Bangor. 29 Severn. 30 Swansea.

Quiz 64 | Pot-Luck 33

Answers – page 70

1 How many packs of cards are needed for a game of Canasta?
2 What is the zodiac sign of the Virgin?
3 Which character did Harrison Ford play in "Star Wars"?
4 What is a sabot?
5 Bill Gates founded which computer corporation?
6 Which Clark was a journalist on "The Daily Planet"?
7 Where would you see fog called the Tablecloth?
8 Whom did Johnny Depp play in the 2005 version of "Charlie and the Chocolate Factory"?
9 In which TV drama series did the character Mubbs Hussein appear for four years?
10 Who recorded the album "Once Upon a Time"?
11 Whom did Sirhan Sirhan assassinate?
12 In which country was the 2005 G8 summit held?
13 What is ruled by the House of Grimaldi?
14 What was the sequel to "Ocean's Eleven" called?
15 What are the two main ingredients of a Bloody Mary?
16 In the rhyme, who killed Cock Robin?
17 What is a world sport, an American vegetable and a British soft drink?
18 Who recorded the album "The Colour of My Love"?
19 Who jumped off the Tallahatchee Bridge?
20 What type of food is consommé?
21 The "Silver Ghost" was what type of car?
22 Who says, "Not many people know that!"?
23 Which day of the week is named after the god Saturn?
24 What was Sam asked to play by Rick in "Casablanca"?
25 Where would you eat if you were eating al fresco?
26 How is Norma Jean Baker better known?
27 What colour features in the title of George Gershwin's Rhapsody?
28 What is the lowest weight in boxing?
29 How many sheets of paper are there in a ream?
30 Who was Sonny's singing partner?

Answers | Pot-Luck 32 (see Quiz 62)

1 He shot himself. 2 There isn't one. 3 Lemar. 4 Elizabeth II (1972 Yugoslavia). 5 The Gondoliers. 6 Three. 7 Sulphur. 8 Mariah Carey. 9 Black Maria. 10 March. 11 Moses. 12 Lady's. 13 Bryn Terfel. 14 The Dukes of Hazzard. 15 Nijinsky. 16 Rhubarb. 17 Earth. 18 A year. 19 16. 20 Knowledge. 21 Ten-pin bowling. 22 Prop. 23 Snagglepuss. 24 Ainsley. 25 Pawn. 26 Jumbo. 27 Jeremy Clarkson. 28 30. 29 Tripe. 30 Jewellery.

Quiz 65 | Pot-Luck 34

Answers – page 75

1 Which country are Qantas airlines from?
2 What is the currency of Russia?
3 What type of plant grows from seed, flowers and dies in a year?
4 Helen Sharman was the first Briton to go where?
5 What is Andy Capp's wife called?
6 Which two members of Bremner, Bird & Fortune share the same first name?
7 In rhyming slang what is Barnet Fair?
8 How is Declan McManus better known?
9 What animal is shown in the painting "The Monarch of the Glen"?
10 Where would you look to discover the Mount of the Moon and the Girdle of Venus?
11 Which insect might be used by a snooker player?
12 In Roman numerals what is MD + MD?
13 What is the first name of Polish film director Polanski?
14 What colour is saffron?
15 What was Al short for in Al Capone's name?
16 How many sides has a trapezium?
17 In which Olympic event would the competitor use ribbons and hoops?
18 Which metal is an alloy of copper and zinc?
19 Which major river flows through Cairo?
20 What is a Blenheim Orange?
21 Which country did Prime Minister Bhutto rule?
22 In which film did John Travolta play Vincent Vega?
23 What number is opposite a one on a dice?
24 Who recorded the album "Made in England"?
25 Which sporting captain called his autobiography "Calling the Shots"?
26 What is the capital of Sweden?
27 Which title gave hits to both Jennifer Rush and Frankie Goes to Hollywood?
28 What is Roget's word book known as?
29 Which Daniel succeeded Pierce Brosnan as 007?
30 Which band took "Crashed the Wedding" to No 1 in 2003?

Answers | Pot-Luck 35 *(see Quiz 67)*

1 Basil Spence. 2 Emily. 3 Nudist. 4 Niven. 5 Weathering. 6 Mario Lanza. 7 Wolves. 8 Mexico. 9 500. 10 Elly May. 11 March. 12 Paul McCartney. 13 Exit. 14 C. S. 15 Jacqueline Wilson. 16 Garden School. 17 Calcium. 18 Jethro Tull. 19 Take That. 20 Sleeve. 21 Beaufort. 22 South Africa. 23 20th. 24 Colt. 25 Aer Lingus. 26 Holidays. 27 Anton. 28 Deuce. 29 Shark. 30 Mineworkers.

73

1 Which Edward became prime minister in 1970?

2 What type of currency was introduced to Britain in 1971?

3 Idi Amin seized power in which country?

4 Henry Cooper retired from which sport?

5 What type of short pants became the fashion craze for women?

6 Bangladesh was formed from the eastern part of which country?

7 Which Sir Anthony was declared to be a Russian spy?

8 Which Mother won a Nobel Peace Prize?

9 Which Conservative leader became prime minister in 1979?

10 The Shah of which country was forced into exile?

11 The strike-bound months of 1978 and 1979 became known as the Winter of what?

12 Which Liberal leader resigned after allegations about his private life?

13 Which princess sought a divorce from the Earl of Snowdon?

14 In which sea off the British coastline was oil discovered?

15 Under Patrick Steptoe's guidance what was produced from a test tube for the first time in July 1978?

16 Whose shroud went on display at St John's Cathedral in Turin?

17 Steve Biko died in a cell in which country?

18 What sport did Kerry Packer try to take over with his cash offers?

19 Which king of rock died in Tennessee in 1977?

20 Freddie Laker brought cut-price travel in what type of transport?

21 Which Jubilee did Queen Elizabeth II celebrate in 1977?

22 The Sex Pistols were the leaders of the movement known as what kind of rock?

23 Which leader of Communist China died in 1976?

24 Which "Lucky" Lord vanished after the murder of his child's nanny?

25 Which scandal forced Richard Nixon to resign as US President?

26 Which countries fought in the 1973 Yom Kippur War?

27 What did the Amoco Cadiz spill off the Brittany coastline?

28 How many days were in a working week during the 1974 power shortage?

29 Which earl was murdered by the IRA in 1979?

30 Which Labour MP James became prime minister?

Answers	Geography *(see Quiz 68)*

1 Spain. 2 India and Pakistan. 3 Northumberland. 4 Peking. 5 Buckingham Palace. 6 Austria. 7 Devon. 8 Red. 9 Derbyshire. 10 Italy. 11 Africa. 12 West. 13 Argentina. 14 Paris. 15 Portugal. 16 Algeria. 17 Scafell Pike. 18 Scotland. 19 Oslo. 20 Africa. 21 Netherlands. 22 Florida. 23 France. 24 Birmingham. 25 Washington. 26 Pacific. 27 Brazil. 28 Europe. 29 Sweden. 30 Belgium.

Quiz 67 | Pot-Luck 35

Answers – page 73

1 Who designed Coventry cathedral?
2 What is the name of Florence's lay-dee companion in "Little Britain"?
3 In 1979, Brighton Council decided to allow what type of beach?
4 Which David told his life story in "The Moon's a Balloon"?
5 Rocks are broken down by the elements by what gradual process?
6 Which tenor took the title role in "The Great Caruso"?
7 The word lupine relates to which animals?
8 In which country is the volcano Popocatépetl?
9 What number does the Roman numeral D stand for?
10 What was Jed Clampett's daughter called in "The Beverley Hillbillies"?
11 In which month is the first day of spring?
12 Who co-wrote a "Liverpool Oratorio" with Carl Davis?
13 Which stage direction means to go off stage?
14 What are the two initials of Narnia creator Lewis?
15 Which best-selling children's writer penned "Diamond Girls" and "Love Lessons"?
16 What type of school did Diarmuid Gavin present on TV?
17 Which element is found in bones, shells and teeth?
18 In the early 1700s who invented a seed drill?
19 What are Gary Barlow, Howard Donald, Jason Orange and Mark Owen better known as?
20 What part of a garment is a raglan?
21 What scale is used to measure wind velocity?
22 In which country is the Table Mountain?
23 Which anniversary on UK screens did Aussie soap "Neighbours" celebrate in 2005?
24 What is a young stallion called?
25 What is the Republic of Ireland's airline called?
26 What does the French word vacances mean?
27 What is the first name of TV cook Mosimann?
28 In tennis, what is a score of 40 all called?
29 Threshers and hammerheads are types of what?
30 The NUM is the National Union of what?

Answers | Pot-Luck 34 *(see Quiz 65)*

1 Australia. 2 Rouble. 3 Annual. 4 Space. 5 Flo. 6 Bird & Fortune (John). 7 Hair. 8 Elvis Costello. 9 A red deer stag. 10 In the palm of your hand. 11 Spider. 12 MMM. 13 Roman. 14 Yellow. 15 Alphonse. 16 Four. 17 Rhythmic gymnastics. 18 Brass. 19 Nile. 20 An apple. 21 Pakistan. 22 Pulp Fiction. 23 A six. 24 Elton John. 25 Michael Vaughan. 26 Stockholm. 27 The Power of Love. 28 Thesaurus. 29 Daniel Craig. 30 Busted.

Quiz 68 | Geography

1 Which country can you easily walk to from Gibraltar?
2 Urdu is an important language in which two Asian countries?
3 Which is England's most northerly county?
4 What did Bejing used to be called?
5 Which is the Queen's London home?
6 In which European country is Salzburg?
7 Which county divides Cornwall from Somerset?
8 What "colour" is the Sea between Egypt and Saudi Arabia?
9 In which county is the Peak District?
10 In which country is the resort of Rimini?
11 Madagascar is to the east of which continent?
12 Is California on the east or west coast of the USA?
13 Which is the nearest country to the Falkland Islands?
14 Near which French city is the Disney Theme Park?
15 In which country is the Algarve?
16 Which is further west, Algeria or Ethiopia?
17 What is the highest point in England?
18 In which country is the county of Tayside?
19 Which Scandinavian capital begins and ends with the same letter?
20 Chad is in which continent?
21 What is Holland also known as?
22 In which US holiday state is Miami?
23 Which country is divided from Spain by the Pyrenees?
24 What is the largest city in the West Midlands?
25 Which town of Tyne and Wear shares its name with the US capital?
26 The Philippines are in which Ocean?
27 What is the largest country of South America?
28 In which continent is Slovenia?
29 Which country originally produced Volvo cars?
30 In which country do most Flemish speakers live?

Answers	70s Newsround (see Quiz 66)

1 Heath. 2 Decimal. 3 Uganda. 4 Boxing. 5 Hot. 6 Pakistan. 7 Blunt. 8 Teresa.
9 Margaret Thatcher. 10 Iran. 11 Discontent. 12 Jeremy Thorpe. 13 Margaret. 14
North Sea. 15 A baby. 16 Jesus Christ. 17 South Africa. 18 Cricket. 19 Elvis Presley.
20 Aircraft. 21 Silver. 22 Punk. 23 Mao Tse-tung. 24 Lucan. 25 Watergate. 26
Egypt, Syria and Israel. 27 Oil. 28 Three. 29 Mountbatten. 30 Callaghan.

1 Which extra title was given to Catherine II of Russia?

2 Which Fiona was Eamonn Holmes' long-running co-presenter on GMTV?

3 Which country is a car from if it has the international registration letter H?

4 Which came first, the House of Tudor or the House of Stuart?

5 Which Norman said, "He got on his bike and looked for work."

6 What was the name of the witch played by Agnes Moorhead in "Bewitched"?

7 Zn is the symbol of which chemical element?

8 In "Coronation Street" what is Ken Barlow's job?

9 According to proverb, one man's meat is another man's what?

10 Which actress played the title role in the movie "Domino"?

11 Williams and Conference are types of what?

12 Who recorded the album "Medusa"?

13 How many times did Will Carling skipper England before giving up the captaincy in '96?

14 What is the capital of Afghanistan?

15 Who was the female lead in the TV sitcom "Terry and June?"

16 Frank Lampard joined Chelsea from which club?

17 Who released the 2005 album "A Time to Live"?

18 Which Irish entertainer Val used to sing in a rocking chair?

19 How many yards in a mile?

20 Who was the only British female singer to have three UK No 1s in the 60s?

21 What was the name of the Ewing ranch in "Dallas"?

22 The USA government is nicknamed which relative?

23 What name is given to poisonous fluid from a snake?

24 Which Biblical town was destroyed with Gomorrah?

25 On what type of farm are horses bred?

26 What famous first in TV advertising is held by Bird's Eye frozen peas?

27 What number is Beethoven's concerto known as the "Emperor"?

28 Which US playwright wrote "The Price"?

29 What name is given to a baby elephant?

30 What colour pottery is Josiah Wedgwood noted for?

Answers | Pot-Luck 37 (see Quiz 71)

1 Spring. 2 Libra. 3 Madagascar. 4 Rolling Stones. 5 Flat. 6 Walt Disney. 7 Plum. 8 Carburettor. 9 Tongue. 10 A rest. 11 Greenwich Mean Time. 12 The Moon. 13 Waistcoat. 14 May. 15 Badminton. 16 An ear. 17 Miser. 18 Les Misérables. 19 Orwell. 20 Only Fools and Horses. 21 Jenny. 22 Fred Flintstone. 23 January. 24 Fleetwood Mac. 25 Lincoln. 26 Labour. 27 Friar. 28 Wall Street. 29 Australia. 30 Ronnie Corbett.

1 What was invented by Lazlo and Georg Biro?
2 Which fashion item is Oscar Levi Strauss responsible for?
3 What nationality was motor vehicle pioneer Gottlieb Daimler?
4 What was developed by André and Edouard Michelin?
5 What type of pen did Lewis Waterman invent?
6 Which air cushion vehicle was invented by Christopher Cockerell?
7 Which engine used in aircraft was invented by Sir Frank Whittle?
8 What did John Logie Baird invent, first called "seeing by wireless"?
9 Which communication system is Alexander Graham Bell famous for?
10 Who invented a code made up of dots and dashes?
11 For whom did Louis Braille develop his writing system?
12 Which method of food preservation did Clarence Birdseye invent?
13 What type of lamp is Humphry Davy famous for?
14 Which predecessor of the CD player did Thomas Edison create?
15 Which breakfast food was developed by Will Keith Kellogg in 1898?
16 Which invention is Marconi known for?
17 Which company, motto "Small is beautiful", was founded in the late 1940s and developed the Walkman?
18 Which explosive was invented by Alfred Nobel?
19 What type of milk did Louis Pasteur give his name to, because of the treatment it undergoes?
20 In which source of power were Volta and Ampère pioneers?
21 What powered James Watt's engine in 1765?
22 What would you use Isaac Singer's invention for?
23 In which room would you be most likely to use the inventions of Kenneth Wood – known to his friends as Ken?
24 At what sort of party might you see the invention of Earl W. Tupper?
25 Which frozen confection was originally called Eskimo pie?
26 Which Earl invented a snack of meat between two slices of bread?
27 What was special about the fabric Charles Macintosh invented?
28 Which essential for foreign tourists was invented by American Express?
29 George Eastman developed an easy to use hand-held what?
30 What type of aircraft is Sikorsky famous for?

Answers | TV: The 80s *(see Quiz 72)*

1 All Creatures Great and Small. 2 Allo Allo. 3 Jersey. 4 Boys from the Blackstuff. 5 Brideshead. 6 Lacey. 7 Fame. 8 French. 9 A Laugh. 10 Grant. 11 Highway. 12 The Galaxy. 13 Boats. 14 Oxford. 15 India. 16 Fire Brigade. 17 Lovejoy. 18 Miami. 19 Not the Nine o'Clock News. 20 All Hours. 21 Spitting Image. 22 Michael Aspel. 23 Dogs. 24 Roland. 25 Holland. 26 Barrister. 27 Japanese. 28 J.R. 29 Watchdog. 30 Sir Humphrey Appleby.

1 Which season does the word vernal relate to?
2 What is the zodiac sign of the Balance?
3 On which island are most lemurs found?
4 Who had a No 1 hit with the song "(I Can't Get No) Satisfaction"?
5 What type of horse racing does not include fences and obstacles?
6 Who created Mickey Mouse?
7 In nursery rhyme, what did Little Jack Horner pull out of a pie?
8 Which device produces the mix of air and petrol in internal combustion engines?
9 What is a butterfly's proboscis?
10 According to proverb, what is a change as good as?
11 What does GMT stand for?
12 Where did Wallace and Gromit visit in "A Grand Day Out"?
13 Called a vest in America, what's the name of this garment in the UK?
14 Hawthorn traditionally blooms in which month?
15 Which game is played with rackets and shuttlecocks?
16 Which part of his anatomy did Van Gogh cut off?
17 What word describes someone mean with money, like Scrooge?
18 In 2005, which musical celebrated 20 years in London's West End?
19 Which George wrote "Animal Farm"?
20 "The Green Green Grass" was a 2005 spin-off from which long-running TV sitcom?
21 What name is given to a female donkey?
22 Who says, "Yabbadabba Doo!"?
23 Which month is named after the god Janus?
24 Who recorded the album "Rumours"?
25 Which city of central England gave its name to a shade of green?
26 Was Clement Attlee a Conservative or Labour politician?
27 What was the profession or calling of Tuck in Sherwood Forest?
28 Where is the New York Stock Exchange?
29 In which country would you see wild wombats?
30 Who was Ronnie Barker's comic partner?

| **Answers** | Pot-Luck 36 *(see Quiz 69)* |

1 The Great. 2 Fiona Phillips. 3 Hungary. 4 The House of Tudor. 5 Tebbit. 6 Endora. 7 Zinc. 8 Teacher. 9 Poison. 10 Keira Knightley. 11 Pear. 12 Annie Lennox. 13 57. 14 Kabul. 15 June Whitfield. 16 West Ham. 17 Stevie Wonder. 18 Doonican. 19 1,760. 20 Sandie Shaw. 21 South Fork. 22 Uncle Sam. 23 Venom. 24 Sodom. 25 Stud. 26 First product advertised in colour. 27 Fifth. 28 Arthur Miller. 29 Calf. 30 Blue.

1 Which series was about Yorkshire vet James Herriot?
2 In which series would you find the Fallen Madonna with the Big Boobies?
3 On which island was "Bergerac" set?
4 Which programme gave the catchphrase "Gissa job"?
5 What was Revisited in the series with Jeremy Irons?
6 Who was Cagney's police partner?
7 What were students at the New York High School of Performing Arts seeking?
8 Which Fields did Hester and William go to after "Fresh Fields"?
9 What was Jeremy Beadle Game for?
10 Which Russell was astrologer on "Breakfast Time"?
11 Which religious programme did Harry Secombe start to present?
12 What was the Hitch Hiker's Guide to?
13 What was being built in the yards in "Howard's Way"?
14 In which university city was Inspector Morse based?
15 In which eastern country was "The Jewel in the Crown" set?
16 Which emergency service is featured in "London's Burning"?
17 Which series featured Ian McShane as an antiques dealer?
18 In which city did Sonny Crockett investigate Vice?
19 What wasn't a news bulletin but did feature Pamela Stephenson and Rowan Atkinson?
20 When was the shop with David Jason and Ronnie Barker Open?
21 Which satirical programme featured latex puppets?
22 Who began presenting "This is Your Life" in 1987?
23 Which pets featured on the programmes with Barbara Woodhouse?
24 Which Rat revived the flagging fortunes of TV-am?
25 Which Jools presented "The Tube"?
26 What was the profession of claret-swigging Horace Rumpole?
27 Whom were the women prisoners of in "Tenko"?
28 Whose shooting in November 1980 was watched by 27 million?
29 What sort of dog became a consumer's champion in the 1980s?
30 Who was MP Jim Hacker's Permanent Under Secretary?

Answers | **Inventors and Inventions** *(see Quiz 70)*

1 Ball-point pen. 2 Jeans. 3 German. 4 Tyres. 5 Fountain pen. 6 Hovercraft. 7 Jet. 8 Television. 9 Telephone. 10 Morse. 11 Blind. 12 Deep freezing. 13 Safety lamp. 14 Gramophone. 15 Cornflakes. 16 Wireless. 17 Sony. 18 Dynamite. 19 Pasteurized. 20 Electricity. 21 Steam. 22 Sewing. 23 Kitchen. 24 Tupperware. 25 Choc ice. 26 Sandwich. 27 Waterproof. 28 Traveller's cheque. 29 Camera. 30 Helicopters.

1 Which country does the airline Iberia come from?
2 What is the currency of South Africa?
3 Who was the youngest leadership contender in the 2005 race for the Tory leadership?
4 Who wrote the Aldwych farces, including "Rookery Nook"?
5 What year is included in the name of the group who recorded "Simon Says"?
6 Which school did Queen Elizabeth II attend as a youngster?
7 In rhyming slang what is dog and bone?
8 What was Frederick Bulsara better known as?
9 The movie "Calendar Girls" was about members of which organization?
10 In the Bible, which book follows Matthew?
11 What famous first did Edward White achieve for America?
12 In which country is the Matterhorn?
13 Who was the first female DJ on Radio 1?
14 What colour is associated with an Oxford or Cambridge sports award?
15 Which rock forms the greater part of the White Cliffs of Dover?
16 Which Coronation Street couple remarried during the week of Charles and Camilla's wedding?
17 In tennis, what name is given to a serve that cannot be returned?
18 Who recorded the album "Bad"?
19 Which major river flows through Gloucester?
20 Who created "Dalziel and Pascoe"?
21 According to Rhoda, in which year was she born in the Bronx, New York?
22 Which card game has the same name as a horse-racing town?
23 Who founded the Rocket record label?
24 What was the first name of Burgess, the spy who defected to Russia?
25 How was Eric Bartholomew better known?
26 What is the capital of Denmark?
27 Who played M in "Die Another Day"?
28 "Just when you thought it was safe to go back in the water..." was the advertising line for which film?
29 In which street is the Bank of England?
30 What does TUC stand for?

| **Answers** | Pot-Luck 39 *(see Quiz 75)* |

1 Keystone. 2 Are You Being Served? 3 Salamander. 4 The Dail. 5 REM.
6 Kuwait City. 7 John Masefield. 8 Susan Hampshire. 9 Wallace and Gromit. 10 Parcel. 11 October. 12 Enya. 13 Matinee. 14 W. B. 15 Heather. 16 Dodd. 17 Bongos. 18 The Bar. 19 Shadows. 20 Head. 21 Dick Dastardly. 22 Andrew. 23 Hamburg. 24 Filly. 25 Status Quo. 26 New Orleans. 27 Whitelaw. 28 Slob. 29 Fiddler on the Roof. 30 Daniel Radcliffe.

Quiz 74 | Jet Setters

Answers – page 84

1 What is the first name of supermodel Evangelista?
2 Which veteran Scottish rock star is married to model Rachel Hunter?
3 Princess Caroline is a member of which royal family?
4 What was the surname of Jackie Onassis's first husband?
5 What is the first name of actress/presenter Ms de Cadenet?
6 Lady Helen, daughter of the Duke and Duchess of Kent, named her son after which famous explorer?
7 What was the first name of tycoon Donald Trump's former wife?
8 What is the first name of actress and model Miss Hurley?
9 Who is the magician partner of model Claudia Schiffer?
10 Which Texan model married Mick Jagger?
11 Which Swedish actress is a former wife of the late Peter Sellers?
12 What is the surname of eight-times married actress Zsa Zsa?
13 What is the first name of celebrity photographer Bailey?
14 Which LA Hills are the home of many of the rich and famous?
15 What is the first name of kilt-wearing designer Gaultier?
16 How is skinny 1960s model Lesley Hornby better known?
17 In which city was George Best's funeral held?
18 What is the first name of actress/model Miss Seymour?
19 Who is the head of the Virgin group?
20 What is the first name of gossip columnist Dempster?
21 Which ski resort is a favourite for Prince Charles for his Xmas break?
22 What is the nationality of Sophia Loren?
23 Which TV show made Pamela Anderson famous?
24 Which princess is known by her husband's first name?
25 Which Lord and celebrity photographer passed away in the autumn of 2005?
26 What is the first name of fashion designer Westwood?
27 Of which country is Juan Carlos king?
28 What was the profession of the Queen's cousin Lord Lichfield?
29 Which Pakistani cricketer married heiress Jemima Goldsmith?
30 Which fuel did the Getty family make their fortune from?

Answers	Sport: The 80s (see Quiz 76)

1 Lineker. 2 Bob Champion. 3 Geoff Boycott. 4 Ovett. 5 Liverpool. 6 Davis. 7 Australia. 8 Hailwood. 9 Watson. 10 Everton. 11 Navratilova. 12 Bolero. 13 Italy. 14 Zola Budd. 15 Los Angeles. 16 Lyle. 17 Brazil. 18 Dennis Taylor. 19 Belgium. 20 Javelin. 21 Boxing. 22 Boris Becker. 23 Maradona. 24 Flo Jo. 25 Bryan Robson. 26 Somerset. 27 France. 28 Czechoslovakia. 29 Rangers. 30 Jack Charlton.

1 Which knockabout Kops were created by Mack Sennett?
2 In which TV programme did the staff of Grace Brothers appear?
3 What is another name for the creature the axolotl?
4 What is the name of the Irish Parliament?
5 Which band features the lyrics of Michael Stipe?
6 What city is the capital of Kuwait?
7 Who wrote the poem "Sea Fever"?
8 Which Susan of "Monarch of the Glen" first found TV fame in the early 1960s?
9 Which duo were the stars of "The Curse of the Were-Rabbit"?
10 In the children's party game, what is passed around and unwrapped?
11 In which month is Halloween?
12 Who recorded the album "Watermark"?
13 What word taken from the French describes an afternoon show?
14 What are the initials of Irish poet Yeats?
15 Which moorland shrub is said to bring good luck?
16 Which comic Ken says, "How tickled I am"?
17 Which instrument is traditionally held between the knees?
18 What name is given to barristers collectively?
19 What are Hank Marvin, Brian Bennett and Bruce Welch better known as?
20 On what part of your body would you wear a homburg?
21 Which cartoon villain exclaimed, "Drat and double drat!"?
22 What is Freddie Flintoff's real first name?
23 In which city did the hamburger originate?
24 What is a young mare called?
25 Which rock group's name is the Latin for the existing state of things?
26 In the song, the House of the Rising Sun is in which city?
27 Which Conservative politician William spoke of a "short, sharp, shock"?
28 What is the surname of the decidedly anti-social TV characters Wayne and Waynetta?
29 The village of Anatevka appears in which musical?
30 Which Daniel played Harry in the Harry Potter films?

Answers | Pot-Luck 38 (see Quiz 73)

1 Spain. 2 Rand. 3 David Cameron. 4 Ben Travers. 5 1910 (Fruitgum Co.) 6 None at all. 7 Phone. 8 Freddie Mercury. 9 The WI. 10 Mark. 11 First to walk in space. 12 Switzerland. 13 Annie Nightingale. 14 Blue. 15 Chalk. 16 Ken and Deidre. 17 Ace. 18 Michael Jackson. 19 Severn. 20 Reginald Hill. 21 1941. 22 Newmarket. 23 Elton John. 24 Guy. 25 Eric Morecambe. 26 Copenhagen. 27 Judi Dench. 28 Jaws II. 29 Threadneedle Street. 30 Trades Union Congress.

1 Which Gary was England's top soccer marksman of the 1980s?
2 Who fought back from cancer to win the Grand National?
3 Which English batsman became the highest run getter in Test history?
4 Which Steve was Sebastian Coe's great rival in mid-distance races?
5 Which club were English soccer champions six times in the 80s?
6 Which Steve became snooker World Champion in 1981?
7 The America's Cup left home for the first time ever to go to where?
8 Which motor-cycle legend Mike was killed in a motor accident in 1981?
9 Which Tom won both the US and British Opens in the same year?
10 Which team were English soccer champions under Howard Kendall?
11 Which Martina dominated Wimbledon in the 1980s?
12 Which piece of music by Ravel did Torvill and Dean use in winning an Olympic gold for ice dancing?
13 Which country beat West Germany to win the 1982 soccer World Cup?
14 The Daily Mail ran a campaign to get which South African athlete to receive a British passport?
15 Where in the USA was the centre for the 1984 Olympic Games?
16 In golf, which Sandy won the 1988 US Masters?
17 Which country is motor racing's Nelson Piquet from?
18 Who became a world snooker champion wearing "upside-down" glasses?
19 In which country was the 1985 Heysel Stadium soccer tragedy?
20 In which event did Tessa Sanderson win Olympic gold?
21 What was Barry McGuigan's sport?
22 Which 17-year-old German won the Wimbledon men's singles?
23 Which Diego benefited from "The hand of God"?
24 What was the nickname of sprinter Florence Griffith-Joyner?
25 Who in soccer was known as "Captain Marvel"?
26 Viv Richards and Ian Botham played together for which county?
27 Which team won the Five Nations tournament from 1986 to 1989?
28 Which country does Ivan Lendl originate from?
29 Which Scottish soccer team was managed by Graeme Souness?
30 Which Englishman became soccer boss of the Republic of Ireland?

Answers | Jet Setters *(see Quiz 74)*

1 Linda. 2 Rod Stewart. 3 Monaco. 4 Kennedy. 5 Amanda. 6 Columbus. 7 Ivana. 8 Elizabeth. 9 David Copperfield. 10 Jerry Hall. 11 Britt Ekland. 12 Gabor. 13 David. 14 Beverly Hills. 15 Jean-Paul. 16 Twiggy. 17 Belfast. 18 Jane. 19 Richard Branson. 20 Nigel. 21 Klosters. 22 Italian. 23 Baywatch. 24 Michael. 25 Lord Lichfield. 26 Vivienne. 27 Spain. 28 Photographer. 29 Imran Khan. 30 Oil.

Quiz 77 | Pot-Luck 40

1 What is another name for the rowan tree?
2 How many hours in four days?
3 Which country is a car from if it has the international registration letter J?
4 Which musical was inspired by the songs of Abba?
5 Which Oscar said, "I have nothing to declare except my genius."
6 In darts, what is the lowest score from three different trebles?
7 Au is the symbol of which chemical element?
8 Which soap features the Woolpack pub?
9 Does Bryn Terfel have a bass/baritone or a tenor singing voice?
10 What name is given to the vast grassy plains of Russia?
11 Who has been married to Gemma Craven and Liz Hobbs?
12 Who recorded the album "Steam"?
13 Bovine relates to which kind of animals?
14 What is the chief ingredient in the production of glass?
15 Which creatures sang, "We All Stand Together"?
16 Which composer had the Christian names Johann Sebastian?
17 Which creature of the horror genre was created by Mary Shelley?
18 Which middle-distance runner became a Dame following the 2004 Olympics?
19 How many sides in three rectangles?
20 On which river does Stoke stand?
21 Which word could go before cab, skirt and van?
22 Six is the lowest of what type of number?
23 Which month is said to come in like a lion and go out like a lamb?
24 What is the name of Bill Clinton's daughter?
25 What did the navigator Amerigo Vespucci give his name to?
26 "Have I Got News for You" is the TV version of which radio show?
27 Who wrote "A Brief History of Time"?
28 How many cards are there in each suit?
29 In "EastEnders" what was Sam's surname before she married Ricky?
30 Which John captained Chelsea to the 2004/5 Premiership title?

Answers | Pot-Luck 41 (see Quiz 79)

1 Mark Spitz. 2 Chris Martin. 3 Chef. 4 John Lennon. 5 Cornet. 6 Honeysuckle.
7 Alfie Moon. 8 Hen party. 9 Tightrope. 10 Small bat. 11 Cannonball. 12 Carla
Laine. 13 Rear light. 14 Joseph Conrad. 15 War of the Roses. 16 Age Concern. 17
Blackburn Rovers. 18 The Bonzo Dog Doo-Dah Band. 19 Black Forest. 20 Pasta. 21
Four. 22 Ten. 23 The Munsters. 24 Twickenham. 25 Captain Hook. 26 Walking in
the Air. 27 Wren. 28 Roy Hudd. 29 Judo. 30 Julie Walters.

1 What relation was Danny de Vito to Arnold Schwarzenegger in their 1988 film?
2 Which Bruce starred in "Die Hard"?
3 Which singer won an Oscar for "Moonstruck"?
4 Out of which continent were Meryl Streep and Robert Redford in 1985?
5 In which film did Dustin Hoffman dress up as a woman to get a job as a soap star?
6 What was Richard Gere in the film with Debra Winger?
7 What does an inventor tell Honey he has Shrunk in the 1989 movie?
8 What does ET stand for in the 1982 film?
9 What sort of Attraction was there between Michael Douglas and Glenn Close?
10 Which bored housewife Shirley had an unforgettable Greek holiday?
11 Which disfigured Man did John Hurt portray in the 1980 film?
12 Which film told the story of two athletes in the 1924 Olympics?
13 What is Australian adventurer Mick Dundee's nickname?
14 Which adventurer Indiana was played by Harrison Ford?
15 Which Indian leader was played by Ben Kingsley?
16 What sort of Busters were Dan Aykroyd and Sigourney Weaver?
17 Which composer did Tom Hulse play in "Amadeus"?
18 Which film with Bob Hoskins is also the name of a painting?
19 Which former actor became president of the USA in 1980?
20 What was the Fish Called in the 1988 movie?
21 Which Naked film was the first in the series with Leslie Nielsen?
22 Who played James Bond in "For Your Eyes Only"?
23 What Strikes Back in the 1980 film?
24 Where was Eddie Murphy a Cop in the film series?
25 Where was Michael J. Fox Back to in 1985?
26 The Return of what in 1983 was the sixth film in the "Star Wars" series?
27 Which US pop superstar starred in "Moonwalker"?
28 Which cartoon Rabbit was Framed in 1988?
29 Which famous ship did they try to Raise in the 1980 film?
30 How many Men looked after Baby in 1987?

Answers	Pop: Sounds of the 80s *(see Quiz 80)*

1 Bermuda. 2 The Jam. 3 Eileen. 4 Twins. 5 Bucks Fizz. 6 Wham! 7 Madonna. 8 Red. 9 Ballet. 10 Police. 11 UB40. 12 Bryan Ferry. 13 Uptown. 14 Phil Collins. 15 Miami. 16 Easton. 17 Duran Duran. 18 Stevie Wonder. 19 Elaine Paige. 20 Love. 21 My Car. 22 Dire Straits. 23 Christmas. 24 Fun. 25 Ultra Vox. 26 In the Street. 27 Nick Berry. 28 Stevens. 29 The Mersey. 30 Kylie Minogue and Jason Donovan.

Quiz 79 | Pot-Luck 41 | Answers – page 85

1 Which swimmer won seven gold medals at the 1972 Olympics?
2 Which Chris from Coldplay married Gwyneth Paltrow?
3 What is the profession of Antony Worrall Thompson?
4 Who had a No 1 hit with the song "Imagine"?
5 Which brass musical instrument shares its name with an ice-cream?
6 What is another name for the plant woodbine?
7 Which character in EastEnders did Kat Slater marry?
8 What type of pre-wedding party is for women only?
9 What is the cord high above the ground which acrobats perform on?
10 What are pipistrelles?
11 Which nickname did saxophonist Julian Adderley acquire?
12 Who wrote "Solo", "Butterflies" and "Luv"?
13 It's a tail lamp in the USA; what's this part of the car called in the UK?
14 Who wrote "Lord Jim"?
15 St Albans started and Bosworth finished which hostilities?
16 Which Concern is a charity about the needs of the elderly?
17 Which club did Chelsea sign Damien Duff from?
18 Which group recorded "I'm the Urban Spaceman"?
19 In which part of Germany might you find a chocolate gâteau with cream and cherries?
20 What type of food is canneloni?
21 How many laps are completed in a speedway race?
22 What was the title of Pearl Jam's first album?
23 In which TV series did Marilyn have an Uncle Herman?
24 Where are the headquarters of the Rugby Union?
25 Which fictional pirate had a bosun named Smee?
26 What is the theme song in the cartoon "The Snowman"?
27 Which bird has the Latin name Troglodytes troglodytes?
28 Who gives his name to Radio 2's "News Huddlines"?
29 In which sport did Neal Adams win Olympic medals?
30 Who is Victoria Wood's comic partner?

Answers	Pot-Luck 40 *(see Quiz 77)*

1 Mountain ash. 2 96. 3 Japan. 4 Mamma Mia!. 5 Wilde. 6 18. 7 Gold. 8 Emmerdale. 9 Bass/baritone. 10 Steppes. 11 Frazer Hines. 12 East 17. 13 Oxen. 14 Sand. 15 Frogs. 16 Bach. 17 Frankenstein's monster. 18 Kelly Holmes. 19 12. 20 Trent. 21 Mini. 22 Perfect number. (It is equal to the sum of its divisions.) 23 March. 24 Chelsea. 25 America. 26 The News Quiz. 27 Stephen Hawking. 28 13. 29 Mitchell. 30 John Terry.

Quiz 80 | Pop: Sounds of the 80s | Answers – page 86

1 Which Triangle did Barry Manilow sing about in 1981?
2 Which "well preserved" group had a hit with "Going Underground"?
3 Who did Dexy's Midnight Runners tell to Come On?
4 What relation were the Thompsons who had hits with "Love on Your Side" and "We are Detective"?
5 Which orange juice/champagne mix were Eurovision winners in 1981?
6 Andrew Ridgeley and George Michael were which group?
7 Who was Like a Virgin in 1984?
8 What colour was Chris de Burgh's Lady in, in 1986?
9 Which type of dance completes the Spandau group's name?
10 Which law enforcers sent a Message in a Bottle?
11 Which band shares its name with a form for the unemployed?
12 Who was a Jealous Guy with Roxy Music in 1981?
13 Where was Billy Joel's Girl in his 1983 Number 1?
14 Which Genesis drummer had three No 1 vocal hits in the 1980s?
15 Where does Gloria Estefan's Sound Machine come from?
16 Which Scottish Modern Girl Sheena had a hit with US singer Prince?
17 Which group did Simon Le Bon sing with?
18 Who Just Called to Say I Love You in 1984?
19 Who sang with Barbara Dickson on the hit "I Know Him So Well"?
20 What did Jennifer Rush sing about The Power of in 1985?
21 Where did Madness say they were Driving in 1982?
22 Which band headed by Mark Knopfler wanted "Money for Nothing"?
23 Band Aid asked Do They Know It's what?
24 What did Cyndi Lauper say Girls wanted to have more of?
25 Which group was Midge Ure chiefly associated with in the 80s?
26 Where were David Bowie and Mick Jagger Dancing in 1985?
27 Which former "EastEnders" and "Heartbeat" star had a hit with "Every Loser Wins" in 1986?
28 Which Shakin' star recorded "This Ole House"?
29 Where was the Ferry going across on the charity record in 1989?
30 Which two stars went from Ramsay Street to the top of the charts?

Answers	80s Films (see Quiz 78)

1 Twin. 2 Willis. 3 Cher. 4 Africa. 5 Tootsie. 6 An Officer and a Gentleman. 7 The Kids. 8 Extra Terrestrial. 9 Fatal. 10 Valentine. 11 Elephant Man. 12 Chariots of Fire. 13 Crocodile. 14 Jones. 15 Gandhi. 16 Ghost. 17 Mozart. 18 Mona Lisa. 19 Ronald Reagan. 20 Wanda. 21 Naked Gun. 22 Roger Moore. 23 The Empire. 24 Beverly Hills. 25 The Future. 26 The Jedi. 27 Michael Jackson. 28 Roger. 29 The Titanic. 30 Three.

1 "I Got Plenty of Nuthin'" comes from which Gershwin work?
2 Who answers the phone by saying, "the lady the house speaking"?
3 What would you find in an arboretum?
4 Which Tess co-hosted "Strictly Come Dancing" with Bruce Forsyth?
5 Which record label turned down the Beatles?
6 In which country is the dong used as currency?
7 What line goes before the line, "In the windmills of you mind"?
8 What is the antirrhinum more commonly known as?
9 Who was Queen of England for nine days before she was beheaded?
10 Which country has had two kings called Carol on the throne this century?
11 What did Madonna fall off to sustain broken bones in the autumn of 2005?
12 Who created the series "Prime Suspect"?
13 What's the surname of cartoon hero Quick Draw?
14 What colour is muscovado sugar?
15 In which unusual way does Yorick first appear on stage in "Hamlet"?
16 How many sides has a cube?
17 What is the currency of Israel?
18 Who was England's first-choice keeper in the 2002 World Cup?
19 Which major river flows through Bristol?
20 What is the surname of rugby players Tony and Rory?
21 Which character has been played by Albert Finney, Peter Ustinov and David Suchet?
22 What is the nationality of Chris de Burgh?
23 Which term means that material can be decomposed by natural means?
24 What sort of vehicle is a limousine?
25 Which veteran male broadcaster has been a long-term presenter of TV's "Children in Need"?
26 Who fronted the Tijuana Brass?
27 What is the largest wild member of the dog family?
28 Who is Magnus Magnusson's TV presenter daughter?
29 Ed Koch was the mayor of which town?
30 What does SNP stand for?

Answers | Pot-Luck 43 *(see Quiz 83)*

1 Edelweiss. 2 Wayne Rooney. 3 Morecambe and Wise. 4 Cape Kennedy. 5 Colin Firth. 6 Henry VIII. 7 Live 8. 8 Holly. 9 240. 10 The Saint. 11 March. 12 Vincent Van Gogh (by Don McLean). 13 Ha'penny. 14 Hertfordshire. 15 Fuchsia. 16 West Indies. 17 Taylor. 18 Shorthand. 19 Wet Wet Wet. 20 Be prepared. Motto of the Boy Scouts, song of Scar. 21 Hops. 22 Kaiser Chiefs. 23 Colin Cowdrey. 24 Joey. 25 British Open. 26 The Outer Limits. 27 Samurai. 28 Cycling. 29 Kylie Minogue. 30 Dungeons and Dragons.

Quiz 82 | Nature: Bird Brains | Answers – page 92

1 Which bird has a red breast?
2 Which birds can be barn, tawny or snowy?
3 What two colours is a magpie?
4 Which birds are associated with the Tower of London?
5 What colour is a female blackbird?
6 The teal belongs to which family group?
7 What word can go in front of sparrow or martin to name a bird?
8 Which bird lays its eggs in the nests of others?
9 Which bird has the same name as a chess piece?
10 Which bird featured in the film "Kes"?
11 Which part of the golden eagle is gold?
12 Which part of a bird was used as a pen?
13 An early riser is said to be up before which bird?
14 What colour is the plumage on the head of a male mallard?
15 What is special about a swallow's tail?
16 Which bird starts its name with the word "Bull"?
17 The jay is a member of which family?
18 Which seashore bird has a colourful triangular bill?
19 Which reddish-brown songbird sings just before dawn or after dusk?
20 What colour is a tufted duck?
21 Which game bird is a word meaning grumble?
22 Which bird is the symbol of peace?
23 Which bird was said to deliver babies?
24 Which bird is so called because of its fast flight?
25 What is the largest bird in the world?
26 Which flying toy shares its name with a bird?
27 What is a baby swan called?
28 Which letter of the alphabet sounds like a bird's name?
29 What is Britain's smallest bird?
30 Is a fledgling a young or old bird?

Answers | **80s Newsround** *(see Quiz 84)*

1 Hitchcock. 2 Zimbabwe. 3 SAS. 4 Poland. 5 John Lennon. 6 Yorkshire Ripper. 7 Ronald Reagan. 8 Edwina Currie. 9 Lockerbie. 10 Paying income tax. 11 Earthquake. 12 Unemployment. 13 Lady Diana Spencer. 14 London. 15 Falkland. 16 Queen Elizabeth II's. 17 A ship. 18 Kinnock. 19 France. 20 Yuppies. 21 North. 22 Two. 23 Car ferry. 24 Guinness. 25 Haiti. 26 Gorbachev. 27 Ethiopia. 28 Oil rig. 29 Bush. 30 Parkinson.

Quiz 83 | Pot-Luck 43

Answers – page 89

LEVEL 1

1 What is the national flower of Austria?
2 Coleen McLoughlin found fame as the fiancée of which football star?
3 The theatre show "The Play What I Wrote" is about which comedy duo?
4 What was the earlier name of Cape Canaveral?
5 Which actor played the children's father in the movie "Nanny McPhee"?
6 Which monarch is credited with writing "Greensleeves"?
7 Which 2005 pop charity concert took place to coincide with the G8 summit?
8 Which spiky tree has the scientific name Ilex aquifolium?
9 How many old pence were there in £1?
10 Which TV sleuth has the car registration number ST1?
11 In which month is St Patrick's Day?
12 The song starting, "Starry, starry night" is about whom?
13 Which pre-decimal coin do you shove in a table game?
14 In which county was the oil depot explosion in Dec 2005?
15 What did German botanist Leonhard Fuchs give his name to?
16 Curtly Ambrose played international cricket for which team?
17 Which name is shared by actress Elizabeth and snooker star Dennis?
18 What sort of quick writing did Pitman invent?
19 What were Marty Pellow, Graeme Clark, Tom Cunningham and Neil Mitchell better known as?
20 What's the link between the Boy Scouts and Uncle Scar?
21 What is dried in an oast house?
22 Who sang "I Predict a Riot" in 2005?
23 Which great English batsmen had the initials M.C.C.?
24 What is a young kangaroo called?
25 Which major golf championship is decided by a four-hole playoff?
26 Which programme started with the words, "There is nothing wrong with your television set...."?
27 Historically, what is the name of Japan's warrior class?
28 Which sport is Chris Boardman famous for?
29 Which Australian had a hit with "I Should be So Lucky"?
30 Which fantasy game has its name made up of places of imprisonment and legendary creatures?

Answers | Pot-Luck 42 (see Quiz 81)

1 Porgy and Bess. 2 Hyacinth Bucket. 3 Trees. 4 Tess Daly. 5 Decca. 6 Vietnam. 7 Like the circles that you find. 8 Snapdragon. 9 Lady Jane Grey. 10 Romania. 11 A horse. 12 Lynda La Plante. 13 McGraw. 14 Brown. 15 Appears as a skull picked up by Hamlet. 16 Six. 17 Shekel. 18 David Seaman. 19 Avon. 20 Underwood. 21 Hercule Poirot. 22 Irish. 23 Biodegradable. 24 A car. 25 Terry Wogan. 26 Herb Alpert. 27 Wolf. 28 Sally Magnusson. 29 New York. 30 Scottish National Party.

91

1 Which Alfred, a master film-maker, died in 1980?

2 What was Southern Rhodesia renamed?

3 Which crack force stormed the Iranian Embassy in London in 1980?

4 Lech Walesa led strikers in which country?

5 Which Beatle was shot dead in New York?

6 What name was given to murderer Peter Sutcliffe?

7 Which former Hollywood actor became US President?

8 Which MP Edwina became "Eggwina" after a salmonella scare?

9 Over 250 people died in an air crash at which Scottish border town?

10 What was Lester Piggott sent to jail for avoiding?

11 What natural disaster hit Armenia in 1988?

12 What topped 3,000,000 in Britain for the first time since the 1930s?

13 Who became a princess by marrying Prince Charles?

14 In which city did the Barbican arts centre open?

15 Which Islands were the cause of a war between Britain and Argentina?

16 Whose London bedroom did Michael Fagin break into?

17 What was "The Mary Rose" which saw sunlight after 400 years?

18 Which Neil became leader of the Labour Party in 1983?

19 In 1988 François Mitterrand was re-elected president of which country?

20 What name was given to young upwardly mobile persons?

21 Which Colonel Oliver starred in the US "Irongate" court hearing?

22 How many general elections did Margaret Thatcher win in the 1980s?

23 What was the "The Herald of Free Enterprise" which met disaster in 1987?

24 Which company, famed for stout, was implicated in a share scandal?

25 President "Baby Doc" fled from which country?

26 Which Mikhail became Soviet leader in 1985?

27 Bob Geldof organized Live Aid to provide food for which country?

28 What was Piper Alpha, scene of a deadly fire?

29 Which George was elected US president?

30 Which cabinet minister Cecil was forced to resign after his jilted mistress told her side of events to the press?

Answers | Nature: Bird Brains *(see Quiz 82)*

1 Robin. 2 Owls. 3 Black and white. 4 Ravens. 5 Brown. 6 Duck. 7 House. 8 Cuckoo. 9 Rook. 10 Kestrel. 11 Neck feathers. 12 Feather. 13 Lark. 14 Green. 15 Forked. 16 Bullfinch. 17 Crow. 18 Puffin. 19 Nightingale. 20 Black and white. 21 Grouse. 22 Dove. 23 Stork. 24 Swift. 25 Ostrich. 26 Kite. 27 Cygnet. 28 Jay. 29 Wren. 30 Young.

1 What is a smolt?
2 Which song contains the words, "If you lose your teeth when you're out to dine borrow mine!"
3 Which country is a car from if it has the international registration letters MEX?
4 Who came first as monarch, Queen Elizabeth I or Henry II?
5 The Charge of the Light Brigade took place during which battle?
6 In snooker, how many points are scored by potting the yellow ball?
7 Cu is the symbol of which chemical element?
8 Which soap pub sells Newton and Ridley?
9 What is the first month of the year to have exactly 31 days and follow a month of 31 days?
10 What are dried plums called?
11 In the past, which animal did doctors use to drain blood from the sick?
12 Who recorded the album "Post"?
13 What is the word for a group of porpoises?
14 What are the two main flavours in a banoffee pie?
15 Which first name was shared by two of the Tory leadership candidates in 2005?
16 What is the medical name for dizziness due to heights?
17 Which county shares its name with a make-up-selling lady?
18 On a map, what are lines called that join places of equal height above sea level?
19 How many pints in three quarts?
20 What is the name of TV cook Floyd?
21 What is a male goose called?
22 In which county is Land's End?
23 Which company created the IPod?
24 "Phiz" illustrated works by which famous writer?
25 What sort of Pie provided a classic hit for Don McLean?
26 Who played the title role of Ray Charles in the movie "Ray"?
27 How many do you get if you add a baker's dozen to a score?
28 Was 1994 a leap year?
29 Who partnered Robbie Williams on the No 1 hit single "Something Stupid"?
30 From which plant is linen obtained?

Answers | Pot-Luck 45 *(see Quiz 87)*

1 Tiny. 2 Capricorn. 3 Fish. 4 Chris de Burgh. 5 Scar. 6 Black and white. 7 School. 8 Leonardo DiCaprio. 9 Jerome. 10 Popes. 11 Member of the European Parliament. 12 Andrew Murray. 13 Turkey. 14 John Wesley. 15 Blocks. 16 Elizabeth I. 17 Hands. 18 Idle hands. 19 South Africa. 20 Fruit. 21 Guinea pig. 22 John McEnroe. 23 Newcastle United. 24 Diving. 25 Led Zeppelin. 26 Ascot. 27 D. 28 Soup. 29 John Wayne. 30 Mel Hutchwright.

1 Who wrote "Jamie's Italy"?
2 Which chef presented "The F Word"?
3 Who wrote the best-selling "How to be a Domestic Goddess"?
4 What type of "Talk" do Gregg Wallace and Charlie Hicks engage in?
5 Nick Nairn hails from which part of the UK?
6 What was the revamped "Masterchef" programme called?
7 Which TV chef broadcasts from River Cottage?
8 What is Jamie Oliver's wife called?
9 Which country does TV chef Bill Granger come from?
10 "How to Cheat at Cooking" was the first cookery book of which chef?
11 Was Ken Hom born in China or the USA?
12 Madhur Jaffrey writes chiefly about the cuisine of which country?
13 Which Manchester football team does Gary Rhodes famously support?
14 Was it Gordon Ramsay or Ainsley Harriott who was on Glasgow Rangers' books as a teenager?
15 Which Antony has presented "Saturday Kitchen"?
16 In 2005 did Jamie Oliver campaign about meals in schools or hospitals?
17 Which cookery programme saw Gary Rhodes doing battle with Jean Christophe Novelli?
18 Which Australian's cookery book was called "Simply Bill"?
19 On his "French Odyssey" did Rick Stein travel by barge or bicycle?
20 Le Gavroche was opened by which French brothers?
21 The third series of "Strictly Come Dancing" featured which chef?
22 Whose 2000 autobiography was called "Out of the Frying Pan"?
23 Which cook from the early days of TV was born Phyllis Primrose-Pechey?
24 Which TV cook's father was Chancellor of the Exchequer?
25 Was Mrs Beeton 21, 31 or 51 when she wrote her famous book of Household Management?
26 Which TV chef has a dog called Chalky?
27 Which TV cook said "Let's be having you" to a football crowd?
28 Was Ross Burden a success on "Masterchef" or "Mastermind"?
29 Has Lesley Waters or Sophie Grigson been a regular on "Ready Steady Cook"?
30 Which county does James Martin hail from?

Answers | Sport: Cricket (see Quiz 88)

1 1987. 2 Surrey. 3 Duck. 4 Devon Malcolm. 5 Lancashire. 6 Bradman. 7 40. 8 Ian Botham. 9 Wide. 10 Wicket keeper. 11 Three. 12 Shane Warne. 13 Slips. 14 Leicestershire. 15 A finger. 16 New Zealand. 17 Chappell. 18 Yorkshire. 19 Lara. 20 Extras. 21 Stumped. 22 Pakistan. 23 A six. 24 A pair. 25 Jonathan Agnew. 26 Edgbaston. 27 Australia. 28 Yes. 29 Glenn McGrath. 30 Simon Jones.

1 What size was Tim in "A Christmas Carol"?
2 What is the zodiac sign of the Goat?
3 What is held in a creel?
4 Who had a No 1 hit with the song "Lady in Red"?
5 What did Al Capone have on his face that gave him his nickname?
6 What two colours are on the flag waved at the end of a motor race?
7 In nursery rhyme, where did Mary's little lamb follow her to?
8 Which actor played the title role in the movie "The Aviator"?
9 Which half of Robson and Jerome played the part of Paddy Garvey?
10 What were Liberius, Sissinius and Constantine?
11 In the political sector, what does MEP stand for?
12 Which Briton entered the tennis top 100 for the first time in 2005?
13 The ancient city of Troy is in which modern country?
14 Who founded the Methodist movement?
15 What do sprinters start from in a track race?
16 Who ordered the execution of Mary Queen of Scots?
17 What do volleyball players hit the ball with?
18 According to the proverb, what does the devil make work for?
19 Which rugby nation was readmitted to international competition in 1993?
20 What type of food is a pomelo?
21 What is another name for a cavy?
22 Who said, "You cannot be serious!"?
23 Which English team did Michael Owen join on his return from Spain?
24 Which Olympic water sport includes twists, tucks and pikes?
25 Who recorded the original track "Stairway to Heaven"?
26 Which race meeting is as famous for its hats as for its horses?
27 What letter features on a snooker table?
28 What type of food is gazpacho?
29 How is Western actor Marion Morrison better known?
30 What was the name of the novelist played by Ian McKellen in "Coronation Street"?

Answers | Pot-Luck 44 *(see Quiz 85)*

1 A young salmon. 2 Friendship (from Anything Goes). 3 Mexico. 4 Henry II. 5 Balaclava. 6 Two. 7 Copper. 8 Rovers' Return. 9 August. 10 Prunes. 11 Leech. 12 Björk. 13 School. 14 Banana and toffee. 15 David (Davies and Cameron). 16 Vertigo. 17 Avon. 18 Contour lines. 19 Six. 20 Keith. 21 Gander. 22 Cornwall. 23 Apple. 24 Charles Dickens. 25 American. 26 Jamie Foxx. 27 33. 28 No. 29 Nicole Kidman. 30 Flax.

1 When did England last win the Ashes before 2005 – was it 1967, 1977 or 1987?
2 The Oval is the home of which county?
3 What bird is linked to a score of nought?
4 Which 1990s English Test pace bowler has the same first name as an English county?
5 Which county has been captained by Mike Atherton?
6 Which Donald became the first Australian to score 300 test runs in a day?
7 At most, how many wickets can fall in a two-innings game?
8 Which former England all-rounder earned the nickname "Beefy"?
9 Which term describes a ball bowled out of the striker's reach?
10 Which specialist position does Adam Gilchrist take when fielding?
11 How many stumps are there on a set of wickets?
12 Which Aussie player is known – among other things – as Shanie?
13 What term describes fielders positioned closely behind the batsmen?
14 Grace Road is the ground of which county?
15 What must an umpire raise to show that a player is out?
16 Which country did all rounder Richard Hadlee play for?
17 What is the surname of Australian brothers Gregg and Ian?
18 Which county side did Fred Trueman play most of his cricket for?
19 Which West Indian batsman Brian started rewriting the record books in 1994?
20 What is added to the scores of the batsmen to make the total?
21 What does the abbreviation "st" stand for?
22 Which country did Abdul Qadir play for?
23 If the umpire raises both arms above his head what is he signalling?
24 What is a batsman said to collect if he scores 0 twice in a match?
25 Which radio commentator is known as "Aggers"?
26 Which Warwickshire ground hosts Test cricket?
27 Lillee and Thomson formed a deadly pace attack for which country?
28 Can a Test Match end in a tie?
29 Which world-class fast bowler made his last visit to England for the 2005 Ashes?
30 In 2005 which Welsh bowler Simon was injured and missed the final Ashes Test?

Answers | **Celebrity Chefs** *(see Quiz 86)*

1 Jamie Oliver. 2 Gordon Ramsay. 3 Nigella Lawson. 4 Veg Talk. 5 Scotland. 6 Masterchef Goes Large. 7 Hugh Fearnley-Whittingstall. 8 Jools. 9 Australia. 10 Delia Smith. 11 USA. 12 India. 13 United. 14 Gordon Ramsay. 15 Worrall Thompson. 16 Schools. 17 Hell's Kitchen. 18 Bill Granger. 19 Barge. 20 Roux brothers. 21 James Martin. 22 Keith Floyd. 23 Fanny Cradock. 24 Nigella Lawson. 25 21. 26 Rick Stein. 27 Delia Smith. 28 Masterchef. 29 Lesley Waters. 30 Yorkshire.

1. Which special birthday did "The Muppets" celebrate in the year 2005?
2. How many Desperate Housewives were there?
3. What is another name for the wildebeeste?
4. What word goes before glove, hound and trot?
5. What is Ryan O'Neal's actress daughter called?
6. Which English queen never married?
7. In rhyming slang what is a north and south?
8. Which PR man Max called his Memoirs "Read All About It"?
9. What was the name of the Elephant Man?
10. To ten years either way, when was the Automobile Association formed?
11. In the plant world, what do the letters RHS stand for ?
12. Between which two African countries are the Victoria Falls?
13. Which country is golfer Ian Woosnam from?
14. Which Mike was the name of the England manager, played by Ricky Tomlinson?
15. What does the word hirsute mean?
16. What word relates to Enya, the Wombles and Venezuela?
17. In feet how wide is a hockey goal?
18. Who wrote "Little Men"?
19. Which major river flows through New Orleans?
20. Whose last words were, "Thank God I have done my duty"?
21. Which country did General Franco rule?
22. Which sisters recorded "I'm in the Mood for Dancing"?
23. Which Hertfordshire town was Britain's first Garden City?
24. What can be HT, floribunda or a rambler?
25. Which word can mean suspicious or to do with seafood?
26. Where is the Sea of Showers?
27. Which king would have been blown up if the Gunpowder Plot had succeeded?
28. For which sport is Lennox Lewis famous?
29. Which purple precious gem is the birthstone for February?
30. Which game is connected with Boris Schapiro?

| **Answers** | Pot-Luck 47 *(see Quiz 91)* |

1 Will Smith. 2 Zoe Salmon. 3 Prescott. 4 Rabbit. 5 Rose. 6 Banjos. 7 ET. 8 Sylvia's Mother. 9 Four. 10 Pressure of gases. 11 March. 12 Toad. 13 Flora. 14 J. R. R. 15 Spiderman. 16 Boxing. 17 Birmingham. 18 Supernanny. 19 Police. 20 Shoulders. 21 Emperor. 22 12. 23 Tin Pan Alley. 24 Three. 25 The clubhouse. 26 The first dog in space. 27 Billy Elliott. 28 Fireball XL5. 29 Wembley. 30 Heavy Goods Vehicle.

1 The Bay of Biscay lies to the north of which country?
2 Which Gulf lies between Iran and Saudi Arabia?
3 Brittany is part of which country?
4 Which US city is known by its initials LA?
5 Which South American country shares its name with a nut?
6 Near which large city is the Wirral?
7 Which is Britain's most southerly point on the mainland?
8 In which country is Shanghai?
9 In which county is Lake Windermere?
10 To which country does the island of Bermuda belong?
11 What is the northernmost town in England?
12 Is San Francisco on the east or west coast of the USA?
13 Which Union was Ukraine once part of?
14 In which country is Zurich?
15 In which country is the holiday destination of Bali?
16 Which island lies to the south of India?
17 In which country would you hear the language Afrikaans?
18 Which group of islands does Gran Canaria belong to?
19 Where would you be if you had climbed Mount Olympus?
20 In which US state is Orlando?
21 Which Ocean is to the west of Portugal?
22 In which country is The Hague?
23 Monte Carlo is in which principality?
24 Which US state has the Arctic Circle running through it?
25 Which Land in Denmark is made up of bricks?
26 Which Falls are on the Canadian/US border?
27 Which country's women might wear a kimono?
28 Which Ocean's name means peaceful?
29 Which country originally produced Peugeot cars?
30 What is the English for what the French call an autoroute?

| **Answers** | Scientists and Inventors *(see Quiz 92)* |

1 Penicillin. 2 X-rays. 3 Greek. 4 Bunsen burner. 5 Curie. 6 Albert. 7 Temperature.
8 Halley. 9 Stephen. 10 Newton. 11 Italian. 12 The atom. 13 Nicotine. 14
Darwin. 15 Microscope. 16 Rutherford. 17 Temperature. 18 Leonardo Da Vinci. 19
Edison. 20 Grass. 21 Attenborough. 22 Atom. 23 Antiseptic. 24 Morris. 25 Blood.
26 Weaving. 27 Pea. 28 Africa. 29 Steam. 30 Spinning Jenny.

1 Who played Muhammad Ali in the movie about the great boxer?
2 Which presenter of "Blue Peter" was Miss Northern Ireland 1999?
3 Which John became deputy Labour leader under Tony Blair?
4 What kind of animal features in the book "Watership Down"?
5 What flower is the emblem of the Labour Party?
6 Which instruments were featured in the hit single that came from the film "Deliverance"?
7 Who used a children's computer to "phone home"?
8 Who did Dr Hook speak to when trying to get through to Sylvia?
9 What number does the Roman numeral IV stand for?
10 What is measured by a manometer?
11 In which month is St David's Day?
12 What type of animal is a natterjack?
13 Which Roman goddess of flowers is the name of a brand of margarine?
14 What are the initials of writer Tolkien?
15 What superhero can Peter Parker turn into?
16 Clint Eastwood's movie "Million Dollar Baby" features which sport?
17 Which city do Aston Villa come from?
18 Jo Frost found TV fame as what?
19 What are Sting, Stewart Copeland and Andy Summers better known as?
20 On what part of your body would you wear a stole?
21 What is the world's largest species of penguin called?
22 In a pack of cards how many jacks' eyes can be seen?
23 London's Denmark Street acquired which nickname?
24 In "Fifteen to One" how many contestants take part in the final round?
25 Where is the 19th hole on an 18-hole golf course?
26 Who or what was Laika?
27 Which story of a boy dancer became a film then a West End musical?
28 Which spacecraft was commanded by Steve Zodiac?
29 In which stadium did England win the 1966 World Cup Final?
30 What do the initials HGV stand for?

---

1 Which drug is Alexander Fleming famous for discovering?
2 Which rays for examining the inside of the body did Röntgen discover?
3 What nationality was philosopher and scientist Aristotle?
4 What was Robert Bunsen famous for?
5 Which Pierre and Marie discovered radium?
6 What was the first name of German scientist Einstein?
7 Fahrenheit is associated with the measurement of what?
8 Which astronomer gave his name to the comet seen every 76 years?
9 What is the first name of physicist Hawking?
10 Which Sir Isaac discovered the law of gravity?
11 What was the nationality of astronomer Galileo?
12 What was Ernest Rutherford the first man to split?
13 Which juice did Jean Nicot extract from tobacco?
14 Which biologist Charles studied the evolution of the species?
15 Which instrument to magnify small objects was invented by Jansen?
16 Which Ernest discovered alpha, beta and gamma rays?
17 What does the scale named after Anders Celsius measure?
18 Which Italian painter drew early ideas for a helicopter?
19 Which American Thomas developed the light bulb?
20 Flymo developed a machine based on the hovercraft for cutting what?
21 Which naturalist Sir David has a film director brother Richard?
22 What did John Dalton define as the smallest particle of substance?
23 What did Lister discover which stopped wounds becoming septic?
24 Which zoologist Desmond broadcast discoveries about man in "The Naked Ape" and "The Human Zoo"?
25 What did Harvey discover is pumped round the body?
26 What was Kay's Flying Shuttle used for in 1733?
27 What is a common vegetable and flower used by Mendel in his theories on genetics?
28 On which continent have the Leakey family made discoveries about man's evolution?
29 What type of engines did George Stephenson develop?
30 What Spinning invention was named after its creator's daughter?

Answers	Geography *(see Quiz 90)*

1 Spain. 2 Persian Gulf. 3 France. 4 Los Angeles. 5 Brazil. 6 Liverpool. 7 Lizard. 8 China. 9 Cumbria. 10 Britain. 11 Berwick-upon-Tweed. 12 West. 13 Soviet. 14 Switzerland. 15 Indonesia. 16 Sri Lanka. 17 South Africa. 18 Canary Islands. 19 Greece. 20 Florida. 21 Atlantic. 22 Holland. 23 Monaco. 24 Alaska. 25 Legoland. 26 Niagara. 27 Japan. 28 Pacific. 29 France. 30 Motorway.

Quiz 93 | Pot-Luck 48

Answers – page 103

LEVEL 1

1 What name is given to the art of clipping hedges into shapes?
2 How many days in two non-leap years?
3 Which country is a car from if it has the international registration letter P?
4 Which Ben played the part of Fagin in Roman Polanski's movie "Oliver Twist"?
5 Which fruit is used to make the drink kirsch?
6 In darts, what is the highest score from three different trebles?
7 U is the symbol of which chemical element?
8 Which former wife of Chris Evans appeared as Dr Who's assistant on TV?
9 What kind of creature is a flying fox?
10 How many miles are there in eight kilometres?
11 What type of canoe is spelt the same backwards and forwards?
12 Who recorded the album "So Far So Good"?
13 What is the word for a squirrel's nest?
14 Which pop star began legal preceedings against Sony in 1993?
15 Which woodland area of Hampshire is noted for its ponies?
16 What is the name of Sharon and Ozzy Osbourne's eldest daughter?
17 Which German philosopher Karl wrote "Das Kapital"?
18 Who was Hare's grave-robbing partner in the 19th century?
19 How many sides in 15 triangles?
20 What is the name of TV cook Berry?
21 What is a male rabbit called?
22 Which Peter, an Australian singer, married Jordan in 2005?
23 What sort of food is Bel Paese?
24 How many athletes are there in an Olympic relay team?
25 What is the opposite of alkali?
26 What traditionally did a fletcher make?
27 What is the first word in the original TV theme song for "Neighbours"?
28 Who rolled down the hill last, Jack or Jill?
29 Who is chat show host Alan Partridge?
30 What part of the human body is treated by a dermatologist?

Answers | Around Ireland (see Quiz 97)

1 Liffey. 2 County Down. 3 Irish Sea. 4 Belfast. 5 Emerald Isle. 6 Shamrock. 7 Dublin. 8 Belfast. 9 Limerick. 10 Whiskey. 11 Atlantic. 12 Irish and English. 13 Crystal. 14 Galway. 15 Blarney Stone. 16 Kildare. 17 Horse racing. 18 Linen. 19 Patrick. 20 Whiskey and cream. 21 Tweed. 22 East. 23 Ferry ports. 24 Dublin. 25 Air. 26 Londonderry. 27 Cork. 28 Giant's Causeway. 29 Guinness. 30 IRL.

1 Which John painted "The Haywain"?
2 What was the surname of outrageous artist Salvador?
3 Which city, famous for its canals, did Canaletto paint?
4 What was the first name of Impressionist painter Cézanne?
5 Which Leonardo painted Mona Lisa?
6 Which parts of the Venus de Milo are missing?
7 Which animals is George Stubbs famous for painting?
8 Which Paul was famous for paintings of the South Seas?
9 Which Vincent lost an ear?
10 What was the first name of pop artist Warhol?
11 How is Francisco de Goya y Lucientes more simply known?
12 Which Greek artist's name means "The Greek"?
13 Which Spanish painter Pablo was the founder of Cubism?
14 Who was famous for his posters of French dance halls and cabarets?
15 What was the nationality of Rembrandt?
16 Edouard and Claude were Manet and Monet. Which was which?
17 Which items useful on a rainy day did Renoir paint?
18 Which branch of the arts was Barbara Hepworth famous for?
19 What was the nationality of Albrecht Dürer?
20 Which art gallery is in Trafalgar Square?
21 Who painted the ceiling of the Sistine Chapel?
22 In late 1995 the painting of which Royal caused controversy?
23 What is the first name of pop artist Hockney?
24 Which Tudor king is Hans Holbein famous for painting?
25 Which metal is sculptress Elisabeth Frink famous for using?
26 What was the nationality of portrait painter Millais?
27 Which member of the royal family has had his paintings reproduced on a set of stamps?
28 Which London art gallery was founded with the financial support of a sugar merchant?
29 What is the first name of sculptor Moore?
30 Which English artist is famous for his matchstalk men pictures?

| **Answers** | Pot-Luck 50 *(see Quiz 96)* |

1 Paris. 2 Peseta. 3 Charles Dickens. 4 USA. 5 Boris Becker. 6 Bolton. 7 Piano. 8 Lulu. 9 David Cornwell. 10 Pig. 11 Earth. 12 Dan Dare. 13 A hurricane. 14 New York Herald. 15 Jason Donovan. 16 Six. 17 Ardiles and Villa. 18 Suicide is Painless. 19 Potomac. 20 Horse. 21 Vietnam. 22 Cash on delivery. 23 Trumpet. 24 White. 25 Nigel Hawthorne. 26 Sunday. 27 Supersonic. 28 Chris Evert. 29 Cologne. 30 Stone.

1 Which cartoon mouse was Pixie's friend?

2 What is the zodiac sign of Aquarius?

3 "An Unearthly Child" was the first episode of which long-running TV series?

4 Who had a No 1 hit with the song "Bridge Over Troubled Water"?

5 What name is given to a person who makes and sells spectacles?

6 In printing and editing what do the letters UC signify?

7 In nursery rhyme, during which season did the Queen of Hearts make the tarts?

8 Which land does Peter Pan come from?

9 What is a young swan called?

10 Which man won both Wimbledon and the US Open in 2005?

11 What life-threatening thing appeared in London for the last time in 1962?

12 At which ground was the first match of the 2005 Ashes series held?

13 Called cotton candy in America, what's this sweet named in the UK?

14 At which famous Hall is the Royal British Legion Festival of Remembrance held?

15 Which Christmas decoration is a parasite of the apple tree?

16 What is the name of the disc used in ice hockey?

17 What vehicles race in the Indianapolis 500?

18 In the Nintendo game what is Mario's job?

19 What is the profession of Paul Rankin?

20 What colour did all lupins used to be?

21 In conservation, what do the letters FOE stand for?

22 Who says, "It's the way I tell 'em!"?

23 What was the ninth month of the Roman calendar?

24 On which day of the week does the Queen distribute Maundy Money?

25 Which part of the foot is between the sole and the heel?

26 What is the wife of an Earl called?

27 What was the first name of Admiral Lord Nelson?

28 Which UK soap staged a murder trial in May 1995?

29 What kind of rays cause a suntan?

30 Who is Steve Punt's comic partner?

Answers	Pot-Luck 48 *(see Quiz 93)*

1 Topiary. 2 730. 3 Portugal. 4 Ben Kingsley. 5 The cherry. 6 171. 7 Uranium. 8 Billie Piper. 9 A bat. 10 Five. 11 Kayak. 12 Bryan Adams. 13 Drey. 14 George Michael. 15 New Forest. 16 Aimee. 17 Marx. 18 Burke. 19 45. 20 Mary. 21 A buck. 22 Peter Andre. 23 Cheese. 24 Four. 25 Acid. 26 Arrows. 27 Neighbours. 28 Jill. 29 Steve Coogan. 30 Skin.

Quiz 96 Pot-Luck 50

Answers – page 102

LEVEL 1

1 In which city is Orly airport?
2 What is the currency of Spain?
3 Back in the West End in 2005, the musical "Scrooge" was based on a novel by which author?
4 The Kentucky Derby is a horse race in which country?
5 Which former tennis champion became a regular on "They Think It's All Over"?
6 Which soccer team moved to the Reebok Stadium in the 1990s?
7 In rhyming slang what is a Joanna?
8 How is Marie McDonald McLaughlin Lawrie better known?
9 What is the real name of John Le Carré?
10 What is a Tamworth a type of?
11 What does the prefix geo mean?
12 With which pilot did Jocelyn Peabody explore space?
13 What destroyed millions of British trees in October 1987?
14 Which newspaper sent Stanley to find Livingstone?
15 Who had a No 1 with "Any Dream Will Do"?
16 How many sides has a cuboid?
17 Which two Argentinian footballers were bought by Spurs after the '78 World Cup?
18 What's the theme song of M*A*S*H?
19 Which major river flows through Washington DC?
20 What do you ride on if you take part in three-day eventing?
21 Which country did Ho Chi Minh rule?
22 What do the initials COD mean?
23 What instrument does Kenny Ball play?
24 What colour gloves does a snooker referee wear?
25 In "The Madness of King George" who played King George?
26 On which day of the week did "EastEnders" first screen an omnibus edition?
27 Which word means faster than the speed of sound?
28 Who was the first woman to win four consecutive US Open tennis titles?
29 Which word is a German city and a light perfume?
30 The first Harry Potter novel concerned the Philospher's what?

Answers	Painters and Sculptors (see Quiz 94)

1 Constable. 2 Dali. 3 Venice. 4 Paul. 5 Da Vinci. 6 Arms. 7 Horses. 8 Gauguin. 9 Van Gogh. 10 Andy. 11 Goya. 12 El Greco. 13 Picasso. 14 Toulouse-Lautrec. 15 Dutch. 16 Edouard Manet, Claude Monet. 17 Umbrellas. 18 Sculpture. 19 German. 20 National Gallery. 21 Michelangelo. 22 Princess of Wales. 23 David. 24 Henry VIII. 25 Bronze. 26 English. 27 Prince Charles. 28 Tate. 29 Henry. 30 L. S. Lowry.

1 Which river runs through through Dublin?
2 In which Irish county are the Mountains of Morne?
3 Which Sea is to the east of the Island of Ireland?
4 What is the capital city of Northern Ireland?
5 What sort of jewelled Isle is Ireland often called?
6 Which plant is the Irish emblem?
7 What is the capital of the Republic of Ireland?
8 In which Irish city is Queens University?
9 Which Irish town gives its name to a saucy rhyme?
10 Spell the Irish version of the drink the Scots call whisky.
11 Which Ocean is to the west of Ireland?
12 What are Ireland's two official languages?
13 Which type of glass is Waterford famous for?
14 Which Irish flute player James shares his name with a Bay ?
15 Which stone is kissed to receive the gift of smooth talking?
16 Which county shares its name with a fictional TV doctor?
17 Which sport is the Curragh famous for?
18 Which fabric made from flax is Ireland famous for?
19 Who is the patron saint of Ireland?
20 What do you put into Gaelic coffee apart from coffee?
21 Which fabric is Donegal famous for?
22 Is Belfast on the east or the west of the province?
23 What do the towns of Dun Laoghaire and Rosslare have in common?
24 O'Connell Street is which Irish city's main street?
25 How would you be travelling if you arrived at Shannon from abroad?
26 Which is further north, Belfast or Londonderry?
27 Which Irish town sounds like something in a wine bottle neck?
28 Which Causeway is said to have been built as a bridge from Ireland to Scotland?
29 Which stout is Dublin world-famous for?
30 What are the international registration letters for Ireland?

Answers | Pot-Luck 49 *(see Quiz 95)*

1 Dixie. 2 Water carrier. 3 Dr Who. 4 Simon and Garfunkel. 5 Optician. 6 Upper case or capital letter. 7 Summer. 8 Never Never Land. 9 Cygnet. 10 Roger Federer. 11 Smog. 12 Lord's. 13 Candy floss. 14 Royal Albert Hall. 15 Mistletoe. 16 Puck. 17 Cars. 18 Plumber. 19 Chef. 20 Blue. 21 Friends of the Earth. 22 Frank Carson. 23 November. 24 Thursday. 25 Instep. 26 Countess. 27 Horatio. 28 Brookside. 29 Ultra violet. 30 Hugh Dennis.

1 In "Little Britain" is it Lou or Andy who has to push the wheelchair?
2 In which TV hospital are Mark and Tricia Williams nurses?
3 The song "I Dreamed a Dream" comes from which musical?
4 Who was the last Viceroy of India?
5 On TV, who played Ryder, the narrator in "Brideshead Revisited"?
6 Which colourless, odourless light gas is used to lift airships?
7 Where in London is the Central Criminal Court?
8 In boxing what do the letters TKO stand for?
9 To a year each way, when was "The Generation Game" first shown?
10 Who created "The Flintstones"?
11 In which month is the Spring Bank Holiday?
12 Which Comic charity promoted National Red Nose Day?
13 How is Marian Fitzwalter more usually known?
14 What are the initials of Victorian writer Mr Gilbert?
15 What is the oldest university in the USA?
16 What was the "profession" of Captain Kidd?
17 What is the main colour of Nigeria's strip?
18 In which game do the players need glass balls?
19 Who wrote "Filthy, Rich and Catflap"?
20 What was Kat Moon's surname before she married Alfie?
21 Sid Vicious was a member of which punk band?
22 Which magazine did Hugh Hefner found?
23 Which sport did Bill Beaumont play?
24 What is a young badger called?
25 Which character did Harry Enfield play in the first series of "Men Behaving Badly"?
26 Which type of headgear did Procol Harum sing about?
27 What type of party or social gathering is for women only?
28 What was the nickname of TV cook Graham Kerr?
29 In boxing which weight is between fly and feather?
30 Which two numbers are missing from this row in Sudoku – 9, 2, 6, 5, 3, 7, 4?

Answers | Pot-Luck 52 *(see Quiz 100)*

1 Aggie. 2 720. 3 Noel Coward. 4 Edward II. 5 Umpire. 6 Ken Livingstone. 7 Silver. 8 Daniel. 9 Reginald Perrin. 10 Van Morrison. 11 Leanne. 12 Bryan Adams. 13 Birds. 14 Pete Best. 15 Neil Diamond. 16 Nancy Sinatra. 17 The Balkan Trilogy. 18 Mowgli. 19 Scaffold. 20 Sophie. 21 Square. 22 The conundrum. 23 Opera singer. 24 Golf. 25 Ealing comedies. 26 Elton John. 27 All Blacks. 28 Crowther. 29 Six. 30 The Shadows.

1 Where was Love in the 1994 record-breaking hit by Wet Wet Wet?
2 Who had a No 1 hit with "Ice Ice Baby"?
3 Who had a hit with the old Osmonds hit "Love Me for a Reason"?
4 Who had a hit in 1992 with "I Will Always Love You", the theme from "The Bodyguard"?
5 Which part of East London sang "Stay Another Day" in 1994?
6 Quite simply, what colour is Mick Hucknall's group?
7 Which two squaddies had new hits with old songs?
8 What sort of Hymns gave Verve a massive No 1 album?
9 Which 50-plus female took "Believe" to the top of the charts?
10 Who said Any Dream Will Do in his Technicolor Dreamcoat?
11 Whose Sister asked you to Stay in 1992?
12 Who wore Crocodile Shoes in 1994?
13 Who took a Stairway to Heaven before going to Animal Hospital?
14 Who joined George Michael on "Don't Let the Sun Go Down on Me"?
15 "Everything I Do (I Do It for You)" came from a film about which hero?
16 During which conflict was the record "Get Here" a UK Forces favourite?
17 Where were Eternal just a step from in 1994?
18 Which Streets did Bruce Springsteen sing about in 1994?
19 What was the name of the dance production Brothers who had a No 1 with "Setting Sun"?
20 Which disbanded group from the 1970s had a chart-topping greatest hits album called "Gold"?
21 Which seven-strong act first hit No 1 with "Bring It All Back"?
22 What nationality is Björk?
23 Who had a No 1 with the "Shoop Shoop Song"?
24 Which cartoon group had a No 1 with "Do the Bartman"?
25 Which Ebenezer was in the tile of the song by the Shamen?
26 Which rock star did Elvis Presley's daughter marry?
27 Which band had a top hit with "Country House"?
28 Which night did Whigfield sing about ?
29 Which Tom, a 1960s veteran, had his biggest ever album success with "Reload" in 1999?
30 How many people made up Steps – three, five or eight?

Answers | Sport: The 90s *(see Quiz 101)*

1 Damon Hill. 2 France. 3 Lancashire. 4 Faldo. 5 Monica Seles. 6 Hastings.
7 Rangers. 8 Phil Taylor. 9 South Africa. 10 Graham Taylor. 11 Grand National.
12 Wigan. 13 Gunnell. 14 George Graham. 15 It was cancelled. 16 Kriss. 17
Swimming. 18 Ireland. 19 Platt. 20 Skis. 21 France. 22 Scotland. 23 Dalglish. 24
John. 25 Conchita. 26 Alex Ferguson. 27 Hingis. 28 Triple Jump. 29 Javelin. 30
David Beckham.

1 Who co-presented "How Clean is Your House" along with Kim?

2 How many minutes in half a day?

3 Who wrote "Don't Let's be Beastly to the Germans"?

4 Who came first, Edward II or George II?

5 How was Rudi Koertzen involved in the 2005 Ashes tour?

6 Who was London's first directly elected Mayor?

7 Ag is the symbol of which chemical element ?

8 In "Coronation Street" what is Ken and Denise's little boy called?

9 David Nobbs created which character made famous by Leonard Rossiter?

10 Who was lead singer with Them?

11 Which Battersby girl returned to "Coronation Street" and had affairs with dad and son Danny and Jamie?

12 Who recorded the album "So Far So Good"?

13 Avian relates to which kind of creatures?

14 Whom did Ringo Starr replace as drummer with the Beatles?

15 How is Noah Kominsky better known?

16 Who sang with Frank Sinatra on the No 1 "Something Stupid"?

17 Which Trilogy was written by Olivia Manning?

18 What was the name of the boy in Disney's "The Jungle Book"?

19 How were Roger McGough, Mike McGear and John Gorman collectively known?

20 What is the first name of TV cook Grigson?

21 What shape is a boxing ring?

22 What is the final round of "Countdown" called?

23 How did Cecilia Bartoli find fame?

24 What game is played at St Andrews?

25 "Passport to Pimlico" was the first in the series of which British-made films?

26 Which legendary pop star wrote the music for the stage show "Billy Elliott"?

27 What is the nickname of the New Zealand rugby team?

28 Which Leslie introduced "The Price is Right" on UK TV?

29 How many time zones does Canada have?

30 Which group backed Cliff Richard in the 1960s?

Answers | Pot-Luck 51 (see Quiz 98)

1 Lou. 2 Holby City. 3 Les Misérables. 4 Lord Mountbatten. 5 Jeremy Irons. 6 Helium. 7 Old Bailey. 8 Technical Knock Out. 9 1971. 10 Hanna-Barbera. 11 May. 12 Relief. 13 Maid Marian. 14 W. S. 15 Harvard. 16 Pirate. 17 Green. 18 Marbles. 19 Ben Elton. 20 Slater. 21 The Sex Pistols. 22 Playboy. 23 Rugby. 24 Cub. 25 Dermot. 26 Homburg. 27 Hen. 28 The Galloping Gourmet. 29 Bantam. 30 1 and 8.

1 Nigel Mansell was the first F1 Champion in the 1990s, who was the second?
2 Barthez, Dugarry and Thuram played for which FIFA World Cup-winning side?
3 England's cricket skipper played for which county side?
4 Which Nick won the British Open in 1990 and 1992?
5 Which tennis player was stabbed while on court?
6 In 1994 which rugby-playing Gavin was made an OBE?
7 Which Scottish team were champions every season in the 90s except 1997/8?
8 Who dominated world darts throughout the 1990s?
9 Which country returned to playing international sport in the 90s?
10 Which England soccer manager became known as a turnip?
11 Which steeplechase did Party Politics win in election year 1992?
12 Which rugby league team won the Challenge Cup every year for the first half of the 1990s?
13 Which Sally won Olympic gold in the 400-metre hurdles?
14 Which manager left Arsenal after taking a "bung"?
15 Why did no horse win the 1993 Grand National?
16 What is the first name of athlete Akabusi?
17 At which sport did Karen Pickering excel?
18 Which country did Sonia O'Sullivan race for?
19 Which former Villa player David became England's soccer captain?
20 What does Alberto Tomba wear on his feet when he competes?
21 Whom does Mary Pierce play tennis for?
22 Which country is snooker star Stephen Hendry from?
23 Which Kenny took Blackburn to the Premiership championship?
24 What is the first name of athlete Regis?
25 Which Miss Martinez beat Martina in a Wimbledon final?
26 Who managed Man Utd in their 1999 triple-winning season?
27 Which teenager Martina won Wimbledon, the US Open and Australian Open in 1997?
28 In which event was Jonathan Edwards world champion in 1995?
29 What does Steve Backley throw?
30 Which English player was hammered by the press after his 1998 World Cup red card?

| **Answers** | Pop: Sounds of the 90s *(see Quiz 99)* |

1 All Around. 2 Vanilla Ice. 3 Boyzone. 4 Whitney Houston. 5 East 17. 6 Red. 7 Robson and Jerome. 8 Urban Hymns. 9 Cher. 10 Jason Donovan. 11 Shakespear's. 12 Jimmy Nail. 13 Rolf Harris. 14 Elton John. 15 Robin Hood. 16 Gulf War. 17 Heaven. 18 Philadelphia. 19 Chemical Brothers. 20 Abba. 21 S Club. 22 Icelandic. 23 Cher. 24 The Simpsons. 25 Goode. 26 Michael Jackson. 27 Blur. 28 Saturday. 29 Tom Jones. 30 Five.

Quiz 102 | Pot-Luck 53

Answers – page 112

1 Which Kimberley was involved with David Blunkett when he resigned in 2004?

2 Rio Ferdinand and Alan Smith have both played for which two Uniteds?

3 How much does it cost to buy a station on a British Monopoly board?

4 Who had a No 1 hit with the song "Bohemian Rhapsody"?

5 In 2005 which Sean was nominated for a lifetime achievement award by the American Film Institute?

6 How many strings are there on a Spanish guitar?

7 How did the notorious witchfinder Matthew Hopkins die?

8 Which country did England cricketers tour after their Ashes win in 2005?

9 Where would you travel to find the Sea of Tranquillity?

10 On which special day in 1964 was "Top of the Pops" first transmitted?

11 In the military sector, what does TA stand for?

12 In which sport does the scoring begin at 15?

13 Called thumbtack in America, what's the name of this in the UK?

14 What game have Spassky, Fischer and Karpov played?

15 What type of hat was worn by Sherlock Holmes?

16 Which sisters had snakes on their heads in place of hair?

17 What was the "Flying Scotsman"?

18 What are you interested in if you study calligraphy?

19 In sailing, what is a warp?

20 What type of food is a profiterole?

21 In which country was Shergar kidnapped?

22 Who said, "Just like that!"?

23 What was the seventh month of the Roman calendar?

24 Which Russian ruler was known as "the Terrible"?

25 Which "copper" tree has reddish brown leaves?

26 What was the surname of landscape gardener Capability?

27 Which musical instrument was played by Larry Adler?

28 Who recorded "Sultans of Swing"?

29 In mythology what is Neptune the god of?

30 Prince William was accepted at which military school after he left university?

Answers | TV: The 90s *(see Quiz 104)*

1 Jennifer Saunders. 2 Soldier Soldier. 3 Time. 4 Baywatch. 5 The Big Breakfast. 6 Leisure Centre. 7 Lenny Henry. 8 Cracker 9 Of May. 10 Dead Donkey. 11 Spain. 12 Goodnight. 13 Police officer. 14 Cards. 15 Eliott. 16 Hurts. 17 Atkinson. 18 Noel Edmonds. 19 Doctors. 20 Nesbitt. 21 Horses. 22 Twin. 23 Year. 24 Hetty. 25 Yes. 26 Stars. 27 Dibley. 28 Panorama. 29 Jill Dando. 30 Rolf Harris.

1 Which English county did ex-Australian captain Allan Border play for?

2 In Parliament what was known as DORA?

3 In sport, who are the Blades?

4 In which musical does the song "Somewhere" appear?

5 Which steam bath originated in Finland?

6 What are protective eyeglasses called?

7 Which comedian created Monsieur Hulot?

8 Which MP Boris has edited the Spectator magazine?

9 What was the original theme song for "Absolutely Fabulous"?

10 Which dance goes, one-two-three-hop?

11 What is the prompting device used by TV presenters called?

12 Which Justin released the chart topping album "Justified"?

13 Who won the world professional snooker championship for the first time back in 1972?

14 In which House was James Herriot's veterinary practice?

15 Which MP has won two Oscars?

16 Who wrote "The History of Mr Polly"?

17 To five years either way, when was the first LP released commercially in Britain?

18 Which political leader appointed in 2005 went to Eton and Oxford?

19 Robin Cousins won an Olympic gold medal in which artistic sport?

20 Who created the Muppets?

21 Which piece of furniture is Benjamin Franklin credited with creating?

22 Which sit com shared its name with a food called the staff of life?

23 The Diamond Sculls takes place at which sporting event?

24 What is a group of five performers called?

25 Which sport do the Harlem Globetrotters play?

26 In soccer, which country did Eusebio play for?

27 Which city devastated in 2005 was a major influence on jazz music?

28 What is the nationality of Tom Conti?

29 If Redknapp was Harry, who was Jim in the Harry and Jim soccer management duo?

30 Which family featured with Gareth Gates on the No 1 single "Spirit in the Sky"?

Answers | Pot-Luck 55 *(see Quiz 105)*

1 Louis Walsh. 2 Dave. 3 Two. 4 Gladioli. 5 Mae West. 6 England. 7 John Bunyan. 8 Albatross. 9 South Pacific. 10 Pastry. 11 The Beach Boys. 12 Marie Curie. 13 Panorama. 14 Patriots. 15 Miss Marple. 16 Michael Fish. 17 Boom Bang-a-Bang. 18 Wisden Cricketers Almanack. 19 Phil Redmond. 20 Northern Ireland. 21 David Cassidy. 22 Canada. 23 Canada. 24 Baseball. 25 R. Kelly. 26 Dollar. 27 Two. 28 Tobacco smoke. 29 Maria. 30 Eddie Fitzgerald.

Quiz 104 TV: The 90s

Answers – page 110

1 Who plays Edina in "Absolutely Fabulous"?

2 In which series did Robson and Jerome star?

3 What Goes By in the sit com with Jean and Lionel?

4 What is the series about LA lifeguards called?

5 What is the Channel 4 Breakfast programme called?

6 In "The Brittas Empire" what is Gordon manager of?

7 Who is the comedian husband of Dawn French who stars in "Chef!"?

8 Which series starred Robbie Coltrane as a police psychologist?

9 Which Darling Buds starred David Jason and Pam Ferris?

10 What did you Drop in the series about a newsroom?

11 In which country was "Eldorado" set?

12 What was said to Sweetheart in the series with Nicholas Lyndhurst?

13 What is Nick's job in "Heartbeat"?

14 What was the House made of in the political drama?

15 Which fashion House did Beatrice and Evangeline head?

16 What does Love do in the drama with Adam Faith and Zoë Wanamaker?

17 Which Rowan played the bumbling Mr Bean?

18 Who hosted a crazy Saturday-night House Party?

19 What was the profession of Jack and Beth in "Peak Practice"?

20 Which Rab C. was a Glasgow street philosopher?

21 Which animals was the series "Trainer" about?

22 Which Peaks provided a mysterious soap series in 1990–91?

23 How long did Peter Mayle spend in Provence?

24 What was the first name of private detective Mrs Wainthropp?

25 Did summer precede winter in Delia Smith's cookery collections?

26 What did contestants have In Their Eyes in the impersonation show?

27 Dawn French played the vicar of which parish?

28 On which long-running current affairs programme did the Princess of Wales give her first solo interview in 1995?

29 Which Breakfast News presenter took over the Holiday programme?

30 Which Australian presented "Animal Hospital"?

Answers | **Pot-Luck 53** *(see Quiz 102)*

1 Quinn. 2 Leeds Utd and Man Utd. 3 £200. 4 Queen. 5 Sean Connery. 6 Six.
7 He was hanged as a wizard. 8 Pakistan. 9 The Moon. 10 New Year's Day. 11
Territorial Army. 12 Tennis. 13 Drawing pin. 14 Chess. 15 Deerstalker. 16 The
Gorgons. 17 A train. 18 Handwriting. 19 Mooring rope. 20 Cake. 21 Ireland. 22
Tommy Cooper. 23 September. 24 Ivan. 25 Beech. 26 Brown. 27 Mouth organ. 28
Dire Straits. 29 The sea. 30 Sandhurst.

1 Who made up the "X Factor" jury with Simon Cowell and Sharon Osbourne?
2 Who is Cockney Chas's singing partner?
3 How many heads did Dr Doolittle's llama have?
4 What are Dame Edna Everage's favourite flowers?
5 Which blonde sex symbol used the pseudonym Jane Mast?
6 Which is the largest country in Great Britain?
7 Who wrote "Pilgrim's Progress"?
8 Which is the only bird capable of flying all day without flapping its wings?
9 "There is Nothing Like a Dame" comes from which musical?
10 What is something wrapped in if it is served "en croûte"?
11 Which 60s group was formed by the Wilson brothers?
12 Who was the first person known to have died from radiation poisoning?
13 Which word for a wide view is the name of a TV news programme?
14 Which New England team won the Super Bowl in 2002 and 2004?
15 Which character has been played by Margaret Rutherford and Joan Hickson?
16 Who assured viewers there were no hurricanes on the way in 1987?
17 Which song did Lulu sing in the Eurovision Song Contest?
18 What sporting publication is nicknamed "The Primrose Bible"?
19 Who created "Brookside"?
20 Which country does Roy Carroll play for?
21 Who shot to fame in the 70s as Keith Partridge?
22 In which country is the Jasper National Park?
23 Which country does snooker star Cliff Thorburn come from?
24 Which sport do the Pittsburgh Pirates play?
25 "Ignition" was a 2003 UK No 1 for which artist?
26 What is the currency of Australia?
27 How many times did Barry Sheene win the 500cc world motor cycle racing championship?
28 What do you dislike if you are misocapnic?
29 What is Mia short for in Mia Farrow's name?
30 What is the full name of the Coltrane character in "Cracker"?

Answers	Pot-Luck 54 *(see Quiz 103)*

1 Essex. 2 Defence Of the Realm Act. 3 Sheffield United. 4 West Side Story. 5 Sauna. 6 Goggles. 7 Jacques Tati. 8 Boris Johnson. 9 This Wheel's on Fire. 10 Polka. 11 Autocue. 12 Justin Timberlake. 13 Alex Higgins. 14 Skeldale House. 15 Glenda Jackson. 16 H. G. Wells. 17 1950. 18 David Cameron. 19 Ice skating. 20 Jim Henson. 21 Rocking chair. 22 Bread. 23 Henley Regatta. 24 Quintet. 25 Basketball. 26 Portugal. 27 New Orleans. 28 Scottish. 29 Jim Smith. 30 The Kumars.

1 Which party won a fourth consecutive term of office in the UK in 1992?
2 Which Middle Eastern country was defeated in the Gulf War?
3 Which country was reunified in 1990?
4 Who became Deputy Prime Minister of the UK in 1995?
5 Which Manchester jail was the scene of rioting in 1990?
6 Which envoy of the Archbishop of Canterbury was released from the Lebanon?
7 Which three-times winner of the Grand National died?
8 Which rock legend's daughter did Michael Jackson marry?
9 Who succeeded Barbara Bush as the USA's First Lady?
10 Which Dimbleby interviewed the Prince of Wales on TV?
11 Who was the first female presenter of the National Lottery Live?
12 Which member of the royal family divorced and remarried?
13 Which Labour leader resigned after the 1992 General Election?
14 Assassinated Prime Minister Rabin was from which country?
15 Which tax was abandoned in favour of the Council Tax?
16 Which country won the Eurovision Contest in consecutive years in the first half of the decade?
17 Who described 1992 as an annus horribilis?
18 Which heavyweight boxing champion served a prison sentence?
19 Which media magnate drowned in mysterious circumstances?
20 George Carey succeeded Robert Runcie in which post?
21 Jill Morrell conducted a campaign to free which Beirut hostage?
22 Who became president of South Africa in 1994?
23 Which US singer celebrated his 80th birthday in December 1995?
24 Benazir Bhutto returned as prime minister of which Asian country?
25 Which Boris became president of the Russian Federation in 1991?
26 Which meat was at the heart of a scare about BSE?
27 Which link between England and France was opened?
28 Which American football star was acquitted of his wife's murder?
29 The imprisonment of Nick Leeson followed the collapse of which bank?
30 What replaced TV am as ITV's weekly breakfast programme?

Answers | 90s Films *(see Quiz 108)*

1 Hugh Grant. 2 Braveheart. 3 Columbus. 4 Mrs Doubtfire. 5 Hook. 6 Sister Act. 7 Jack Lemmon. 8 List. 9 A dog. 10 A ghost. 11 Tom Hanks. 12 Patrick Swayze. 13 Kevin Costner. 14 The Silence of the Lambs. 15 Alone. 16 The Lion King. 17 Indecent. 18 Trousers. 19 Julia Roberts. 20 Sally. 21 Jurassic. 22 Seattle. 23 Pocahontas. 24 Batman. 25 Mohicans. 26 Aladdin. 27 Tom Cruise. 28 Dredd. 29 34th. 30 Golden.

Quiz 107 | Pot-Luck 56

Answers – page 117

LEVEL 1

1 Which Glasgow comedian is married to actress Pamela Stephenson?
2 Who were the parents of Cain, Able and Seth?
3 Which was the first British soccer side to win the European Cup?
4 What is the flavour of Tia Maria?
5 Which Joyce said, "George, don't do that!"
6 In snooker, what is the score from potting the pink?
7 N is the symbol of which chemical element ?
8 In "EastEnders" who is Kathy Mitchell's son by Pete Beale?
9 What is the second month of the year to have exactly 30 days?
10 Which Rupert played Ron in the Harry Potter films?
11 In England, where is the National Water Sports Centre?
12 In which US state is Jack Daniel's whiskey distilled?
13 How much was a groat worth?
14 Who hosted "The Last Resort"?
15 What was special about the size of the disc developed by Philips and Sony in the late 1970s?
16 Which two fruits were crossed to produce a nectarine?
17 In which country did judo develop?
18 Which rapper featured on The Pussycat Dolls' No 1 hit "Don't 'Cha"?
19 Which pop star was Jeff Banks married to?
20 What is the first name of TV cook Harris?
21 Who is the patron saint of travellers?
22 A caravan is a group of which animals?
23 In the pop song, who wore a "crimson dress that clings so tight"?
24 Which striker Andy has played for both City and United in Manchester?
25 Who picked up the nickname the "Louisville Lip"?
26 From which film did Duran Duran get their name?
27 Whose summer residence is at Castel Gandolfo?
28 In which city did the charity Oxfam originate?
29 How many games did Arsenal lose in winning the 2003/4 Premiership?
30 Which fashion item was Imelda Marcos famous for collecting?

Answers | Pot-Luck 57 *(see Quiz 109)*

1 Coldplay. 2 Japan. 3 USA. 4 Ram. 5 Deputy Dawg. 6 Bobby Robson. 7 Smoked cod's roe. 8 Campion. 9 Gene Roddenberry. 10 One horse power. 11 Greenland. 12 Sari. 13 Rubella. 14 April Fool's Day. 15 Metro Goldwyn Mayer. 16 An anchor. 17 Derbyshire. 18 Smoke. 19 Barbie. 20 Rudolph Valentino. 21 Antiques. 22 Nettle. 23 The Olympic Games. 24 Sahara. 25 FBI. 26 Outside. 27 Snap. 28 Gascoigne. 29 Gimme! Gimme! Gimme! (A Man After Midnight). 30 Plums.

115

Quiz 108 | 90s Films

Answers – page 114

1 Which male star shot to fame in "Four Weddings and a Funeral"?

2 In which film shot in Ireland did Australian Mel Gibson play a Scot?

3 Who had to "Carry On" 500 years after the discovery of America?

4 In which film did Robin Williams dress up as a Scottish nanny?

5 What was the name of the Dustin Hoffman film about Peter Pan?

6 In which film did Whoopi Golberg first get into the habit?

7 Who joined Walter Matthau in the film "Grumpy Old Men"?

8 What did Schindler draw up in the Spielberg film?

9 What is Beethoven in the 1992 film?

10 What is Casper?

11 Who won an Oscar for "Forrest Gump" and "Philadelphia"?

12 Who starred with Demi Moore in "Ghost"?

13 Who was Whitney Houston's Bodyguard?

14 In which film did Anthony Hopkins play the role of Hannibal Lecter?

15 How was Macaulay Culkin left at Home in 1990?

16 What did the cub Simba become in the 1994 Disney film?

17 What kind of Proposal did Robert Redford make concerning Demi Moore?

18 What was Wrong in the Wallace and Gromit Oscar-winning film?

19 Who was the Pretty Woman in the 1990 film?

20 Whom did Harry meet in the film with Billy Crystal?

21 Which Park was the Spielberg film about dinosaurs?

22 Where was someone Sleepless in the film with Meg Ryan?

23 Which Disney release told the story of an American Indian heroine?

24 In which series of films would you find Robin and the Joker?

25 Daniel Day-Lewis starred in the Last of what in 1992?

26 In which film was Robin Williams the voice of the genie?

27 Who was Nicole Kidman's co star in "Far and Away" whom she later married?

28 Which Judge does Sylvester Stallone play in the comic cult movie?

29 On which street was there A Miracle in the Xmas movie with Richard Attenborough?

30 What colour is the Eye in the 007 film?

Answers | 90s Newsround *(see Quiz 106)*

1 Conservatives. 2 Iraq. 3 Germany. 4 Michael Heseltine. 5 Strangeways. 6 Terry Waite. 7 Red Rum. 8 Elvis. 9 Hillary Clinton. 10 Jonathan. 11 Anthea Turner. 12 Princess Royal. 13 Neil Kinnock. 14 Israel. 15 Poll tax. 16 Ireland. 17 The Queen. 18 Mike Tyson. 19 Robert Maxwell. 20 Archbishop of Canterbury. 21 John McCarthy. 22 Nelson Mandela. 23 Frank Sinatra. 24 Pakistan. 25 Yeltsin. 26 Beef. 27 Channel Tunnel. 28 OJ Simpson. 29 Barings. 30 GMTV.

Quiz 109 | Pot-Luck 57

Answers – page 115

LEVEL 1

1 "X&Y" is the third album from which group?
2 Which country co-hosted the 2002 World Cup with South Korea?
3 Which country does tennis player Pete Sampras come from?
4 What is a male sheep called?
5 Who exclaims "Dagnabit!"?
6 Who was manager of Ipswich when they first won the FA Cup in '78?
7 What is taramasalata made from?
8 Which sleuth drove round East Anglia in a vintage Lagonda?
9 Who created "Star Trek"?
10 What is 1 Cheval-Vapeur equivalent to?
11 From which country's language does anorak come from?
12 What is a traditional Indian dress called?
13 The MMR vaccine covers measles, mumps and what else?
14 Boob Day is the Spanish equivalent of what in Britain?
15 In cinema, what does MGM stand for?
16 What is tattooed on Popeye's arm?
17 Which county did England's wicket keeper Bob Taylor play for?
18 If a sign in Germany announced Rauchen Verboten, what could you not do?
19 In the toy world, who is Ken's girlfriend?
20 Which film star's funeral in 1926 was attended by more than 100,000 mourners?
21 What did Lovejoy deal in?
22 Which stinging weed can be used to make a kind of beer?
23 What was held in Britain in 1908 and 1948?
24 In which desert did Mark Thatcher go missing?
25 Which organization's motto is "Fidelity, Bravery, Integrity"?
26 Would a Scotsman wear a sporran under or outside the kilt?
27 Which card game involves quickly spotting matching pairs?
28 Which ex-England soccer great Paul got the push as boss of Kettering in 2005?
29 Which ABBA hit did Madonna sample for her single "Hung Up"?
30 What is the drink slivovitz made from?

Answers | Pot-Luck 56 (see Quiz 107)

1 Billy Connolly. 2 Adam and Eve. 3 Celtic. 4 Coffee. 5 Grenfell. 6 Six. 7 Nitrogen. 8 Ian. 9 June. 10 Rupert Grint. 11 Nottingham. 12 Tennessee. 13 4d (four old pence). 14 Jonathan Ross. 15 Compact. 16 Peach and plum. 17 Japan. 18 Busta Rhymes. 19 Sandie Shaw. 20 Valentina. 21 St Christopher. 22 Camels. 23 Pretty Flamingo. 24 Andy Cole. 25 Muhammad Ali. 26 Barbarella. 27 The Pope. 28 Oxford. 29 None. 30 Shoes.

117

1 Which singer starred in "The Bodyguard"?
2 Which actress Keaton starred in "Father of the Bride II"?
3 "Walk the Line" was a biopic of which country music legend?
4 Which Holly won an Oscar for a silent role in "The Piano"?
5 Which silent movie star was played by Robert Downey Jr in 1992?
6 Which Welsh actor starred with Jodie Foster in "The Silence of the Lambs"?
7 Which Bob starred in "Mona Lisa" before finding it "good to talk"?
8 Which Steven directed "Schindler's List"?
9 Which actor Sylvester has the nickname Sly?
10 Who is Donald Sutherland's actor son?
11 What is the first name of "Pulp Fiction" director Tarantino?
12 Which actress Melanie married Don Johnson – twice?
13 Which Nick co-starred with Barbra Streisand in "The Prince of Tides"?
14 What is the first name of actress Sarandon ?
15 Which Johnny starred as Edward Scissorhands?
16 Which Scottish actor Sean has an actor son Jason?
17 Which Emilio starred in "Young Guns" I and II?
18 Which Macaulay became one of the highest-paid child stars ever?
19 Which actress Glenn had a "Fatal Attraction"?
20 Which Al starred in "The Godfather" and "Scent of a Woman"?
21 Which actor Mel was born in the US but brought up in Australia?
22 What is the surname of father and daughter Peter and Bridget?
23 Which Robin became Mrs Doubtfire?
24 Which blond Daryl had adventures with the Invisible Man?
25 Who was Alec Baldwin's real and screen wife in "The Getaway"?
26 What is the first name of Joanne Whalley-Kilmer's husband?
27 Liza Minnelli and Lorna Luft are daughters of which Hollywood great?
28 Which actor succeeded Timothy Dalton as James Bond?
29 Which film director's real name is Allen Stewart Konigsberg?
30 Which actor won an Oscar as director of "Dances with Wolves"?

Answers | **Pot-Luck 60** *(see Quiz 114)*

1 Somerset. 2 Jessica Fletcher. 3 Piccadilly. 4 Nancy. 5 Grant. 6 Casino Royale. 7 Bruce Forsyth. 8 Circus. 9 1963. 10 Two. 11 None. 12 Sixpence. 13 Peter Davison. 14 Casino Royale. 15 George VI. 16 Jack. 17 Manchester. 18 James Blunt. 19 Balmoral. 20 Clive Dunn. 21 Bridge. 22 UB40. 23 Roll call. 24 Poet Laureate. 25 Armstrong. 26 Wall Street. 27 Eight. 28 Jeremy Isaacs. 29 Wear. 30 ASLEF.

Quiz 111 | Pot-Luck 58

Answers – page 121

LEVEL 1

1 What is the seventh commandment?
2 What sport takes place in a velodrome?
3 Who had UK No 1s with "Independent Women" and "Survivor"?
4 Who sang the theme song for "The Man with the Golden Gun"?
5 Who said, "I shall hear in heaven"?
6 In which card game do you "peg out"?
7 Which bingo number is clickety click?
8 What was Ivan Lendl's first Wimbledon tournament win?
9 What is another name for Lady's Fingers?
10 Which member of the Monkees appeared in "Coronation Street"?
11 What colour is ebony?
12 What do you have at the bottom of a colander?
13 Who wrote the TV musical drama "Lipstick on Your Collar"?
14 Who was England's captain in the 2002 World Cup?
15 In which track event do you get wet even when it's not raining?
16 On which track at Pennsylvania Station did the Chattanooga Choo Choo leave?
17 What colour are French post boxes?
18 What does the letter U stand for in URL?
19 Who played Len Fairclough?
20 When during a meal would you have an hors d'oeuvre?
21 Which team did Alf Garnett support?
22 What is the US military academy called?
23 Over what type of food did Edwina Currie resign a ministerial post?
24 Which classical composer did Richard Chamberlain play in "The Music Lovers"?
25 What is the name of the cat which dips its paw in the food tin?
26 Who coached England's 2003 rugby World Cup-winning team?
27 What name is given to the style of riding when both the rider's legs are on the same side of the horse?
28 Who tragically died while appearing on Live at Her Majesty's?
29 Where might you find a breeze block?
30 Whose motto is "Nation shall speak unto nation"?

Answers	Pot-Luck 61 *(see Quiz 115)*

1 Honolulu. 2 Mozart. 3 Gondola. 4 A hater of mankind. 5 Israel. 6 Somerset. 7 Donna Karan New York. 8 Arsenal. 9 Sharon Stone. 10 Demi Moore. 11 Bill Gates. 12 Irvine Welsh. 13 Gareth Gates. 14 Anfield, Liverpool. 15 Dublin. 16 Sett. 17 Centrepoint. 18 Gaggle. 19 Brian Lara. 20 They are all royal boroughs. 21 Emma Hamilton. 22 Amadeus. 23 Charles. 24 Sergeant Uhuru. 25 Andrew Flintoff. 26 King Harold. 27 Sancho Panza. 28 Myxamatosis. 29 A. A. Milne. 30 York.

1 What did Iran used to be called?
2 In which World are underdeveloped countries said to be?
3 Normandy is part of which country?
4 In which Sea is the island of Majorca?
5 Which country does the island of Rhodes belong to?
6 In which US state is Disney World?
7 Which county is abbreviated to Oxon?
8 In which country is the Costa del Sol?
9 Which is further south, Great Yarmouth or Brighton?
10 Is Torremolinos on the coast or inland?
11 Which sea lies between Italy and the former Yugoslavia?
12 On which coast of France are Cannes and St Tropez?
13 If you took a holiday in Gstaad what sport would you practise?
14 In which country is Buenos Aires?
15 In which continent is the holiday destination of Ibiza?
16 Where would you speak English and Maltese?
17 Which island lies at the eastern end of the Mediterranean?
18 Which group of islands does Tenerife belong to?
19 What is the Matterhorn?
20 What is the continent around the South Pole called?
21 Which country does the Loire flow through?
22 What is the world's second highest mountain?
23 In which Ocean is Greenland?
24 On which continent is the Kalahari desert?
25 What is the chief official language of Israel?
26 The Arctic Ocean is not covered mainly by water but by what?
27 Which tiny princedom is situated between France and Spain?
28 In which Sea is Cuba?
29 Which Falls are on the border between Zimbabwe and Zambia?
30 On which continent is the Amazon river?

| **Answers** | Hollywood *(see Quiz 110)* |

1 Whitney Houston. 2 Diane. 3 Johnny Cash. 4 Hunter. 5 Charlie Chaplin. 6 Anthony Hopkins. 7 Hoskins. 8 Spielberg. 9 Stallone. 10 Kiefer. 11 Quentin. 12 Griffith. 13 Nolte. 14 Susan. 15 Depp. 16 Connery. 17 Estevez. 18 Culkin. 19 Close. 20 Pacino. 21 Gibson. 22 Fonda. 23 Williams. 24 Hannah. 25 Kim Basinger. 26 Val. 27 Judy Garland. 28 Pierce Brosnan. 29 Woody Allen. 30 Kevin Costner.

1 What sort of Circle do conjurers join?
2 The biopic movie "The Aviator" was about which person?
3 Which city hosted the 2004 Olympic Games?
4 Which musical includes the characters Sky Masterson and Nathan Detroit?
5 What can be the name of a hat and a member of a cricket team?
6 Which sign of the zodiac follows Capricorn?
7 Which game might you be watching if you were at the Belfry?
8 Variola is more commonly called what?
9 Who wrote the play "An Inspector Calls"?
10 What is Diana Prince's other identity?
11 Which Scottish group took their name from a Scritti Politti lyric?
12 Which section do you look for in the newspaper to read what the stars have in store for you?
13 Which musical instrument does Nigel Kennedy play ?
14 Which residence of the Queen's was opened to the public in 1993?
15 In which month is the Le Mans 24-hour race held?
16 Who wrote the theme song to "Harry's Game"?
17 After what is London's Fleet Street named?
18 Which "Knight Rider" travelled to "Baywatch"?
19 Whom did Frank Bruno beat to become WBC heavyweight champion in 1995?
20 What is a cassoulet?
21 In which sport would you have an Eskimo roll?
22 What is another name for a Chinese gooseberry?
23 What is a 200th anniversary called?
24 How many players are there in a basketball team?
25 In ads, what was BT's bird called?
26 Which striker Jimmy has played soccer for Leeds, Chelsea and Middlesbrough?
27 What was the name of Hamlet's father?
28 On which day of the week did "The Archers" first have an omnibus edition?
29 What is the English name for Firenze?
30 To five years either way, when was the Royal Variety show first televised?

Answers | Pot-Luck 58 *(see Quiz 111)*

1 Thou shalt not commit adultery. 2 Cycling. 3 Destiny's Child. 4 Lulu. 5 Beethoven. 6 Cribbage. 7 66. 8 Junior Wimbledon. 9 Okra. 10 Davy Jones. 11 Black. 12 Holes. 13 Dennis Potter. 14 David Beckham. 15 Steeplechase. 16 Track 29. 17 Yellow. 18 Uniform. 19 Peter Adamson. 20 Beginning. 21 West Ham. 22 West Point. 23 Eggs. 24 Tchaikovsky. 25 Arthur. 26 Sir Clive Woodward. 27 Side saddle. 28 Tommy Cooper. 29 In a wall. 30 The BBC.

Quiz 114 | Pot-Luck 60

LEVEL 1

1 In which English county are Taunton and Wells?
2 Which fictional detective wrote "The Corpse Danced at Midnight"?
3 On the London Underground, on which line is Knightsbridge station?
4 What is the name of Frank Sinatra's daughter?
5 What is the name of Phil's brother in "EastEnders"?
6 In which Ian Fleming novel did James Bond first appear?
7 Whom did 1975 Miss World Wilnelia Merced marry in the 1980s?
8 What type of entertainment is the musical "Barnum" about?
9 In which year did "Dr Who" first appear on BBC?
10 Over how many days is an Olympic decathlon held?
11 How many World Cup final stages has Ryan Giggs played in?
12 In June 1980, which coin ceased to be legal tender?
13 Whom is actress Sandra Dickinson married to?
14 What was the title of the first movie in which Daniel Craig played James Bond?
15 Who was the first British monarch to visit America?
16 What is the first name of comedian Dee?
17 0161 is the dialling code for which city?
18 "Back to Bedlam" is the debut album by which singer?
19 At which Scottish home of the Queen did Charles and Camilla spend their honeymoon?
20 Which member of "Dad's Army" had a chart-topping hit?
21 At which game has Omar Sharif represented his country?
22 Which group features the children of 50s and 60s folk singer Ian Campbell?
23 What does Tenko mean in English?
24 C. Day Lewis and John Betjeman have both held which title?
25 Which Lance monopolized the Tour de France in the first years of the new millennium?
26 On which Street is the New York Stock Exchange?
27 How many times do you sing "Happy Birthday" if you sing two verses of the song?
28 Who left Channel 4 to become Director of the Royal Opera House?
29 Sunderland lies at the mouth of which river?
30 Of which union was Ray Buckton once a leader?

Answers | Geography (see Quiz 112)

1 Persia. 2 Third World. 3 France. 4 Mediterranean. 5 Greece. 6 Florida. 7 Oxfordshire. 8 Spain. 9 Brighton. 10 On the coast. 11 Adriatic. 12 South. 13 Skiing. 14 Argentina. 15 Europe. 16 Malta. 17 Cyprus. 18 Canary Islands. 19 Mountain. 20 Antarctica. 21 France. 22 K2. 23 Arctic. 24 Africa. 25 Hebrew. 26 Ice. 27 Andorra. 28 Caribbean. 29 Victoria. 30 South America.

Quiz 115 | Pot-Luck 61

Answers – page 119

LEVEL 1

1 What is the capital city of Hawaii?
2 The birth of which musical genius was celebrated in 2006?
3 What boat is found on the canals of Venice?
4 What is a misanthrope?
5 Where would you find a kibbutz?
6 Where are the Quantocks?
7 What do the initials DKNY stand for?
8 Which London underground station was named after a football club?
9 Who uncrossed their legs to much ado in "Basic Instinct"?
10 Who was the female lead in a harassment case in the film "Disclosure"?
11 Who founded the Microsoft Corporation?
12 Who wrote the novel "Trainspotting"?
13 Who had a No 1 with "The Long and Winding Road" coupled with "Suspicious Minds"?
14 Where are the Shankly Gates ?
15 In which city did Molly Malone wheel her wheelbarrow?
16 What is the name of the badger's residence?
17 Which office block is located at the junction of Charing Cross Road and Tottenham Court Road?
18 What is the collective noun for geese?
19 Who is the only cricketer to score 501 in first-class cricket?
20 What have Tunbridge Wells, Windsor and Kensington & Chelsea got in common?
21 Who was Admiral Lord Nelson's lover?
22 What was Mozart's middle name?
23 Which Prince moved into Clarence House after the Queen Mother died?
24 Who was the principal communications officer on the Starship Enterprise?
25 Who was voted Professional Cricketers' Association Player of the Year in 2004 and 2005?
26 Who got one in the eye at the Battle of Hastings?
27 Who was Don Quixote's sidekick?
28 What is the viral disease of rabbits?
29 Who wrote Winnie the Pooh?
30 Where is the Jorvik centre?

Answers | Pot-Luck 59 *(see Quiz 113)*

1 Magic. 2 Howard Hughes. 3 Athens. 4 Guys and Dolls. 5 Bowler. 6 Aquarius. 7 Golf. 8 Smallpox. 9 J. B. Priestley. 10 Wonderwoman. 11 Wet Wet Wet. 12 Horoscope. 13 Violin. 14 Buckingham Palace. 15 June. 16 Clannad. 17 The river Fleet. 18 David Hasselhoff. 19 Oliver McCall. 20 A French stew. 21 Canoeing. 22 Kiwi fruit. 23 Bicentenary. 24 5. 25 Buzby. 26 Jimmy Floyd Hasselbaink. 27 Hamlet. 28 Sunday. 29 Florence. 30 1960.

123

The Medium Questions

This next selection of questions is getting a little more like it. For an open entry quiz then you should have a high percentage of medium level questions – don't try to break people's spirits with the hard ones just make sure that people play to their ability.

Like all questions this level of question can be classed as either easy or impossible depending on whether you know the answer or not and although common knowledge is used as the basis for these questions there is a sting in the tail of quite a few. Also, if you have a serious drinking squad playing then they can more or less say goodbye to the winner's medals, but that isn't to say they will feel any worse about it.

Specialists are the people to watch out as those with a good knowledge of a particular subject will doubtless do well in these rounds so a liberal sprinkling of pot-luck questions are needed to flummox them.

1 The first book title was Harry Potter and what?
2 What do J. K. Rowling's initials stand for?
3 What is the most popular sport among wizards?
4 Which Harry Potter novel was first published in 2005?
5 What is the first name of the giant Hagrid?
6 Which Emma played Hermione in the Harry Potter films?
7 What is Ron's surname?
8 What is the third word of all the book titles?
9 In the US version what did "The Philosopher's Stone" become in the book title?
10 Who is "You know who" and "He Who Must not be Named"?
11 Which actor played Hagrid in the Harry Potter films?
12 Which company bought J. K. Rowling's first script and published the novel?
13 Cornelius Fudge is the Minister for what?
14 Which city is a favoured venue for midnight launches with J. K. Rowling present?
15 Which Chris directed the first Harry Potter movie?
16 What is the name of the Slytherin Student who keeps company with Draco Malfoy?
17 Which character did the late Richard Harris play on film?
18 Parselmouth is the name for a wizard that can do what special thing?
19 What type of transport appears on the cover of the children's edition of The Philosopher's Stone?
20 What is the name of Ron's pet rat?
21 In "The Half-Blood Prince" is Harry is in his fourth, fifth or sixth year at Hogwarts?
22 What was the second book to be published?
23 Which book has Ron inviting Harry to the Quidditch World Cup?
24 Which university did J. K. Rowling attend?
25 What did "DA" stand for?
26 What is the name of the soul-sucking guards from Azkaban?
27 Which Mike directed the movie The Goblet of Fire?
28 What is the name of the national wizarding newspaper?
29 Which book cover depicts a creature rising above some flames?
30 What has happened to Harry's parents?

Answers | Nature: Animals *(see Quiz 3)*

1 Starfish. 2 Adult. 3 Tadpole. 4 Colour. 5 Skin. 6 Venom. 7 Africa. 8 Bat. 9 Grizzly. 10 Caribou. 11 Seven. 12 Insects. 13 Grey, red. 14 Cheetah. 15 Scottish. 16 Blue. 17 Man. 18 Trees. 19 Chihuahua. 20 Yes. 21 Horn. 22 Tiger. 23 Goat. 24 Kangaroo. 25 Two. 26 Panther. 27 Earthworms. 28 China. 29 Elk. 30 Dams.

1 Which world leader's funeral took place the day Charles and Camilla were due to be married?
2 In which country is Baden-Baden?
3 Who captained England in the famous 5–1 victory in Germany in 2001?
4 Whom did Michael Howard succeed as Tory Party leader?
5 Which English king was nicknamed Rufus?
6 Which county gives its name to a horse known as a Punch?
7 The Angel of the North was erected next to which major road?
8 Obstetrics is the study of what?
9 Which bird gave Fleetwood Mac a No 1 instrumental?
10 In proverb speech is silver but what is golden?
11 Who became known as "The King of the Wild Frontier"?
12 What is the heavy rain of summer called in Asia ?
13 What is alopecia?
14 Which London station would you arrive at if you travelled from Ipswich?
15 What fruit are you said to be if you are accompanying a courting couple?
16 Frederick the Great was king of which country?
17 Before going solo Beyoncé Knowles fronted which female band?
18 Which city was built on seven hills?
19 What type of creature is a painted lady?
20 What is a lift for food in a restaurant known as?
21 Which Latin phrase means in good faith?
22 What does a misogynist hate?
23 Which American president had a wife known as Ladybird?
24 What name is given to animals that eat grass and plants?
25 What is Delft in Holland famous for?
26 In the Bible, which king had to decide which of two women was the mother of a child?
27 Fletcher Christian led a mutiny on which ship?
28 Who wrote "Under Milk Wood"?
29 What is the capital of Hawaii?
30 What is the post code known as in America?

Answers	Pot-Luck 2 (see Quiz 4)

1 Iris. 2 Mime. 3 Charles Kennedy. 4 Juventus. 5 Bristol. 6 Natasha Kaplinsky. 7 Mrs Brown. 8 Thomas More. 9 Kennedy. 10 Cuba. 11 Phoenix. 12 Marx Brothers. 13 Piebald. 14 Stoat. 15 Sea sickness. 16 Poland. 17 Thomas à Becket. 18 Animal Farm. 19 Cup and lip. 20 Rhesus. 21 Acute. 22 Isle of Wight. 23 Beethoven. 24 Testator. 25 Violin. 26 Black. 27 Coast. 28 Chlorophyll. 29 Louisiana. 30 Quicksilver.

1 What is a common name for the asteroidea which have five arms?
2 At what stage of development is the imago stage of an insect?
3 What is the aquatic larva of an amphibian more commonly called?
4 What is a chameleon capable of changing?
5 What does a reptile shed in the process of sloughing?
6 What is another name for snake poison?
7 The aardvark is a native of which continent?
8 Which is the only mammal able to fly?
9 Which type of dark-coloured bear is the largest?
10 What do Americans call reindeer?
11 Man has seven vertebrae in his neck. How many does a giraffe have?
12 What is the main diet of hedgehogs?
13 Which two colours are wolves?
14 What is the fastest land animal?
15 From which border do Border collies originate?
16 What colour is a chow chow's tongue?
17 What is the mammal homo sapiens better known as?
18 Where does an arboreal animal live?
19 What is the smallest breed of dog?
20 Do dolphins have teeth?
21 Which part of the rhino is regarded as an aphrodisiac?
22 Which is the largest of the cats?
23 The ibex is a member of which animal family?
24 Which is generally larger, a wallaby or a kangaroo?
25 How many sets of teeth do most mammals have?
26 What is the black leopard more commonly known as?
27 What do moles mainly feed on?
28 Which country does the breed of dog, shih tzu, come from?
29 What would the Europeans call what the Americans call a moose?
30 What do beavers build?

| **Answers** | Harry Potter *(see Quiz 1)* |

1 The Philosopher's Stone. 2 Joanne Kathleen. 3 Quidditch. 4 Harry Potter and the Half Blood Prince. 5 Rubeus. 6 Emma Watson. 7 Weasley. 8 And. 9 The Sorcerer's Stone. 10 Lord Voldemort. 11 Robbie Coltrane. 12 Bloomsbury. 13 Magic. 14 Edinburgh. 15 Chris Columbus. 16 Pansy Parkinson. 17 Dumbledore. 18 Talk to snakes. 19 Train. 20 Scabbers. 21 His sixth year. 22 Chamber of Secrets. 23 Goblet of Fire. 24 Exeter. 25 Dumbledore's Army. 26 Dementors. 27 Mike Newell. 28 The Daily Prophet. 29 Order of the Phoenix. 30 Killed (by Lord Voldemort).

1 What is the coloured part of the eye called?
2 With what type of entertainment is Marcel Marceau associated?
3 The wife of which party leader gave birth to a son during the 2005 election campaign?
4 Thierry Henry joined Arsenal from which club?
5 In which British city is the station Temple Meads?
6 Who was the first female winner of "Strictly Come Dancing"?
7 Judi Dench won a Golden Globe in 1998 for which film?
8 Which Tudor figure is the main character in "A Man for All Seasons"?
9 Which American president had the first names John Fitzgerald?
10 In which country is Havana?
11 In legend, which bird rose from its own ashes?
12 Which brothers starred in the film "Duck Soup"?
13 What term describes a black and white horse?
14 Which animal does ermine come from?
15 If you have "mal de mer" what are you suffering from?
16 The Solidarity movement began in which country?
17 In 1170, which Archbishop of Canterbury was murdered?
18 What kind of farm did George Orwell write about?
19 In proverb, there is "many a slip 'twixt" what and what?
20 Which monkey possesses a blood factor that is shared with humans?
21 What type of angle is less than 90 degrees?
22 On which Isle is Osborne House?
23 Who composed the piece of music known as the "Moonlight Sonata"?
24 What name is given in law to a person who makes a will?
25 Stéphane Grappelli is famous for playing which instrument?
26 What colour were the shirts of Mussolini's Italian Fascists?
27 What was the title of the 2005 TV series about Britain's borders with the sea?
28 What is the green colouring matter in plants known as?
29 Which American state does cajun music come from?
30 What is another name for mercury?

Answers Pot-Luck 1 (see Quiz 2)

1 Pope John Paul II. 2 Germany. 3 David Beckham. 4 Iain Duncan Smith. 5 William II. 6 Suffolk. 7 A1. 8 Childbirth. 9 Albatross. 10 Silence. 11 Davy Crockett. 12 Monsoon. 13 Baldness. 14 Liverpool Street. 15 Gooseberry. 16 Prussia. 17 Destiny's Child. 18 Rome. 19 Butterfly. 20 A dumb waiter. 21 Bona fide. 22 Women. 23 Lyndon Johnson. 24 Herbivore. 25 Pottery. 26 Solomon. 27 HMS Bounty. 28 Dylan Thomas. 29 Honolulu. 30 Zip code.

1 What were the full first names of the founders of the House of Eliott?
2 Which was the then most expensive TV series ever when it was first broadcast in 2005?
3 Which family lived at 165 Eaton Place, London?
4 Which actress played wife No 1 in "The Six Wives of Henry VIII" and Mrs Victor Meldrew?
5 Whom did Demelza marry in the drama set in Cornwall?
6 Which 1970s series was based on novels by Anthony Trollope ?
7 Which shipping line did the "Charlotte Rhodes" belong to?
8 Which mistress of Edward VII was played by Francesca Annis?
9 Derek Jacobi played the title role as which Roman emperor?
10 Which saga was about Soames, Irene, Jolyon and their family?
11 In which country was "The Far Pavilions" set?
12 During which war was "By the Sword Divided" set?
13 In "Brideshead Revisited" what was Aloysius?
14 What is the profession of Eleanor Bramwell in the Victorian series?
15 Who played the title role in the series about Elizabeth I?
16 Which compass points formed the title of an American Civil War drama?
17 What was the profession of the Duchess of Duke Street?
18 Which James Bond once played Mr Rochester in a TV version of "Jane Eyre"?
19 Who links "Ab Fab" Saffron and "Pride and Prejudice" Lydia Bennet?
20 In "Upstairs, Downstairs" what was butler Hudson's first name?
21 The drama "Whatever Love Means" was about which love triangle?
22 Which daughter of Vanessa Redgrave played Mrs Simpson in the 2005 drama "Wallis and Edward"?
23 Which "Good Lifer" starred on TV as Edward VII's sister?
24 Which romantic hero was played by Colin Firth in 1995?
25 Which series was "Thomas and Sarah" a spin-off from?
26 Which movement was the series "Shoulder to Shoulder" about?
27 Which tyrannical Italian family was the subject of a series in 1981?
28 Which drama featured Peggy Ashcroft and Geraldine James in wartime India?
29 Who played Churchill in "The Wilderness Years"?
30 Who wrote "Middlemarch", the novel the TV serial was based on?

Answers   Theatre and Musicals *(see Quiz 7)*

1 Anthony Andrews. 2 Sarah Brightman. 3 David Essex. 4 Sunset Boulevard. 5 La Cage aux Folles. 6 The Sound of Music. 7 Tony. 8 Chicago. 9 Kiss Me, Kate. 10 Theatre Royal. 11 Michael Ball. 12 Don Black. 13 Tim Rice. 14 Show Boat. 15 Happy Talk. 16 Siam (now Thailand). 17 West Side Story. 18 Stripper. 19 Stephen Sondheim. 20 Carousel. 21 Michael Crawford. 22 Joyce Grenfell. 23 Gaston Leroux. 24 Mary Magdalen. 25 Chess. 26 Roger Moore. 27 Petula Clark. 28 Cats. 29 Hair. 30 A Chorus Line.

1 Which animal appears on the front of a British passport with a lion?

2 What does a theodolite measure?

3 Which poisonous gas is given off from a car exhaust?

4 In Scotland, what are Eigg, Muck and Rhum?

5 In Channel 4's 2005 historical drama about the life of Elizabeth I, who played Elizabeth?

6 Robert Menzies was prime minister of which country?

7 What is the currency of Poland?

8 "The Two of Us" was an autobiography about which actress and her late husband?

9 In maths, what is meant by three dots in a triangular formation?

10 Traditionally, what does a cooper make?

11 Which motorway goes from east to west across the Pennines?

12 What are workers and drones types of?

13 What is the middle name of Winston S. Churchill?

14 On what calendar date is Burns Night?

15 What is the home of a beaver called?

16 How many railway stations are there on a Monopoly board?

17 What was the title of the movie sequel to "The Mask of Zorro"?

18 What has the body of a lion and the head of a human?

19 Who invented the method by which the blind can read by touch?

20 Who sang the Bond theme "Goldfinger"?

21 What does a costermonger sell?

22 What did the Italian soldier Garibaldi give his name to?

23 How many Premiership sides did Millwall beat to reach the 2004 FA Cup Final?

24 Which sea is north of Turkey?

25 What colour are the flowers of St John's Wort?

26 Segovia is associated with which musical instrument?

27 Cold meat and cold potatoes can produce what dish?

28 Which king is supposed to have hidden in a tree after the Battle of Worcester?

29 Which brothers flew the first manned, powered aeroplane?

30 The Heriot-Watt university is in which city?

Answers   Pot-Luck 4 *(see Quiz 8)*

1 We Will Rock You – The Queen Musical. 2 Leeds United. 3 Sharp. 4 White and yellow. 5 24. 6 Bishop. 7 Animal. 8 South Africa. 9 Van Gogh. 10 Berkshire. 11 Radius. 12 Mont Blanc. 13 Six. 14 H. G. Wells. 15 Runnymede. 16 90 degrees. 17 Bakewell. 18 Yellow. 19 Bad breath. 20 Enid Blyton. 21 Mediterranean. 22 Pontoon. 23 Sue MacGregor. 24 Mexico and USA. 25 5. 26 20. 27 Three. 28 Princess Anne. 29 Raymond Chandler. 30 Geology.

1 Which Anthony has starred in "My Fair Lady" and "The Woman in White" on the West End stage?
2 Which musical star was Andrew Lloyd Webber's second wife?
3 Who played Che in the original stage production of "Evita"?
4 Which was Elaine Paige's first musical on Broadway?
5 Which musical does the song "I am What I am" come from?
6 In which musical is Maria von Trapp the heroine?
7 Which theatre award is named after actress Antoinette Perry?
8 The characters of Billy Flynn, Mama Morton and Velma Kelly appear in which musical?
9 Which musical is based on "The Taming of the Shrew"?
10 What is the name of the most famous theatre in London's Drury Lane?
11 Who originally played the role of Alex in "Aspects of Love"?
12 Who wrote the lyrics for "Tell Me on a Sunday" and "Sunset Boulevard"?
13 Who co-produced the revival of "Anything Goes" with Elaine Paige?
14 Which musical is the song "Ol' Man River" from?
15 Which song from "South Pacific" was recorded by Captain Sensible?
16 In which country is "The King and I" set?
17 Which musical are the songs "Tonight" and "Somewhere" from?
18 What was the profession of the heroine in "Gypsy"?
19 Who wrote "Into the Woods" and "A Little Night Music"?
20 In which musical does "You'll Never Walk Alone" appear?
21 Who played the title role in "Barnum" and "Billy"?
22 Which actress was Maureen Lipman's show "Re Joyce" about ?
23 Who wrote the novel that forms the basis of the musical "Phantom of the Opera"?
24 Which character sings "I Don't Know How to Love Him" in "Jesus Christ Superstar"?
25 Which musical is "I Know Him So Well" from?
26 Which former Saint turned down a musical role in "Aspects of Love"?
27 Who replaced Elaine Paige as Norma Desmond in the London production of "Sunset Boulevard"?
28 In which musical do they sing about a "Jellicle Ball"?
29 Which musical hailed the dawning of the age of Aquarius?
30 Which musical is the song "One" from?

Answers	TV: Costume Drama *(see Quiz 5)*

1 Beatrice and Evangeline. 2 Rome. 3 Bellamy family. 4 Annette Crosbie. 5 Ross Poldark. 6 The Pallisers. 7 Onedin Line. 8 Lillie Langtry. 9 Claudius. 10 Forsyte Saga. 11 India. 12 English Civil War. 13 A teddy. 14 Doctor. 15 Glenda Jackson. 16 North and South. 17 Cook. 18 Timothy Dalton. 19 Julia Sawalha. 20 Angus. 21 Charles, Diana and Camilla. 22 Joely Richardson. 23 Felicity Kendal. 24 Mr Darcy. 25 Upstairs, Downstairs. 26 The suffragettes. 27 The Borgias. 28 The Jewel in the Crown. 29 Robert Hardy. 30 George Eliot.

Quiz 8 | Pot-Luck 4

Answers – page 130

LEVEL 2

1 The characters Killer Queen and Scaramouche feature in which musical?
2 Jonathan Woodgate was first capped for England while at which club?
3 In music, a flat sign lowers a note but what sign raises a note?
4 What are the two main colours on the Vatican flag?
5 Chemically pure gold contains how many carats?
6 In chess, which piece always moves diagonally?
7 Are sea-urchins animal, vegetable or mineral?
8 In which country did the England team play Test cricket in January 2005?
9 Which artist painted "Sunflowers"?
10 In which county is Windsor Castle?
11 What term is given to the distance from the centre of a circle to the outer edge?
12 Which is the highest mountain in the Alps?
13 How many points are there on a snowflake?
14 Who wrote the story "The Invisible Man"?
15 On which island did King John set his seal to the Magna Carta?
16 How many degrees in a right angle?
17 Which Derbyshire town gives its name to a Tart?
18 Jonquil is a shade of which colour?
19 What is halitosis?
20 Who created the character Kiki the parrot?
21 Which sea does the River Rhone flow into?
22 In which card game can you stick and twist?
23 Which female presenter introduced Radio 4's "Today" programme from 1994 to 2002?
24 The Rio Grande separates which two countries?
25 What do 2 + 2 = according to Radiohead?
26 How many decades are there in two centuries?
27 How many stripes does a police sergeant have on his arm?
28 Which royal was quoted by the press as saying "Why don't you naff off"?
29 Which writer created Philip Marlowe, the private eye?
30 What is the name for the study of rocks and the earth's crust?

Answers | Pot-Luck 3 (see Quiz 6)

1 Unicorn. 2 Angles. 3 Carbon monoxide. 4 Islands. 5 Helen Mirren. 6 Australia. 7 Zloty. 8 Sheila Hancock. 9 Therefore. 10 Barrels. 11 M62. 12 Bees. 13 Spencer. 14 25th January. 15 Lodge. 16 Four. 17 The Legend of Zorro. 18 The Sphinx. 19 Louis Braille. 20 Shirley Bassey. 21 Fruit and vegetables. 22 A biscuit. 23 None. 24 Black Sea. 25 Yellow. 26 Guitar. 27 Bubble and squeak. 28 Charles II. 29 Wright Brothers. 30 Edinburgh.

132

1 What team is known as The Baggies?
2 In which year did Arsène Wenger join Arsenal as manager?
3 What two colours are in Derby's home strip?
4 Who said, "When seagulls follow the trawler it is because they think the sardines will be thrown into the sea"?
5 In which country was the Final of the 2002 World Cup played?
6 Which city has a team of the same name and a United team?
7 Hernan Crespo joined Chelsea in 2003 from which club?
8 Bobby Gould and Phil Neal have both managed which club?
9 Who plays home games at the New Den?
10 Which club is linked with the playing career of Tom Finney?
11 Who managed Liverpool to the 1986 FA Cup and League double?
12 Which country do Brondby come from?
13 Which famous first will always be held by Keith Peacock?
14 Which club did Mark Atkins play for in a Premiership-winning season?
15 Which country did Mike England play for?
16 What is the home colour of Crystal Palace?
17 Which country does Craig Bellamy play for?
18 Which team had Radford and Kennedy as a strike force?
19 Which club broke the Auld Firm dominance to win the Scottish League Cup in 2004?
20 Michael Carrick joined Spurs from which other London club?
21 To two years, when did the late, great George Best leave Man Utd?
22 Who has managed both Southampton and Celtic?
23 Who was the manager when England won the 1966 World Cup?
24 Which country did Alan Brazil play for?
25 Who made comments implying some Man Utd fans were only there for the prawn sandwiches?
26 Which player was involved in Britain's first million-pound transfer?
27 David Murray has been an influential chairman of which Scottish club?
28 Which club has been managed by Bobby Robson, Kevin Keegan and Ruud Gullit?
29 Which Arsenal player followed Robert Pires as the Football Writers' Player of the Year?
30 Who went to Newcastle from Man Utd in the Andy Cole transfer deal?

Answers | Pot-Luck 5 *(see Quiz 11)*

1 Alice Cooper. 2 Colditz. 3 Iraq. 4 Decibels. 5 Egypt. 6 Yorkshire. 7 Shoes. 8 Golf. 9 Tchaikovsky. 10 60. 11 Sandringham House. 12 Batman. 13 Morocco. 14 Dublin. 15 Elysée Palace. 16 144. 17 Canoeing. 18 June. 19 Boats. 20 When it is about to leave port. 21 Comet. 22 Hansard. 23 Judaism. 24 Australia and New Zealand. 25 Vertical. 26 Five. 27 Four. 28 The eye. 29 Sheila. 30 H and N.

1 How long is a Member of Parliament elected for?

2 In which year in the 1970s were there two general elections?

3 Which party won Bethnal Green & Bow at the 2005 general election?

4 After the 2005 election had the Liberals got more or fewer parliamentary seats than before?

5 Which candidate stood down from the Lib Dem leadership election in 2006?

6 Who was Britain's first black woman MP?

7 Who was Tory leader at the time of the 2005 general election?

8 Who became Labour leader after the 1992 election defeat?

9 Which future PM failed to win Dartford for the Tories in 1950 and 1951?

10 Which two Davids headed the Alliance party in 1983?

11 Which prime minister's father was a trapeze artist?

12 The House of Commons consists of how many members?

13 Who replaced Alan Clark as MP for Kensington & Chelsea?

14 Who gave up the title of Viscount Stansgate to remain an MP?

15 Which MP is the son-in-law of Alf Garnett's son-in-law?

16 Who was the leader of the opposition at the time of the 2001 general election?

17 What was the first name of the wife of the leader of the opposition in the 2005 general election?

18 Who wrote the novel "A Parliamentary Affair"?

19 Who resigned as a government minister over the Sara Keays affair?

20 Which party won the general election in 1945?

21 Which former minister has presented "Six O Six" on Radio 5 Live?

22 Name the 1992 Tory party chairman who lost his Bath seat?

23 Which former deputy Labour leader, whose father was once a Catholic priest, stood down after the 1992 General Election?

24 What was Norman Tebbitt's job before entering Parliament?

25 Which party did Screaming Lord Sutch represent?

26 Who became deputy Labour leader after the 1992 General Election?

27 Which constituency did the late Mo Mowlam represent?

28 What did the Ecology Party change its name to in 1985?

29 What was Dennis Skinner's job before he entered Parliament?

30 Which MP won gold medals at the 1980 and 1984 Olympics?

Answers	Heavy Metal (see Quiz 12)

1 Yardbirds. 2 Black Night. 3 John. 4 Black Sabbath. 5 Iron Maiden. 6 Led Zeppelin III. 7 Metallica. 8 Def Leppard. 9 Birmingham. 10 Deep Purple. 11 AC/DC. 12 Ozzy Ozbourne. 13 Drums. 14 Sandy Denny. 15 Bat Out of Hell. 16 David Coverdale's Whitesnake. 17 Machine Head. 18 Dennis Wheatley. 19 Bass guitar. 20 Ian Gillan. 21 Jimmy Page. 22 Playing guitar solos. 23 An arm. 24 Rick Wakeman. 25 Pyromania. 26 Phil Collins. 27 But I Won't Do That. 28 Rainbow. 29 Iommi. 30 Iron Maiden.

Quiz 11 | Pot-Luck 5 | Answers – page 133 | LEVEL 2

1 Which gender-bender name did rock star Vincent Furnier adopt?
2 Which German prison camp did Pat Reid try to escape from?
3 Kurds, Shias and Sunnis were involved in elections in which country in 2005?
4 What measure is used for sound or noise?
5 Farouk was king of which country?
6 Which county used to be divided into Ridings?
7 Which item of clothing is linked with the name Jimmy Choo?
8 Which sport is played at Sunningdale?
9 Who composed the "1812 Overture"?
10 What is the mean of 40, 60 and 80?
11 Which royal residence is in Norfolk?
12 In comics, by what name is Bruce Wayne known?
13 Marrakesh is in which country?
14 In the traditional song, in which city did Molly Malone sell cockles and mussels?
15 What is the official residence of the French president?
16 How many square inches in a square foot?
17 In which sport are there wild water, sprint and slalom events?
18 In which month is the longest day in Britain?
19 Smack and sampan are types of what?
20 When is the Blue Peter flag raised on a ship?
21 What type of heavenly body is named after Edmund Halley?
22 Which book records debates in Parliament?
23 Which religion observes the Passover?
24 Anzac troops come from which two countries?
25 In aviation VTOL stands for what type of take-off and landing?
26 How many lines in a limerick?
27 How many years is the term of office of the American president?
28 In which part of the body is the cornea located?
29 What is the first name of John Peel's widow?
30 Which two letters of the alphabet identify the virus known as bird flu?

Answers | Sport: Football *(see Quiz 9)*

1 West Bromwich Albion. 2 1996. 3 Black and white. 4 Eric Cantona. 5 Japan. 6 Dundee. 7 Inter Milan. 8 Coventry. 9 Millwall. 10 Preston. 11 Kenny Dalglish. 12 Denmark. 13 First substitute in a League game. 14 Blackburn. 15 Wales. 16 Red and blue. 17 Wales. 18 Arsenal. 19 Livingston. 20 West Ham. 21 1974. 22 Gordon Strachan. 23 Alf Ramsey. 24 Scotland. 25 Roy Keane. 26 Trevor Francis. 27 Rangers. 28 Newcastle United. 29 Thierry Henry. 30 Keith Gillespie.

1 Which group was Jimmy Page in before forming Led Zeppelin?
2 What was Deep Purple's first hit in the singles charts?
3 What is Ozzy Ozbourne's actual first name?
4 Which group were "Paranoid" in the charts?
5 Which group took its name from a medieval instrument of torture?
6 They were known for imaginative cover designs, but what was the title of Led Zeppelin's third album?
7 Which band released the album "St Anger" that topped the US charts in 2003?
8 Which group founded the Bludgeon Riffola label?
9 Which city did Black Sabbath come from?
10 Ian Gillan, Graham Bonnet and David Coverdale sang for which group?
11 In which group did Angus Young wear short trousers?
12 Who recorded "Bark at the Moon"?
13 What instrument did Ian Paice play?
14 Which folk singer sang on Led Zep's "The Battle of Evermore"?
15 Which album from 1978 was reissued in 1991 and led to a 1993 sequel?
16 How were Whitesnake credited on their first recordings?
17 "Smoke on the Water" came from which album?
18 Terry Butler changed his group's name to Black Sabbath after reading a novel by which author?
19 What instrument does Iron Maiden founder Steve Harris play?
20 "Naked Thunder" was the first solo album by which singer?
21 Who wrote "Stairway to Heaven"?
22 On stage, Nugent, Kramer and Pinera indulged in what kind of duels?
23 What did Def Leppard drummer Rick Allen lose in a car accident?
24 Which Yes keyboard player was on "Sabbath Bloody Sabbath"?
25 "Rock of Rages" was on which Def Leppard album?
26 Who was guest drummer for Led Zeppelin at the Live Aid concert?
27 What words in brackets end the title "I Would Do Anything for Love?"
28 Which group did Ritchie Blackmore form on leaving Deep Purple?
29 Which guitarist Tony was an original member of Black Sabbath?
30 Which band released the album "Dance of Death" in 2003?

Answers | **Election Fever** *(see Quiz 10)*

1 Five years. 2 1974. 3 Respect – The Unity Coalition. 4 More. 5 Mark Oaten. 6 Diane Abbott. 7 Michael Howard. 8 John Smith. 9 Margaret Roberts (later Thatcher). 10 Owen and Steel. 11 John Major's. 12 651. 13 Michael Portillo. 14 Tony Benn. 15 Tony Blair. 16 William Hague. 17 Sandra. 18 Edwina Currie. 19 Cecil Parkinson. 20 Labour. 21 David Mellor. 22 Chris Patten. 23 Roy Hattersley. 24 Airline pilot. 25 Monster Raving Loony Party. 26 Margaret Beckett. 27 Redcar. 28 Green Party. 29 Miner. 30 Sebastian Coe.

1 Who had the first No 1 with "Unchained Melody"?
2 Which rogue trader brought about the downfall of Barings Bank?
3 Which jockey rode over 200 winners in both 1997 and 1998?
4 In which country is the Dordogne?
5 What kind of creature is a natterjack?
6 Which team were on the receiving end of Man Utd's 9–0 record Premier victory?
7 Which cricket team plays home county games at Edgbaston?
8 How is the letter S represented in morse code?
9 If something is Cantonese which country does it come from?
10 Whose murder conviction was overturned after 45 years in 1998?
11 What is the background colour of motorway signs?
12 In which resort was "Fawlty Towers" set?
13 Orthodontics involves what parts of the body?
14 In China what was the colour of Chairman Mao's "little book"?
15 In which film does Professor Higgins appear?
16 How many ribs does a human have?
17 Zen is a form of what type of religion?
18 What does a pathologist study?
19 In which European country is Malmö?
20 What name is given to a book in which a sea captain charts events on a voyage?
21 What type of pet animal can be Chinchilla or Dutch?
22 What is the longest word that appears in the film "Mary Poppins"?
23 On the road, what does a red circular sign with a white band across it mean?
24 In which city is the Doge's Palace?
25 In the past, what was an Iron Horse?
26 Buff Orpingtons and Plymouth Rocks are types of what?
27 Which city in North Wales has the name of a Welsh saint?
28 In which sport is the Curtis Cup awarded?
29 Which canal takes food through your body?
30 Who wrote the controversial "Satanic Verses"?

| **Answers** | Pot-Luck 7 *(see Quiz 15)* |

1 20. 2 Valletta. 3 In the neck. 4 A hawk. 5 The Beatles. 6 Spanish. 7 Princess Margaret. 8 Rabbit. 9 Pontius Pilate. 10 Bootlegger. 11 Skye. 12 Caron Keating. 13 Golf. 14 Mullion. 15 A flower grows. 16 Ball. 17 Black. 18 Sheep. 19 Nepotism. 20 Neville Chamberlain. 21 Aurora Borealis. 22 James I. 23 Hippocratic Oath. 24 Susan. 25 AS Monaco. 26 Two. 27 Baloo. 28 Blue or violet. 29 Salisbury. 30 Maeve Binchy.

Quiz 14 | Food and Drink

Answers – page 140

1 What country is Pecorino cheese from?
2 What type of pastry are profiteroles made from?
3 Which fruits are usually served "belle hélène"?
4 What is the main flavour of aïoli?
5 Which vegetable can be oyster, chestnut or shitaki?
6 What is wiener schnitzel?
7 How is steak tartare cooked?
8 Which drink is Worcester sauce traditionally added to?
9 Which fish is the main ingredient of Scotch Woodcock?
10 Which area of England are Singing Hinnies from?
11 What is beef fillet cooked in puff pastry called?
12 What gives Windsor Red cheese its colour and flavour?
13 What is a Worcester Pearmain?
14 Which meat is used in Glamorgan sausages?
15 Which vegetables can be Pentland Crown or Maris Bard?
16 What type of food is basmati?
17 What is Roquefort cheese made from?
18 What are the two main ingredients of angels on horseback?
19 Which fruit is a cross between a blackberry and a raspberry?
20 Which type of pasta's name means "little worms"?
21 What ingredient is included in food in a florentine style?
22 What is pancetta?
23 What is the main ingredient of a black pudding?
24 Which herb is in pesto sauce?
25 In Indian cookery what is naan?
26 What type of food is Cullen Skink?
27 What type of fish is in an Omelette Arnold Bennett?
28 What shape is the pasta called rigatoni?
29 What is couscous made from?
30 What does a Pomfret or Pontefract cake taste of?

Answers	Sci-Fi Movies *(see Quiz 16)*

1 Robocop. 2 Carrie Fisher. 3 Arthur C. Clarke. 4 Planet of the Apes. 5 Vulcan.
6 2000 A.D. 7 Steven Spielberg. 8 Barbarella. 9 451. 10 Superman. 11 Arnold
Schwarzenegger. 12 Queen. 13 The Death Star. 14 Peter Jackson. 15 Ants. 16 The
Invisible Man. 17 David Bowie. 18 The Omega Man. 19 Cars. 20 Logan's Run. 21
The Day the Earth. 22 Forbidden Planet. 23 Scream. 24 20,000. 25 Dr Strangelove.
26 Alec Guinness. 27 The Night of the Living Dead. 28 Keanu Reeves. 29 Dale Arden.
30 Spider.

Quiz 15 | Pot-Luck 7

Answers – page 137

LEVEL 2

1 In Sudoku, what is the total of the even numbers in a completed row?
2 What is the capital city of Malta?
3 Where in the body is the thyroid gland?
4 In politics what is the opposite of a dove?
5 Which group have had most British No 1 single hits?
6 What is the main language spoken in Mexico?
7 Which late Royal was the subject of a Channel 4 biopic broadcast in November 2005?
8 A cony is what sort of animal?
9 When Jesus was crucified, which Roman was governor of Jerusalem?
10 In the United States what name was given to a seller of illegal alcohol?
11 Which Scottish Isle became linked to the mainland by a bridge in 1995?
12 Who was Gloria Hunniford's daughter, subject of the book "Next to Me"?
13 Henry Cotton became famous in which sport?
14 What name is given to a vertical divide in a window?
15 In the song "I Believe", what happens for every drop of rain that falls?
16 Which word of four letters can go after beach and before gown to make new words?
17 What colour is the Northern Line on a London Underground map?
18 Astrakhan comes from which creature?
19 What is the name given to the practice of favouring your own relatives?
20 Which British prime minister spoke of "peace in our time"?
21 What is another name for the Northern Lights?
22 Who was monarch directly after Elizabeth I?
23 What is the name of the medical oath taken by doctors?
24 What is the name of the elder of the two girls in "The Lion, the Witch and the Wardrobe"?
25 Fabien Barthez joined Man Utd from which club?
26 How many packs of cards are needed to play bezique?
27 What is the name of the singing bear in Disney's "Jungle Book"?
28 What colour are the flowers of a periwinkle?
29 Which English city was once known as Sarum?
30 Who wrote the novel "The Glass Lake"?

Answers | Pot-Luck 6 (see Quiz 13)

1 Jimmy Young. 2 Nick Leeson. 3 Kieren Fallon. 4 France. 5 A toad. 6 Ipswich Town. 7 Warwickshire. 8 Dot dot dot. 9 China. 10 Derek Bentley. 11 Blue. 12 Torquay. 13 The teeth. 14 Red. 15 My Fair Lady. 16 24. 17 Buddhism. 18 Diseases. 19 Sweden. 20 Log. 21 Rabbit. 22 Supercalifragilisticexpialidocius. 23 No entry. 24 Venice. 25 Steam locomotive. 26 Chickens. 27 St Asaph. 28 Golf. 29 Alimentary. 30 Salman Rushdie.

Quiz 16 | Sci-Fi Movies

Answers – page 138

1 Which character was described as "part man, part machine, all cop"?

2 Who played the part of the rebel princess in "Star Wars"?

3 "2001: A Space Odyssey" was based on a short story by whom?

4 What was the first in the five-film series of man and monkey conflict?

5 What planet did long-eared Mr Spock come from?

6 "Judge Dredd" was based on the character from which comic?

7 Which director said, "I'm embarrassed and ashamed that I get paid for doing this"?

8 In which film did Jane Fonda "do her own thing" in the 40th century?

9 What was the Fahrenheit reading in Truffaut's 1960s film?

10 Which hero has been portrayed by Christopher Reeve and Kirk Alyn?

11 Who was the star of "The Terminator" films?

12 Which rock band did the score for the 1970s romp "Flash"?

13 What was Darth Vader's spacecraft in "Star Wars"?

14 Who directed the 2005 version of "King Kong"?

15 Which creatures mutated in "Them"?

16 In which film did Claude Rains star as someone who was not seen?

17 Which rock star played Newton in "The Man Who Fell to Earth"?

18 In which film does Charlton Heston think he is Earth's last survivor?

19 Which vehicles set out to devour Paris?

20 In which film are people terminated at the age of 30?

21 In titles, which words go before "Stood Still" and "Caught Fire"?

22 Robbie the Robot and Dr Morbius appear in which film?

23 "Alien" posters said that "in space no one can hear you" do what?

24 In the 1953 film how many fathoms did the Beast come from?

25 "How I Learned to Stop Worrying and Love the Bomb" is known by what shorter title?

26 Which veteran actor played Ben (Obi-Wan) Kenobi?

27 In which 1960s film does rocket radiation activate flesh-eating zombies?

28 Who was the main star of "The Matrix" series of movies?

29 Who is the female companion of Flash Gordon?

30 In "The Incredible Shrinking Man" which creature does the man fight off with a needle?

Answers | **Food and Drink** *(see Quiz 14)*

1 Italy. 2 Choux pastry. 3 Pears. 4 Garlic. 5 Mushroom. 6 Veal. 7 It's served raw. 8 Tomato juice. 9 Anchovy. 10 North East. 11 Beef Wellington. 12 Red wine. 13 Apple. 14 None, they are made from cheese. 15 Potatoes and cabbage. 16 Rice. 17 Ewe's milk. 18 Oysters and bacon. 19 Tayberry. 20 Vermicelli. 21 Spinach. 22 Bacon. 23 Blood. 24 Basil. 25 Bread. 26 Soup. 27 Smoked haddock. 28 Tube-shaped. 29 Semolina. 30 Liquorice.

1 Which two countries agreed in November 2005 to field a joint team at the Beijing Olympics?

2 If two straight lines are always the same distance apart what are they said to be?

3 Kate Bush released the album "Aerial" in 2005 – how many years had gone by since her last album?

4 Nat Lofthouse was famous in which sport?

5 In the 14th century what was the bubonic plague called in England?

6 What is another word for a sleepwalker?

7 What do the initials WO stand for as a rank in the army?

8 Which Italian city was painted by Canaletto?

9 Who composed the "Enigma Variations"?

10 In politics, how many readings does a bill have in the House of Commons?

11 Yum Yum and Ko-Ko appear in which opera?

12 In which war was the Victoria Cross first awarded?

13 An ampersand is a sign for which word?

14 In Spanish, which word is used to address a young, or unmarried, lady?

15 The Suez Canal connects the Red Sea with which other Sea?

16 Which country did composer Aaron Copland come from?

17 Where did the Norse gods live?

18 In financial terms, what is the IMF?

19 Who was the first woman to edit the Sun newspaper?

20 Who composed the music for "West Side Story"?

21 "The City of Dreaming Spires" is which English city?

22 David Ben-Gurion was the first prime minister of which country?

23 What word means to gradually get louder and louder?

24 Troglodytes lived in what particular type of dwelling?

25 The borders of Turkey make up most of the land around which sea?

26 "Somewhere My Love" was the theme tune of which film?

27 How many players are there in a netball team?

28 If you are sinistral, what are you?

29 Mahmoud Ahmadinejad was Prime Minister of which country?

30 Mount Parnassus is in which country?

---

1 Little Rock is the capital of which US state?
2 On which granite cliff are the faces of four presidents carved?
3 Which language is the first language of 6% of the population?
4 Which natural disaster is the San Andreas Fault prone to?
5 What does DC stand for in Washington DC?
6 In which city is the University of Virginia located?
7 In which state is the Grand Canyon?
8 What are a group of six states on the northeast coast known as collectively?
9 Which Kander and Ebb musical was set in a city in Illinois?
10 Which was the first of the original 13 states of the United States?
11 Where is the main space exploration centre in Florida?
12 In which city is almost half of the population of Illinois to be found?
13 How long is the motor race which Indianapolis is famous for?
14 Which town is famous for its jazz music?
15 Which mountainous forest state has a settlement of Crow Indians?
16 What is traditionally easily available in Reno?
17 In which city is La Guardia airport?
18 Which US state has the highest population?
19 Which two New York boroughs begin with B?
20 Key West and Key Largo are off the coast of which state?
21 Which US state used to be called the Sandwich Islands?
22 Which New York street is famous for its fashion stores?
23 The name of which state has four letters, the first and last the same?
24 The discovery of what in 1848 led to the expansion of California?
25 Kansas is the United States' chief producer of which grain?
26 Which Michigan town is famous for the production of motor vehicles?
27 Which New York borough is noted for its skyscraper skyline?
28 Other than White Americans what is the largest racial group on Hawaii?
29 Which US state is the title of a musical by Rodgers and Hammerstein?
30 Which city, the capital of Tennessee, is famous for its music?

Answers Pot-Luck 9 *(see Quiz 20)*

1 Kirsten Dunst. 2 The Albatross. 3 The Dandie Dinmont. 4 The Moskva. 5 Mount Olympus. 6 Gene Kelly. 7 Michael and John. 8 The Moonstone. 9 Roses. 10 The Brave. 11 Biology. 12 Mercury. 13 The Crimean War. 14 Catherine Parr. 15 William Brown. 16 Officer of the Order of the British Empire. 17 Jason. 18 Peter Phillips. 19 German. 20 Destiny's Child. 21 Tchaikovsky. 22 Labrador Retriever. 23 William IV. 24 Helium. 25 Trinidad & Tobago. 26 China. 27 Anne Brontë. 28 St Mary Mead. 29 The Clock Tower. 30 His ear.

1 Which county did Huntingdonshire become part of in 1974?
2 What is High Wycombe famous for manufacturing?
3 Which atomic energy establishment used to be called Windscale?
4 Which two London boroughs begin with E?
5 Which seaside resort is on the Fylde?
6 What is the low-lying area of East Anglia called?
7 Which city was a Roman fortress called Deva and retains its medieval walls?
8 How many tunnels under the Mersey link Liverpool to the Wirral?
9 In which northern city is the National Railway Museum?
10 The Ribble is the chief river of which county?
11 In which city is the University of East Anglia?
12 Which county is Thomas Hardy associated with?
13 Which part of Oxford was famous for motor car manufacture?
14 Which Devon port has a famous Hoe?
15 Which county is also known as Salop?
16 Which Isle has Needles off its west coast?
17 Where would you find the 18th-century Assembly Rooms and Royal Crescent?
18 Which county does not exist: North, South, East or West Yorkshire?
19 In which town is the shopping complex, the Metro Centre?
20 Where would you find the Backs and the Bridge of Sighs?
21 Alphabetically what is the last county?
22 In which Metropolitan county are Trafford and Tameside?
23 In which National Park is Scafell Pike?
24 On which bank of the Thames is the City of London?
25 In which town is the modernist De La Warr Pavilion to be found?
26 Which city is served by John Lennon Airport?
27 Which county lies between the North Sea and Greater London?
28 What is Lindisfarne also known as?
29 In which county is Hadrian's Wall?
30 From which London station are there trains direct to the continent through the Channel Tunnel?

Answers | Pot-Luck 8 (see Quiz 17)

1 North & South Korea. 2 Parallel. 3 12 years. 4 Football. 5 The Black Death. 6 Somnambulist. 7 Warrant officer. 8 Venice. 9 Elgar. 10 Three. 11 Mikado. 12 Crimean. 13 And. 14 Señorita. 15 Mediterranean. 16 United States. 17 Valhalla. 18 International Monetary Fund. 19 Rebekah Wade. 20 Leonard Bernstein. 21 Oxford. 22 Israel. 23 Crescendo. 24 Caves. 25 Marmara. 26 Dr Zhivago. 27 Seven. 28 Left-handed. 29 Iran. 30 Greece.

Quiz 20 Pot-Luck 9

1 Who was Orlando Bloom's female co-star in the movie "Elizabethtown"?
2 What was the nickname of German swimmer Michael Gross?
3 Which breed of dog is named after a character in a novel by Sir Walter Scott?
4 On which river does Moscow stand?
5 Where do the Greek gods live?
6 Which dancer sang in the rain?
7 What were the names of Wendy Darling's brothers in "Peter Pan"?
8 Which Wilkie Collins book is said to be the first detective story written in English?
9 Ena Sharples and Elizabeth of Glamis are types of what?
10 What was the title of the first movie that was directed by Johnny Depp?
11 Which "ology" is the study of human life?
12 Which planet is nearest to the sun?
13 In which war was the Charge of the Light Brigade?
14 Who was Henry VIII's last wife?
15 Which William led a gang called the Outlaws?
16 If you were awarded an OBE what would you be?
17 Who led the Argonauts in their quest for the Golden Fleece?
18 Who is the Queen's eldest grandchild?
19 What nationality was Richard Wagner?
20 "No, No, No" was the first UK top ten hit for which girl group?
21 Who wrote the music for "The Nutcracker"?
22 What is the most common breed of guide dog?
23 Which William did Queen Victoria succeed to the throne?
24 Which gas is used in modern airships?
25 Which country does footballer Dwight Yorke play for?
26 In which country were fireworks invented?
27 Who wrote "Agnes Grey"?
28 Where does Miss Marple live?
29 In which tower is Big Ben?
30 Which part of Captain Jenkins was cut off to start a war?

Answers	**Around the United States** *(see Quiz 18)*

1 Arkansas. 2 Mount Rushmore. 3 Spanish. 4 Earthquakes. 5 District of Columbia. 6 Charlottesville. 7 Arizona. 8 New England. 9 Chicago. 10 Delaware. 11 Cape Canaveral. 12 Chicago. 13 500 miles. 14 New Orleans. 15 Montana. 16 Divorce. 17 New York. 18 California. 19 Bronx, Brooklyn. 20 Florida. 21 Hawaii. 22 Fifth Avenue. 23 Ohio. 24 Gold. 25 Wheat. 26 Detroit. 27 Manhattan. 28 Japanese. 29 Oklahoma. 30 Nashville.

1 How many countries took part in the 2004 Olympic Games – 188, 202, 218?

2 What type of medal did boxer Amir Khan win at the 2004 Olympic Games?

3 How many gold medals did Mark Spitz win in Munich in 1972?

4 Which country is 1972 Pentathlon winner Mary Peters from?

5 What colour medal did Sharron Davies win in Moscow?

6 In which two successive Olympics did Daley Thompson win gold?

7 In which team game did Britain's men win gold in Seoul in 1988?

8 Which country has won most summer Olympic medals since 1896?

9 Whose long-jump record in the 1968 Olympics lasted for 24 years?

10 Which boxer won gold for Canada in Seoul in 1988?

11 Which country did athletes with FRG after their names represent?

12 Who won silver at 100 metres in '88 and gold in the same event in '92?

13 Which country won most gold medals in 2004?

14 Which gymnast scored the first perfect ten in Olympic history?

15 Which Cathy lit the cauldron at the start of the 2000 Sydney Olympics?

16 Who was disqualified after a drugs test in the Men's 100 metres in 1988?

17 Who collided with Zola Budd in the 3000 metres in 1984?

18 Who won Britain's first men's swimming gold for 68 years in 1976?

19 At which sport was Katarina Witt an Olympic champion?

20 In which city were the Winter Olympics held when Torvill and Dean won gold in 1984?

21 Which gold medal winner in 2004 was born in Pembury, Kent in 1970?

22 Which swimming event was introduced to the Olympics in 1984?

23 In which month was the Athens 2004 Olympics?

24 Which British skater won gold in 1980?

25 What are the five colours of the Olympic rings?

26 In 1984 who won gold in the Men's 800 metres and the 1500 metres?

27 In which country were the first modern Olympics held in 1896?

28 Who won the Women's 400-metre hurdles in Barcelona in 1992?

29 How many judges out of nine gave Torvill and Dean full marks for artistic impression in 1984?

30 Who was Britain's first-ever gold medallist in a throwing event in 1984?

| **Answers** | Royals *(see Quiz 23)* |

1 Twice. 2 Grand National. 3 Prince Harry. 4 Blue. 5 Timothy Lawrence. 6 Prince Andrew. 7 Gordonstoun. 8 Income tax. 9 Norman Hartnell. 10 Sophie. 11 John Bryan. 12 As the bride's mother. 13 Duke of Kent. 14 One. 15 Highgrove. 16 The Prince's Trust. 17 Zara Phillips. 18 HSBC. 19 Prince Charles. 20 Kiri Te Kanawa. 21 Elizabeth and David Emanuel. 22 Queen Mother. 23 Princess Alexandra. 24 Lord Mountbatten. 25 Princess Michael of Kent. 26 Louise. 27 Wales. 28 Ruby. 29 Queen Elizabeth II. 30 Royal Marines.

1 Which club became the first to win the FA Cup ten times?
2 St Stephen's Day is better known as which day?
3 Who recorded the original of "Love is All Around"?
4 Who became the first First Minister of the new Scottish Parliament?
5 A scallop sculpture on Aldeburgh beach in Suffolk is a tribute to which composer?
6 Which watch is from 8pm to midnight at sea?
7 Which two countries are divided by the Palk Strait?
8 Which Derbyshire town is noted for a church with a crooked spire?
9 In which field of writing is Simon Armitage mainly concerned?
10 What type of stone is the Koh-i-noor?
11 What is the study of family history called?
12 Which creature sends down share values on the stock exchange?
13 Which sport has its headquarters in St John's Wood, London?
14 Which language was invented for international use?
15 What was climbed "Because it is there"?
16 The Lutine bell is in which London institution?
17 The inspiration for which children's book character died in April 1996?
18 Which drug is obtained from foxglove leaves?
19 In which county is Romney Marsh?
20 Which magazine is the flagship of the Consumers Association?
21 Which four words follow "To be or not to be..."?
22 In France what title was given to the eldest son of the king?
23 What are the colours of the berries of the Mountain Ash?
24 What part of Cyrano de Bergerac's anatomy was particularly large?
25 In Japan what name is given to ritual sacrifice?
26 Whom did Flora Macdonald rescue?
27 Purchase tax was abolished in 1973, but what replaced it?
28 In the song, who regrets she is unable to lunch today?
29 Who was the god of war in Roman mythology?
30 The Gobi Desert is in which continent?

| **Answers** | Pot-Luck 11 *(see Quiz 24)* |

1 Carbon. 2 Bryan McFadden. 3 Zeus. 4 The Volga. 5 Sir Isaac Newton. 6 Sonny.
7 Lisa Marie Presley. 8 Carmen. 9 Four. 10 Surbiton. 11 Fred Astaire. 12 Nagasaki.
13 Normandy. 14 Catch 22. 15 Brown. 16 Twentieth. 17 Light. 18 Black Sea.
19 Mandy Rice-Davis. 20 Simba. 21 Black Rod. 22 Astrologists. 23 Orchestra. 24
Skye Terrier. 25 John Dillinger. 26 Tosca. 27 The North Sea. 28 Butcher. 29 Die
Fledermaus. 30 West Germany.

Quiz 23 | Royals

Answers – page 145

LEVEL 2

1 How many times had Wallis Simpson been married before she married Edward VIII?

2 Which major sporting event took place on the same day that Charles and Camilla were married?

3 Which prince's last three names are Charles Albert David?

4 What colour was the suit Diana Spencer wore in her engagement photograph in 1981?

5 What is the name of the Princess Royal's second husband?

6 What was Prince Philip's father called?

7 Which Scottish school did Prince Charles go to?

8 What did the Queen agree to pay for the first time in 1992?

9 Who created Princess Elizabeth's wedding dress in 1947?

10 What is the Queen's youngest daughter-in-law called?

11 Who was the Duchess of York's financial adviser in 1992?

12 In what capacity was Mrs Susan Barrantes invited to the wedding of Prince Andrew and Sarah Ferguson?

13 Whom did Katharine Worsley marry in 1961?

14 How many official speeches did Camilla, Duchess of Cornwall, make on her first official visit to the US?

15 Where is the Prince of Wales' home in Gloucestershire?

16 Which organization did Prince Charles set up in 1976?

17 Who is the Queen's second eldest grandchild?

18 Which bank did Prince William work for on work experience in 2005?

19 Who is Earl of Chester?

20 Which opera singer sang at the wedding of Charles and Diana?

21 Who designed Diana Spencer's wedding dress?

22 Whose Christian names are Elizabeth Angela Marguerite?

23 Who is the Duke of Kent's sister?

24 Who was known as Uncle Dickie?

25 Which princess's first names are Marie Christine?

26 What is the Queen's youngest granddaughter-in-law called?

27 Royal wedding rings are made from gold from which country?

28 Which coloured stone was in Fergie's engagement ring?

29 Who as a child was known to her family as Lilibet?

30 Which branch of the armed forces did Prince Edward briefly join in 1986?

| **Answers** | The Olympics (see Quiz 21) |

1 202. 2 Silver. 3 Seven. 4 Northern Ireland. 5 Silver. 6 1980 and 1984. 7 Hockey. 8 United States. 9 Bob Beamon's. 10 Lennox Lewis. 11 West Germany. 12 Linford Christie. 13 United States. 14 Nadia Comaneci. 15 Cathy Freeman. 16 Ben Johnson. 17 Mary Decker. 18 David Wilkie. 19 Ice skating. 20 Sarajevo. 21 Kelly Holmes. 22 Synchronized swimming. 23 August. 24 Robin Cousins. 25 Black, yellow, red, green, blue. 26 Sebastian Coe. 27 Greece. 28 Sally Gunnell. 29 Nine. 30 Tessa Sanderson.

1 Coal is composed of which element?
2 Who left Westlife in March 2004?
3 Who was chief of the Greek gods?
4 What is the longest river in Russia?
5 Who formulated the law of gravity?
6 What was Sophie Ellis Bextor's first male child called?
7 Who has been married to Michael Jackson and Nicolas Cage?
8 In which opera does the heroine work in a cigarette factory?
9 When Steve Redgrave won his fifth Olympic gold how many rowers were there in the boat?
10 In which surburban district of London was the "Good Life" set?
11 Who was Ginger Rogers' most famous dancing partner?
12 Two Japanese cities were hit by atomic bombs in World War II. Hiroshima was one: what was the other?
13 William of where won the Battle of Hastings?
14 In which novel does the character Major Major Major Major appear?
15 What is the colour of the live wire in a three-pin plug?
16 In which century did Queen Victoria die?
17 Which word goes after lime and before house to make two new words?
18 What sea lies between Turkey and Russia?
19 Who said, "Well he would say that, wouldn't he?"
20 In Disney's "The Lion King" who is king at the end of the picture?
21 Whom does the monarch send to summon the Commons to her at the State Opening of Parliament?
22 Which 'ologists study the future through the movement of the planets?
23 What musical word is an anagram of cart-horse?
24 What breed of dog was Greyfriars Bobby?
25 Which 1930s US criminal was known as "Public Enemy No 1"?
26 Of which opera is Floria Tosca the heroine?
27 Which sea provides much of Britain's domestic gas?
28 To what trade had highwayman Dick Turpin been apprenticed?
29 Which Viennese opera title when translated is "The Bat"?
30 Which country were beaten finalists in the 2002 FIFA World Cup?

Answers | Pot-Luck 10 (see Quiz 22)

1 Man Utd. 2 Boxing Day. 3 The Troggs. 4 Donald Dewar. 5 Benjamin Britten. 6 First watch. 7 India and Sri Lanka. 8 Chesterfield. 9 Poetry. 10 Diamond. 11 Genealogy. 12 Bear. 13 Cricket. 14 Esperanto. 15 Mount Everest. 16 Lloyds. 17 Christopher Robin. 18 Digitalis. 19 Kent. 20 Which? 21 That is the question. 22 Dauphin. 23 Red. 24 His nose. 25 Hara-kiri. 26 Bonnie Prince Charlie. 27 VAT – Value Added Tax. 28 Miss Otis. 29 Mars. 30 Asia.

1 Was bird flu first detected in America, Asia or Europe?
2 What species of kite breeds in Britain?
3 What is the study of birds' eggs called?
4 An exaltation is a group of which birds?
5 What would you see if there was a Turdus on your window sill?
6 What colour are wild budgerigars?
7 A scapular on a bird is a type of what?
8 Which bird song sounds like chiff-chaff chiff-chaff?
9 Which bird is sacred in Peru?
10 What is the smallest British bird?
11 What type of birds are ratites?
12 Which birds group to mate and are shot in braces?
13 What name is given to a flock or gathering of crows?
14 What is special about the bones of most birds?
15 Which family of birds does the robin belong to?
16 Golden and argus are varieties of which bird?
17 Which of the senses is poorly developed in most birds?
18 What is special about a palmiped?
19 Which bird lays the largest egg?
20 What is the oldest known fossil bird?
21 What is the main food of the oyster catcher?
22 What is the shaft of a feather called?
23 Which extinct bird was last sighted in Mauritius?
24 What does a syrinx help a bird to do?
25 Which three features distinguish birds from other creatures?
26 What name is given to a castrated cockerel?
27 What is the common name for all small birds of prey?
28 Which bird is the symbol of the RSPB?
29 What name is given to a flock or gathering of starlings?
30 What is the main group in the family Phasianidae?

Answers | Karaoke (see Quiz 27)

1 Is this just fantasy? 2 Unchained Melody. 3 My, my, my Delilah. 4 My Way. 5 Advertising Space. 6 In his kiss. 7 Your head. 8 Chris de Burgh. 9 The curtain. 10 In the wind. 11 She was a showgirl. 12 New York. 13 Eton Rifles. 14 Matchstalk cats and dogs. 15 I feel it in my fingers. 16 Ten. 17 Jolene. 18 All right. 19 Thought control. 20 Midnight. 21 Your lips. 22 This feeling inside. 23 Rosemary and thyme. 24 Guitar George. 25 Tell me more. 26 Hospital Food. 27 River deep mountain high. 28 Eleanor Rigby. 29 Make me cry. 30 A whiter shade of pale.

1 Which principality lies between France and Spain in the Pyrenees?
2 Canaan Banana was the first president of which country?
3 What was the name of the Queen of Faeries in "A Midsummer Night's Dream"?
4 Who was divorced from Mark Phillips?
5 What was the name of the girl who visited the Wizard of Oz?
6 Who came directly after Pope John Paul I?
7 Which team did Arsenal beat in the FA Cup Final in 2002 to complete the double?
8 Which "EastEnders" actress has a daughter named Tallulah Lilac?
9 Which stretch of water separates Alaska from the Russian mainland?
10 What did Sandie Shaw bare in the Eurovision Song Contest?
11 Who was the last chemist to be prime minister of Britain?
12 In 1979, who sang about "Walking on the Moon"?
13 Which Jane married Gerald Scarfe?
14 How many letters are there in the Greek alphabet?
15 Which camels have more humps, Dromedaries or Bactrians?
16 "If I were a Rich Man" comes from which stage show?
17 Which word follows "paper" and precedes "gammon" to make two new words?
18 Who was lead singer with the Boomtown Rats?
19 What was the name of Lady Penelope's puppet chauffeur?
20 What was St Luke's profession?
21 Which Michael Caine film was about the battle at Rorke's Drift?
22 In mythology, Minerva was the goddess of what?
23 What is exactly 26 miles and 385 yards long?
24 If you betray your country what crime do you commit?
25 Which politician was the subject of TV's "A Very Social Secretary"?
26 What in France is "Le Figaro"?
27 The musical "Blood Brothers" is based in which city?
28 What is the middle name of Cruz Beckham?
29 Who took over as England cricket captain from Graham Gooch?
30 The Lorelei rock is on which river?

Answers	TV: Police Serials *(see Quiz 28)*

1 Glasgow. 2 Frank. 3 Terry Venables. 4 Dixon of Dock Green. 5 Ruth Rendell. 6 Kojak. 7 Martin Shaw. 8 Jim. 9 Robert Lindsay. 10 Pierce Brosnan. 11 Metropolitan Police. 12 Pepper. 13 Jemima Shore. 14 Tubbs. 15 Juliet Bravo. 16 Dave and Ken. 17 Hawaii Five-O. 18 Morse Code. 19 Magnum. 20 The Avengers. 21 Poetry. 22 Sweeney Todd – Flying Squad. 23 Van de Valk. 24 Basset hound. 25 Cambridge. 26 Los Angeles. 27 Maigret. 28 Z Cars. 29 Radio presenter. 30 Cagney and Lacey.

Quiz 27 Pop: Karaoke

Answers – page 149

LEVEL 2

1 What line follows "Is this the real life"?
2 "Time goes by so slowly, And time can do so much," comes from which song?
3 What line comes before "Why, why, why, Delilah?"?
4 "And so I face the final curtain" comes from which song?
5 Which Robbie Williams song names Marlon Brando?
6 Finish the line: "If you want to know if he loves you so, It's..."
7 What do you hold up high when you walk through a storm?
8 Who sang "Never seen you looking so gorgeous as you did tonight"?
9 Jason Donovan closed his eyes and drew back what?
10 "The answer, my friend, is blowing..." where?
11 What line comes after "Her name was Lola"?
12 Where are you if you "wake up in a city that never sleeps"?
13 In which song by the Jam is there "a row going on, down in Slough"?
14 What did he paint apart from "Matchstalk Men"?
15 What line comes before "I feel it in my toes"?
16 How many times do you sing "Yeah" in the chorus of "She Loves You"?
17 To whom did Dolly Parton beg "Please don't take my man"?
18 If tonight is the night how is Whitney Houston feeling?
19 According to Pink Floyd, "We don't need no education, We don't need no..." what?
20 What word comes before "Not a sound from the pavement"?
21 Finish the line: "You never close your eyes anymore when I kiss..."
22 Which Elton John line follows "It's a little bit funny"?
23 Which two herbs go with "parsley, sage"?
24 In "Sultans of Swing" who "knows all the chords"?
25 In "Grease", what line comes before "Did she put up a fight?"?
26 Which David Gray song features the line, "Tell me something I don't already know"?
27 What four words go after "Do I love you, My oh my"?
28 Who was "wearing a face that she keeps in a jar by the door"?
29 "Do you really want to hurt me? Do you really want to" do what?
30 "Her face at first just ghostly turned" what colour?

Answers Nature: Birds *(see Quiz 25)*

1 Asia. 2 Red. 3 Oology. 4 Larks. 5 A thrush. 6 Green. 7 Feather. 8 Chiffchaff. 9 Condor. 10 Wren. 11 Flightless. 12 Pheasants. 13 Murder. 14 They are hollow. 15 Thrush. 16 The pheasant. 17 Smell. 18 It has webbed feet. 19 Ostrich. 20 Archaeopteryx. 21 Mussels. 22 Quill. 23 The dodo. 24 Sing. 25 Beaks, feathers and wings. 26 Capon. 27 Hawks. 28 Avocet. 29 A chattering. 30 Pheasants.

1 In which city is "Taggart" set?
2 What is "The Bill"'s DI Burnside's first name?
3 Who was co-creator of "Hazell" with Gordon Williams?
4 Which police series had the theme music "An Ordinary Copper"?
5 Who created the character of Chief Inspector Wexford?
6 Which detective called people "Pussycat"?
7 Which actor links "The Chief" and "The Professionals"?
8 What was Bergerac's first name?
9 Who played the part of Jericho in the 2005 series?
10 Who played the title role in "Remington Steele"?
11 Whom did Spender work for before being posted back to Newcastle?
12 In "Police Woman" what was Sgt Anderson's nickname?
13 Which series starred Patricia Hodge in the title role?
14 Who was Crockett's partner in "Miami Vice"?
15 In which series did Jean Darblay, then Kate Longton, appear?
16 What were Starsky and Hutch's first names?
17 In which series did Steve Garrett say "Book 'em Danno!"?
18 What sound was the theme music for "Inspector Morse" based on?
19 Which detective shares his name with a chocolate covered ice-cream bar?
20 Which long-running crime series was a spin-off from a programme called "Police Surgeon"?
21 What sort of literature does Commander Adam Dalgliesh write?
22 How did "The Sweeney" get its name?
23 Which series had the chart-topping "Eye Level" as its theme tune?
24 What breed of dog was Columbo's companion Fang?
25 In "Dempsey and Makepeace" which university had Lady Harriet graduated from?
26 In which city did "Burke's Law" take place?
27 Which detective has been played by Richard Harris and Michael Gambon?
28 Which series was set in Seaport and Newtown?
29 What was the occupation of Eddie Shoestring?
30 In which series did cops Petrie and Isbecki appear?

Answers	Pot-Luck 12 *(see Quiz 26)*

1 Andorra. 2 Zimbabwe. 3 Titania. 4 Princess Anne. 5 Dorothy. 6 John Paul II. 7 Chelsea. 8 Jessie Wallace. 9 Bering Strait. 10 Her feet. 11 Margaret Thatcher. 12 The Police. 13 Asher. 14 24. 15 Bactrian camels. 16 Fiddler on the Roof. 17 Back. 18 Bob Geldof. 19 Parker. 20 Doctor. 21 Zulu. 22 Wisdom. 23 The Marathon. 24 Treason. 25 David Blunkett. 26 Newspaper. 27 Liverpool. 28 David. 29 Mike Atherton. 30 Rhine.

1 Which gas shares its name with Superman's home planet?

2 In politics, to whom does the expression "Father of the House" refer?

3 On which island is Wall Street?

4 Who made the first full state visit to the UK by a US President?

5 What is the study of fluids moving in pipes?

6 What type of person studies the relationship between living organisms and their environment?

7 Who wrote the River Cottage cookery books?

8 Which English town is an anagram of ancestral?

9 Where, in Baker Street, did Sherlock Holmes live?

10 What does the word "Bolshoi" mean?

11 In mythology, who was banished by his son Jupiter?

12 Which London borough is the "G" in GMT?

13 Where in London is the Royal Opera House?

14 What is Eric Clapton's middle name?

15 How many dancers feature in a pas de deux?

16 Which William wrote a poem about daffodils?

17 What was the name of the World War I ace nicknamed "The Red Baron"?

18 Who produced the works of art "My Bed" and "Everyone I Have Ever Slept With"?

19 Who invented frozen food?

20 What unit is used to measure the gas we use in our homes?

21 What title did Harold Macmillan take?

22 In "Billy Elliot" what does Billy's father want him to train at instead of ballet?

23 Which Shakespeare play is in three parts?

24 What is a mordant?

25 Which "ology" is the art of ringing bells?

26 How was Achilles killed?

27 Matt Holland and Hermann Hreidarsson were together at Charlton and which other soccer club?

28 Which precinct does Ed McBain write about?

29 Who wrote the novel "Dr Zhivago"?

30 Who was prime minister of Britain at the outbreak of World War II?

Answers | Pot-Luck 14 *(see Quiz 31)*

1 Edward Heath. 2 Alan Sheppard. 3 Crufts. 4 Ireland. 5 Psychology. 6 Formic acid. 7 George III. 8 Fred Perry. 9 The Crimea. 10 Meal. 11 Richard Dunwoody. 12 Terpsichore. 13 Jimi Hendrix. 14 China. 15 Germany. 16 Red. 17 Man City. 18 The Times. 19 Flowers. 20 21. 21 Nitrous oxide. 22 Egypt. 23 1990s 24 Dermatology. 25 Sulphuric acid. 26 Plastering. 27 Edward Gibbon. 28 Poland. 29 Dorothy L. Sayers. 30 Children.

1 What is the plate connecting two lengths of railway track called?
2 What, according to tradition, takes four years to paint from end to end?
3 Which letter do post-war tanks all begin with?
4 Outside which London building were traffic lights first installed?
5 In World War II what was a McRobert's Reply?
6 What did LNER stand for?
7 Which Alistair was Secretary of State for Transport at the start of Labour's third term in office?
8 Which was the first true jet to enter passenger service?
9 What is the popular name for the Boeing 747 and the European airbus?
10 What links the Pacific Ocean with the Caribbean?
11 Who introduced the C5 in 1985?
12 Which motorway goes from London to Winchester?
13 Which nickname is given to aircraft such as the Harrier?
14 Who developed the Mini?
15 Which type of transport is Zeppelin associated with?
16 Where is O'Hare International airport?
17 What is the distress word for ships and aircraft?
18 Which four-wheel drive vehicle was launched in 1940?
19 Which word is used to describe the frame, wheels and machinery of a car?
20 The first motor car race was held to Bordeaux and back to where?
21 Which country has the international registration letter M?
22 Which US car manufacturer makes Astra, Corsa and Chevrolet?
23 What is the distance between two rails on a track called?
24 What colour is the District Line on a London Underground map?
25 From which two London stations could you travel to Scotland direct?
26 Which two classes of travel are there on Inter City trains?
27 In terms of tonnes of cargo handled, which is Europe's busiest port?
28 What does 'Volkswagen' mean?
29 On which side of the road do the Japanese drive?
30 In which city is Lime St Station?

Answers	**Religious Fervour** *(see Quiz 32)*

1 Jesus Christ's. 2 Brazil. 3 Ecumenical Movement. 4 Jehovah's Witnesses. 5 The Salvation Army. 6 Ramadan. 7 Jihad. 8 Buddhism. 9 Japan. 10 Russia. 11 Quakers. 12 Hinduism. 13 Mecca. 14 Hare Krishna. 15 Sikhs. 16 Scientology. 17 Chinese. 18 Mormons. 19 Transcendental Meditation. 20 Rastafarianism. 21 Temple. 22 Islam. 23 Kosher. 24 Eskimos. 25 Unitarians. 26 Church of Christ, Scientist. 27 John and Charles. 28 Immersion. 29 Moonies. 30 Sunday.

1 Whom did Margaret Thatcher replace as leader of the Tory Party?
2 Who hit a golf shot on the moon?
3 Which dog show was first held in Islington in 1891?
4 Darina Allen specializes in food that comes from which country?
5 In which "ology" were Freud and Jung active?
6 What acid gives nettles their sting?
7 Which king was nicknamed "Farmer George"?
8 Who was the last Briton to win the men's singles at Wimbledon?
9 On which peninsula is the city of Sevastopol situated?
10 Which word goes after piece and before times to make two new words?
11 Which jockey produced an autobiography titled "Obsessed"?
12 Who was the Greek muse of dance?
13 Which rock guitarist prophetically said, "When you're dead you're made for life"?
14 In which country is Puccini's "Turandot" set?
15 Which country did "Kaiser Bill" rule?
16 What colour of ballet shoes did Hans Christian Andersen write about?
17 Which club did David Seaman join on a free transfer after leaving Arsenal?
18 Which British newspaper is nicknamed "The Thunderer"?
19 What according to Scott McKenzie did you wear in your hair in San Francisco?
20 After 1928, women over what age were given the vote?
21 What is the correct name for laughing gas?
22 In which country was Harrods owner Mohamed al Fayed born?
23 In which decade of the last century did the Church of England vote for women priests?
24 Which "ology" is concerned with the human skin?
25 What is H_2SO_4?
26 Finish and browning are used in which building trade?
27 Who wrote the "Decline and Fall of the Roman Empire"?
28 In which country was Catherine the Great born?
29 Who chronicled the cases of Lord Peter Wimsey?
30 Whom is UNICEF responsible for?

Answers | Pot-Luck 13 *(see Quiz 29)*

1 Krypton. 2 The longest-serving MP. 3 Manhattan. 4 George W. Bush. 5 Hydraulics. 6 Ecologist. 7 Hugh Fearnley Whittingstall. 8 Lancaster. 9 221B. 10 Big. 11 Saturn. 12 Greenwich. 13 Covent Garden. 14 Patrick. 15 Two. 16 Wordsworth. 17 Baron von Richthofen. 18 Tracey Emin. 19 Clarence Birdseye. 20 Therms. 21 Earl of Stockton. 22 Boxing. 23 Henry VI. 24 A substance used to fix colours in dyeing. 25 Campanology. 26 By an arrow in his heel. 27 Ipswich Town. 28 The 86th Precinct. 29 Boris Pasternak. 30 Neville Chamberlain.

Quiz 32 | Religious Fervour | Answers – page 154

1 Whose birth shaped the calendar of the Western world?

2 Which country has the largest number of Roman Catholics?

3 Which movement promotes understanding between different branches of the Christian faith?

4 What are members of the Watchtower Movement better known as?

5 Whose newspaper is called "The Warcry"?

6 During which month do Muslims fast from before sunrise to sunset?

7 What term is used in Islam for "Holy War"?

8 Which religion is based on the teaching of Siddhartha Gautama?

9 Shintoism is the native religion of which country?

10 Which country has the largest Orthodox Church?

11 What are members of the Society of Friends called?

12 In which religion are Shiva and Vishnu major gods?

13 Where should Muslims make a pilgrimage to once in their lifetime?

14 How is the International Society for Krishna Consciousness known?

15 Who have uncut hair worn in a turban and uncut beards?

16 Which religion was founded by a science fiction author?

17 What nationality was Confucius?

18 What are members of the Church of Jesus Christ of Latter Day Saints better known as?

19 What does TM stand for in the movement founded by the Maharishi?

20 Dreadlocks in the hair and a musical style are hallmarks of which movement linked with Ethiopia?

21 In Hinduism what is a mandir?

22 Which religion has Sunnis and Shiites?

23 In Judaism treifa foods are forbidden. Which foods are allowed?

24 Shamanism is the dominant religion of which Arctic people?

25 Which Christian group deny the idea of the Trinity?

26 Which Church was founded by Mary Baker Eddy in the USA in 1879?

27 Which two Wesleys founded Methodism?

28 What sort of baptism does the Baptist Church practise?

29 What are members of the Unification Church better known as?

30 In Judaism what is the first day of the week?

Answers	Transport (see Quiz 30)

1 Fishplate. 2 Forth Railway Bridge. 3 C. 4 Houses of Parliament. 5 Bomber. 6 London and North Eastern Railway. 7 Alistair Darling. 8 Comet. 9 Jumbo jet. 10 Panama Canal. 11 Clive Sinclair. 12 M3. 13 Jump jet. 14 Alec Issigonis. 15 Airships. 16 Chicago. 17 Mayday. 18 Jeep. 19 Chassis. 20 Paris. 21 Malta. 22 General Motors. 23 Gauge. 24 Green. 25 Euston and Kings Cross. 26 First and standard. 27 Rotterdam. 28 People's Car. 29 Left. 30 Liverpool.

Quiz 33 | Pot-Luck 15 | Answers – page 159

1 Who was elected Governor of California in 2003?
2 Which of the seven deadly sins begins with G?
3 What was Ghana's former name?
4 The Dutch royal family acquired its name from which French town?
5 Is the corncrake a bird, mammal or reptile?
6 What name is given to animals that do not hunt or eat meat?
7 Over which continent did the ozone hole form?
8 Which tanker suffered a severe oil spill in Alaska in 1989?
9 Where is the pituitary gland?
10 Which structural tissue is found in between the vertebral discs?
11 The five-year marriage of Ethan Hawke and which actress ended in August 2005?
12 In which country was former Tory leader Iain Duncan Smith born?
13 In which country would you find polders?
14 In which country are the Angel Falls?
15 After her "Strictly Come Dancing" triumph, Jill Halfpenny landed a role in which West End musical?
16 In which two cities would you find Cleopatra's Needles?
17 In which African country is Timbuktu?
18 Which BBC journalist was at the centre of the controversy over a weapons expert's report on the Iraq war?
19 Which English prime minister was known as "the Great Commoner"?
20 Who was the first person to notice that the Sun had spots?
21 Which metal is the best conductor of electricity?
22 Which actress's real name is Julia Wells?
23 Which secret society refers to God as "the great architect of the Universe"?
24 Which building is used for the election of a pope?
25 With whom did Bing Crosby sing "True Love" in the film "High Society"?
26 Which two colours appear on the UN flag?
27 What is the name of the Welsh Nationalist party?
28 What kind of stone is marble?
29 What name is given to the thousands of small bodies that orbit the Sun?
30 Which island was held by the Knights of St John from 1530 to 1798?

Answers	Soul and Motown *(see Quiz 35)*

1 Reach Out, I'll be There. 2 Berry Gordy. 3 Dave. 4 Aretha Franklin. 5 Holland. 6 Otis Redding. 7 The Broken Hearted. 8 Jackie Wilson. 9 The Isley Brothers. 10 James Brown. 11 The Supremes. 12 After the song Tammy by Debbie Reynolds. 13 You Keep Me Hangin' On. 14 Wilson Pickett. 15 The Vandellas. 16 Arthur Conley. 17 I'm Still Waiting. 18 Lionel Richie. 19 Gladys Knight. 20 Bobby Brown. 21 Stevie Wonder. 22 The Temptations. 23 Jimmy Mack. 24 William. 25 Midnight. 26 Reflections. 27 Marvin Gaye. 28 Atlantic. 29 Edwin Starr. 30 Junior Walker.

Quiz 34 | Sports Bag

1 In darts, what is the maximum check-out score?
2 Who has won most international soccer caps for England?
3 Which country did boxer Lennox Lewis represent at the Olympics?
4 How many points did England score in the 2003 rugby union World Cup Final of 2003?
5 Which group were England in for the 2006 FIFA World Cup?
6 Which country turned Rugby Union's Five Nations into the Six Nations Championship in 2000?
7 Boxer Amir Khan comes from which north west town?
8 In 2005 Eddie Jones got sacked as rugby coach of which country?
9 For what sport is Ellery Hanley famous?
10 Is snooker's Jimmy White left-handed or right-handed?
11 What important role did Oliver McCall play in Frank Bruno's career?
12 At which Grand Prix circuit did Ayrton Senna lose his life?
13 Who was the first man to do the 100-metre breast stroke in under a minute?
14 The WDC is the World Darts Council, but what is the PDC?
15 Where was Barry Sheene involved in a 175 mph crash in 1975?
16 Which twisting circuit on the Grand Prix calendar is only 1.95 miles long?
17 Has croquet ever been a sport in the Olympics?
18 Which boxer used to enter the ring to Tina Turner's "Simply the Best"?
19 Whose shoulder was injured during Martin Johnson's 2005 testimonial?
20 In Rugby Union, who is Australia's record try scorer?
21 What make of car has made Michael Schumacher F1 World Champion in his triumphs this century?
22 In speedway racing, how many laps of the track does a race consist of?
23 Apart from England which European country took part in cricket's 1996 World Cup?
24 Which world heavyweight boxing champion died in an air-crash in 1969?
25 Who won a 100-metre breast stroke gold in the 1980 Olympics?
26 In badminton, how many points win a single game?
27 Which trainer is known as the "Queen of Aintree"?
28 Is an own goal allowed for in the rules of hockey?
29 Which two sports take place on a piste?
30 Which club side does Jonny Wilkinson play for?

Answers	Pot-Luck 16 *(see Quiz 36)*

1 Piano. 2 Southampton. 3 Ukraine. 4 1990. 5 Rome. 6 New Zealand. 7 Le Mans. 8 Brazil and Colombia. 9 Quito. 10 Inert gases. 11 Nucleus. 12 Peter Wright. 13 Samuel Beckett. 14 Adelaide. 15 Rainbow Warrior. 16 Sally Gunnell. 17 The Nag's Head. 18 Laurence Olivier. 19 You're So Vain. 20 Rembrandt. 21 The Brothers Grimm. 22 Danish. 23 Robert Baden-Powell. 24 Chuck Berry. 25 Alchemy. 26 William Bragg. 27 Imran Khan. 28 India. 29 Laura. 30 Paddy Ashdown.

Quiz 35   Pop: Soul and Motown   Answers – page 157   LEVEL 2

1 The Four Tops had only one British No 1. What was it?
2 Who was the boss of Tamla Motown?
3 Who sang with Sam on the hit "Soul Man"?
4 Which female soul star has recorded with Elton John, George Michael and George Benson?
5 Who made up the songwriting trio with Holland and Dozier?
6 Who was sitting on the dock of the bay?
7 Who according to Jimmy Ruffin "had love that has now departed"?
8 Which soul singer died in 1984 after lying in a coma for eight years?
9 Rudolph, Ronald and O'Kelley were which singing Brothers?
10 Who is known as "The Godfather of Soul"?
11 Which group featured Cindy Birdsong?
12 The Motown label was nearly called Tammy. After which Tammy?
13 Which Tamla song starts, "Set me free, why don't you babe"?
14 In the 1960s who was known as "The Wicked Pickett"?
15 Which group backed Martha Reeves?
16 Who recorded the soul classic "Sweet Soul Music"?
17 What was Diana Ross's first solo British No 1?
18 Which singer went solo after performing with the Commodores?
19 Who was backed by the Pips?
20 Which soul singer married Whitney Houston in 1992?
21 Who sang "I Was Made to Love Her"?
22 Eddie Kendricks and David Ruffin were lead singers with which group?
23 Whom did Martha Reeves want to "hurry back"?
24 What was Smokey Robinson's real first name?
25 Which hour did Cropper and Pickett write about?
26 Which was the first single in which the Supremes were billed as Diana Ross and the Supremes?
27 Who originally heard it through the grapevine?
28 On which label did Aretha Franklin record in the 1960s?
29 Who had a Tamla hit with "War"?
30 Who fronted the All Stars?

| **Answers** | Pot-Luck 15 *(see Quiz 33)* |

1 Arnold Schwarzenegger. 2 Gluttony. 3 Gold Coast. 4 Orange. 5 Bird. 6 Herbivore. 7 Antarctic. 8 Exxon Valdez. 9 In the brain. 10 Cartilage. 11 Uma Thurman. 12 Scotland. 13 Netherlands. 14 Venezuela. 15 Chicago. 16 London and New York. 17 Mali. 18 Andrew Gilligan. 19 William Pitt the Elder. 20 Galileo. 21 Silver. 22 Julie Andrews. 23 Freemasons. 24 Sistine Chapel. 25 Grace Kelly. 26 Blue and white. 27 Plaid Cymru. 28 Limestone. 29 Asteroids. 30 Malta.

1 Which instrument did Franz Liszt play?
2 Graeme Le Saux finished his soccer playing days with which club?
3 In which republic of the former USSR is Chernobyl?
4 In which year were East and West Germany unified?
5 Where was the treaty signed that established the EEC?
6 Who won the first Rugby Union World Cup, held in 1987?
7 On which circuit is motor racing's Grand Prix d'Endurance run?
8 Which two South American countries produce the most coffee?
9 What is the capital of Ecuador?
10 Helium belongs to which group of elements?
11 Where in the cell is DNA stored?
12 Who was the author of "Spycatcher" in 1987?
13 Who wrote the play "Waiting for Godot"?
14 Which Australian city is named after William IV's queen?
15 Which Greenpeace ship was sunk in Auckland harbour in 1985?
16 Who was the first female Brtish athlete to win world, Olympic, European and Commonwealth titles?
17 What is Del Boy's local?
18 Who was the first director of Britain's National Theatre Company?
19 Which song features the line "I bet you think this song is about you"?
20 Who painted "The Nightwatch?"
21 Which German brothers collected such stories as "Hansel and Gretel"?
22 What nationality was Hans Christian Andersen?
23 Who said, "A Scout smiles and whistles under all circumstances"?
24 Who first urged Beethoven to "roll over" in 1956?
25 What name was given to the practice that tried to turn lead into silver and gold?
26 Who shared a Nobel Prize for physics with his son?
27 Who entered Pakistani politics in 1995 after a successful career as a cricketer?
28 In which country was Rudyard Kipling born?
29 What is Prince Charles's step daughter called?
30 Who was Liberal Democrat leader immediately before Charles Kennedy?

Answers	Sports Bag *(see Quiz 34)*

1 170 – two treble 20s plus bull. 2 Peter Shilton. 3 Canada. 4 20. 5 Group B.
6 Italy. 7 Bolton. 8 Australia. 9 Rugby League. 10 Left-handed. 11 Bruno beat
McCall to become the WBC Heavyweight champion. 12 San Marino, Italy. 13 Adrian
Moorhouse in 1987. 14 Professional Darts Council. 15 Daytona. 16 Monaco. 17
Yes. 18 Chris Eubank. 19 Jonah Lomu. 20 David Campese. 21 Ferrari. 22 Four. 23
Netherlands. 24 Rocky Marciano. 25 Duncan Goodhew. 26 15 points. 27 Jenny
Pitman. 28 Yes. 29 Fencing and skiing. 30 Newcastle.

Quiz 37 War Films

Answers – page 163

1 About which conflict is the Sam Mendes film "Jarhead" about?

2 During which war was "Platoon" set?

3 Which Hollywood legend played Kurtz in "Apocalypse Now"?

4 Who played Hawkeye and Trapper John in "M*A*S*H"?

5 How was the film "Patton" known in the UK?

6 For which Robert de Niro film was "Cavatina" the theme music?

7 Who won an Oscar as the Colonel in "The Bridge on the River Kwai"?

8 In "The Colditz Story" what type of building was Colditz?

9 In which English county were the GIs billeted in "Yanks"?

10 What type of soldiers were the four Britons in "The Wild Geese"?

11 Which 1963 film about Allied POWs starred James Garner and Steve McQueen?

12 Hits from which decade were on the soundtrack of "Good Morning, Vietnam"?

13 Which George was the star of "Three Kings"?

14 How were the 12 convicts recruited for a suicide mission known in the 1967 movie?

15 Which novel was "Schindler's List" based on?

16 Which US singer played Von Ryan in "Von Ryan's Express"?

17 Whose café was a meeting place for war refugees in "Casablanca"?

18 Who wrote the novel on which "Where Eagles Dare" was based?

19 Which musical satire on war was directed by Richard Attenborough?

20 Where was it "All Quiet" in the classic film made in 1930?

21 At the time of which World War II event is "From Here to Eternity" set?

22 In "A Town Like Alice" what does "Alice" refer to?

23 Which anti-Vietnam War activist starred in "Coming Home"?

24 Who was the subject of the film "The Desert Fox"?

25 Which 1940 film starred Charlie Chaplin as despot Adenoid Hynkel?

26 Who directed "Born on the Fourth of July"?

27 Whose heroes were Clint Eastwood and Telly Savalas in 1970?

28 "The Eagle Has Landed" centres on a plot to kidnap whom?

29 Who won the Oscar for best actress in 1982 for "Sophie's Choice"?

30 In which country is "The Killing Fields" set?

Answers | Literature (see Quiz 39)

1 Serpent. 2 Hercule Poirot. 3 John Grisham. 4 The Prodigal Daughter. 5 Antonia.
6 10/6. 7 John McCarthy. 8 Australia. 9 Brian Keenan. 10 John Le Carré.
11 Shrewsbury. 12 Margaret Thatcher's. 13 Nancy Sinatra. 14 Ben Elton. 15 Gamekeeper. 16 Jack Higgins. 17 Maureen Lipman. 18 The Camomile Lawn. 19 Ian Fleming. 20 Sharpe. 21 Edwina Currie. 22 Georges Simenon. 23 Nelson Mandela. 24 Rudyard Kipling. 25 China. 26 Julian Fellowes. 27 Bunter. 28 Mercenaries. 29 Les Misérables. 30 Dan Brown.

1 What is Terry Wogan's real first name?
2 What name was given to the 19th-century group who wrecked machines?
3 What is the name of Orson Welles' first film, made when he was 26?
4 Which party did George Galloway belong to when he was elected to Parliament in 2005?
5 Which river runs through the Grand Canyon?
6 Name the geological fault that runs the length of California.
7 Which bandmaster composed "The Stars and Stripes Forever"?
8 Which drug is derived from the willow, Salix alba?
9 Where was Captain Cook killed?
10 Which star actor links "Charlie and the Chocolate Factory" and "The Libertine"?
11 Which hurricane threatened Texas shortly after hurricane Katrina struck in 2005?
12 What is the full name for DNA?
13 Other than the "Odyssey", which work is Homer famed for?
14 Name the art of making decorative lacework with knotted threads?
15 To which family does the chive belong?
16 Which indoor game was invented by British Army Officers in India in 1875?
17 Which microbe is the basis of the brewing and baking industry?
18 In 2005, which birthday did Thomas the Tank Engine celebrate?
19 In bluegrass music who is Flatt's partner?
20 Philip Glass wrote an opera about which scientist?
21 Who led the crew of the "Argo" in their search for the golden fleece?
22 What planet was home for the aliens in Wells's "The War of the Worlds"?
23 Who is credited with the invention of scat singing?
24 Which group consisted of Les, Eric, Woody, Alan and Derek?
25 Name Mary Quant's shop, which revolutionized fashion in the 1960s?
26 Which mountain was first climbed by Edward Whymper in 1865?
27 In fiction, Michael Henchard became mayor of which town?
28 Which Kray twin survived the other?
29 Who discovered that the universe is expanding?
30 In music, what is meant by pianissimo?

Answers   Pot-Luck 18 *(see Quiz 40)*

1 One. 2 Tea. 3 Pole or North Star. 4 Two. 5 Anton Chekhov. 6 Black Prince. 7 Bees. 8 Myxomatosis. 9 The inner ear. 10 Nuts. 11 Crete. 12 Katie Price. 13 Napoleon Bonaparte. 14 Anaemia. 15 Chelsea. 16 Saudi Arabia. 17 South Korea. 18 Aneurin Bevan. 19 Golden Gate. 20 Capability Brown. 21 Praying Mantis. 22 Yellowstone, Wyoming. 23 Trachea. 24 William Hague. 25 Istanbul. 26 Dinar. 27 Cadiz. 28 Joanne Harris. 29 Oxygen. 30 Nineteen Eighty-Four.

1 Which creature features on the adult edition of "The Chamber of Secrets"?

2 Which fictional detective is assisted by Captain Hastings?

3 Who wrote "The Firm" and "The Pelican Brief"?

4 What was Jeffrey Archer's sequel to "Kane and Abel" called?

5 What is the first name of the novelist A. S. Byatt?

6 In "Alice in Wonderland" what price did the Mad Hatter have on his hat?

7 Who co-wrote "Some Other Rainbow" with Jill Morrell?

8 In which country is the beginning of "The Thorn Birds" set?

9 Which former Beirut hostage wrote "An Evil Cradling"?

10 How is adventure writer David Cornwell better known?

11 Which town is the main setting for the Cadfael novels?

12 Part of whose life story is called "The Path to Power"?

13 Who wrote the biography "Frank Sinatra: An American Legend"?

14 Which alternative comedian wrote "Gridlock"?

15 What was the job of Mellors in "Lady Chatterley's Lover"?

16 Under which pseudonym does Harry Paterson also write?

17 Which comedy actress wrote "When's It Coming Out"?

18 Which Mary Wesley novel transferred to TV with Felicity Kendal and Paul Eddington?

19 Which suspense novelist was the cousin of horror movie actor Christopher Lee?

20 What is the name of Bernard Cornwell's hero, played on TV by Sean Bean?

21 Which politician wrote "A Woman's Place"?

22 Who created the detective Maigret?

23 Whose autobiography is called "Long Walk to Freedom"?

24 Who wrote the tales on which the film "The Jungle Book" was based?

25 In which country was the best-seller "Wild Swans" set?

26 Which Oscar-winning script writer wrote the novel "Snobs"?

27 What was the name of Lord Peter Wimsey's butler?

28 What were the "Dogs of War" in Frederick Forsyth's novel?

29 Which novel by Victor Hugo became a long-running musical?

30 Which mega-selling author wrote "Deception Point"?

Answers | War Films *(see Quiz 37)*

1 1991 Gulf War. 2 Vietnam War. 3 Marlon Brando. 4 Donald Sutherland and Elliott Gould. 5 Patton – Lust for Glory. 6 The Deer Hunter. 7 Alec Guinness. 8 A castle. 9 Lancashire. 10 Mercenaries. 11 The Great Escape. 12 The 1960s. 13 Clooney. 14 The Dirty Dozen. 15 Schindler's Ark. 16 Frank Sinatra. 17 Rick's Café. 18 Alistair MacLean. 19 Oh! What a Lovely War. 20 On the Western Front. 21 Pearl Harbor. 22 Alice Springs. 23 Jane Fonda. 24 Rommel. 25 The Great Dictator. 26 Oliver Stone. 27 Kelly's Heroes. 28 Winston Churchill. 29 Meryl Streep. 30 Cambodia.

1 The poster advertising "Mamma Mia" features how many people?
2 What popular drink was known in China as early as 2737 BC?
3 What is the other name for the star Polaris?
4 On how many stone tablets were the Ten Commandments engraved?
5 Who wrote "The Three Sisters"?
6 What was the nickname of Edward Prince of Wales, son of Edward III?
7 Which insects communicate with one another by dancing?
8 Which disease was deliberately introduced in rabbits in the UK?
9 Where are the semicircular canals in the body?
10 What part of a cola tree is used to flavour drinks?
11 Which is the largest Greek island?
12 Who wrote "Being Jordan"?
13 Who married Joséphine de Beauharnais and Princess Marie Louise?
14 Lack of iron in the diet may cause which disease?
15 Marcel Desailly joined which club after winning the World Cup with France?
16 Riyadh is the capital of which country?
17 In which Far Eastern country was the Unification Church (Moonies) founded in 1954?
18 Which minister of health inaugurated the National Health Service?
19 Which strait links San Francisco Bay with the Pacific?
20 Which famous gardener helped landscape Blenheim and Stowe?
21 Which insect sometimes eats its male mate during copulation?
22 What was the first national park established in the United States in 1872?
23 What is the scientific name for the windpipe?
24 Who became Tory party leader immediately after John Major?
25 In which city would you find the Blue Mosque?
26 What is the currency of Algeria?
27 In which port did Sir Francis Drake "singe the King of Spain's beard"?
28 Who wrote "Chocolat" and "Gentlemen and Players"?
29 What is the commonest element in the Earth's crust?
30 Which George Orwell novel showed the dangers of excessive state control?

Answers | Pot-Luck 17 *(see Quiz 38)*

1 Michael. 2 Luddites. 3 Citizen Kane. 4 Respect. 5 Colorado. 6 San Andreas fault. 7 John Philip Sousa. 8 Aspirin. 9 Hawaii. 10 Johnny Depp. 11 Rita. 12 Deoxyribonucleic acid. 13 The Iliad. 14 Macramé. 15 Onion. 16 Snooker. 17 Yeast. 18 60th. 19 Scruggs. 20 Albert Einstein. 21 Jason. 22 Mars. 23 Louis Armstrong. 24 The Bay City Rollers. 25 Bazaar. 26 Matterhorn. 27 Casterbridge. 28 Reggie survived Ronnie. 29 Edwin Hubble. 30 Very softly.

1 Claret wine is produced in the region surrounding which French city?
2 What would be the term to describe a dry champagne?
3 In which country is the wine-growing Barossa Valley?
4 Which white wine grape variety is most widely planted in California?
5 In which country is the Marlborough wine region?
6 Retsina is native to which country?
7 Which wine has the varieties Malmsey and Sercial?
8 What is the normal capacity for a bottle of wine?
9 In which country is Rioja produced?
10 Along which river is most of France's Sauvignon Blanc cultivated?
11 What colour are most English wines?
12 Which scientist discovered that yeast causes fermentation?
13 What is a crate of twelve bottles of wine called?
14 Which country does Sukhindol wine come from?
15 In which part of the United States is the Zinfandel grape chiefly cultivated?
16 What is the first name of wine writer Ms Robinson?
17 In which country is the wine-making area of Stellenbosch?
18 How many normal-size wine bottles would you have in a Methuselah?
19 How are fizzy wines, other than champagnes, described?
20 In which area of Italy is Chianti Classico produced?
21 Would a French wine described as "doux" be medium sweet or medium dry?
22 What are the three styles of port?
23 What colour are most of the wines from France's Anjou region?
24 In which South American country is Casablanca Valley?
25 Which red wine is drunk when young and is called "nouveau"?
26 In which country was a vine variety called "vegetable dragon pearls"?
27 Which wine can be "fino" or "oloroso"?
28 What is Moët et Chandon?
29 Who is the female wine expert on the BBC's "Food and Drink" programme?
30 Along which river and its tributaries do the German vineyards lie?

Answers | Premiership Soccer (see Quiz 43)

1 Wayne Rooney. 2 Liverpool. 3 Wigan. 4 Charlton. 5 Eric Cantona. 6 Iceland. 7 Bryan Robson. 8 Dean Kiely. 9 Chelsea. 10 Ipswich. 11 Preston. 12 Facundo Sava. 13 Alan Shearer. 14 Laurent Blanc. 15 Spurs. 16 Leeds. 17 Liverpool. 18 Argentina. 19 Birmingham. 20 16 years old. 21 Anderton. 22 Denis Irwin. 23 Liverpool. 24 West Ham. 25 Glenn Hoddle. 26 Sunderland. 27 Lee Bowyer. 28 Graham Taylor. 29 James Beattie. 30 2002-03.

1 Who preceded Jose Mourinho as Chelsea manager?

2 Picardy is in the northeast of which country?

3 NUPE was the National Union of what?

4 Which cathedral has the highest spire in Britain?

5 Who sang "Hey, babe, take a walk on the wild side"?

6 The Brenner Pass links which two countries?

7 Which two fruits are anagrams of each other?

8 What is the chief member of a lifeboat crew called?

9 In geography, which term means the joining of two rivers?

10 Which musical note follows fah?

11 How many phases of the moon are there in a lunar month?

12 Which river flows through Cambridge?

13 In geometry what type of line bisects a circle?

14 Which university is based at Milton Keynes?

15 What on your body would a trichologist be concerned with?

16 Which former butler to the Princess of Wales was involved in a pending court case that collapsed in October 2002?

17 What was Gilbert White's field of work?

18 In the board game Cluedo what is the name of the Reverend?

19 Brussels, Honiton and Nottingham are all renowned for which product?

20 Which radio serial is "an everyday story of country folk"?

21 What was David Blunkett's government job when he resigned in 2004?

22 Who wrote that "The workers have nothing to lose but their chains"?

23 What have you done if you have committed patricide?

24 Which donkey is Winnie the Pooh's friend?

25 In which district are Hawes and Ullswater?

26 Which major art gallery was opened in London in 2000?

27 In the Bible, where was the traveller going to in the parable of the Good Samaritan?

28 To what kind of meeting was Mahatma Gandhi going when he was assassinated?

29 What colour are Aylesbury ducks?

30 Which stage musical, based on a Disney movie, opened in London's West End in December 2004?

| **Answers** | Nature: Fish *(see Quiz 44)* |

1 The tail. 2 Red/orange. 3 Tuna. 4 Herring. 5 Roe. 6 Tench. 7 Salmon. 8 Whale shark. 9 Sardine. 10 Blue/black. 11 Liver. 12 Carp. 13 Fish rearing. 14 Silver bream. 15 Whelk. 16 Small shark. 17 Rock salmon. 18 Hermit crab. 19 On its back. 20 Trout. 21 Ten. 22 Izaak Walton. 23 Flatfish. 24 Sprats. 25 Round its mouth. 26 A grain of sand. 27 Pike. 28 Red mullet. 29 Dover sole. 30 Clam.

Quiz 43 | Premiership Soccer | Answers – page 165

1 Who scored Man Utd's first goal following the death of George Best?
2 Milan Baros first played in the Premiership with which club?
3 Which club enjoyed their first ever season in the top division in 2005–06?
4 Charlton, Man Utd, Spurs, West Ham – which club has Teddy Sheringham not played for?
5 Who was the first footballer to win the Premier League Championship with two different clubs?
6 Which country does Bolton's super shot stopper Jussi Jaaskelainen play for?
7 Which manager masterminded WBA's escape from relegation, 2004–05?
8 Which Dean of the Republic of Ireland has been a keeper for Charlton?
9 Joe Cole played for which club during their relegation season?
10 At which club did Richard Wright first play in the Premier League?
11 Which club did David Moyes manage before going to Everton?
12 Which Fulham player donned a Zorro mask after scoring?
13 Which striker has played for Southampton, Blackburn and Newcastle?
14 Which defender of the French World Cup-winning squad went to Man Utd?
15 Kasey Keller and Neil Sullivan have both kept goal for which club?
16 Which club had O'Leary, Venables and Reid as managers in this new millennium?
17 At which club did Henchoz and Hyypia form a defensive pairing?
18 Juan Veron had spells with Man Utd and Chelsea, but which country did he play for?
19 Frenchman Christophe Dugarry had a spell with which Midlands club?
20 How old was Wayne Rooney when he first played in the Premiership?
21 Which Darren earned the nickname "Sicknote" at Tottenham?
22 Which former Oldham defender played over 300 games for Man Utd?
23 Which club had a group of high-living players dubbed "The Spice Boys"?
24 Which club did Nigel Winterburn move to after 400-plus games for Arsenal?
25 Who was the last Englishman to manage Chelsea?
26 Reid, Wilkinson, Cotterill and McCarthy all managed which club in a relegation season?
27 Who was sent off for an on field fight with his Newcastle team-mate Kieron Dyer?
28 David O'Leary took over at Aston Villa from which manager?
29 Which England striker James went from Southampton to Everton?
30 In which season did Roy Keane last win the Premiership with Man Utd?

Answers	Food and Drink: Wine *(see Quiz 41)*

1 Bordeaux. 2 Brut. 3 Australia. 4 Chardonnay. 5 New Zealand. 6 Greece. 7 Madeira. 8 75 centilitres. 9 Spain. 10 Loire. 11 White. 12 Louis Pasteur. 13 Case. 14 Bulgaria. 15 California. 16 Jancis. 17 South Africa. 18 Eight. 19 Sparkling. 20 Tuscany. 21 Medium sweet. 22 Ruby, tawny and vintage. 23 Rosé. 24 Chile. 25 Beaujolais. 26 China. 27 Sherry. 28 Champagne. 29 Jilly Goolden. 30 Rhine.

1 Where is a fish's caudal fin?
2 What colour are the spots on a plaice?
3 What sort of fish is a skipjack?
4 Which family does the anchovy belong to?
5 Caviare is which part of the sturgeon?
6 Tinca tinca is the Latin name of which fish?
7 Alevin and parr are stages in the development of which fish?
8 What is the world's largest fish?
9 What is a young pilchard called?
10 What colour is a live lobster?
11 From which part of the cod is a beneficial oil produced?
12 The minnow is the smallest member of which family?
13 What is pisciculture?
14 Which fish has been nicknamed "tin plate"?
15 What is a buckie another name for?
16 What sort of fish is a dogfish?
17 What is a dogfish called when it is bought for food?
18 Which type of crab lives in hollow objects such as snail shells?
19 Where is a fish's dorsal fin?
20 Which fish has the varieties brown, sea or rainbow?
21 How many arms does a squid have?
22 Who wrote "The Compleat Angler"?
23 Flounder is a common name for which type of fish?
24 What are brisling also called?
25 Where would you find barbels on a fish?
26 What starts an oyster developing a pearl in its shell?
27 Which fish has the same name as an early infantry weapon?
28 Which fish is also called goatfish or surmullet?
29 What is another name for the common European sole?
30 What is a geoduck?

Answers | **Pot-Luck 19** *(see Quiz 42)*

1 Claudio Ranieri. 2 France. 3 Public Employees. 4 Salisbury. 5 Lou Reed. 6 Austria and Italy. 7 Lemon and melon. 8 Coxswain. 9 Confluence. 10 Soh. 11 Four. 12 The Cam. 13 Diameter. 14 Open University. 15 Hair. 16 Paul Burrell. 17 Naturalist. 18 Green. 19 Lace. 20 The Archers. 21 Home Secretary. 22 Karl Marx. 23 Murdered your father. 24 Eeyore. 25 Lake District. 26 Tate Modern. 27 Jericho. 28 Prayer meeting. 29 White. 30 Mary Poppins.

1 In Sudoku, what is the total of a square containing each number used once?

2 Which device is used on a guitar fretboard to raise the pitch of the strings?

3 Which king was reigning in Britain at the start of the First World War?

4 In imperial measurement, how many yards are in a chain?

5 What kind of tree is an osier?

6 On TV, "who was feared by the bad, loved by the good"?

7 With what do you play a vibraphone?

8 On a ship what are the scuppers?

9 At which club did Stuart Pearce end his playing days?

10 Who became ruler of Spain after the Spanish Civil War?

11 In literature, how many Arabian Nights were there?

12 Which singer said, "You're not drunk if you can lie on the floor without holding on"?

13 Black, Italian and Lombardy are all types of which tree?

14 In which war was the Battle of Jutland?

15 What is the square root of 169?

16 Which star of the movie "Mr and Mrs Smith" is a Goodwill Ambassador to the UN?

17 What is the name given to the lowest layer of the atmosphere?

18 What was added to rum to make the drink grog?

19 In London where is Poet's Corner?

20 In which country did the former Foreign Secretary Robin Cook die?

21 For which of these games would you use dice: ludo, whist, hopscotch, snakes-and-ladders?

22 What instrument would you use to measure the diameter of a cylinder?

23 In which month is Michaelmas Day?

24 In which English county would you find the coastal resort of California?

25 Which former Spice Girl recorded the album "Beautiful Intentions"?

26 For what is Elizabeth Fry chiefly remembered?

27 What fruit do we get from a rose?

28 What was Cleo Laine's job before she was a singer?

29 Which ocean is crossed to sail from San Francisco to Sydney?

30 Who was the British member of the Monkees?

Answers | Pot-Luck 21 (see Quiz 47)

1 Yew. 2 Greece. 3 Maurice Gibb. 4 Portugal. 5 Gordon Strachan. 6 It had no toes.
7 Computer languages. 8 Five and a half. 9 Michael Ball. 10 Model T Ford. 11 Max
Wall. 12 Watt. 13 Straws. 14 A spy or informer. 15 The Gruffalo's Child. 16 Stitches.
17 The Merchant of Venice. 18 Bob Dylan. 19 Adam Ant. 20 By rubbing its legs
against its wings or together. 21 Massachusetts. 22 Stephen. 23 Tennis. 24 Wore
them. They are very wide trousers. 25 Paris. 26 Charles Edward Stuart. 27 Brendan
Cole. 28 Georgia. 29 George Clooney. 30 Thomas.

Quiz 46 | Pop: Dance and Disco | Answers – page 172

1 Which dance favourite became Kylie's first UK million-seller?
2 Which Village People chart hit was made up of initial letters?
3 Which boy's name took Sister Sledge to No 1 in 1985?
4 Cheryl Jones and Sandra Denton spiced up their names to what?
5 Who recorded the 2002 No 1 album "Come with Us"?
6 Which Doors song was given the disco treatment by Amii Stewart?
7 In which song does the line "Too Ra Loo Ra Loo Rye Aye" appear?
8 Which girl group backed Disco Tex?
9 Who was too sexy in 1991?
10 Whose name comes before the Mastermixers?
11 Which Richie Valens 1950s hit charted for Los Lobos in 1987?
12 Who was "Never Gonna Give You Up" in 1987?
13 Who did Madonna tell "don't preach" in the 1986 No 1?
14 Which country do Black Box come from?
15 Who recorded "Funky Stuff" and "Jungle Boogie"?
16 Which group found success in the 1970s with "Night Fever"?
17 Who teamed up with Take That in "Relight My Fire"?
18 Who recorded "Wham Rap"?
19 Who else was on "Keep On Pumpin' It" along with the Visionmasters and Tony Knight?
20 What was on the B side of Boney M's "Rivers of Babylon"?
21 Which disco hit singer thought that "Love's Unkind"?
22 What was a No 1 for The Simpsons?
23 Who had "A Night to Remember" in 1982?
24 While Tina Charles loved to love, what did her baby love to do?
25 In his baggy trousers, what name is rapper Stanley Burrell known as?
26 Who had "Heartache" in 1987?
27 Who had a 2001 dance hit with "Clint Eastwood"?
28 Who recorded the 1970s disco song "You're My First My Last My Everything"?
29 Who is credited on "Lady Marmalade" along with Christina Aguilera, Lil' Kim and Mya?
30 How is Robert Bell better known?

Answers	Around Europe *(see Quiz 48)*

1 Albania. 2 Oberammergau. 3 Yugoslavia. 4 Malta. 5 Austria's. 6 Spain and Portugal. 7 The Hague. 8 Strait, Turkey. 9 Munich. 10 Greece. 11 Italy. 12 Liechtenstein. 13 Baltic. 14 France, Italy, Switzerland and Austria. 15 Russia. 16 Cologne. 17 Iceland. 18 Denmark and Norway. 19 Moldova. 20 The Netherlands. 21 Belgium. 22 Lorraine and Nancy. 23 Denmark. 24 Mont Blanc. 25 Germany's. 26 Bulgaria. 27 Finnish and Swedish. 28 Red Cross. 29 The Algarve. 30 Ukraine.

1 From which wood were longbows made?

2 In which country is the Corinth Canal?

3 Which member of the Bee Gees died following a stomach operation in 2003?

4 Of which European country are Madeira and the Azores a part?

5 Who managed Southampton when they reached the 2003 FA Cup Final?

6 In a poem by Edward Lear, what was peculiar about the "Pobble"?

7 Pascal, Cobol and Basic are all types of what?

8 In yards, how long was a rod, pole, or perch?

9 Which musical theatre star released his "Love Changes Everything" album in 2004?

10 What is or was a tin lizzie?

11 Which comedian's catch phrase was, "Now there's a funny thing"?

12 What name is given to the unit of electrical power?

13 According to the proverb what do drowning men clutch?

14 What is a copper's nark?

15 What was the sequel to the popular children's picture book "The Gruffalo" called?

16 Back, blanket and buttonhole are all types of what?

17 In which Shakespeare play is Shylock introduced?

18 Which folk singer wrote the song "The Times They are A-Changin'"?

19 In pop, who was King of the wild frontier?

20 How does a grasshopper produce its distinctive sound?

21 Of which US state is Boston the capital?

22 Who came to the throne of England on the death of Henry I?

23 With which sport do you associate Rosemary Casals?

24 What did people do with Oxford bags?

25 In which city is Sacré Coeur?

26 Who assumed the guise of Betty Burke?

27 Whom did both Natasha Kaplinsky and Fiona Phillips partner on "Strictly Come Dancing"?

28 Which is the home state of former president Jimmy Carter?

29 Who co starred with Catherine Zeta Jones in the movie "Intolerable Cruelty"?

30 What is Sean Connery's real first name?

Answers | Pot-Luck 20 (see Quiz 45)

1 45 (Numbers 1 to 9). 2 Capo. 3 George V. 4 22. 5 Willow. 6 Robin Hood. 7 With small mallets. 8 Holes to allow water to run off the deck. 9 Man City. 10 General Franco. 11 1001. 12 Dean Martin. 13 Poplar. 14 First World War. 15 13. 16 Angelina Jolie. 17 The troposphere. 18 Water. 19 Westminster Abbey. 20 Scotland. 21 Ludo and snakes-and-ladders. 22 Callipers. 23 September (29th). 24 Norfolk. 25 Melanie C. 26 Prison reform. 27 Hips. 28 Hairdresser. 29 Pacific. 30 Davy Jones.

1 Which country's capital is Tirana?

2 Where is a passion play staged every ten years?

3 Which state was Macedonia part of from 1945 to 1991?

4 Which island holds the George Cross?

5 Which country's highest mountain is the Grossglockner?

6 Which countries are on the Iberian Peninsula?

7 Where is the Netherlands' seat of government and administration?

8 What are the Dardanelles and where are they?

9 Which southern German city is famous for its October beer festival?

10 Which country is called Elleniki Dimokratia or Hellenic Republic?

11 Which country's chief river is the Po?

12 Which country, whose capital is Vaduz, has no armed forces?

13 Which sea lies to the north of Poland?

14 In which four countries are the Alps?

15 Which country covers 10% of the globe's land surface?

16 By what English name is Köln known?

17 Which country's landscape is made up of volcanoes and geysers?

18 Between which countries does the Skagerrak lie?

19 What are Bessarabia, Moldavia and a former part of the USSR now known as?

20 Which country has had a prime minister called Wim Kok?

21 Albert II became king of which country in 1993?

22 A region of eastern France has a girl's name with another girl's name as its capital. What are they?

23 Which country do Greenland and the Faeroe Islands belong to?

24 What is France's highest point?

25 Whose upper house of Parliament is called the Bundesrat?

26 Which country's currency is the lev?

27 What are the two official languages of Finland?

28 Which aid organization's emblem is the Swiss flag with its colours reversed?

29 Which Portuguese province borders Spain and the Atlantic Ocean?

30 Which is Europe's largest country after Russia?

Answers	Pop: Dance and Disco *(see Quiz 46)*

1 Can't Get You Out of My Head. 2 YMCA. 3 Frankie. 4 Salt 'N' Pepa. 5 Chemical Brothers. 6 Light My Fire. 7 Come On Eileen by Dexy's Midnight Runners. 8 The Sex-O-Lettes. 9 Right Said Fred. 10 Jive Bunny. 11 La Bamba. 12 Rick Astley. 13 Papa. 14 Italy. 15 Kool and the Gang. 16 The Bee Gees. 17 Lulu. 18 Wham! 19 Kylie Minogue. 20 Brown Girl in the Ring. 21 Donna Summer. 22 Do the Bartman. 23 Shalamar. 24 Dance. 25 M. C. Hammer. 26 Pepsi and Shirlie. 27 Gorillaz. 28 Barry White. 29 Pink. 30 Kool, of Kool and the Gang.

1 What is the longest-running children's TV programme?
2 Who host Dick and Dom in "Da Bungalow"?
3 "Can We Fix It" relates to which handyman?
4 In which country is "Balamory" set?
5 Which village's postmistress is called Mrs Goggins?
6 What was "Fingermouse" made from?
7 Who fought against Bulk and Texas Pete?
8 Who presented his own "Cartoon Time" and "Cartoon Club"?
9 Which three singers from "Rainbow" were given their own series?
10 Which show ended ruefully with "Bye bye, everybody, bye bye"?
11 Which show was first presented by Emma Forbes and Andi Peters?
12 Was the 2005 show "Raven" a fantasy game show or a wildlife programme?
13 Which family had a daily help called Mrs Scrubbitt?
14 Which magazine programme had a mascot called Murgatroyd?
15 What sort of animal was Parsley in "The Herbs"?
16 Who had magical adventures and lived at 52 Festive Road?
17 Which pre-school programme was the first programme on BBC2?
18 The characters Bella and Milo appeared in which show?
19 Who were Andy Pandy's two best friends?
20 In which 1980s/1990s series did Robin of Islington and Little Ron appear?
21 In which show for the under fives did the Muppets first appear?
22 In "Rag, Tag and Bobtail" which was the hedgehog?
23 What was the registration number of Lady Penelope's pink Rolls?
24 Who is associated with the catchphrase "Get down, Shep"?
25 Which show was TV's answer to the Guinness Book of Records?
26 Where do the Hoobs come from?
27 Who took over from Phillip Schofield as presenter of Children's BBC?
28 In which county was Camberwick Green?
29 Who gave his name to the early bulletins of "Newsround"?
30 What is the logo on a Blue Peter badge?

1 Two. 2 Stone. 3 Oak or blackthorn. 4 Belfast. 5 Shannon. 6 Lough Neagh. 7 Lead-zinc. 8 Lava. 9 Enniskillen. 10 Mountains of Mourne. 11 Cork. 12 Abbey Theatre. 13 Macgillicuddy's Reeks. 14 Golden Vale. 15 Antrim, Armagh. 16 Queen's. 17 Mountain peaks. 18 St Brigit. 19 TV listings. 20 Smoking. 21 Waterford. 22 The Twelve Bens. 23 Hills. 24 Queen's County. 25 Leinster. 26 Bells. 27 Kerry, Kildare, Kilkenny. 28 Sligo. 29 University of Ulster. 30 Armagh, Belfast, Derry/Londonderry.

1 Which country staged the last FIFA World Cup Final of the 20th century outside Europe?

2 Who created a garden at Sissinghurst in Kent?

3 Who recorded the album "Odyssey"?

4 What is Prince William's second name?

5 What chicken dish is named after a battle of the Napoleonic Wars?

6 In 2005 at which ground did England beat Australia by two runs?

7 Which "Cutting It" star appeared in the movie "The Wedding Date"?

8 Which famous writer was married to archaeologist Sir Max Mallowan?

9 Who invented the Flying Shuttle in 1733?

10 What kind of gas was used in the trenches during World War I?

11 Who sang "Islands in the Stream"?

12 Which Sondheim musical tells the story of a murdering barber?

13 What breed of retriever takes its name from a North American bay?

14 What does a Geiger Counter measure?

15 In which "ology", founded in the early 1950s, is self-awareness paramount?

16 Which star of "The X Files" appeared in the 2005 UK TV drama "Bleak House"?

17 Who defeated Richard III at Bosworth in 1485?

18 Which Hollywood actress's real name was Lucille Le Sueur?

19 Beaumaris, Conway and Harlech are famous for what type of building?

20 Whom did the religious assassins known as Thugs worship?

21 If you were an LLD what profession would you be involved in?

22 Which famous brothers made a movie called "A Night at the Opera"?

23 What is a tine?

24 Who was the first regular female presenter of "Points of View"?

25 Which William featured in the title of a Benjamin Britten opera?

26 Which country was invaded during Operation Barbarossa?

27 Which famous children's author and artist lived and worked in the Lake District for much of her life?

28 How many of Henry VIII's wives were called Anne?

29 What did miners use to find out if there was gas in a pit?

30 Of which party were Bill Rodgers and Roy Jenkins founder members?

Answers | Pot-Luck 23 *(see Quiz 52)*

1 Henry Cooper. 2 Her father, King George VI. 3 Barium. 4 Sociology. 5 For the Good Times. 6 William III and Mary II. 7 New Zealander. 8 Greek Orthodox. 9 Leda. 10 Sealed with a loving kiss. 11 Alec Guinness. 12 The stamen. 13 The Prince of Wales. 14 William Wilberforce. 15 Marshal Blücher. 16 Lee Dixon. 17 Independent on Sunday. 18 Rare (noble or inert gases). 19 Canterbury. 20 The Acts of the Apostles, 1. 21 Laurence Dallaglio. 22 Nicole. 23 Physiologists. 24 Ombrophobia. 25 Dollywood. 26 Ewan McGregor. 27 Susan Coolidge. 28 Odin. 29 Delano. 30 Lieutenant Pinkerton.

Quiz 51

Around Ireland

Answers – page 173

1 How many wheels does a jaunting car have?
2 On what would you see Ogham writing?
3 Which of two kinds of wood can a shillelagh be made from?
4 In which city is the Maze Prison?
5 Which is Ireland's chief river?
6 Which lake is the British Isles' largest?
7 What is the mine at Navan famous for?
8 What are the columns of the Giant's Causeway made from?
9 What is the county town of Fermanagh?
10 Which mountains stretch from Carlingford Lough to Dundrum Bay?
11 Which county's Irish name is Corcaigh?
12 What is Dublin's most famous theatre called?
13 What are the highest uplands in Ireland?
14 What is the name of the fertile vale in Limerick?
15 Which two of the counties of Northern Ireland begin with A?
16 What is Belfast's university called?
17 What are Slieve Donard and Slieve Commedagh?
18 Whose Saint's day is celebrated on 2nd February?
19 If you bought the RTE Guide what information would you receive?
20 In the early years of this millennium what was banned from pubs in Ireland?
21 Which is further north, Waterford or Cork?
22 What are the quartzite mountains in Connemara called?
23 What are drumlins?
24 What did Laoighis used to be called?
25 Which province of southeast Ireland includes the counties of Wexford and Wicklow?
26 What is St Ann's Shaldon Church famous for?
27 Which three counties of the Republic of Ireland begin with K?
28 Which county do Westlife come from?
29 Which university is at Coleraine?
30 Which three places in Northern Ireland may officially use the title "city"?

Answers | Children's TV (see Quiz 49)

1 Blue Peter. 2 Richard McCourt & Dominic Wood. 3 Bob the Builder. 4 Scotland. 5 Greendale. 6 Paper. 7 SuperTed. 8 Rolf Harris. 9 Rod, Jane and Freddy. 10 Sooty. 11 Live and Kicking. 12 Fantasy game show. 13 The Woodentops. 14 Magpie. 15 Lion. 16 Mr Benn. 17 Play School. 18 The Tweenies. 19 Teddy and Looby Loo. 20 Maid Marian and Her Merry Men. 21 Sesame Street. 22 Rag. 23 FAB1. 24 John Noakes. 25 Record Breakers. 26 Hoobland. 27 Andy Crane. 28 Trumptonshire. 29 John Craven. 30 Ship.

Quiz 52 | Pot-Luck 23 | Answers – page 174

1 Which English boxer had Muhammad Ali (Cassius Clay) on the floor?
2 Who bought Queen Elizabeth II her first corgi?
3 Which highly insoluble substance is opaque to X-rays?
4 What is the study and functioning of human societies called?
5 "Lay your head upon my pillow" appears in which Perry Como song?
6 Which king and queen ruled Britain jointly from 1689 to 1694?
7 What nationality was detective writer Ngaio Marsh?
8 What branch of Christianity still flourishes in Russia?
9 Whom did Zeus seduce when he assumed the guise of a swan?
10 What does "SWALK" stand for?
11 On TV, who played George Smiley in "Smiley's People"?
12 What is the male reproductive organ of a plant called?
13 In the song, "I danced with a man, who danced with a girl who danced with..." whom?
14 Which William was concerned with abolishing slavery?
15 Who commanded the Prussian troops at the Battle of Waterloo?
16 Which veteran full-back was part of Arsenal's 2002 double winning squad?
17 Which Sunday newspaper first featured extracts from Bridget Jones's Diary in the mid 1990s?
18 Krypton, neon, radon, xenon and helium are what kind of gases?
19 Mo Mowlam spent her final days in which city?
20 In the Bible, which book comes after Saint John?
21 Who resigned as England Rugby captain in 1999 following allegations concerning drugs?
22 Who is papa's daughter in the Renault ad?
23 The functioning of living organisms is the concern of which "ologists"?
24 What is fear of rain called?
25 What is Dolly Parton's theme park in Tennessee called?
26 Which star of "Star Wars" also starred in "Guys and Dolls" in the West End?
27 Who wrote the "What Katy Did Next"?
28 Who was Thor's father?
29 What did the "D" stand for in Franklin D. Roosevelt?
30 Which American told Madam Butterfly that he loved her?

Answers | Pot-Luck 22 *(see Quiz 50)*

1 USA. 2 Vita Sackville-West. 3 Hayley Westenra. 4 Arthur. 5 Chicken Marengo.
6 Edgbaston. 7 Sarah Parish. 8 Agatha Christie. 9 John Kay. 10 Mustard gas. 11 Kenny Rogers and Dolly Parton. 12 Sweeney Todd. 13 Chesapeake Bay Retriever. 14 Radioactivity. 15 Scientology. 16 Gillian Anderson. 17 Henry VII. 18 Joan Crawford. 19 Castles. 20 The goddess Kali. 21 The legal profession (Doctor of Law). 22 The Marx Brothers. 23 The prong of a fork. 24 Anne Robinson. 25 Billy Budd. 26 USSR. 27 Beatrix Potter. 28 Two. 29 Caged birds. 30 The Social Democratic Party.

Quiz 53 | Sport: Tennis

Answers – page 179

1 Who was the first unseeded man to win Wimbledon?
2 Which tennis star married Tatum O'Neal?
3 How many times did Martina Navratilova win the Wimbledon singles?
4 What was Evonne Goolagong's married name?
5 Which Australian pair dominated the men's doubles in the late 1960s?
6 Who is the only black American to have won the men's singles at Wimbledon?
7 Who is Czech Cyril Suk's famous sister?
8 In which year did Ivan Lendl win Wimbledon?
9 Which British pair won the Wimbledon mixed doubles in 1987?
10 Roger Federer hails from which country?
11 Which woman French player won the Australian Open in 1995?
12 Who is the elder of the two tennis-playing Williams sisters?
13 Which cup for women was contested between the US and Britain?
14 Where is the final of the US Open played?
15 Which US champion was married to British player John Lloyd?
16 Who was the first male tennis player to win 100 tournaments?
17 Which two women competed in the all-British Wimbledon final in 1961?
18 What is the international team competition for men called?
19 What are the colours of the All England Lawn Tennis Club?
20 In 1996, 1997, 2003 and 2004 Tim Henman went out of Wimbledon at which stage?
21 What did line judge Dorothy Brown do in a 1964 Wimbledon match?
22 Whom did Virginia Wade beat in the final to win Wimbledon in 1977?
23 Which German won the Wimbledon men's singles in 1991?
24 Who won his first US Open title in 1990?
25 Which American won the ladies' singles and doubles at Wimbledon in 1999?
26 What is the surface of the courts at Roland Garros in Paris?
27 Why did Catherine McTavish make Wimbledon history in 1979?
28 Which Greek Cypriot lost the men's final at the Australian Open in 2006?
29 What is the score in tennis when the tie break is introduced?
30 Which sisters won Olympic gold in tennis in 2000?

Answers	Pop: Duos *(see Quiz 55)*

1 Chas and Dave. 2 Wake Up Little Suzie. 3 Husband. 4 Wham! 5 Sweet Dreams (are Made of This). 6 Donkey. 7 Simon and Garfunkel. 8 Lionel Richie. 9 Opportunity Knocks. 10 Kiki Dee. 11 Esther and Abi. 12 L. S. Lowry. 13 Gimme Dat Ding. 14 Love you. 15 Marvin Gaye. 16 Everly Brothers. 17 Mel and Kim. 18 One. 19 Charles and Eddie. 20 Soft Cell. 21 Phil Spector. 22 John Travolta and Olivia Newton-John. 23 The World. 24 Roger Whittaker, Des O'Connor. 25 Erasure. 26 Chemical Brothers. 27 Nomad. 28 One. 29 Homeward Bound. 30 Pet Shop Boys.

1 What kind of dancer was Mr Bojangles?

2 Who secretly married Kevin Federline in 2005?

3 Where did William III defeat a French and Irish army in 1690?

4 In the 1990s, which British manager won successive titles with PSV Eindhoven?

5 What was American inventor Thomas Edison's middle name?

6 What does hydrogen combine with to form water?

7 Where in the House of Lords do peers with no party loyalties sit?

8 What is the northernmost point of the British mainland?

9 Which cartoon cat is the creation of Jim Davis?

10 What is the process by which plants use light to make food?

11 Which branch of medical science is concerned with muscle?

12 Which actor's real name was Reginald Carey?

13 Prince George of Denmark was the husband of which English queen?

14 What was the true vocation of the detective in the stories by G. K. Chesterton?

15 In darts, who won the World Masters five times between 1977 and 1984?

16 Whom did Orpheus attempt to rescue from the underworld?

17 In the song, how many little girls were in the back seat a-kissin' and a-huggin' with Fred?

18 What does ENO stand for?

19 A plant produced by crossing different species is known as what?

20 What was the Birmingham Royal Ballet previously known as?

21 Who were the hosts of football's African Cup of Nations in 2006?

22 On what day in 1939 did Britain declare war on Germany?

23 Which French writer lived with the composer Chopin?

24 Which TV chef presented a "French Odyssey" in 2005?

25 What is the most abundant gas in the atmosphere?

26 Who was the first woman elected to the British Parliament?

27 Where on the human body is the skin the thinnest?

28 What nationality was the Pope who succeeded Pope John Paul II?

29 Which actress replaced Amanda Burton as the forensic scientist in "Silent Witness"?

30 Which "ology" is concerned with the study and treatment of crime?

Answers | Pot-Luck 25 *(see Quiz 56)*

1 Pythagoras. 2 Taxi driver. 3 Michael Foot. 4 She was her half-sister. 5 Jacqueline Wilson. 6 The Arctic Ocean. 7 Scandinavian. 8 Two. 9 Guy Ritchie. 10 Pampas grass. 11 Swan Lake. 12 Ewart. 13 Robert Baden-Powell. 14 Colleen McCullough. 15 The 1920s. 16 Hydrogen. 17 Glenn Hoddle. 18 Red. 19 Borzoi. 20 212 degrees. 21 Palaeontology. 22 Michael Buerk. 23 James VI of Scotland, who was James I of England. 24 Call for the Dead. 25 David and Victoria Beckham. 26 Diana. 27 M. 28 Mimi's (in La Bohème). 29 Lancelot. 30 Andrew Lloyd Webber.

1 How are Messrs Hodges and Peacock better known?
2 "It's four o'clock and we're in trouble deep" comes from which Everly Brothers song?
3 What relation was Sonny to Cher in their single-making days?
4 Pepsi and Shirlie provided backing vocals for which superstar group?
5 What was the first Eurythmics top ten single back in 1983?
6 What little animal did Nina and Frederick sing about?
7 Which duo were made up of Paul and Art?
8 Whom did Diano Ross duo with on "Endless Love"?
9 Which TV show gave Peters and Lee their first break?
10 Whom did Elton John sing with on his first British No 1?
11 What were the first names of the Ofarims?
12 Which artist did Brian and Michael sing about?
13 What was the Pipkins' only hit?
14 According to Peter and Gordon, to know you is to do what?
15 "It Takes Two" featured Tammi Terrell and who else?
16 Which duo has spent most weeks in the UK single charts?
17 Who were respectable in 1987?
18 How many of duo Miki and Griff were female?
19 Which duo had a No 1 with "Would I Lie to You"?
20 Which duo comprised Marc Almond and David Ball?
21 Who produced Ike and Tina Turner's "River Deep Mountain High"?
22 Which male/female singing duo had 16 weeks at No 1 in 1978?
23 According to "Tears for Fears", what did everyone want to rule?
24 Which duo charted with the "The Skye Boat Song"?
25 Which duo appeared in drag in an Abba tribute?
26 Tom Rowlands and Ed Simons make up which production dance duo?
27 Who charted with "(I Wanna Give You) Devotion"?
28 How many girls in the duo Everything but the Girl?
29 Which Simon and Garfunkel song starts "I'm sitting in a railway station"?
30 How are Christopher Lowe and Neil Tennant better known?

Answers | Tennis (see Quiz 53)

1 Boris Becker. 2 John McEnroe. 3 Nine. 4 Cawley. 5 Newcombe and Roche. 6 Arthur Ashe. 7 Helena Sukova. 8 He never won it. 9 Jeremy Bates & Jo Durie. 10 Switzerland. 11 Mary Pierce. 12 Venus. 13 Wightman Cup. 14 Flushing Meadow. 15 Chris Evert. 16 Jimmy Connors. 17 Christine Truman and Angela Mortimer. 18 Davis Cup. 19 Green and purple. 20 Quarter-finals. 21 Fell asleep. 22 Betty Stove. 23 Michael Stich. 24 Pete Sampras. 25 Lindsay Davenport. 26 Clay. 27 Its first woman umpire. 28 Marcos Baghdatis. 29 Six games all. 30 Venus and Serena Williams.

1 Whose famous theorem is concerned with the sums of the squares of the sides of right-angled triangles?

2 What was "Mastermind" winner Fred Housego's job?

3 Whom did Neil Kinnock succeed as leader of the Labour Party?

4 What relation was Mary I to Elizabeth I?

5 Which lady novelist was children's laureate in 2005?

6 Which ocean lies to the north of Russia?

7 In which mythology does Yggdrasil feature?

8 How many step children does Prince Charles have?

9 Who directed the 2005 movie "Revolver"?

10 What is Cortaderia selloana better known as?

11 Of which ballet is Prince Siegfried hero?

12 What was William Gladstone's middle name?

13 Who led the British forces during the Siege of Mafeking?

14 Who wrote "The Thorn Birds"?

15 In which decade did John Logie Baird invent television?

16 What gas is given off by pouring dilute sulphuric acid on to granulated zinc?

17 Who was England's coach in France 98?

18 What colour is the "This is Your Life" book?

19 What is another name for the Russian wolfhound?

20 What is the boiling point of water on the Fahrenheit Scale?

21 Which "ology" is concerned with fossils?

22 Which reporter fronted the film footage that sparked off Band Aid?

23 Whose nickname was "the Wisest Fool in Christendom"?

24 In which book did John le Carré's George Smiley first appear?

25 The aftershave Instinct was created by which married couple?

26 A temple to whom was sited at Ephesus?

27 Who was 007's boss?

28 In opera, whose tiny hand was frozen?

29 What was landscape gardener Capability Brown's real first name?

30 Which composer had a Broadway hit with "Song and Dance"?

Answers | Pot-Luck 24 *(see Quiz 54)*

1 A tap dancer. 2 Britney Spears. 3 At the Battle of the Boyne. 4 Bobby Robson. 5 Alva. 6 Oxygen. 7 On the cross benches. 8 Dunnet Head. 9 Garfield. 10 Photosynthesis. 11 Myology. 12 Rex Harrison. 13 Queen Anne. 14 He was a Catholic priest. 15 Eric Bristow. 16 Eurydice. 17 Seven. 18 English National Opera. 19 A hybrid. 20 Sadlers Wells Opera Ballet. 21 Egypt. 22 3rd September. 23 George Sand. 24 Rick Stein. 25 Nitrogen. 26 Countess Markievicz. 27 On the eye. 28 German. 29 Emilia Fox. 30 Criminology.

1 In which month in 1914 did the First World War begin?

2 What were people told to "keep burning" in the hit song of 1914?

3 What was the occupation of Edith Cavell, who was shot by the Germans on a spying charge?

4 Who became Prime Minister of Britain in 1916?

5 What did George V ban in his household to encourage others to do the same, and help the war effort?

6 In the 1915 song where did you "Pack Up Your Troubles"?

7 How did Lord Kitchener die?

8 At which battle in 1916 were there said to be a million fatalities?

9 Which new weapon was introduced in battle in 1916?

10 What was the 1914–18 war known as until 1939?

11 What was the nationality of dancer Mata Hari, shot as a spy?

12 In which year did the United States enter the First World War?

13 Why were British soldiers called Tommies (short for Tommy Atkins)?

14 Which new British military force was established in 1918?

15 The German attack on which country caused Britain to enter the Second World War?

16 Which German word meaning "lightning war" entered the English language?

17 According to the World War II poster what did "Careless Talk" do?

18 What was the nickname of anti-British broadcaster, William Joyce?

19 According to Churchill he had nothing to offer in 1940 but what?

20 Which great evacuation of 1940 was called Operation Dynamo?

21 What was the German air force called?

22 What were the Local Defence Volunteers renamed?

23 Which fruit was no longer imported after 1940?

24 Which US bandleader went missing over the Channel in 1944?

25 Where did the Bevin Boys work?

26 What was the popular name for pilotless aircraft, V-1s?

27 What was snoek?

28 Who commanded the Allied forces that invaded Europe on D-Day?

29 Which scantily clad female had a daily strip in the "Daily Mirror"?

30 In which French city did Germany surrender in World War II?

Answers | Pot-Luck 26 *(see Quiz 59)*

1 France. 2 Car crash. 3 Boris Karloff. 4 Henry Morton Stanley discovered David Livingstone. 5 Hydrogen. 6 Mrs Malaprop in Sheridan's The Rivals. 7 The Gordon setter (after the Duke of Richmond and Gordon). 8 John Mortimer. 9 Borsetshire. 10 George IV. 11 Sheridan. 12 Helicopter. 13 Phrenologists. 14 Richmal Crompton. 15 St Petersburg. 16 Two. 17 Kilohertz. 18 Nigeria. 19 Ivy 20 Scottish country dancing. 21 Flanders and Swan. 22 Rik Mayall. 23 Iris Murdoch. 24 Uranus. 25 One. 26 The Return of the King. 27 Nanette Newman. 28 Estonia. 29 Menelaus. 30 Congress.

1 Which country is Kiri Te Kanawa from?
2 What are the Christian names of the three tenors?
3 Which German composer's only opera was "Fidelio"?
4 Which Gilbert and Sullivan opera is set in the Tower of London?
5 Which composer from East Anglia wrote the opera "Peter Grimes"?
6 What was the nationality of ballet composer Aaron Copland?
7 What was the name of Gounod's opera based on Doctor Faustus?
8 How did Lehár describe the Widow in his operetta?
9 Who wrote "Madame Butterfly" and "La Bohème"?
10 Which opera does "Nessun Dorma" come from?
11 Which work did the Who call a rock opera?
12 Where was the Barber from in the title of Rossini's opera?
13 How is Kurt Weill's "Die Dreigroschenoper" better known?
14 What does an operetta have which an opera usually doesn't?
15 Which Russian dancer gave his name to a famous racehorse?
16 Who wrote the ballets "Swan Lake" and "The Nutcracker"?
17 Which surname is shared by composers Johann and Richard?
18 What was the profession of Frederick Ashton?
19 Which controversial dancer died when her scarf caught in the wheels of her sports car?
20 What is the religious equivalent of opera without costumes and scenery?
21 Which Russian ballerina gave her name to a meringue dessert?
22 Who was Margot Fonteyn's most famous dancing partner?
23 Which 2005 ballet was based on a Tim Burton/Johnny Depp film?
24 What is the nationality of Alicia Markova?
25 For which sporting event was "Nessun Dorma" a TV theme tune?
26 What is Lesley Garrett's home county?
27 Which Italian composer's English name would be Joseph Green?
28 Which Russian-born composer wrote "The Rite of Spring"?
29 In ballet what is a jeté?
30 In 2005, which Royal Ballet production did not have matinees as it was deemed too shocking?

Answers	Movies: Comedies *(see Quiz 60)*

1 My Big Fat Greek Wedding. 2 Daniel. 3 (Bend It Like) Beckham. 4 Bruce Willis. 5 Arnold Schwarzenegger. 6 City Under Siege. 7 Ghostbusters. 8 Jessica Lange. 9 Julia Roberts. 10 Paul Newman and Robert Redford. 11 Manhattan. 12 Dolly Parton. 13 Disney. 14 Mel Gibson. 15 Michael Caine. 16 Meg Ryan and Billy Crystal. 17 Stockbroker. 18 Carry On Sergeant. 19 Clouseau. 20 Priscilla Presley. 21 Three Men and a Little Lady. 22 Butch Cassidy and the Sundance Kid. 23 Scottish. 24 Maggie Smith. 25 A pig. 26 The Mafia. 27 Big. 28 St Valentine's Day Massacre. 29 Woody Allen. 30 Harpo and Groucho (Marx).

1 Yasser Arafat died in November 2004 in which country?
2 How did Princess Grace of Monaco die?
3 Which horror movie actor's real name is William Pratt?
4 Who "discovered" whom at Ujiji in 1871?
5 Which gas has the chemical symbol H?
6 Which character says, "He is the very pineapple of politeness"?
7 Which breed of setter is named after a British duke?
8 Who wrote "Paradise Postponed"?
9 In which fictional county do the Archers live?
10 Which George did the Prince Regent become?
11 What is Hyacinth Bucket's absentee son called?
12 The poster advertising "Miss Saigon" featured what type of transport?
13 Which "ologists" study bumps on the human head?
14 Who wrote the book "William the Detective"?
15 Which Russian city used to be called Leningrad?
16 How many faces did the Romans believe Janus to have?
17 kHz is an abbreviation for what?
18 Kanu of Arsenal and WBA played international football for which country?
19 Hedera helix is better known as what?
20 What kind of dances are Hamilton House and Petronella?
21 Which duo wrote and first recorded "Mud Mud, Glorious Mud"?
22 Who played the part of George in the TV family drama "All About George"?
23 Who wrote the novel "The Bell"?
24 Which planet did Herschel discover in 1781?
25 How many atoms of oxygen are there in one molecule of water?
26 What was the title of the third "Lord of the Rings" movie?
27 Who is Emma Forbes's mother?
28 The USSR annexed three Baltic states in 1940. Latvia and Lithuania were two: what was the third?
29 Who was Helen of Troy's husband?
30 What does the "C" in TUC stand for?

Answers | World Wars (see Quiz 57)

1 August. 2 Home fires. 3 Nurse. 4 Lloyd George. 5 Alcohol. 6 In your old kit bag.
7 Lost at sea. 8 Somme. 9 Tank. 10 The Great War. 11 Dutch. 12 1917. 13 Sample
name on recruitment form. 14 RAF. 15 Poland. 16 Blitzkrieg. 17 Costs Lives. 18
Lord Haw Haw. 19 Blood, toil, tears and sweat. 20 Dunkirk. 21 Luftwaffe. 22 Home
Guard. 23 Bananas. 24 Glenn Miller. 25 Coalmines. 26 Doodle-bug or buzz bomb.
27 Fish. 28 Eisenhower. 29 Jane. 30 Reims.

1 In which 2002 movie did Nia Vardalos play a frumpy waitress in her Greek family's restaurant?

2 Who is Bridget Jones' boss in "Bridget Jones' Diary"?

3 In the 2001 movie directed by Gurinder Chadha, which footballer's surname is in the title?

4 Who was the baby's voice in "Look Who's Talking"?

5 Which tough guy was the star of "Kindergarten Cop"?

6 What was the subtitle of "Police Academy 6"?

7 Which film was about the activities of unemployed parapsychologists in New York?

8 Who won an Oscar for "Tootsie"?

9 Who was Richard Gere's co-star in "Pretty Woman"?

10 Which actors played the two revenging con men in "The Sting"?

11 In which area of New York is "Crocodile Dundee" set?

12 Which country singer starred in "Nine to Five"?

13 Which studios produced "Honey I Shrunk the Kids"?

14 Who plays the chauvinistic advertising executive in "What Women Want"?

15 Which English actor starred in "The Muppet Christmas Carol"?

16 Who played the title roles in "When Harry Met Sally"?

17 What was the profession of the Patrick Swayze character in "Ghost"?

18 Which was the first "Carry On" film?

19 Who is the police inspector in "The Pink Panther" films?

20 Which late superstar's wife stars in "The Naked Gun" films?

21 What was the sequel to "Three Men and a Baby"?

22 Which film included the song "Raindrops Keep Fallin' on My Head"?

23 What was the nationality of Mrs Doubtfire in the film of the same name?

24 Who played the role of Wendy in "Hook"?

25 In the film "Babe" who or what is "Babe"?

26 Who is Whoopi Goldberg hiding from in "Sister Act"?

27 In which film is Tom Hanks a small boy in a grown man's body?

28 Which historic event triggers the plot in "Some Like It Hot"?

29 Who directed "Annie Hall" and "Match Point"?

30 Who were Chico, Gummo and Zeppo's two brothers?

Answers | Opera and Ballet *(see Quiz 58)*

1 New Zealand. 2 Placido (Domingo), José (Carreras) and Luciano (Pavarotti). 3 Beethoven. 4 The Yeomen of the Guard. 5 Benjamin Britten. 6 American. 7 Faust. 8 Merry. 9 Puccini. 10 Turandot. 11 Tommy. 12 Seville. 13 The Threepenny Opera. 14 Spoken dialogue. 15 Nijinsky. 16 Tchaikovsky. 17 Strauss. 18 Choreographer. 19 Isadora Duncan. 20 Oratorio. 21 Pavlova. 22 Rudolf Nureyev. 23 Edward Scissorhands. 24 English. 25 1990 World Cup. 26 Yorkshire. 27 Giuseppe Verdi. 28 Stravinsky. 29 Jump. 30 The Lesson.

1 Who wrote the music for the "The Threepenny Opera"?
2 Which botanist gave his name to fuchsias?
3 What nationality was ballet star Rudolf Nureyev?
4 Who is known as "The Big Yin"?
5 Which two countries fought for supremacy in the Punic Wars?
6 Who left an unfinished novel called "Sanditon"?
7 In which country did broadcaster John Peel die?
8 Sara Paretsky is known for writing what type of novels?
9 Who carried the spirits of dead warriors to Valhalla?
10 The Soviet secret police were known by their initials: what were they?
11 Who succeeded George Carey as Archbishop of Canterbury?
12 In the children's fiction what type of creature is the ballerina Angelina?
13 Which William was married to Mary II?
14 Who said, "To err is human but it feels divine"?
15 In which TV programme did John Humphrys take over from Magnus Magnusson?
16 In Indian cuisine, what vegetable is referred to as "Aloo"?
17 If an elderly couple are happily married whom are they likened to?
18 Who's real name is Sofia Scicolone?
19 Which sport is played at Rosslyn Park?
20 What do we call a period of play in polo?
21 Which country's name means the Saviour?
22 How many cents are there in a US nickel?
23 With which country do you associate the drink pernod?
24 Rudi Voller took which team to the 2002 World Cup tournament?
25 What do we call what the Spaniards call an autopista?
26 Of which country is Tripoli the capital?
27 If you had an escutcheon, what would be shown on it?
28 Which city has given its name to a wheelchair and to a bun?
29 Which animal is associated with Paddy McGinty?
30 How much in old money was a tanner?

1 How many of the four majors did Tiger Woods win in 2003 and 2004?
2 Which European No 1 golfer won the Hong Kong Open in 2005?
3 Who is nicknamed "The Great White Shark"?
4 Which actress did Sam Torrance marry?
5 What is the women's equivalent of the Ryder Cup?
6 Which European Open gave Seve Ballesteros his first-ever European win back in 1976?
7 Where does Ernie Els hail from?
8 What does the D stand for in Arnold D. Palmer?
9 What is a bunker known as in the United States?
10 What is the maximum number of clubs permitted in a golf bag?
11 Which English player scored a hole in one on the final day of the 1995 Ryder Cup?
12 Who was the first German to win the German Open?
13 Where is the "home of golf"?
14 In which year did Tiger Woods win his first Open Championship?
15 Which country does Michael Campbell come from?
16 In stroke play, what is the penalty for playing the wrong ball?
17 What do the initials PGA stand for?
18 What is the amateur's equivalent of the Ryder Cup?
19 At which "appetizing" course did Sandy Lyle win the 1985 British Open?
20 Who is "The Golden Bear"?
21 Which is the oldest golf club in England?
22 At what age can a player join the Seniors' Tour?
23 Name Europe's 1997 Ryder Cup captain?
24 Which Henry won his first British Open in 1934?
25 What nationality is golfer Vijay Singh?
26 Which British golfer won the British Open in 1969?
27 Which famous American played his last British Open in 1995?
28 In which tournament does a player win a green jacket?
29 Which country does former Open winner Paul Lawrie come from?
30 Ernie Els had surgery on which part of his anatomy in 2005?

Answers | Jazz and Blues *(see Quiz 64)*

1 Satchmo. 2 The Yardbirds. 3 Harry Connick Jnr. 4 Moscow. 5 Bessie Smith. 6 Petite Fleur. 7 Dave Brubeck. 8 Twentysomething. 9 Bluesbreakers. 10 Piano. 11 Kenny G. 12 Ronnie Scott. 13 Diana Ross. 14 Benny Goodman. 15 John Lee Hooker. 16 Cleo Laine. 17 Humphrey Lyttelton. 18 Little Walter. 19 Saxophone. 20 Peggy Lee. 21 Muddy Waters. 22 Buddy Rich. 23 France. 24 Long John Baldry. 25 Paramount. 26 Piano. 27 Clarinet. 28 Gary Moore. 29 John Dankworth. 30 Cream.

1 Who was the last person to hold both water and land speed records?
2 Who starred opposite Richard Gere in "Shall We Dance"?
3 Which high-profile UK serial killer was found hanged in his prison cell in January 2004?
4 In which park is the Serpentine?
5 Of which country is Baffin Island a part?
6 Who wrote the novel "Lord of the Flies"?
7 In South America, what is a gaucho?
8 What colour are the flowers of the hawthorn?
9 Which US writer created Tarzan?
10 Ipswich is the administrative headquarters of which English county?
11 What job is done by a concierge?
12 Which astronaut was the second man to set foot on the moon?
13 With what industry is the inventor Richard Arkwright associated?
14 What is the common name for calcium carbonate?
15 What do we call what the Germans call "Strumpfhose"?
16 In chess, how many squares can the king move at a time?
17 With which industry is the Royal Smithfield Show concerned?
18 On what type of surface is the sport of curling played?
19 Which militant Islamic group won a landslide victory in the 2006 Palestinian elections?
20 Whose book about her ex-husband was simply called "John"?
21 Who were the first landlords of the Rovers' Return?
22 Which French king was husband to Marie Antoinette?
23 What are bespoke clothes?
24 What can cats do with their claws that dogs cannot do?
25 According to the proverb, what shouldn't call the kettle black?
26 What sort of a holiday is it if you do the same thing as in your job?
27 Who played Elizabeth Bennet in the 2005 film of "Pride and Prejudice"?
28 What is a peruke?
29 England's Owen Hargreaves first played in a European Cup final for which club?
30 Luciana Barroso married which Hollywood actor in December 2005?

Answers | Pot-Luck 27 *(see Quiz 61)*

1 Kurt Weill. 2 Leonhard Fuchs. 3 Russian. 4 Billy Connolly. 5 Rome and Carthage. 6 Jane Austen. 7 Peru. 8 Crime novels. 9 The Valkyries. 10 KGB. 11 Rowan Williams. 12 Mouse. 13 William III. 14 Mae West. 15 Mastermind. 16 Potatoes. 17 Darby and Joan. 18 Sophia Loren. 19 Rugby Union. 20 Chukka. 21 El Salvador. 22 Five. 23 France. 24 Germany. 25 Motorway. 26 Libya. 27 Your coat of arms. 28 Bath. 29 Goat. 30 Six pence.

Quiz 64 | Jazz and Blues

Answers – page 186

1 What was Louis Armstrong's nickname?
2 Which 1960s band featured Eric Clapton and Jimmy Page?
3 Which singer recorded the "When Harry Met Sally" soundtrack?
4 In which city were Kenny Ball and his jazzmen at midnight?
5 Which 1920s blues singer recorded "Down Hearted Blues"?
6 What was Chris Barber's only hit single?
7 Whose quartet famously decided to "Take Five"?
8 What was Jamie Cullum's breakthrough album?
9 What was John Mayall's group known as?
10 What instrument did Earl Hines play?
11 Which jazz-funk saxophonist had a hit in 1987 with "Songbird"?
12 Which jazz musician opened a London club in 1959?
13 Who played Billie Holiday in the film "Lady Sings the Blues"?
14 Which clarinettist lived from 1909 to 1986 and had his "Story" told in a 1955 film?
15 Which veteran blues performer recorded "The Healer"?
16 How is singer Clementina Dinah Campbell better known?
17 Which trumpeter talks of Mornington Crescent in a radio panel game?
18 Under what name did Marion Walter Jacobs record?
19 What instrument is associated with Courtney Pine?
20 Who sang "He's a Tramp" in Disney's "Lady and the Tramp"?
21 Who recorded "Hoochie Coochie Man" and "Got My Mojo Working"?
22 Which virtuoso jazz drummer started out in a vaudeville act as Baby Trapps the Drum Wonder?
23 In which country was Alexis Korner born?
24 Which bluesman had a No 1 with "Let the Heartaches Begin"?
25 What was the name of Mr Acker Bilk's Jazz Band?
26 Which instrument does Jamie Cullum play?
27 What instrument is associated with Monty Sunshine?
28 Which guitarist released the album "Ballads and Blues"?
29 Who turned "Three Blind Mice" into "Experiments with Mice"?
30 Which group were formed by Bruce, Baker and Clapton?

Answers | Sport: Golf *(see Quiz 62)*

1 None. 2 Colin Montgomerie. 3 Greg Norman. 4 Suzanne Danielle. 5 Curtis Cup. 6 Dutch Open. 7 South Africa. 8 Daniel. 9 Trap. 10 14. 11 Howard Clark. 12 Bernhard Langer. 13 St Andrews. 14 2000. 15 New Zealand. 16 Two strokes. 17 Professional Golfers' Association. 18 Walker Cup. 19 Sandwich. 20 Jack Nicklaus. 21 Royal Blackheath, Kent. 22 50 years. 23 Seve Ballesteros. 24 Cotton. 25 Fijian. 26 Tony Jacklin. 27 Arnold Palmer. 28 US Masters. 29 Scotland. 30 Knee.

1 Which entertainer returned to London's West End as Scrooge in 2005?
2 Which ex-England soccer manager wrote "Farewell But Not Goodbye"?
3 By what name is Formosa now known?
4 What have Thistle, Brent and Ninian in common?
5 Who became queen of the Netherlands in 1980?
6 Who wrote the poem that begins, "Shall I compare thee to a summer's day"?
7 Singer Daniel Powter is from which country?
8 What is Al Pacino's full first name?
9 Provence and Brittany are both parts of which country?
10 Who played the scarecrow, Worzel Gummidge, on television?
11 Nowadays, who might wear a wimple?
12 Which country lies immediately south of Estonia?
13 In geography, what is a cataract?
14 Which English soccer team plays at home at Molyneux?
15 In America what is Airforce One?
16 With which sport do you associate Karen Pickering?
17 Who was the lead singer of the group, the Who?
18 What does the reference book, Crockfords, list?
19 What is Prince Charles' step son called?
20 Where in the body is the humerus?
21 In which country is the city of Jakarta?
22 As what did Grimaldi achieve fame?
23 In which US city is Grand Central Station?
24 Of which ancient empire was Nebuchadnezzar king?
25 In which art did Sir Henry Irving become famous?
26 When the sun is at its zenith, where is it?
27 The tears of which creatures are said to be a sign of insincere grief?
28 In which sport does the Harlequin Club compete?
29 For what achievement is Valentina Tereshkova famous?
30 In 2004, members of which organization attacked the PM with flour in the House of Commons?

Answers | Around Africa *(see Quiz 67)*

1 Zambia, Zimbabwe. 2 Sahara Desert. 3 Ethiopia. 4 Organization of African Unity. 5 Burkina Faso. 6 A wind. 7 Uganda. 8 Namibia. 9 Cocoa. 10 Victoria. 11 Kilimanjaro. 12 Portuguese. 13 Libya. 14 Nigeria. 15 Rwanda. 16 Dutch. 17 Victoria Falls. 18 Sahel. 19 Gold. 20 Casablanca. 21 Botswana. 22 Sudan. 23 Wildlife. 24 South Africa. 25 None, it is native to Asia not Africa. 26 Dams. 27 North. 28 Somalia. 29 A click, made in the throat. 30 Pretoria.

1 Which 2004 Oscar-winning actress was the face of L'Oréal in 2005?
2 Which former model is married to actor Leigh Lawson?
3 Which singer collaborated with Tommy Hilfiger on the "true star" series of perfumes?
4 Which model has been married to rock star Bill Wyman and footballer Pat Van Den Hauwe?
5 Which daughter of David Arquette and Courteney Cox shares a first name with a fashion legend?
6 Which supermodel's name was linked with Babyshambles front man Pete Doherty during a drugs scandal in 2005?
7 Who released a perfume called Stella in 2005?
8 Which cosmetic house did Liz Hurley become the face of in 1995?
9 Which famous photographer was Marie Helvin married to?
10 Which Oscar winner for "The Hours" advertised Chanel No 5?
11 Which designer is well known for her pink hair?
12 Which fruit gave its name to ex-model Debbie Moore's dance studio?
13 Which former model did Ringo Starr marry?
14 Who is the designer daughter of food critic Egon Ronay?
15 In what area of fashion is Barbara Daly famous?
16 Which famous hairdresser married Lulu?
17 Which garment is Jean-Paul Gaultier famous for wearing?
18 Who is the Frost half of the FrostFrench lingerie label?
19 Who said, "A woman is as young as her knees"?
20 Who designed Liz Hurley's famous "safety pin" dress?
21 Which model did Peter Andre marry in 2005?
22 What is the first name of designer St Laurent?
23 Which cosmetic house did Charles Revson found?
24 Which model has a daughter called Lila Grace?
25 Which pop singer was designer/TV presenter Jeff Banks married to?
26 Woodall and Constantine are the surnames of which fashion experts?
27 Which London street was famous for its 1960s boutiques?
28 Which hairdresser pioneered the geometric haircut in the 1960s?
29 Which Italian city is at the heart of the fashion industry?
30 Which Vivienne is famous for her outrageous designs?

Answers | Pot-Luck 30 (see Quiz 68)

1 Half a loaf. 2 Cat. 3 Bizet. 4 A rope. 5 Worcestershire sauce. 6 Kensington Gardens. 7 Franz Ferdinand. 8 Having the same centre. 9 Pinocchio. 10 The Pickwick Papers. 11 Bread. 12 Terry Pratchett. 13 Orlando. 14 Wines. 15 Cheeses. 16 Gwen Stefani. 17 Fashion leader. 18 Scotland. 19 Bob Monkhouse. 20 Fish. 21 Theatres. 22 South Africa. 23 John Bunyan. 24 Dressing. 25 1605. 26 D. H. Lawrence. 27 Candles. 28 You Raise Me Up. 29 Swan. 30 Silvio Berlusconi.

1 The names of which two African countries begin with the letter Z?
2 What covers 85% of Algeria?
3 Famine in which country triggered the Band Aid Charity?
4 What do the initials OAU stand for?
5 Of which country is Ouagadougou the capital?
6 What is the Harmattan?
7 Which is further west, Uganda or Kenya?
8 Which country used to be called South West Africa?
9 Which substance, used to make a drink, is Ghana's main export?
10 Which lake lies between Kenya, Tanzania and Uganda?
11 What is Africa's highest mountain?
12 Which European language is an official language of Angola?
13 In which African country is El Alamein, scene of a World War II battle?
14 Which country is the main economic power in West Africa?
15 Which country is further north, Rwanda or Burundi?
16 Which language is Afrikaans derived from?
17 Near which major landmark is the Boiling Pot?
18 What is the area of savanna in West Africa called?
19 South Africa is the world's leading exporter of what?
20 Which Moroccan city is the name of a famous film?
21 The Kalahari Desert lies chiefly in which country?
22 What is the largest country in Africa?
23 What is the Okavango Swamp famous for?
24 In which country are the political parties ANC and Inkatha?
25 Which African country is the tiger native to?
26 Which man-made structures would you see at Aswan and Kariba?
27 Does most of Africa lie to the north or to the south of the Equator?
28 Which country occupies the Horn of Africa?
29 Which sound is unique to many African languages including Xhosa?
30 What is the administrative capital of South Africa?

Answers | Pot-Luck 29 *(see Quiz 65)*

1 Tommy Steele. 2 Bobby Robson. 3 Taiwan. 4 All are (North Sea) oilfields. 5 Beatrix. 6 Shakespeare. 7 Canada. 8 Alfredo. 9 France. 10 Jon Pertwee. 11 A nun. 12 Latvia. 13 Waterfall. 14 Wolverhampton Wanderers. 15 The president's plane. 16 Swimming. 17 Roger Daltry. 18 The clergy of the Church of England. 19 Tom. 20 Upper arm. 21 Indonesia. 22 Clown. 23 New York. 24 Babylonia. 25 Theatre. 26 Directly overhead. 27 Crocodile. 28 Rugby Union. 29 She was the first woman in space. 30 Fathers 4 Justice.

Quiz 68 Pot-Luck 30

1 According to the proverb, what is better than no bread?
2 What kind of animal is a Persian Blue?
3 Who composed the opera "Carmen"?
4 On a ship or boat what is a painter?
5 What condiment is manufactured by Lea & Perrins?
6 Where in London is the statue of Peter Pan?
7 Alex Kapranos is the front man for which band?
8 In geometry, what is meant by concentric?
9 Which wooden puppet was first written about by Carlo Collodi?
10 In which of Dickens's novels does Sam Weller appear?
11 Which food, not rationed during World War II, was rationed after it?
12 Whose novels include "Going Postal" and "Thud!"?
13 What is the name of the marmalade cat created by Kathleen Hale?
14 For what is the Médoc area of France famous?
15 What are Cheshire, Gouda and Gorgonzola?
16 LAMB is the clothing line designed by which singer?
17 As what did Beau Brummel achieve fame?
18 Which country used to have a coin called a bawbee?
19 Who was the first presenter of "Family Fortunes"?
20 What do we call what the Italians call pesce?
21 In London, the Cambridge, the Lyric and the Adelphi are all what?
22 Of which country was Field-Marshal Smuts prime minister?
23 Which religious writer was born in Elstow, near Bedford?
24 What word can go after salad and before gown?
25 In which year was the Gunpowder Plot?
26 Who wrote the novels "Sons and Lovers" and "The Rainbow"?
27 What does a chandler make?
28 Westlife won the award of Britain's Record of the Year 2005 for which song?
29 Black, Whooper, and Bewick are all types of which bird?
30 Which Italian Prime Minister also had the distinction of being the country's richest man?

Answers	Supermodels and Fashion *(see Quiz 66)*

1 Charlize Theron. **2** Twiggy. **3** Beyoncé. **4** Mandy Smith. **5** Coco (Chanel). **6** Kate Moss. **7** Stella McCartney. **8** Estée Lauder. **9** David Bailey. **10** Nicole Kidman. **11** Zandra Rhodes. **12** Pineapple. **13** Barbara Bach. **14** Edina Ronay. **15** Make-up. **16** John Frieda. **17** Kilt. **18** Sadie Frost. **19** Mary Quant. **20** Versace. **21** Katie Price (Jordan). **22** Yves. **23** Revlon. **24** Kate Moss. **25** Sandie Shaw. **26** Trinny and Susannah. **27** Carnaby Street. **28** Vidal Sassoon. **29** Milan. **30** Westwood.

1 What do conifers have in their cones?
2 Which tree's leaves are the symbol of the National Trust?
3 Which three coniferous trees are native to Britain?
4 Which garden tree with yellow flowers has poisonous seeds?
5 What colour are the flowers of the horse chestnut tree?
6 In which country did the bonsai technique develop?
7 Which tree do we get turpentine from?
8 In which continent did the monkey-puzzle tree originate?
9 Which tree produces cobs and filberts?
10 Aspen is from which family of trees?
11 Is the wood of a coniferous tree hard or soft?
12 What is the more common name for the great maple?
13 What sort of environment do alder trees grow in?
14 Which tree is cork obtained from?
15 In which county is England's largest forest?
16 Which tree is sago obtained from?
17 Which beech tree has purplish leaves?
18 What is the Spanish chestnut also called?
19 Which tree can be English, American or Eurasian?
20 To which family does the umbrella tree belong?
21 The teak is native to which continent?
22 Which wood is used for piano keys?
23 Which maple's sap is used to make maple syrup?
24 To which family does the osier belong?
25 Which is thought to be the tallest tree in the world and one of the longest-lived?
26 Which tree produces "keys"?
27 What colour flowers does a jacaranda tree have?
28 Which tree produces the seeds from which cocoa is made?
29 To which group of trees do blue gum and red gum belong ?
30 What is the linden tree also called?

Answers | Sport: Cricket *(see Quiz 71)*

1 County. 2 2003. 3 Gary Sobers. 4 Ian Botham. 5 Keedie. 6 Richie Benaud.
7 All maidens – no runs conceded. 8 Brian Close. Played at 18 and finally at 45. 9
Inzamam ul-Haq. 10 11. 11 Somerset, Worcestershire and Durham. 12 Yorkshire. 13
Canterbury. 14 Middlesex. 15 Wilfred Rhodes. 16 Mark and Steve. 17 Lord's. 18
Jamaica. 19 Danish. 20 Warwickshire. 21 Harold Larwood. 22 Grace. 23 Colin and
Christopher Cowdrey. 24 Jim Laker. 25 Malcolm Nash. 26 22. 27 Right arm raised in
horizontal position. 28 Javed Miandad of Pakistan. 29 Durham. 30 Viv Richards.

1 In which country did the poets Keats and Shelley both die?
2 How many tusks does a warthog have?
3 What is the nearest star to the solar system?
4 Who wrote "Porgy and Bess"?
5 Who was king of France at the time of the French Revolution?
6 Which card game has two forms, called auction and contract?
7 In which country does the Amazon rise?
8 Graphite is composed of which element?
9 Who was the first English captain to lift the Webb Ellis Trophy?
10 What can be seen from Earth only once every 76 years?
11 Who was prime minister of Australia from 1983 to 1991?
12 Where was the Mount Pinatubo eruption?
13 What was notable about all the dancers in Matthew Bourne's version of Swan Lake?
14 What is the nationality of opera singer Renee Fleming?
15 Who became potter to King George III in 1806?
16 What does "m" stand for in Einstein's equation $E=mc^2$?
17 Which sign of the zodiac is represented as a man pouring water from a jug?
18 Who preferred "50,000 rifles to 50,000 votes"?
19 Who devised the modern system for naming and classifying plants and animals?
20 Whose fan did Oscar Wilde write about?
21 What name is given to the set of fans at the front of a jet engine?
22 How many gold medals did Michael Phelps win at the Athens Olympics in 2004?
23 On the shores of which lake does Toronto stand?
24 What is the scientific name for the lemon tree?
25 On which day in 1066 was William the Conqueror crowned king of England?
26 What is the currency of the British colony of Bermuda?
27 Sir Christopher Wren was a professor in which scientific field?
28 What is the first name of the second Mrs Paul McCartney?
29 Who was Pinocchio's father?
30 Where are the Tivoli Gardens?

| **Answers** | Pot-Luck 32 *(see Quiz 72)* |

1 XY. 2 Bernard Hill. 3 Atmospheric pressure. 4 Donovan. 5 Gamma. 6 Orange. 7 Indonesia's. 8 Thirty. 9 Ralph Fiennes. 10 Miles Davis's. 11 James Chadwick. 12 Emporio. 13 Opera. 14 Lyle Lovett. 15 Edward Heath. 16 Solomon Grundy. 17 Dr No. 18 Pink Floyd. 19 The binary system. 20 1995–96. 21 Tuna fishing. 22 Pancreas. 23 17th century. 24 Victoria. 25 Crystal Palace. 26 Atlas Mountains. 27 American Civil War. 28 Della Street. 29 Periodic table. 30 Osiris.

Quiz 71 | **Sport: Cricket** | Answers – page 193

1 What does the first C stand for in TCCB?
2 In which year did Michael Vaughan take over as England captain?
3 Which West Indies star with bat and ball scored over 8,000 Test runs?
4 Who was the last cricketer to be named BBC Sports Personality of the Year before Freddie Flintoff?
5 Which lady sang on the 2005 England squad's version of "Jerusalem"?
6 Which popular figure wrote "My Spin on Cricket"?
7 What was remarkable about the 16 overs that South Africa's Hugh Tayfield bowled against England at Durban in 1957?
8 Who was England's youngest and later oldest post-war Test player?
9 Who skippered Pakistan in the 2005 series victory over England?
10 In 1995, Jack Russell took how many catches in a Test to create a new world record?
11 Which three counties did Ian Botham play for?
12 Which county have won the championship most times?
13 Where is Kent's cricket ground headquarters?
14 Edmonds and Emburey were the spinning duo for which county?
15 Which all-rounder took 100 wickets and scored 1000 runs in 16 seasons between 1903 and 1926?
16 What are the Christian names of Australia's Waugh brothers?
17 Where do Middlesex play home matches?
18 On which West Indian island is Sabina Park?
19 Which name of Pakistani wrist spinner Kaneria suggests he comes from Scandinavia?
20 Which English county has Brian Lara played for?
21 Who was the "bodyline" bowler?
22 Gloucestershire cricketers of the 1870s W. G. and E. M. had what surname?
23 Who are the only father and son to captain England?
24 Which Englishman took 19 wickets in a 1956 Test against Australia?
25 Who was bowling for Glamorgan when Sobers hit six sixes in an over?
26 How many Test centuries did Geoff Boycott score for England?
27 What is the umpire's signal for a no-ball?
28 Who was selected for all World Cups from 1975 to 1995?
29 Which was the first new county to join the championship in the 1990s?
30 Who was West Indian captain before Richie Richardson?

Answers | Nature: Trees *(see Quiz 69)*

1 Seeds. 2 Oak. 3 Yew, Scots Pine, Juniper. 4 Laburnum. 5 White/cream. 6 Japan. 7 Pine. 8 South America. 9 Hazel. 10 Poplar. 11 Soft. 12 Sycamore. 13 Wet. 14 Cork oak. 15 Northumberland. 16 Palm. 17 Copper beech. 18 Sweet chestnut. 19 Elm. 20 Magnolia. 21 Asia. 22 Ebony. 23 Sugar maple. 24 Willow. 25 Redwood. 26 Ash. 27 Blue/violet. 28 Cacao. 29 Eucalyptus. 30 Lime.

1 Which sex chromosomes are possessed by a human male?
2 Who played King Theoden of Rohan in the last two parts of the "Lord of the Rings" trilogy?
3 What does a barometer measure?
4 Which pop star from the 1960s called his autobiography "The Hurdy Gurdy Man"?
5 What is the third letter of the Greek alphabet?
6 What is the flavour of Grand Marnier?
7 Whose national airline is called Garuda?
8 How many counters are on a backgammon board at start of play?
9 Who voiced Victor Quartermaine in "Wallace and Gromit: The Curse of the Were-Rabbit"?
10 In the 1950s whose quintet did John Coltrane play with?
11 Who discovered the neutron?
12 Under what label did Giorgio Armani design clothes?
13 What word can go after soap and before house?
14 Which country singer married Julia Roberts in 1993?
15 Which prime minister brought in a 10.30pm TV curfew in 1973?
16 In the nursery rhyme who was married on a Wednesday?
17 Which Bond movie featured the partially dressed Ursula Andress?
18 Which British rock band had Syd Barrett among its founders?
19 Which number code system is based on the digits 1 and 0?
20 David Beckham first won the Premiership with Man Utd in which season?
21 What type of driftnet fishing caused the deaths of hundreds of dolphins in the 1980s?
22 Which organ of the body secretes insulin?
23 In which century was tea first brought to Europe?
24 Of which Australian state is Melbourne the capital?
25 What was built in Hyde Park for the Great Exhibition of 1851?
26 Mount Toubkal is the highest peak of which mountain range?
27 Which war started with the bombardment of Fort Sumter?
28 Who was Perry Mason's secretary?
29 What name is given to the most used table of the elements?
30 Who was the Egyptian god of the underworld?

Answers | Pot-Luck 31 (see Quiz 70)

1 Italy. 2 Four. 3 Alpha Centauri. 4 George Gershwin. 5 Louis XVI. 6 Bridge. 7 Peru. 8 Carbon. 9 Martin Johnson. 10 Halley's Comet. 11 Bob Hawke. 12 The Philippines. 13 They were all men. 14 American. 15 Josiah Spode. 16 Mass. 17 Aquarius. 18 Benito Mussolini. 19 Linnaeus. 20 Lady Windermere's. 21 Compressor. 22 Six. 23 Lake Ontario. 24 Citrus limon. 25 Christmas Day. 26 Bermuda dollar. 27 Astronomy. 28 Heather. 29 Geppetto. 30 Copenhagen.

1 Which method of fast writing did Isaac Pitman develop?
2 Which two major electronics companies developed the compact disc in 1979?
3 What was invented by US students using aluminium flan cases?
4 In which country was the first modern motorway created?
5 Who registered the first patents for the railway sleeping car?
6 Which Swiss company developed the first widely used instant coffee?
7 Which rubber-based product was patented in the United States in 1869?
8 Why was the invention of the electric iron useless in America in 1882?
9 What was American Mr Bissel's dust-collecting invention?
10 What was the surname of King Camp who invented the safety razor?
11 What was the occupation of Dom Pierre Perignon who developed the champagne process?
12 What type of pens did Pentel invent?
13 Which building toy was designed by a Dane, Ole Kirk Christiansen?
14 What is unusual about Mark Button's invention, the Koosh ball?
15 Which Kimberley Clark Co invention was first called Celluwipes?
16 Which form of precautionary medicine was discovered by Edward Jenner?
17 What was the nationality of saxophone inventor Adolphe Sax?
18 Which type of transport did John Outram invent in 1775?
19 Which sauce did Henry Heinz invent in 1876?
20 JVC launched VHS format in 1976, but what does VHS stand for?
21 Which drink was created when Indian army officers added quinine to soda water to help fight malaria?
22 In which country were cultured pearls first obtained?
23 What was Alka-Seltzer first marketed as?
24 The Penny Black was the first adhesive stamp, how was the Penny Red a first?
25 In which country were banknotes first used?
26 Which weapon did Samuel Colt develop and popularize?
27 Which musical instrument did American Rickenbacher create?
28 What was based on the Victorian game called Magic Square?
29 What did the owner of the Humpty Dumpty store in Oklahoma invent?
30 Which type of fastening was first used on snow boots?

Answers | Pop: Solo Stars *(see Quiz 75)*

1 No. 2 The Day I Met Marie. 3 Elvis Presley. 4 Holiday. 5 Rod Stewart. 6 Bryan Hyland. 7 Perry Como. 8 Bonnie Tyler. 9 Green Door. 10 Bobby Brown. 11 Christina Aguilera. 12 RSVP. 13 Thunderball. 14 Gene Pitney. 15 Marti Webb. 16 Will Young. 17 Maggie May. 18 Frank Ifield. 19 Careless Whisper. 20 Sam Cooke. 21 In Dreams. 22 They Call the Wind Mariah. 23 Seal. 24 Elton John. 25 Belinda Carlisle. 26 Tamla Motown. 27 25 mph. 28 Bruce Springsteen. 29 Cher – Gypsies, Tramps and Thieves. 30 Georgia.

1 What is the Aurora Australis also called?
2 Which three South American countries does the Equator cross?
3 What was the first X-rated film to win an Oscar?
4 What is the name of the national airline of Israel?
5 Which pop star earned his bus pass and became an official OAP on 14 October 2005?
6 Which female cookery writer wrote "Climbing the Mango Trees"?
7 What did Little Polly Flinders spoil?
8 Who wrote "Anna Karenina"?
9 What metallic element is mixed with tin to form the alloy bronze?
10 Who was the founder of the Christian Science movement?
11 Made this millennium, in which decade was the detective series "Jericho" set?
12 In which city did Karl Marx write "Das Kapital"?
13 How is the Caribbean island of St Christopher more familiarly known?
14 Which planet has a pink appearance?
15 Who was world professional billiards champion from 1968 to 1980?
16 Which is the most northerly capital city in Europe?
17 Which New York baseball player who married Marilyn Monroe?
18 Which country is the world's leading producer of copper?
19 Which acid builds up in the muscles during severe exercise?
20 Who circumnavigated the world solo in "Gipsy Moth IV" in 1966–67?
21 Which Australian city stands near the mouth of the Yarra river?
22 What common mineral is formed by the fossilization of vegetation?
23 Which stand-up comedian created the character the Pub Landlord?
24 Which comic playwright wrote the trilogy "The Norman Conquests"?
25 Who took over the movie role of Clarice Starling from Jodie Foster?
26 Who was George Logan better known as?
27 What form of energy is produced by an electric motor?
28 Which beautiful youth did the Greek goddess Aphrodite love?
29 Who said "When you are as great as I am, it's hard to be humble"?
30 Which country's flag shows a green star on a red background?

Answers | Painting and Scupture *(see Quiz 76)*

1 Gainsborough. 2 Renoir. 3 Mona Lisa. 4 Jack Russell. 5 The Rake's. 6 The Laughing Cavalier. 7 Sphinx. 8 Op Art. 9 Wet plaster. 10 Statue of Liberty. 11 Nude. 12 Engravings. 13 Mount Rushmore. 14 Sculpture. 15 Millais. 16 Henry Moore. 17 Salvador Dali. 18 Rembrandt. 19 Andy Warhol. 20 Portraits. 21 Buddha. 22 Van Gogh. 23 Glue. 24 Picasso. 25 Impressionist. 26 Pop Art. 27 Dancers. 28 Russia. 29 Suffolk. 30 Jacob.

Quiz 75 | Pop: Solo Stars | Answers – page 197

1 Did John Lennon have a solo single No 1 in his lifetime?
2 Which Cliff Richard hit starts "Imagine a still summer's day"?
3 Colonel Tom Parker launched which star?
4 Which was Madonna's first UK top ten hit?
5 Which singer recorded "Every Picture Tells a Story"?
6 Who had a hit with the original version of "Sealed with a Kiss"?
7 Which former barber charted from 1953 to 1973?
8 Which lady was "Lost in France"?
9 What was a hit for both Frankie Vaughan and Shakin' Stevens?
10 Britney Spears had a hit with "My Prerogative", but who had the original hit?
11 Who had No 1s with both "Dirrty" and "Beautiful"?
12 Which Jason Donovan single is made up of initials?
13 Tom Jones sang for which Bond film?
14 Which solo star had his first No 1 in a duo with Marc Almond in 1989?
15 Apart from Michael Jackson, which female singer charted with "Ben"?
16 Who had a No 1 in 2003 with "Friday's Child"?
17 Which Rod Stewart hit starts "Wake up, Maggie..."?
18 Can you remember who sang "I Remember You"?
19 What was George Michael's first solo No 1?
20 Whose "Wonderful World" was a bigger hit as a reissue 26 years after the original?
21 Which Roy Orbison hit begins, "A candy-coloured clown they call the sandman"?
22 Mariah Carey was named after which song in "Paint Your Wagon"?
23 Which singer was "Crazy" with his first single success?
24 Which superstar has been chairman of Watford football club?
25 Which female singer recorded "Heaven is a Place on Earth"?
26 Which label did Michael Jackson first record on?
27 According to Tina Turner, what was the speed limit in Nutbush?
28 Who was born in the United States of Irish-Italian parents and with the middle names Frederick Joseph ?
29 Who sang that she was "born in the wagon of a travelling show"?
30 Which country does Katie Melua come from?

Answers | Hi-Tech: Inventions *(see Quiz 73)*

1 Shorthand. 2 Sony and Philips. 3 Frisbee. 4 Italy. 5 Pullman. 6 Nestlé. 7 Chewing gum. 8 Homes did not have electricity. 9 Carpet sweeper. 10 Gillette. 11 Monk. 12 Felt tips. 13 Lego. 14 It doesn't bounce. 15 Paper handkerchiefs. 16 Vaccination. 17 Belgian. 18 Tram. 19 Tomato ketchup. 20 Video Home System. 21 Tonic water. 22 Japan. 23 Cold cure. 24 Perforated. 25 Sweden. 26 Revolver. 27 Electric guitar. 28 Crossword puzzles. 29 Supermarket trolley. 30 Zip.

1 Who painted "The Blue Boy" and "Mr and Mrs Andrews"?
2 Which Pierre-Auguste painted "Umbrellas" and "The Bathers"?
3 What is Leonardo da Vinci's "La Gioconda" also known as?
4 Which English cricketer is a keen amateur watercolour artist?
5 Whose Progress did William Hogarth paint?
6 What is arguably the most famous painting by Dutchman Frans Hals?
7 Which Egyptian sculpture is more than 73 metres long?
8 Which 1960s art vogue was based on optical illusion?
9 What is paint applied to in a fresco?
10 Which sculpture did Auguste Bartholdi give to the United States?
11 What is notable about the woman in Ingres' "Valpinçon Bather"?
12 What type of work is Albrecht Dürer famous for?
13 Where in the United States would you find Washington's head 18 metres high?
14 What art form is a Japanese netsuke?
15 Who painted "Bubbles", which has been used in a soap ad?
16 Which English sculptor produced rounded forms such as "Reclining Figure"?
17 Which Spaniard is known for his hallucinatory paintings?
18 Which Dutch painter is well known for his self-portraits?
19 Who painted Campbell soup tins and Marilyn Monroe?
20 What type of paintings is Joshua Reynolds famous for?
21 A statue in Afghanistan of which religious teacher standing 53 metres high was destroyed by the Taliban in 2001?
22 Whose "Irises" and "Sunflowers" were two of the world's most expensive paintings at auction?
23 What is the binding medium in gouache technique?
24 Which Spaniard founded the Cubist movement?
25 Of which school of painting was Claude Monet a leading exponent?
26 For which art style is David Hockney famous?
27 Which performers were a favourite subject for painter/sculptor Degas?
28 In which country was the French painter Marc Chagall born?
29 In which county is "Constable country", named after its famous son?
30 What was the first name of sculptor Epstein?

Answers | Pot-Luck 33 *(see Quiz 74)*

1 The Southern Lights. 2 Brazil, Colombia and Ecuador. 3 Midnight Cowboy. 4 El-Al.
5 Cliff Richard. 6 Madhur Jaffrey. 7 Her nice new clothes. 8 Leo Tolstoy. 9 Copper.
10 Mary Baker Eddy. 11 1950s. 12 London. 13 St Kitts. 14 Mars. 15 Rex Williams.
16 Helsinki. 17 Joe DiMaggio. 18 Chile. 19 Lactic acid. 20 Francis Chichester.
21 Melbourne. 22 Coal. 23 Al Murray. 24 Alan Ayckbourn. 25 Julianne Moore.
26 Evadne Hinge (of Hinge and Brackett). 27 Mechanical energy. 28 Adonis. 29
Muhammad Ali. 30 Morocco.

1 The year 2006 marks which anniversary of Mozart's birth?
2 Goalkeeper Richard Wright joined Everton from which club?
3 In which movie did Nicolas Cage play the character Yuri Orlov?
4 What source of light is used in producing a hologram?
5 Which Bond movie was a hit for Sheena Easton?
6 Which instrument does the musician Einaudi play?
7 Where in Canada is the world's second-largest French-speaking city?
8 Which character did Clark Gable play in "Gone with the Wind"?
9 Which tsar conquered Kazan and Siberia in the 16th century?
10 What was the subtitle of the movie "Miss Congeniality 2"?
11 In which year did Britain abandon the gold standard?
12 Which Italian artist included Halley's comet in a fresco of the Nativity?
13 Which object took almost seven hours to rise from the Solent in 1982?
14 Which "Dad's Army" actor was married to Hattie Jacques?
15 What name is given to the genetic make-up of an individual?
16 Where did chess originate in the second century AD?
17 What happened to the main character in Kafka's "Metamorphosis"?
18 What style of music was pioneered by jazzmen Charlie Parker and Dizzy Gillespie?
19 Which 18th-century priest discovered that plants absorb air?
20 Cecil Beaton won Oscars for his designs for which two films?
21 In the rhyme, what is Friday's child?
22 What is the name given to the chief religious leader of a synagogue?
23 What were the surnames of the tennis doubles stars known as the Woodies?
24 What did Mahatma Gandhi train to become?
25 Where would you find an avenue of sphinxes?
26 Which instrument did Lionel Hampton introduce to jazz?
27 Who played the Riddler in "Batman Forever"?
28 Who was the last prisoner to be held at Spandau?
29 Which rock star, known as "Slowhand", received an OBE in 1995?
30 Which theme from a film did the BBC use for the 1984 Olympics?

Answers | Pot-Luck 35 *(see Quiz 79)*

1 Spanish. 2 Hamlet. 3 Hindu. 4 Madeleine Albright. 5 Squirrel. 6 Zimbabwe. 7 The Medway. 8 Nigella Lawson. 9 November. 10 Keith Richard. 11 Isaac. 12 James II. 13 Canary. 14 Manitoba. 15 Italy. 16 Battle of Bosworth. 17 Noel Coward. 18 Bench. 19 Canada. 20 Eyes. 21 Tea. 22 Anne Boleyn. 23 Etna. 24 The Seagull. 25 Salome. 26 Magyar. 27 On its tail. 28 Gerald Ford. 29 Steffi Graf. 30 Suez Canal.

1 In "Doctor Who" what does TARDIS stand for?
2 Which film starts with a telephone conversation between Cypher and Trinity?
3 In which series did scientist Dr Sam Beckett appear?
4 What was the Six Million Dollar Man's previous occupation?
5 In which sci-fi series did Joanna Lumley and David McCallum star?
6 What was unusual about Dr Peter Brady and Dr Daniel Westin?
7 What was the name of Dr Who's assistant as played by Billie Piper?
8 Which Edwardian adventurer, trapped in ice, thawed out in 1966?
9 What was Steve Zodiac's spacecraft?
10 Where were the Robinson family lost in the 1960s series?
11 What is Doctor Who always called in the series?
12 Which series has had Eartha Kitt in the role of Catwoman?
13 Who played Jamie in "Doctor Who" and Joe Sugden in "Emmerdale"?
14 What were Captain Kirk's two Christian names?
15 How was Diana Prince better known?
16 What did "A" stand for in the name of the 1960s series?
17 What was special about the Man from Atlantis, Mark Harris?
18 Which 11th-century wizard became trapped in the 20th century?
19 In "Doomwatch" what was Doomwatch?
20 Who travelled in "The Liberator" fighting the Federation?
21 What was the surname of Professor Bernard whose name has become synonymous with early TV sci-fi?
22 What was the title of the Star Trek series that resumed in 1990?
23 Which series preceded "Galactica 80"?
24 In "Doctor Who" what was the Daleks' most famous command?
25 In "Star Trek" what colour was Mr Spock's blood?
26 Which children's series featured Spectrum and Colonel White?
27 Which series is remembered for Diana seeming to swallow a mouse?
28 What was the surname of global rescuers Jeff, Scott and Virgil?
29 In which 1970s series had 95% of the world's population been wiped out by a killer virus?
30 What sort of vehicle was Stingray?

Answers	New Millennium Milestones *(see Quiz 80)*

1 Arnold Schwarzenegger. 2 Tate Modern. 3 Millennium Bridge. 4 Hillary Clinton. 5 Submarine. 6 The Guardian. 7 Indonesia. 8 Routemaster bus. 9 101. 10 December. 11 Ukraine. 12 Angela Merkel. 13 Buncefield. 14 Mars. 15 Yasser Arafat. 16 Two. 17 Shed (Shed-Boat-Shed). 18 Rudolph Giuliani. 19 Bali. 20 Nepalese. 21 Kelly Holmes. 22 Three. 23 Pete Sampras. 24 Martin Johnson. 25 George Best. 26 Cats. 27 Israel. 28 Fountain. 29 M25. 30 The Mousetrap.

Quiz 79 Pot-Luck 35

1 What is the main language spoken in Chile?
2 In which Shakespeare play do we meet two grave diggers?
3 Which Eastern religion includes the caste system?
4 Which prominent US politician was born Madeleine Korbel in Czechoslovakia in the 1930s?
5 What animal lives in a drey?
6 In which African country is the city of Bulawayo?
7 On which river do Rochester, Chatham and Gillingham stand?
8 Who wrote the cookery book "Feast", which featured two large cooking pots on its cover?
9 In which month in 2003 did England triumph to win the Rugby World Cup?
10 Who said, "I never had any problems with drugs, only with policemen"?
11 In the Bible, name the son whom Abraham was asked to sacrifice?
12 Who was the last Roman Catholic king of England?
13 What sort of bird is a Cinnamon Norwich?
14 Winnipeg is the capital of which Canadian province?
15 Of which country was Aldo Moro prime minister?
16 At which battle was Richard III killed?
17 Who wrote the operetta "Bitter Sweet" and the play "Private Lives"?
18 What do we call a group of bishops?
19 Which country does a car come from if it shows CDN as the international registration letters?
20 What part of the body would be affected if you suffered from myopia?
21 What cargo did the ship "Cutty Sark" carry?
22 Who was the mother of the first Queen Elizabeth?
23 What is the name of the famous active volcano on the island of Sicily?
24 Which bird is also the name of a play by Chekhov?
25 Who asked for the head of John the Baptist?
26 Which is the main language spoken in Hungary?
27 Whereabouts on a whale are its flukes?
28 Who succeeded Richard Nixon as president of the United States in 1974?
29 Who is Jaz Elle Agassi's mum?
30 Which important ship canal was built by Ferdinand de Lesseps?

Answers | Pot-Luck 34 (see Quiz 77)

1 250th. 2 Arsenal. 3 Lord of War. 4 Laser. 5 For Your Eyes Only. 6 Piano. 7 Montreal. 8 Rhett Butler. 9 Ivan the Terrible. 10 Armed & Fabulous. 11 1931. 12 Giotto. 13 The Mary Rose. 14 John Le Mesurier. 15 Genotype. 16 India. 17 Turned into an insect. 18 Bebop. 19 Stephen Hales. 20 Gigi and My Fair Lady. 21 Loving and giving. 22 Rabbi. 23 Woodford and Woodbridge. 24 Lawyer. 25 Luxor, Egypt. 26 Vibraphone. 27 Jim Carrey. 28 Rudolf Hess. 29 Eric Clapton. 30 Chariots of Fire.

1 Who became Governor of California in 2003?
2 What was the name of the then largest modern art gallery opened by the Queen in 2000?
3 Which was London's first new river crossing for 100 years, opened in 2000?
4 In 2000 who became the first First Lady to join the US Senate?
5 What type of vessel was the Kursk, involved in an accident in 2002?
6 Which broadsheet British newspaper changed to Berliner format in 2005?
7 In which country is Aceh, a region badly devastated by the 2004 tsunami?
8 Which form of London Transport ceased in December 2005?
9 How old was the Queen Mother when she died in 2002?
10 In what month in 2005 were gay 'marriages' allowed through civil partnership registrations?
11 In 2004, which part of the former USSR witnessed an Orange Revolution?
12 Who became Germany's first Chancellor from the former Eastern bloc?
13 An explosion at which oil depot caused the biggest peace time blaze seen in England?
14 Beagle 2 was launched to probe which planet?
15 Mahmoud Abbas replaced whom as leader of the PLO in 2005?
16 How many Popes were there in 2005?
17 The "shed" that won the Turner Prize in 2005 started life as a what?
18 Michael Bloomberg replaced whom as mayor of New York?
19 Which island was the scene of a terrorist attack in 2002?
20 Which Royal Family suffered a mass massacre of its members in June 2001?
21 In May 2005 which record breaker was crowned Laureus World Sportswoman of the Year in Portugal?
22 How many airliners attacked the Pentagon on 11 September 2001?
23 Which tennis star became the man with most Grand Slam tournament titles?
24 Who was the captain of the 2003 Rugby World Cup winners?
25 Which former Northern Ireland and Man United legend died in 2005?
26 Which musical became the first to establish a 20-year West End run?
27 In September 2005 which country pulled out of the Gaza Strip?
28 What type of memorial to Princess Diana was built in Hyde Park?
29 Which road carried Britain's first 12-lane stretch of motorway?
30 Which stage show clocked up a 50-year run in London's West End?

Answers   TV: Sci Fi *(see Quiz 78)*

1 Time And Relative Dimensions In Space. 2 The Matrix. 3 Quantum Leap. 4 Astronaut.
5 Sapphire and Steel. 6 Invisible. 7 Rose. 8 Adam Adamant. 9 Fireball XL5. 10
Space. 11 The Doctor. 12 Batman. 13 Frazer Hines. 14 James Tiberius. 15 Wonder
Woman. 16 Andromeda. 17 Half man, half fish. 18 Catweazle. 19 Government
department. 20 Blake's Seven. 21 Quatermass. 22 The Next Generation. 23 Battlestar
Galactica. 24 Exterminate. 25 Green. 26 Captain Scarlet and the Mysterons. 27 V.
28 Tracy. 29 Survivors. 30 Submarine.

1 When a cow stands up, which legs does it get up on first?
2 Who sang "On the good ship Lollipop"?
3 According to the proverb, what is the better part of valour?
4 How many teams started the Euro 2004 tournament in Portugal?
5 The oil storage terminal at Buncefield, scene of a major explosion, was near which English town?
6 From which London railway station do you normally travel to Bristol?
7 In which film is the Harry Lime theme?
8 Which American city is named after a British prime minister?
9 Where would you find a dead man's handle?
10 Who wrote the Orange Prize-winning book "Small Island"?
11 On which river does swan-upping take place?
12 Which country lies immediately east of Iraq?
13 Which London building is nicknamed "Ally Pally"?
14 Who claimed that "History is Bunk"?
15 In which English city is the cathedral known as "Paddy's Wigwam"?
16 From which port was the bulk of the British Expeditionary Force in France evacuated in 1940?
17 Which architect designed New York's Guggenheim Museum?
18 Who wrote "Gulliver's Travels"?
19 In which city was General Gordon put to death?
20 What kind of animal is a pipistrelle?
21 According to the proverb which fruit tastes sweetest?
22 What was the name for the ancient Egyptian good luck charm in the shape of a beetle?
23 Who was Spain's first ever F1 World Champion?
24 Who said "Father, I cannot tell a lie"?
25 Nitrous oxide is more commonly known as which gas?
26 In German fable who sold his soul to Mephistopheles?
27 What do Bluebell, the Watercress, and the Severn Valley all have in common?
28 What is Freddie Starr's real name?
29 Which sport did David Duckham play?
30 Which major political figure became MP for Witney in 2001?

Answers | Pot-Luck 37 (see Quiz 83)

1 Slander. 2 July. 3 Jet. 4 The Crusades. 5 1961. 6 Newfoundland. 7 Aardvark.
8 Dr Crippen. 9 Tom & Jerry. 10 Can-can. 11 Susan Hill. 12 All work and no play.
13 Daisy. 14 House of Lords. 15 Bulgaria. 16 Sikh. 17 Mushrooms or toadstools.
18 Canada. 19 Equipment. 20 Marchioness. 21 Tunisia. 22 The Salvation Army. 23
Joshua. 24 Coldplay. 25 Tasman Sea. 26 Limited. 27 Grapefruit. 28 Heart surgery.
29 Ernest. 30 The Dam Busters.

1 Which Rio-based club is named after a Portuguese navigator?
2 Which Japanese city is home to Grampus Eight?
3 Who was dubbed "El Beatle" by fans in Portugal?
4 On which day of the week do the Spanish usually play football?
5 Former Celtic favourite Henrik Larsson represented which country?
6 Which Dutch side play their games in the Philips Stadium?
7 Which country does Michael Essien play for?
8 Which country was in three of the first four European finals?
9 Which city is home to Racing Club and River Plate?
10 At which ground do the Republic of Ireland play home games?
11 Which former goalie coached both Juventus and Lazio?
12 In which European country are the headquarters of UEFA?
13 Who did England play in their final 2006 World Cup Group qualifier?
14 Where did Aston Villa win the European Cup in 1982?
15 Where in France is the ground known as Le Stadium?
16 Who scored two goals in the 2002 Final of the World Cup?
17 Who was FIFA World Footballer of the Year in 1998, 2000 and 2003?
18 In what year was the first ever European Cup match played?
19 Who was the first manager to coach both Australia and England?
20 Independiente are a leading club in which country?
21 Which side beat Arsenal in the 1995 European Cup Winners' Cup with a goal in the last minute of extra time?
22 In which country was the 1992 European Championship staged?
23 Name the the beaten finalists in the 1994 World Cup final?
24 2003 was the year that which English ground first hosted a European Champion Clubs' Cup Final?
25 Figo, Raul and Zidane played together at which club?
26 Who won the Club World Championship final in 2005?
27 Which was the first British team to lift the European Cup after a penalty shoot-out?
28 Alfredo di Stefano played international football for three countries – Argentina, Spain and which other country?
29 Which item of kit was made compulsory by FIFA in 1990?
30 Who is the only player to score a hat-trick in a World Cup final?

Answers | Trouble Spots *(see Quiz 84)*

1 Shah of Iran. 2 Afghanistan. 3 Kenya. 4 Six Days. 5 Jackie Mann. 6 General Belgrano. 7 Hungary. 8 Nicaragua. 9 Nasser. 10 Bay of Pigs. 11 Algeria. 12 Canary Wharf. 13 Palestine Liberation Organization. 14 Zimbabwe (Southern Rhodesia). 15 Corazón Aquino. 16 Gulf War. 17 Cyprus. 18 Iraq. 19 Korean War. 20 Martin Luther King, Robert Kennedy. 21 China. 22 Vietnam. 23 Galtieri. 24 Nigeria. 25 South Africa. 26 Prague's. 27 France. 28 Entebbe airport. 29 Yugoslavia. 30 Tiananmen.

1 If libel is a written defamation, what is oral defamation?
2 On which month in 2005 was it announced that London had won its bid to host the 2012 Olympics?
3 Which word can go after jumbo and before black?
4 What name was given to the mediaeval warlike expeditions to the Holy Land?
5 In which year was the first manned space flight?
6 In Canada, of which province is St John's the capital?
7 Which animal's name literally means "earth pig"?
8 Who was the first major criminal to be arrested as a result of the use of radio?
9 Who made their screen debut in "Puss in Boots"?
10 Which dance is usually performed to "Orpheus in the Underworld"?
11 Who wrote the novel which formed the basis for the play "The Woman in Black"?
12 According to the proverb what makes Jack a dull boy?
13 Of which flower is ox-eye a type?
14 In Britain which is the ultimate court of appeal?
15 Which country did tennis-playing sisters Katerina and Manuela Maleeva come from?
16 Amritsar is a holy city for the followers of which religion?
17 What are ink-caps, death caps and puffballs all types of?
18 Which country was once called New France?
19 What does the second E in the acronym ERNIE stand for?
20 What is the wife of a marquis called?
21 In which country is the ruined city of Carthage?
22 Which religious body publishes a magazine called "The War Cry"?
23 In the Bible, who led the Israelites to the Battle of Jericho?
24 Who won the Best UK and Ireland award at the 2005 MTV Awards?
25 Which sea lies between New Zealand and Australia?
26 The initials plc stand for what type of public company?
27 What is the common name for the fruit Citrus grandis?
28 Sir Magdi Yacoub is an expert in which field?
29 What was Sergeant Bilko's first name?
30 What daring raid was led by Guy Gibson?

Answers | Pot-Luck 36 (see Quiz 81)

1 Back. 2 Shirley Temple. 3 Discretion. 4 16. 5 Hemel Hempstead. 6 Paddington. 7 The Third Man. 8 Pittsburgh. 9 In an electric train, tube train. 10 Andrea Levy. 11 The Thames. 12 Iran. 13 Alexandra Palace. 14 Henry Ford. 15 Liverpool. 16 Dunkirk. 17 Frank Lloyd Wright. 18 Jonathan Swift. 19 Khartoum. 20 A bat. 21 Forbidden fruit. 22 The scarab. 23 Fernando Alonso. 24 George Washington. 25 Laughing gas. 26 Faust. 27 Railways. 28 Freddie Starr. 29 Rugby Union. 30 David Cameron.

Quiz 84 | Trouble Spots

Answers – page 206

LEVEL 2

1 Who fled his "Peacock Throne" into exile in 1979?

2 Where did the mujahideen resist Soviet attack?

3 Which country was the scene of the Mau Mau rebellion in the 1950s?

4 How long did the Arab-Israeli War of 1967 last?

5 Which English World War II veteran was a Beirut kidnap victim?

6 Which Argentinian cruiser was sunk outside an exclusion zone during the Falklands War?

7 Where did Russian troops crush an anti-Soviet uprising in 1956?

8 Where did the Sandinistas overthrow the government in 1979?

9 Who was president of Egypt during the Suez Crisis in 1956?

10 In which Bay was there a failed attempt by exiled Cubans to invade Cuba?

11 Where in North Africa did a war for independence take place between 1954 and 1962?

12 In 1996, where in London was an IRA bomb planted to end a ceasefire?

13 In the Middle East conflict what does PLO stand for?

14 Where did ZANU and ZAPU fight for independence?

15 Who ousted Ferdinand Marcos as president of the Philippines?

16 In which war was Operation Desert Storm?

17 Where did Greeks and Turks clash in major unrest in 1964?

18 Who fought against Iran in the 1980–88 conflict?

19 Which war was fought along the 38th parallel?

20 Which two public figures were assassinated in the United States in 1968?

21 Where in the 1960s was there a Cultural Revolution?

22 In which country did the My Lai massacre take place?

23 Who was the Argentinian president during the Falklands conflict?

24 Biafra was a breakaway state from which African country?

25 In which country did Steve Biko die in detention ?

26 Which city's "Spring" was ended by a Soviet invasion in 1968?

27 Whom did Vietnam gain independence from in 1954?

28 Where in Uganda was a hijacked Air France plane stormed in 1976?

29 Which country disintegrated following the outbreak of civil war in 1992?

30 In which Peking square were pro-democracy demos violently suppressed?

Answers | **World Soccer** *(see Quiz 82)*

1 Vasco da Gama. 2 Nagoya. 3 George Best. 4 Sunday. 5 Sweden. 6 PSV Eindhoven. 7 Ghana. 8 USSR. 9 Buenos Aires. 10 Lansdowne Road. 11 Dino Zoff. 12 Switzerland. 13 Poland. 14 Rotterdam. 15 Toulouse. 16 Ronaldo. 17 Zinedine Zidane. 18 1955. 19 Terry Venables. 20 Argentina. 21 Zaragoza. 22 Sweden. 23 Italy. 24 Old Trafford. 25 Real Madrid. 26 Sao Paulo (Brazil). 27 Liverpool. 28 Colombia. 29 Shin guard. 30 Geoff Hurst.

1 Which novel is about a boy called Billy Casper who trains a hawk?

2 Martina Navratilova won most doubles trophies with which partner?

3 With what is Threadneedle Street associated?

4 In which art has Beryl Grey achieved fame?

5 Who lives in a kraal?

6 Who was the first female to get the top job of director general of MI5?

7 What colour is angelica?

8 With which country is the famous soldier Robert Clive associated?

9 What happens in a vortex?

10 To which section of the orchestra does the tuba belong?

11 In the song, who stuck a feather in his hat called macaroni?

12 What was the first Ealing Comedy?

13 Whom did George W. Bush appoint as Secretary of Defence in 2001?

14 In which sporting event does the winning team move backwards?

15 What is a fandango?

16 Eau-de-nil is a shade of what colour?

17 Which revolution began in 1917?

18 Who is said to have introduced the habit of smoking into this country?

19 After seven which is the next highest prime number?

20 In boxing at what weight do you fight if you weigh over 12 stone 7 pounds?

21 Who wrote the novel "Jane Eyre"?

22 In 1990 and 1991 Matthew Pinsent rowed for which winning Boat Race crews?

23 Which author wrote "The Flood" and "Mortal Causes"?

24 In which country were turkeys first found?

25 What is a carillon?

26 How many moves are there in a chess game in which White opens and wins with Fool's Mate?

27 In which month each year is Battle of Britain week?

28 In a bullfight who kills the bull?

29 What size of bottle is a magnum?

30 What is David Frost's middle name?

Answers | Pot-Luck 39 *(see Quiz 87)*

1 Genesis. 2 A space. 3 Crab. 4 Richard Burton. 5 Belgium. 6 The Importance of Being Earnest. 7 In your foot. 8 Renee Zellwegger. 9 Places of the same height. 10 The parson. 11 Beauty. 12 Laurel and Hardy. 13 Swan. 14 B. 15 Joe Louis. 16 China. 17 British admirals. 18 Long-distance running. 19 Charles. 20 The Merchant of Venice. 21 At the base of the neck. 22 Spain. 23 Sahara. 24 P. D. James. 25 To smell. 26 Ronnie Barker. 27 72 (accept 65–79). 28 Wimbledon. 29 Toyota. 30 New Year's Eve.

Quiz 86 | Folk and Country | Answers – page 212

1 Who was known as "Gentleman Jim"?

2 Which country anthem starts "Sometimes it's hard to be a woman"?

3 Which John Denver song did Peter, Paul and Mary take into the charts?

4 Which Dolly Parton song was a chart hit for Whitney Houston?

5 Which country music legend died in 2003 at the age of 71?

6 Which country star had a hit with "Kiss an Angel Good Morning"?

7 Which singer/songwriter penned "The Last Thing on My Mind"?

8 Which country star has had five husbands, including George Jones, and been kidnapped?

9 Which group was fronted by singer/songwriter Dave Cousins?

10 Which folk singer was called "Judas" for going electric?

11 Which city in eastern England has been the venue for a long-standing folk festival?

12 Who wrote "Your Cheatin' Heart"?

13 Which Rochdale Cowboy was a 1970s folk club favourite?

14 Who recorded the album "No Fences"?

15 Who is the long-time lead singer with Steeleye Span?

16 Who declared "Thank God I'm a Country Boy"?

17 In what language was Fairport Convention's only English hit sung?

18 Which guitarist teamed up with Mark Knopfler on "Neck and Neck"?

19 Who wrote US dust-bowl songs and "This Land is Your Land"?

20 How did Patsy Cline die?

21 Who took "There But for Fortune" into the UK single charts?

22 Under what name did Brenda Gail Webb become famous?

23 Who wrote the folk club classic "Streets Of London"?

24 Who wrote "Where Have All the Flowers Gone"?

25 How is Alexandra Denny better known?

26 Who recorded the album "Shotgun Willie"?

27 How are the trio of Yarrow, Stookey and Travers better known?

28 Who was on "Honky Tonk Angels" with Dolly Parton and Tammy Wynette?

29 Which Latin carol gave Steeleye Span a chart hit?

30 Which boy with a girl's name did Johnny Cash sing about?

Answers	**Action Movies** *(see Quiz 88)*

1 Long Island. 2 Sean Connery. 3 Bruce Willis. 4 The Godfather. 5 Superman. 6 The Philosopher's Stone. 7 The architect. 8 Dr No. 9 The Return of the King. 10 Lee Van Cleef. 11 Raiders of the Lost Ark. 12 William Wallace. 13 Chicago. 14 Stallone. 15 Live and Let Die. 16 Daniel Day-Lewis. 17 David Lean. 18 Patriot Games. 19 Directing. 20 On Her Majesty's Secret Service. 21 Robert De Niro. 22 Unforgiven. 23 Faye Dunaway. 24 Kathleen Turner. 25 Car chase. 26 The Spy Who Loved Me. 27 True Grit. 28 Dirty Harry. 29 Liam Neeson. 30 Lois Maxwell.

Quiz 87 | Pot-Luck 39

Answers – page 209

LEVEL 2

1 Which book of the Bible tells us about the creation of the world?
2 What is a lacuna?
3 Edible, blue and hermit are all types of which creature?
4 Who played Thomas à Becket to Peter O'Toole's Henry II?
5 In which country is Waterloo, site of the Napoleonic battlefield?
6 In which play does Miss Prism appear?
7 Where is the metatarsal arch?
8 Which actress played opposite Russell Crowe in the movie "Cinderella Man"?
9 On a map, which places are joined by a contour?
10 In the song, which official is waiting "for me and my gal"?
11 What is pulchritude?
12 Which film comedians are associated with the phrase, "That's another fine mess you got me in"?
13 Which creature's song refers to a final speech or performance?
14 Which letter of the alphabet is used to describe a soft lead pencil?
15 Who was nicknamed the Brown Bomber?
16 In which country were there originally mandarins?
17 Who or what are Effingham, Grenville, Benbow and Collingwood?
18 For which sport is Gordon Pirie remembered?
19 What was Buddy Holly's real first name?
20 Which of Shakespeare's plays involves a pound of flesh?
21 Where are your clavicles?
22 A lady would wear a mantilla in which country?
23 In area, which is the world's largest desert?
24 First published in October 2005, who wrote the novel "The Lighthouse"?
25 What do your olfactory organs help you do?
26 Which comic actor who died in 2005 used the pseudonym Gerald Wiley as a writer?
27 To within a margin of seven more or less, what is a grown man's normal pulse rate in beats per minute?
28 What was Venus Williams' first tennis Grand Slam title?
29 Which motor company developed the Pivo, which can swivel to assist when parking?
30 Which festival is called Saint Sylvestre or San Silvestro in certain countries?

Answers | Pot-Luck 38 *(see Quiz 85)*

1 Kestrel for a Knave, by Barry Hines (Kes). 2 Pam Shriver. 3 Bank of England. 4 Ballet (dance). 5 A Zulu. 6 Stella Rimington. 7 Green. 8 India. 9 Everything swirls around. 10 Brass. 11 Yankee Doodle. 12 Passport to Pimlico. 13 Donald Rumsfeld. 14 Tug of war. 15 Dance. 16 Green/blue-green. 17 Russian Revolution. 18 Sir Walter Raleigh. 19 Eleven. 20 Heavyweight. 21 Charlotte Brontë. 22 Oxford. 23 Ian Rankin. 24 North America. 25 Set of bells. 26 7. 27 September. 28 Matador. 29 Holds two ordinary bottles. 30 Paradine.

211

1 Off which island is "Jaws" set?
2 Who played Harrison Ford's father in "Indiana Jones and the Last Crusade"?
3 Who is the cop battling with terrorists in "Die Hard"?
4 Which films are about the Corleone family?
5 What is Christopher Reeve's most famous role?
6 What is the name of the gem Harry Potter is looking for in the first Harry Potter movie?
7 In "Towering Inferno" Steve McQueen was the fireman: what was Paul Newman?
8 Which was the first Bond movie?
9 What was the final Lord of the Rings movie called?
10 Who was Bad in Spaghetti Westerns?
11 Which was the first of the "Indiana Jones" films to be released?
12 Which hero did Mel Gibson play in "Braveheart"?
13 In which city is "The Untouchables" set?
14 Who was involved in the writing of the "Rocky" and "Rambo" films?
15 Which was the first Bond film with Roger Moore?
16 Who played the starring role in "Last of the Mohicans"?
17 Who directed "Lawrence of Arabia"?
18 Which film starred Harrison Ford as an ex-CIA man?
19 For what did Kevin Costner win an Oscar in "Dances with Wolves"?
20 Which was George Lazenby's only Bond film?
21 Who starred as Jake La Motta in "Raging Bull"?
22 Which Clint Eastwood film won an Oscar for Gene Hackman as the sheriff of Big Whiskey?
23 Who played Bonnie to Warren Beatty's Clyde?
24 Who co-starred with Michael Douglas in "Romancing the Stone"?
25 What was the memorable, and at that time innovative, scene in "Bullitt"?
26 Which Bond film had the song "Nobody Does It Better"?
27 In which film did John Wayne win his only Oscar?
28 Which movie preceded "Magnum Force" and "The Enforcer"?
29 Who plays the title role in "Rob Roy"?
30 Who plays Miss Moneypenny in the early Bond films?

Answers	Folk and Country *(see Quiz 86)*

1 Jim Reeves. 2 Stand by Your Man. 3 Leaving on a Jet Plane. 4 I Will Always Love You. 5 Johnny Cash. 6 Charlie Pride. 7 Tom Paxton. 8 Tammy Wynette. 9 The Strawbs. 10 Bob Dylan. 11 Cambridge. 12 Hank Williams. 13 Mike Harding. 14 Garth Brooks. 15 Maddy Prior. 16 John Denver. 17 French. 18 Chet Atkins. 19 Woody Guthrie. 20 In an air crash. 21 Joan Baez. 22 Crystal Gayle. 23 Ralph McTell. 24 Pete Seeger. 25 Sandy Denny. 26 Willie Nelson. 27 Peter, Paul, Mary. 28 Loretta Lynn. 29 Gaudete. 30 Sue.

1 Which country has been officially called Myanmar since 1989?
2 Which country is made up of over 800 islands including Viti Levu?
3 Which desert covers part of China and Mongolia?
4 What title does the head of state of Nepal have?
5 Which 7000-island country lies in the Pacific, northeast of the South China Sea?
6 How is the Republic of China better known?
7 To which country does East Timor belong?
8 Which neighbouring countries' currency is the won?
9 What was the name of Bangladesh between 1947 and 1972?
10 In which country are the Cameron Highlands?
11 What are the majority of the islands of Micronesia composed of?
12 Which country is bordered by Laos, Vietnam and Thailand?
13 Which sea lies to the north of Iran?
14 What is Japan's highest mountain?
15 How many vowels are there in Kyrgyzstan?
16 Which country's official name in Hindi is Bharat?
17 What are China's famous "warriors" made from?
18 Which country's capital is Ulan Bator?
19 In which two countries is the Thar desert?
20 Which social system is divided into brahmins, ksatriyas vaisyas and sundras?
21 Where were Gurkhas originally from?
22 Which area of Russia has had the lowest temperatures in the world recorded there?
23 When "The Sound of Music" was shown in Korea what was missing?
24 What are the Seychelles' three official languages?
25 What is the capital of Singapore?
26 Which country's flag is a red circle on a green background?
27 Which Pacific islands share their name with a wise man in the Bible?
28 What did Ho Chi Minh City used to be called?
29 Which country has designated Chachoengsao as its new capital?
30 How many rivers does Tonga have?

Answers | **Around Scotland** *(see Quiz 91)*

1 Distillery. 2 Sir Walter Scott. 3 Southwest. 4 Extinct volcano. 5 Bird sanctuary. 6 St Giles Cathedral. 7 Bute. 8 Holyrood House. 9 Aberdeen. 10 Nuclear power. 11 Two. 12 Princes Street. 13 Glamis Castle. 14 Silicon Glen. 15 Caledonian Canal. 16 Iona. 17 Meadowbank. 18 Tay Bridge. 19 Bell's. 20 Blair Castle. 21 Fingal's Cave. 22 Scone Palace. 23 Loch Ness. 24 Perth. 25 Culloden. 26 Dee. 27 Abbeys. 28 Stone Age. 29 Loch Lomond. 30 Tomatin.

1 Of which country is Freetown the capital?
2 What is the term for a group of partridges?
3 What was the occupation of the legendary "Casey Jones"?
4 According to the proverb what is the mother of invention?
5 What is an area of water separated from the open sea by a coral reef?
6 How many countries starting with a letter J reached Euro 2004 in Portugal?
7 In the London theatre what is the longest-running play ever?
8 Which actor played Nicole Kidman's husband in the movie "The Stepford Wives"?
9 In astronomy what are falling stars properly called?
10 What are Hickling, Barton, and Breydon Water?
11 In 1989, which electronic giant bought Columbia Pictures?
12 What is meant by the Italian phrase "che sara sara"?
13 What does an American mean when he talks of a check in a restaurant?
14 Whom might you expect to see working in a dig?
15 If a ship runs up a yellow flag what does it mean?
16 Which is the smallest bird in the world?
17 Which Saint's day falls on 30 November?
18 In fiction who lived in the stables at Birtwick Hall?
19 Who was Oberon?
20 Which name is shared by David Beckham and Kevin Keegan?
21 In cookery, what is meant by coddling?
22 Which trade is especially likely to use an awl?
23 Who played President Bartlet in "West Wing"?
24 In World War II on what were we "going to hang out the washing"?
25 In which city was there formerly a parliament building called the Reichstag?
26 In which London building is the Whispering Gallery?
27 Which duo have produced songs for Tottenham Hotspur?
28 Who became President of Ireland in 1997?
29 What name was given to an airship that could be steered?
30 What was Darkness's follow up album to "Permission to Land"?

Answers | Pot-Luck 41 *(see Quiz 92)*

1 35p. 2 Powys. 3 Arsenal. 4 On a staircase. 5 Naturalist, entomologist. 6 Archbishop of Canterbury. 7 81. 8 Loudspeakers. 9 Bury St Edmunds, Suffolk. 10 In a low voice. 11 Atlantic. 12 Wagons, carts. 13 Rosary. 14 Leonardo. 15 Postage stamps. 16 It turns blue. 17 Margaret Mitchell. 18 Gerald Durrell. 19 Anatomy. 20 Seizure of power. 21 Clown (mime). 22 Revelation. 23 Anna Ford. 24 At right angles. 25 Venezuela. 26 Birmingham. 27 Brussels. 28 Channel Islands. 29 Michael Caine. 30 Teacher.

1 Edradour is the smallest what in Scotland?
2 Which famous Scottish writer lived at Abbotsford by the Tweed?
3 In which direction from Edinburgh do the Pentland Hills lie?
4 What is Berwick Law?
5 What is the Bass Rock famous as?
6 Which cathedral is also known as the High Kirk of Edinburgh?
7 Rothesay is the chief town of which island?
8 What is at the foot of the Royal Mile in Edinburgh?
9 Which city is at the mouth of the rivers Don and Dee?
10 What is produced at Torness?
11 How many bridges are there over the Firth of Forth?
12 What lies between Charlotte Square and St Andrew's Square?
13 Where was the childhood home of the Queen Mother?
14 What is the industrial area in and around Livingston nicknamed?
15 Which canal links the lochs of the Great Glen?
16 Which historic island is off the southwest tip of the Isle of Mull?
17 What is the name of Edinburgh's stadium where the Commonwealth Games have been held?
18 Which rail bridge is the longest in Europe?
19 Which famous whisky is made at Blair Athol?
20 Which baronial castle is the seat of the only British subject allowed to maintain his own private army?
21 What is the most famous cave on Staffa?
22 Which palace was once the site of a famous coronation stone?
23 Which loch contains the largest volume of fresh water in the British Isles?
24 Which city is often called the Fair City?
25 Leanach farmhouse can be seen on which moorland field of battle?
26 On which river does Balmoral stand?
27 Remains of what type of building are at Kelso and Jedburgh?
28 What type of village can be seen at Skara Brae?
29 Which loch is the largest stretch of inland water in Britain?
30 Where is Scotland's largest malt whisky distillery?

Answers	**Around Asia** *(see Quiz 89)*

1 Burma. 2 Fiji. 3 Gobi. 4 King. 5 Philippines. 6 Taiwan. 7 Indonesia.
8 North and South Korea. 9 East Pakistan. 10 Malaysia. 11 Coral. 12 Cambodia. 13 Caspian. 14 Mount Fujiyama. 15 One. 16 India. 17 Terracotta. 18 Mongolia's. 19 India and Pakistan. 20 Caste system. 21 Nepal. 22 Siberia. 23 Music. 24 English, French and Creole. 25 Singapore. 26 Bangladesh. 27 Solomon Islands. 28 Saigon. 29 Thailand. 30 None.

1 If VAT is 17.5% what is the VAT on an item costing £2?
2 In which county are the Brecon Beacons?
3 Emmanuel Petit was at which English club when he scored in a World Cup final?
4 Where would you find treads and risers close together?
5 As what did Henri Fabre achieve fame?
6 Whose official residence is Lambeth Palace?
7 How many individual squares are there in a standard Sudoku puzzle?
8 What are woofers and tweeters?
9 Restored in the 21st century, in which town is St Edmundsbury Cathedral?
10 What is meant by "sotto voce"?
11 In which ocean is the Sargasso Sea?
12 What are made by wainwrights?
13 What do Catholics call the string of beads they use when praying?
14 Who painted the most famous version of "The Last Supper"?
15 What is the subject matter covered by a Gibbons's catalogue?
16 What happens when red litmus paper is put in an alkaline solution?
17 Who wrote the novel "Gone with the Wind"?
18 Which naturalist is the author of "My Family and Other Animals"?
19 What word is used for the science dealing with the body structure?
20 What is a coup d'état?
21 As what kind of entertainer did Grock achieve fame?
22 Which is the last book of the Bible?
23 Which TV newsreader was married to cartoonist Mark Boxer?
24 How do bevel gears engage with one another?
25 Of which country is Caracas the capital?
26 Which soccer side plays at St Andrews?
27 In which capital is the statue of a small boy, the Mannekin Pis?
28 Where, today, would you find a bailiwick?
29 Which actor played Dr Larch in "The Cider House Rules"?
30 Before becoming famous, what was opera star Katherine Jenkins' profession?

Answers | Pot-Luck 40 *(see Quiz 90)*

1 Sierra Leone. 2 A covey. 3 Railroad engineer. 4 Necessity. 5 Lagoon. 6 None.
7 The Mousetrap. 8 Matthew Broderick. 9 Meteors. 10 Norfolk Broads. 11 Sony.
12 What ever will be, will be. 13 The bill. 14 Archaeologist. 15 No disease aboard, and it needs clearance. 16 Hummingbird. 17 St Andrew. 18 Black Beauty. 19 King of the fairies. 20 Joseph. 21 Simmering briefly. 22 Leather worker/shoemaker. 23 Martin Sheen. 24 Siegfried Line. 25 Berlin. 26 St Paul's. 27 Chas & Dave. 28 Mary McAleese. 29 Dirigible. 30 One Way Ticket to Hell... and Back.

Quiz 93 | Nature: Flowers | Answers – page 219

1 What is the common name for the antirrhinum?
2 Which hanging basket favourite is also called pelargonium?
3 What qualities do the flowers helichrysum and acroclinium have?
4 By what name is Solidago known?
5 What type of bell is a campanula?
6 Which yellow, pink-flushed rose was bred by Meilland in 1945?
7 Which wild flower is also known as the knapweed?
8 Which flower has rung-like leaflets?
9 What would you find in an anther on a stamen?
10 What is the common name for the plant Impatiens?
11 Which flowers are said to symbolize the Crucifixion?
12 Which flower, also called chalk plant or baby's breath, is a favourite with flower arrangers ?
13 Bachelor's buttons are a variety of which yellow wild flower?
14 Which flower's seeds are pickled to make capers?
15 Which animals love nepeta, giving the latter its common name?
16 What sort of hyacinth is a muscari?
17 Which flower – Lychnis – shares its name with a fictional detective?
18 Which two flowers would you find in an orchestra?
19 Which flower gets its name from a Persian or Turkish word for turban?
20 Which plant is grown not for its flowers but for its silvery seed pods?
21 Which family do azaleas belong to?
22 Jonquils are members of which family?
23 Which plant is also called the torch lily?
24 Which climbing plant has the variety Nelly Moser?
25 Which flower's foundation varieties are alba, gallica and damascena?
26 Which plant was named after the Greek goddess of the rainbow?
27 What sort of purplish-blue daisies are types of aster?
28 Which bloom's name means golden flower, although it can be many different colours?
29 What colour is the rose Silver Jubilee?
30 Which country sent the first dahlia seeds to Europe?

Answers | Pop: Worldwide (see Quiz 96)

1 Switzerland. 2 Greece. 3 Germany. 4 Italy. 5 Norway. 6 Germany. 7 José Carreras. 8 Dannii. 9 Montserrat Caballé. 10 Denmark. 11 Jason Donovan. 12 Ireland. 13 Jamaica. 14 France. 15 Two Little Boys. 16 Eddy Grant. 17 Chariots of Fire. 18 Chris de Burgh. 19 Perez Prado. 20 Boyzone. 21 Riverdance. 22 Yoko Ono. 23 West Indies. 24 Boogie. 25 Placido Domingo. 26 Sweden. 27 Maurice, Jean-Michel. 28 Sinead O'Connor. 29 Je t'aime. 30 España.

1 ICBM stands for Inter-Continental what?
2 What was a matchlock?
3 In which TV show did creatures cry "Exterminate!"?
4 What is the male equivalent of a ranee?
5 In chemistry, what is a substance which cannot be split into simpler substances?
6 According to the Germans, who were the 'Ladies from Hell'?
7 Who created "Till Death Us Do Part"?
8 In "Two Little Boys", what did each boy have that was wooden?
9 Which American rodent builds dams and fells trees?
10 In which river was Jesus Christ baptized?
11 In which Shakespeare play does a forest apparently move?
12 What do Americans call a pack of cards?
13 Who were the beaten finalists when France first won the World Cup?
14 What was the name of the first nuclear-powered submarine?
15 Who played Tony Blair on television in "A Very Social Secretary"?
16 Which word can go after funny and before china?
17 If you were driving at 50 miles per hour, at how many kilometres per hour would you be going (approximately)?
18 Which English king died at the age of 15?
19 In which sport are stones and a broom used?
20 Which surname links a Spice Girl and the first US Vice President?
21 Of which country was John George Diefenbaker prime minister?
22 In which language did Aristophanes write his plays?
23 Of which country was Archbishop Makarios prime minister?
24 Which member of U2 has the real name of Paul Hewson?
25 Of which US state is Little Rock the capital?
26 Which part of the body is described by the word labial?
27 In which West Country city is the railway station St David's?
28 For which country did Dennis Law play soccer?
29 Who created the Rebus novels?
30 Who was the youngest member of England's Rugby World Cup-winning squad in 2003?

Answers   Pot-Luck 43 *(see Quiz 97)*

1 Eros. 2 Green. 3 Friday. 4 Sailing/yachting. 5 Flyweight. 6 Sheep. 7 David Lloyd George. 8 Christine Keeler. 9 Sean Penn. 10 Yellow. 11 Karl Jenkins. 12 El Dorado. 13 Bank manager. 14 Dark blue. 15 La Paz. 16 Sculpture. 17 Ireland. 18 Hymn book. 19 Raven. 20 Astro. 21 Netherlands. 22 Colorado river. 23 Archery. 24 Femur. 25 Atlantic. 26 Kookaburra. 27 Greyfriars. 28 Calvary or Golgotha. 29 Colin Montgomerie. 30 Polo.

1 Which is the oldest British flat classic race?
2 Which jockey won the Derby, Oaks and St Leger in 2001?
3 Which jockey riding Shergar in 1981 won in his first Derby ride?
4 Which jockey won the Prix de l'Arc de Triomphe from 1985 to 1987 on three different horses?
5 Where did Britain's first evening meeting take place?
6 Who rode Henbit, Nashwan and Erhaab to Derby victories?
7 Which horse, in 1977, became the first to win the Mackeson and Hennessy in the same season?
8 Which horse had a hat-trick of wins in the Cheltenham Gold Cup from 2002 to 2004?
9 Who was the first woman to ride a winner over fences in Britain?
10 In 1925 at Windsor, bookmakers went on strike. Against what?
11 Where was the Derby held during the two World Wars?
12 On which course in Australia is the Melbourne Cup run?
13 Which jockey had most Classic wins before Lester Piggott?
14 Which was the first racecourse equipped with a photo-finish camera?
15 On which horse did Princess Anne win her first flat race?
16 Diomed was the first winner of which great race?
17 Which race came first, the 1000 Guineas or 2000 Guineas?
18 What is Dick Hern's real first name?
19 Who was Champion National Hunt jockey for four years before the new millennium and four after it?
20 Where is the Happy Valley racecourse?
21 What is the first name of Peter Scudamore's father?
22 In betting, how much is a monkey?
23 In which Surrey town is Sandown racecourse?
24 Lester Piggott shares his birthday with which annual event?
25 In which country did Steve Donoghue ride his first winner?
26 What is the real first name of Richard Dunwoody?
27 Son of a famous father, who had his first winner at Kempton in 1978?
28 Who won the Derby on Kris Kin in 2003 and North Light in 2004?
29 How many individual bets make up a Yankee?
30 How many Grand Nationals did Desert Orchid win?

Answers | **Nature: Flowers** *(see Quiz 93)*

1 Snapdragon. 2 Geranium. 3 Everlasting. 4 Golden Rod. 5 Canterbury bell. 6 Peace. 7 Cornflower. 8 Jacob's ladder. 9 Pollen. 10 Busy Lizzie. 11 Passion flower. 12 Gypsophila. 13 Buttercups. 14 Nasturtium. 15 Cats (Catmint). 16 Grape hyacinth. 17 Campion. 18 Viola, Bugle. 19 Tulip (tuliban). 20 Honesty. 21 Rhododendron. 22 Narcissus. 23 Red hot poker. 24 Clematis. 25 Rose. 26 Iris. 27 Michaelmas daisy. 28 Chrysanthemum. 29 Pink. 30 Mexico.

1 Whom did Celine Dion represent in the 1988 Eurovision Song Contest?
2 What is Demis Roussos' home country?
3 Which country does James Last come from?
4 U Got 2 Know where Cappella are from, do you?
5 Their first No 1 was "The Sun Always Shines on TV". Where were they from?
6 Members of Los Bravos were from Spain and from where else?
7 Which opera singer had a hit with "Amigos Para Siempre" (Friends for Life) in 1992?
8 Which Minogue sister had a hit with "Love and Kisses"?
9 Who duetted with Freddie Mercury on "Barcelona"?
10 Where does Whigfield hail from?
11 Which Australian had three consecutive No 1s between December 1988 and June 1989?
12 Which country won the Eurovision Song Contest in 1992, 1993 and 1994?
13 Which country are Bob and Ziggy Marley associated with?
14 Where is 70s chart topper Charles Aznavour from?
15 Which Rolf Harris record went to No 1 in 1969?
16 Who said "I Don't Wanna Dance" in 1982?
17 Which film theme gave Vangelis a hit in 1981?
18 Who was "Missing You" in 1988?
19 Who had a hit with "Guaglione" nearly 40 years after his first No 1?
20 Which Irish group sang "Love Me for a Reason" in 1994?
21 Which song and show started as a Eurovision interval filler?
22 Which famous widow was "Walking on Thin Ice" in 1981?
23 From which island group did Boney M hail?
24 In 1977 Baccara said "Yes, Sir, I Can..." what?
25 Who sang "Perhaps Love" with John Denver?
26 Whom did Abba win Eurovision for in 1974?
27 What are the first names of father and son musicians Jarre?
28 Whose first No 1 was "Nothing Compares 2 U"?
29 What was Jane Birkin and Serge Gainsbourg's famous recording?
30 Swedish Sylvia sang "Y Viva" where?

| **Answers** | Pot-Luck 42 *(see Quiz 94)* |

1 Ballistic missile. 2 Gun. 3 Dr Who. 4 Rajah. 5 Element. 6 Scottish Highland soldiers in kilts. 7 Johnny Speight. 8 Horse. 9 Beaver. 10 The Jordan. 11 Macbeth. 12 A deck. 13 Brazil. 14 Nautilus (in 1955). 15 Robert Lindsay. 16 Bone. 17 80 kilometres per hour. 18 Edward VI. 19 Curling. 20 Adams (Victoria and John). 21 Canada. 22 Greek. 23 Cyprus. 24 Bono. 25 Arkansas. 26 The lips. 27 Exeter. 28 Scotland. 29 Ian Rankin. 30 Jonny Wilkinson.

Quiz 97 | Pot-Luck 43

Answers – page 218

1 In Greek mythology, who is the god of love?
2 At night what colour light is shown on the starboard side of a ship?
3 Which day of the week is the Muslim holy day?
4 If you were using a spinnaker, what would you be doing?
5 What is the lightest weight in boxing?
6 What kind of animal is a merino?
7 Who was the first prime minister to make use of Chequers?
8 In a political scandal, who said, "Discretion is a polite word for hypocrisy"?
9 Who was Nicole Kidman's co star in the movie "The Interpreter"?
10 What colour jersey is worn by the leader in the Tour de France?
11 Who composed the choral work "The Armed Man"?
12 What was the name of the mythical South American city of gold?
13 In "Dad's Army" what was Captain Mainwaring's day job?
14 On a London Underground map, what colour is the Piccadilly line?
15 What is the capital of Bolivia?
16 In which art has Barbara Hepworth become famous?
17 Which country shares its name with the daughter of Alex Baldwin and Kim Basinger?
18 What sort of book was compiled by Moody and Sankey?
19 Which bird did Noah first send out of the ark?
20 How is Terence Williams of UB40 better known?
21 Of which country is Ajax a famous football team?
22 Which river flows through the Grand Canyon in the United States?
23 What sport would you practise if you were a toxophilite?
24 What is the name of the bone in your thigh?
25 In which ocean are the Azores?
26 Which Australian bird is famous for laughing?
27 Which school did Billy Bunter go to?
28 What is the name of the hill where Jesus Christ was crucified?
29 Who was runner up to Tiger Woods in the Open of 2005?
30 Which royal sport would you see at Cowdray Park and Hurlingham?

Answers	Sport: Horse Racing (see Quiz 95)

1 St Leger. 2 Michael Kinane. 3 Walter Swinburn. 4 Pat Eddery. 5 Hamilton. 6 Willie Carson. 7 Bachelor's Hall. 8 Best Mate. 9 Jane Thorne. 10 Betting tax. 11 Newmarket. 12 Flemington Park. 13 Frank Buckle. 14 Epsom. 15 Gulfland. 16 Derby. 17 2000 Guineas in 1809. 18 William. 19 Tony McCoy. 20 Hong Kong. 21 Michael. 22 £500. 23 Esher. 24 Guy Fawkes Night. 25 France. 26 Thomas. 27 Walter Swinburn, Jnr. 28 Kieren Fallon. 29 11. 30 One.

Quiz 98 | Celebs: Jet Setters

Answers – page 224

LEVEL 2

1 Which Oscar-winning actress adopted children Maddox and Zahara?
2 Which Welsh singer's name was linked with rugby's Gavin Henson in 2005?
3 Which rock star became dad to Alistair at the age of 60 in 2005?
4 Which French actor announced his retirement in 2005?
5 What is the first name of the crown prince of Spain?
6 Before their resignations in 1996 whom did Patrick Jephson and Steve Davies work for?
7 What were George Best's two wives called?
8 Which "Baywatch" star married Tommy Lee?
9 What were the two married names of the late Jacqueline Bouvier?
10 Whom did actress Jennifer Garner marry in 2005?
11 At the start of his career, which footballer's name was linked to Coleen McLoughlin?
12 What nickname was given to the group of artists which included Dean Martin, Frank Sinatra and Peter Lawford ?
13 Which superstar and former playboy is Annette Bening married to?
14 Which one-time Hollywood pair have a daughter called Dakota ?
15 Which film actress did Ashton Kutcher marry in 2005?
16 Which actress is the wife of Simon MacCorkindale?
17 Which heiress to a hotel chain appeared in the TV series "The Simple Life"?
18 Who got engaged to Jude Law on Christmas Day 2004?
19 Who was Athina Roussel's multi-millionairess mother?
20 What is the first name of Michael Caine's wife?
21 From which US state does model Jerry Hall come?
22 Who was Mrs Larry Fortensky until early 1996?
23 Who is Lady Helen Taylor's mother?
24 Who was widowed in 1990 when her husband's boat went out of control?
25 Who was married to and also separated from country singer Kenny Chesney in 2005?
26 Which southern French resort holds a yearly film festival?
27 Which film star is Mrs Carlo Ponti?
28 Which singer made a documentary called "I Want to Tell You a Secret"?
29 Which supermodel married British film producer Matthew Vaughn?
30 Which husband of Sarah Jessica Parker appeared in the 2005 movie version of "The Producers"?

Answers	Popular Classics (see Quiz 100)

1 Handel. 2 Enigma Variations. 3 Beethoven. 4 Finlandia. 5 The Pearl Fishers. 6 Iolanthe. 7 Washington Post. 8 Air on a G String. 9 Pachelbel. 10 From the New World. 11 The Four Seasons. 12 Frederick Delius. 13 Guitar. 14 Elijah. 15 Eine Kleine Nachtmusik (A Little Night Music). 16 Ravel. 17 Animals. 18 Purcell. 19 The Thieving Magpie. 20 The Planets. 21 Choral Symphony. 22 Violin. 23 Peter and the Wolf. 24 Ballet. 25 The Ring. 26 Computer. 27 Land of Hope and Glory. 28 Danube. 29 Britannia rules the waves. 30 France.

1 The River Ganges is a holy place for the followers of which religion?
2 What is the name for the home of an eagle?
3 Where was Robbie Burns born in Ayrshire?
4 Which Shakespearian play takes place in Illyria?
5 Which two leaders had a meeting in the Brenner Pass in World War II?
6 Tom Thumb, Tennis Ball and Winter Density are all types of what?
7 Which flower is particularly associated with Mary, the Madonna?
8 On which Yorkshire moor was a battle fought on July 2nd, 1644?
9 Which music hall comedian was known as the "Cheeky Chappie"?
10 In which industry was Lord Nuffield a pioneer?
11 Which word describes architecture dating from the time of James I?
12 What word describes the minimum number of members on a committee in attendance for it to reach valid decisions?
13 Who composed the "Thunder and Lightning" Polka?
14 Which war was fought in the Far East from 1950 to 1953?
15 What type of animal is a Kerry Blue?
16 In which year was the evacuation of Dunkirk?
17 Who won the Best Male Performer award at the 2005 MTV Awards?
18 What does an anemometer measure?
19 What is a filbert?
20 Which strait links the Black Sea and the Sea of Marmara?
21 What does a lexicographer write or make?
22 What was the name of the prison in "Porridge"?
23 Who or what live in a holt?
24 Which city was once known as Eboracum?
25 Which country's Royal family include Crown Prince Frederik and Crown Princess Mary?
26 What is the name of the largest art gallery in Russia, situated in St Petersburg?
27 By what name is mid-Lent Sunday popularly known?
28 What was the name of Britney Spears' first son?
29 Of the Seven Wonders of the World, where was the Colossus?
30 Which gorge is crossed by the Clifton suspension bridge?

Answers | Pot-Luck 45 *(see Quiz 101)*

1 Ways of ringing church bells. 2 Goat. 3 Nigeria. 4 Eye. 5 Its passion play (held every ten years). 6 Carlisle. 7 Jay Leno. 8 Forehead. 9 Palm Sunday. 10 Spain. 11 Ivor Novello. 12 A watch. 13 Jerusalem. 14 Lemmings. 15 Tax collector. 16 Nicolas Cage. 17 Dr Samuel Johnson. 18 Hamlet. 19 Evening. 20 Sheep. 21 Journalists, the press. 22 Edinburgh. 23 A wreath. 24 Sparking plug. 25 Norwegian. 26 Anthea Redfern. 27 Composer. 28 Bernard Montgomery. 29 Zidane. 30 Stephen Daldry.

1 Who wrote "The Hallelujah Chorus"?
2 From which work does the piece "Nimrod" come from?
3 Who wrote the concerto called "The Emperor"?
4 Which work by Sibelius represented the defiance of the Finns?
5 Which Bizet opera features the duet "Au Fond du Temple Saint"?
6 In which Gilbert and Sullivan opera do fairies take over Parliament?
7 Which US newspaper shares its name with a march by Sousa?
8 Which work by Bach became famous in a cigar advertisement?
9 Who wrote Pachelbel's Kanon?
10 What is Dvorak's 9th Symphony, written in the US, often called?
11 Which Vivaldi composition did Nigel Kennedy popularize?
12 Who wrote "On Hearing the First Cuckoo in Spring"?
13 For which instrument is Joaquín Rodrigo most famous?
14 Which Old Testament prophet was the subject of an oratorio by Mendelssohn?
15 Which title of a composition by Mozart was translated by Stephen Sondheim into the name of a musical?
16 Who wrote the Bolero Torvill and Dean danced to?
17 What was in the Carnival in the Saint-Saëns composition?
18 Which English composer's 300th anniversary took place in 1995?
19 What is the English title of "La gazza ladra" by Rossini?
20 Which suite is Gustav Holst's most famous composition ?
21 What is Beethoven's 9th Symphony known as?
22 For which instrument did Paganini chiefly compose?
23 Which famous piece by Prokofiev is for orchestra and narrator?
24 What type of performance was "The Rite of Spring" written for?
25 What is the Wagner opera cycle which includes "Siegfried" and "Die Walküre"?
26 What are pieces by Iannis Xenakis written with the aid of?
27 How is the "Pomp and Circumstance March" better known?
28 Which river is celebrated in Johann Strauss's most famous waltz?
29 Which line follows "Rule Britannia" in the chorus of the song?
30 Who is Russia's opponent in the campaign commemorated in the "1812 Overture"?

Answers	Celebs: Jet Setters (see Quiz 98)

1 Angelina Jolie. 2 Charlotte Church. 3 Rod Stewart. 4 Gérard Dépardieu. 5 Felipe. 6 The Princess of Wales. 7 Angie and Alex. 8 Pamela Anderson. 9 Kennedy, Onassis. 10 Ben Affleck. 11 Wayne Rooney. 12 Rat Pack. 13 Warren Beatty. 14 Don Johnson and Melanie Griffith. 15 Demi Moore. 16 Susan George. 17 Paris Hilton. 18 Sienna Miller. 19 Christina Onassis. 20 Shakira. 21 Texas. 22 Elizabeth Taylor. 23 The Duchess of Kent. 24 Princess Caroline of Monaco. 25 Renee Zellweger. 26 Cannes. 27 Sophia Loren. 28 Madonna. 29 Claudia Schiffer. 30 Matthew Broderick.

Quiz 101 Pot-Luck 45

Answers – page 223

1 What are Steadman triples, Plain Bob Caters and Gransire triples?
2 What kind of animal is a chamois?
3 In which African country is the city of Ibadan?
4 Which part of the body would be affected by astigmatism?
5 For what is Oberammergau famous?
6 Which city is the administrative headquarters of Cumbria?
7 Which Jay has hosted "The Tonight Show" in the US?
8 Where in your body is the frontal bone?
9 On which day does the Church celebrate Jesus entering Jerusalem?
10 This century, Prince Felipe has been heir to which throne?
11 Who wrote "The Dancing Years" and "King's Rhapsody"?
12 What is the collective noun to describe a number of nightingales?
13 With which holy city is the name Zion associated?
14 Which Scandinavian animals are famous for running over cliff tops?
15 Before he became a disciple of Jesus, what was Matthew's job?
16 Which actor co stars with Ethan Hawke in the movie "Lord of War"?
17 Boswell wrote the biography of which famous writer?
18 Ophelia appears in which Shakespeare play?
19 To what does the adjective crepuscular refer?
20 In Australia, what animal is a jumbuck?
21 Who or what is meant the Fourth Estate?
22 Which city has or had the nickname Auld Reekie?
23 What was awarded to winners in the original Olympic Games?
24 In a car what is the device called that secures electrical ignition?
25 What nationality was the playwright Ibsen?
26 Who was Bruce Forsyth's second wife?
27 As what did Bela Bartók achieve fame?
28 Who commanded the Allied ground forces in the Normandy invasion of 1944?
29 Which player hit two goals in the 1998 World Cup final?
30 Which theatre director was Oscar nominated for the movie "Billy Elliot"?

| **Answers** | Pot-Luck 44 *(see Quiz 99)* |

1 Hinduism. 2 Eyrie. 3 Alloway. 4 Twelfth Night. 5 Hitler and Mussolini. 6 Lettuce. 7 Lilies. 8 Marston Moor. 9 Max Miller. 10 Motor car manufacturing. 11 Jacobean. 12 Quorum. 13 Johann Strauss the Younger. 14 Korean War. 15 Dog. 16 1940. 17 Robbie Williams. 18 Wind speed. 19 A hazelnut. 20 The Bosporus. 21 Dictionaries. 22 HMP Slade. 23 Otters. 24 York. 25 Denmark. 26 The Hermitage. 27 Mothering Sunday. 28 Sean Preston. 29 Rhodes. 30 The Avon Gorge.

Quiz 102 | Pop: Shock Rock | Answers – page 228

1 Nancy Spungeon was the girlfriend of which punk performer?

2 Which grunge purveyor blew his brains out in 1994?

3 Which glam rocker proclaimed himself the "Godfather of Punk"?

4 Who was murdered by his father on his birthday in 1984?

5 Who had No1 albums in 1982 with "Number of the Beast" and "Seventh Son of a Seventh Son" in 1988?

6 Which interviewer challenged the Sex Pistols to swear on TV?

7 Which 1960s hit singer was famous for his trousers splitting on stage?

8 Which group made the top ten in 1991 after 20 minor hits over 15 years?

9 Which rock superstar did Mark Chapman gun down?

10 "Aquarius" came from which show that shocked 1960s audiences?

11 Who started life as John Lydon?

12 Who recorded "Grimly Fiendish" with the record number GRIM 1?

13 Who recorded – and set himself on – "Fire"?

14 Which group recorded the album "Nevermind"?

15 In 1993 what was Snoop Doggy Dogg arrested for?

16 Which Frankie Goes to Hollywood hit was banned by the BBC?

17 Which group was formed by Jello Biafra in the late 1970s?

18 Who was manager of the Sex Pistols?

19 The film "The Rose" was loosely based on whose life?

20 Which actress should have partnered Serge Gainsbourg on "Je t'aime" but withdrew from the project?

21 Which Sinatra song did Sid Vicious record?

22 Who were the "Hersham Boys"?

23 What is Boy George's real name?

24 Whose stage act included simulated "killings" of a doll and a chicken?

25 Reg Presley was said to be "too suggestive" with which group?

26 Which cult hero did Val Kilmer play in a 1991 Oliver Stone movie?

27 Who in 1966 spoke of being "more popular than Jesus'"?

28 Who released the solo album "Blaze of Glory" which included tracks from "Young Guns II"?

29 Which Australasian rock band included singer Michael Hutchence?

30 Who released the then extremely controversial "Let's Spend the Night Together" in 1967?

Answers | Around Australia *(see Quiz 104)*

1 Sydney. 2 Great Barrier Reef. 3 Ayers Rock or Uluru. 4 Canberra. 5 Pacific and Indian. 6 Bondi Beach. 7 The Northern Territory. 8 Botany Bay. 9 Brisbane river. 10 Queensland. 11 Western Australia. 12 The Blue Mountains. 13 Alice Springs. 14 Melbourne. 15 Wave Rock. 16 The Gold Coast. 17 Kakadu National Park. 18 Kuranda, Queensland. 19 Fraser Island. 20 Cairns. 21 Great Dividing Range. 22 Surfers' Paradise. 23 Cape Tribulation. 24 Perth. 25 The Bungle Bungle Range. 26 The Twelve Apostles. 27 Mount Bartle Frere. 28 Adelaide. 29 The Pinnacles. 30 Cape York.

1 Who said, "Anyone who hates children and dogs can't be all bad"?

2 In our solar system which planet takes the least time to orbit the sun?

3 What is the name of René's wife in "Allo Allo"?

4 Whose cave inspired Mendelssohn to compose his Hebrides overture?

5 Who wrote the Waverley novels?

6 Which word can go after blue and before neck?

7 Who was George W. Bush's first Vice President?

8 Is an okapi animal or vegetable or mineral?

9 Which musical was voted Britain's favourite in a 2005 Radio 2 poll?

10 On which country's stamps would you find the words Magyar Posta?

11 Whom did Joe Bugner defeat in his comeback fight in Sydney, in 1986?

12 Where was Marat when Charlotte Corday murdered him?

13 Nickelodeon was a name given to a juke box. What was it originally?

14 At what did Antonio Stradivari achieve fame?

15 To one place of decimals, how many centimetres equal one inch?

16 By what English name is the mountain Yr Wyddfa known?

17 Is the suburb of Southgate in the north, south, east or west of London?

18 Which famous British film company was associated with the symbol of a man striking a gong?

19 In Greek tragedy, which king married his own mother?

20 Which star sign is shared by Pat Cash and Steffi Graf?

21 Whose real name is Steveland Judkins?

22 In geometry, how many degrees are there in a complete circle?

23 In which kind of building is there a transept?

24 In London, which road runs from Charing Cross to Fleet Street?

25 Which alloy of tin and lead is used for making tankards and mugs?

26 What Egyptian obelisk stands on the Thames Embankment?

27 In which country did Boavista win their first league title in 2001?

28 What was Serena Williams' first tennis Grand Slam title?

29 What does a Frenchman mean when he says "Quel dommage"?

30 Who was the second wife of Tom Cruise?

Answers	American Sport *(see Quiz 105)*

1 National Football League. 2 Ice hockey. 3 Pittsburgh Stealers. 4 Baseball. 5 No-one. It was cancelled because of a strike by players. 6 Ice hockey. 7 Houston. 8 Washington. 9 Georgman Herman Ruth. 10 Florida. 11 Brad Friedel. 12 London Ravens. 13 American football. 14 Boston Red Sox. 15 1970. 16 Six. 17 Basketball. 18 Yogi. 19 New York. 20 Basketball. 21 The visiting team. 22 1994. 23 American football. 24 Canada. 25 Scott Hamilton and Brian Boitano. 26 The Pro Bowl. 27 LA Lakers. 28 Green Bay Packers. 29 Baseball. 30 Nine.

1 Which city with 3 million inhabitants is Australia's largest?
2 What is the name of the world's longest reef?
3 Which sacred rock is the world's largest monolith?
4 What is the capital of Australia?
5 Which two oceans are to the east and west of Australia?
6 What is the name of the surfing beach on the outskirts of Sydney?
7 Darwin is the capital of which state?
8 At which famous east coast bay did James Cook arrive in April 1770?
9 Which meandering river is Brisbane built around?
10 Which state is commonly called the Sunshine State?
11 Perth is the capital of which Australian state?
12 Which mountain range to the west of Sydney was partly destroyed by bush fires in December 1993?
13 Which is the nearest major town to the southwest of Ayers Rock?
14 What is the capital of the state of Victoria?
15 Which granite formation, formed by the wind, is to the east of Perth?
16 What is the coastline to the south of Brisbane called?
17 Which national park, known for its Aboriginal rock paintings and wildlife, lies to the east of Darwin?
18 Which "village in the rainforest" at the highest end of the Barron Gorge is the home to the only permanent Aboriginal theatre in Australia?
19 What is the world's largest sand island northeast of Brisbane?
20 What is Queensland's most northerly city?
21 Which mountain range runs parallel to the east coast for 4000 kilometres?
22 Which famous surfing beach is to the south of Brisbane?
23 Where does the rainforest meet the sea in northern Queensland?
24 Which state capital lies on the Swan River?
25 Which range of domed mountains lies in Purnululu National Park?
26 Along the Great Ocean Road in Victoria what 12 off-coast formations would you discover?
27 Which mountain, at 1611 metres, is the highest in Queensland?
28 Which Australian city hosted its final Formula 1 race in 1995?
29 Which fossilized remains of an ancient forest are found in the Nambung?
30 Which cape is at the northernmost tip of Australia in Queensland?

Answers | Pop: Shock Rock *(see Quiz 102)*

1 Sid Vicious. 2 Kurt Cobain. 3 Marc Bolan. 4 Marvin Gaye. 5 Iron Maiden. 6 Bill Grundy. 7 P. J. Proby. 8 Clash. 9 John Lennon. 10 Hair. 11 Johnny Rotten. 12 Damned. 13 Arthur Brown. 14 Nirvana. 15 A charge of murder. 16 Relax. 17 Dead Kennedys. 18 Malcolm McLaren. 19 Janis Joplin. 20 Brigitte Bardot. 21 My Way. 22 Sham 69. 23 George Alan O'Dowd. 24 Alice Cooper. 25 The Troggs. 26 Jim Morrison. 27 John Lennon – about the Beatles. 28 Jon Bon Jovi. 29 INXS. 30 The Rolling Stones.

1 In American football was does NFL stand for?

2 Which sport do the Buffalo Sabres play?

3 Which club was the first to win the Super Bowl two years in succession on two occasions?

4 Which sport has a Hall of Fame at Cooperstown, New York?

5 Who won the Baseball World Series in 1994?

6 In which sport is the Stanley Cup awarded?

7 Where are the Astros baseball team from?

8 Which city do the Redskins American football team come from?

9 What were "Babe" Ruth's real first names?

10 Where do World Series winners in 1997 and 2003 the Marlins come from?

11 Which Blackburn Rovers keeper played for the United States in the 2002 FIFA World Cup?

12 The first Budweiser Bowl in the UK in 1986 was won by which team?

13 The Princetown College rules drawn up in 1867 affect which sport?

14 Who lifted "The Curse of the Bambino" in 2004?

15 In American football in which year did the AFL and the NFL merge?

16 How many people are there in an ice hockey team?

17 What game is played by the Detroit Pistons?

18 What was the nickname of baseball's Lawrence Peter Berra?

19 Giants and Jets have triumphed in the Super Bowl for which city?

20 The invention of which sport is credited to Dr J. A. Naismith?

21 In baseball, which team bats first?

22 Which year were American professionals first allowed to enter the World Basketball Championships?

23 Which sport do the Miami Dolphins play?

24 In which country were the rules for modern ice hockey formulated?

25 Which two American men won ice skating Olympic gold in the 1980s?

26 Which trophy do teams from AFC and NFC players contest?

27 Which LA team had a 2000 to 2002 hat-trick of triumphs in basketball's NBA Championship?

28 Which team won the first Super Bowl?

29 Which sport do the Atlanta Braves play?

30 How many players are there in a baseball team?

Answers | Pot-Luck 46 *(see Quiz 103)*

1 W. C. Fields. 2 Mercury. 3 Edith. 4 Fingal's. 5 Sir Walter Scott. 6 Bottle. 7 Dick Cheney. 8 Animal. 9 Les Misérables. 10 Hungary's. 11 James Tillis. 12 In his bath. 13 US cinema (admission was a nickel). 14 Violin maker. 15 2.5. 16 Snowdon. 17 North. 18 The Rank Organization. 19 Oedipus. 20 Gemini. 21 Stevie Wonder. 22 360. 23 Church (or cathedral). 24 The Strand. 25 Pewter. 26 Cleopatra's Needle. 27 Portugal. 28 US Open. 29 "What a pity". 30 Nicole Kidman.

Quiz 106 Pot-Luck 47

Answers – page 232

1 Who composed the opera "The Tales of Hoffman"?
2 Which letters could David Beckham add to his name following a presentation in 2003?
3 For what is Frank Lloyd Wright famous?
4 Who wrote a novel about Kenilworth in Warwickshire?
5 What are the Howard League concerned with?
6 Mount Ararat is the traditional resting place of which ship or boat?
7 In "Treasure Island", which sailor dreamed of toasted cheese?
8 In South America what kind of building is a hacienda?
9 Which country won the Battle of Flodden?
10 In a fairy story a queen had to guess the name of a little man or lose her baby. What was his name?
11 In which book would you find Mrs Do-as-you-would-be-done-by?
12 What did the M stand for in the name of writer Louisa M. Alcott?
13 The play "And Then There were None" is based on a book by which author?
14 What term is given to the making of patterns by inlaying different coloured pieces of wood?
15 In which art did John and Ethel Barrymore achieve fame?
16 Which Oscar winner, for "Fargo", married director Joel Coen?
17 In the United States what item of clothing do they call suspenders?
18 Fashion designer Giorgio Armani studied for which profession in Milan?
19 Which is these is not a freshwater fish: cod, pike, carp, roach?
20 In 2001, which individual won the Nobel Peace Prize jointly with the UN?
21 Who wrote the Inspector Morse novels?
22 What is a mazuka?
23 In which Libyan seaport did Australian forces endure a long siege in World War II?
24 What is the common name for solidified carbon dioxide?
25 Nowadays, which is the largest British bird?
26 With which composer is the German town of Bayreuth associated?
27 Which university is situated at Uxbridge in Middlesex?
28 Which is the highest female voice?
29 What kind of material is cheesecloth?
30 Under Hitler, who was Nazi minister of propaganda?

Answers | Pot-Luck 48 (see Quiz 108)

1 Katherine Jenkins. 2 Cinque Ports (the original five). 3 Colgate. 4 Its stomach. 5 First female taxi driver. 6 Jerusalem (Christian, Jewish and Muslim). 7 Tartan. 8 Asia. 9 Denmark. 10 Music hall. 11 John Lowe. 12 Shooting. 13 A bevy. 14 Lindsay Davenport. 15 Two. 16 Euston. 17 Othello. 18 Jodie Marsh. 19 Purgatory. 20 Dead Cert. 21 Roman. 22 The Worst Witch books. 23 Fern. 24 Dr Kildare. 25 1961. 26 Job. 27 Jeremy Paxman. 28 Mars. 29 Bayern Munich. 30 Strong, warrior women.

1 In which film does Robert De Niro ask "are you talkin' to me?"?
2 Who wrote the book on which "The Russia House" was based?
3 Whom was the Jackal trying to assassinate in "The Day of the Jackal"?
4 Which president is being referred to in "All the President's Men"?
5 Who won an Oscar for "The Accused"?
6 Which movie was the first collaboration between Steven Spielberg and Tom Cruise?
7 What is Hitchcock said to have used for the blood in "Psycho"?
8 Which three actors have each played Richard Hannay in "The 39 Steps"?
9 Who played the role of South African Donald Woods in "Cry Freedom"?
10 What sort of establishment is the setting for "The China Syndrome"?
11 For which film did the reviewer write "Enough to make you kick the next pigeon you come across"?
12 What relation is Carter to Cain in "Raising Cain"?
13 On whose novel is the Sissy Spacek film "Carrie" based?
14 Who play the getaways in the remake of "The Getaway"?
15 What is the relationship between Tippi Hedren of Hitchcock's "Marnie" and Melanie Griffith of "A Stranger Among Us"?
16 What was the nationality of Alfonso Cuaron, who directed the third Harry Potter movie?
17 In which classic film do Mrs Danvers and Maxim de Winter appear?
18 Whose "Fatal Attraction" to Glenn Close cost him dear?
19 For which film did Steven Spielberg win his first Oscar as Director?
20 Who were the first performers to win the Best Actor and Actress Oscars in the same film after Henry Fonda and Katharine Hepburn in 1981?
21 Who starred in Hitchcock's "Dial M For Murder" and "Rear Window"?
22 Where was Jack Lemmon's son "Missing"?
23 In which classic film is "Rosebud..." a piece in the jigsaw puzzle?
24 In Hitchcock's "Frenzy" what are the victims strangled with?
25 Who costarred with Oscar-winner Jane Fonda in "Klute"?
26 In "The Crying Game" to which organization does the gunman belong?
27 Which filmed Anthony Shaffer play starred Michael Caine and Laurence Olivier?
28 Which Apollo mission was the subject of a film with Tom Hanks?
29 What was described as "Five criminals. One line up. No coincidence"?
30 Who causes terror in "The Hand That Rocks the Cradle"?

| **Answers** | Hi-Tech: Scientists (see Quiz 109) |

1 Hertz. 2 Becquerel. 3 Copernicus. 4 Stephen Hawking. 5 Nuclear fission. 6 Trigonometry. 7 Kelvin. 8 Atomic particles. 9 Bessemer. 10 Radar. 11 DNA. 12 Ampère. 13 Descartes. 14 Davy. 15 HIV. 16 Chadwick. 17 Hydrogen bomb. 18 Cathode ray tube. 19 Boyle. 20 Faraday. 21 First woman. First person to receive it twice. 22 Andrei Sakharov. 23 Werner von Braun. 24 Logarithms. 25 Polonium, radium. 26 Multiply. 27 Taxonomy. 28 Metric. 29 Galapagos. 30 Explosion of the atomic bomb.

1 "Living The Dream" was the third album released by which singer?
2 What name links Hastings, New Romney, Hythe, Dover and Sandwich?
3 In ads, which toothpaste gave you a ring of confidence?
4 According to Napoleon, what does an army march on?
5 In April 1967, what famous first did Shirley Preston achieve in London?
6 Which city is a holy one for three religions?
7 In Scotland what style of cloth was illegal from 1745 to 1782?
8 In land area which is the world's largest continent?
9 Of which country is Jutland a part?
10 In what kind of theatre did Vesta Tilley become famous?
11 Who in 1984 scored the first nine-dart 501 finish in a major event?
12 In the Wild West, for what was Annie Oakley famous?
13 Which word is used for a group of quails?
14 Which female tennis player finished 2004 ranked as World No 1?
15 How many Bond films did Timothy Dalton star in?
16 From which London station would you leave if travelling to Carlisle?
17 In a Shakespeare play who kills Desdemona?
18 Which glamour model wrote an autobiography entitled "Keeping It Real"?
19 What do Roman Catholics call the state or place where souls are purified after death?
20 What was the title of Dick Francis's first horse-racing thriller?
21 Which empire was ruled by Titus?
22 Which series of children's books are set in Miss Cackle's Academy for Witches and Wizards?
23 What kind of plant is maidenhair?
24 On TV, whose boss was Dr Gillespie?
25 Which was the last year which looked the same when the figures were looked at upside down?
26 Which Old Testament book is about the sufferings of one man?
27 Who has presented both "Newsnight" and "University Challenge"?
28 Which planet is also known as the Red Planet?
29 Which German team was first to win the European Cup?
30 In mythology who were the Amazons?

Answers   Pot-Luck 47 *(see Quiz 106)*

1 Offenbach. 2 OBE. 3 Architecture. 4 Sir Walter Scott. 5 Prison reform. 6 Noah's Ark. 7 Ben Gunn. 8 (Large) estate/farmhouse. 9 England. 10 Rumpelstiltskin. 11 The Water Babies (by Charles Kingsley). 12 May. 13 Agatha Christie. 14 Marquetry. 15 Acting. 16 Frances McDormand. 17 Braces. 18 Medicine. 19 Cod. 20 Kofi Annan. 21 Colin Dexter. 22 A dance. 23 Tobruk. 24 Dry ice. 25 Mute swan. 26 Wagner. 27 Brunel University. 28 Soprano. 29 Muslin. 30 Goebbels.

1 Who discovered radio waves?

2 Who gave his name to a unit of radioactivity?

3 Which 16th-century scientist proposed that the Earth orbited the Sun?

4 Who is best known for his theory of black holes?

5 On what did Otto Hahn, Lise Meitner and Fritz Strassman work?

6 In which branch of mathematics was Hipparchus a pioneer?

7 Which Baron of Largs gave his name to the degrees on the absolute scale?

8 What does Hans Geiger's Geiger counter detect?

9 Whose process decarbonized iron?

10 Which tracking device did Sir Robert Watson-Watt develop?

11 What did Crick, Watson and Wilkins determine the structure of?

12 Who formulated a law of electromagnetism and pioneered techniques in measuring electricity?

13 Which French philosopher created analytical geometry?

14 Which English chemist discovered the most elements?

15 Which virus was Robert Gallo one of the first to identify?

16 Which English physicist discovered the neutron?

17 What type of bomb did Edward Teller develop?

18 What sort of tube did William Crookes invent?

19 Who gave his name to the law that states that the pressure of gas is proportional to its volume?

20 Which physicist and chemist gave his name to the law of induction?

21 In terms of Nobel prizes how did Marie Curie achieve two "firsts"?

22 Which physicist who contributed to the development of Soviet nuclear weapons was also a civil rights campaigner?

23 Which German-born rocket engineer worked on the space programme?

24 Which aids to calculation did John Napier devise?

25 Which two elements did the Curies discover?

26 Leibniz's calculating machine was the first to perform which function?

27 Which word was Candolle the first to use in the classification of plants?

28 For which measuring system did Joseph Louis Lagrange lay the foundations?

29 Which Islands inspired Darwin write "The Origin of Species"?

30 For which Soviet development was Igor Kurchatov team leader?

Answers | Movies: Thrillers (see Quiz 107)

1 Taxi Diver. 2 John Le Carré. 3 Charles de Gaulle. 4 Richard Nixon. 5 Jodie Foster. 6 Minority Report. 7 Chocolate sauce. 8 Robert Donat, Kenneth More, Robert Powell. 9 Kevin Kline. 10 Nuclear power plant. 11 The Birds. 12 Twin brother. 13 Stephen King's. 14 Alec Baldwin and Kim Basinger. 15 Mother and daughter. 16 Mexican. 17 Rebecca. 18 Michael Douglas. 19 Schindler's List. 20 Anthony Hopkins and Jodie Foster. 21 Grace Kelly. 22 Chile. 23 Citizen Kane. 24 Necktie. 25 Donald Sutherland. 26 IRA. 27 Sleuth. 28 13. 29 The Usual Suspects. 30 The nanny.

Quiz 110 | Pot-Luck 49

Answers – page 236

1 When it is made in Europe, what are the three main ingredients of a kedgeree?

2 If a violinist is playing pizzicato, what is he doing?

3 For what kind of building is Rievaulx in North Yorkshire famous?

4 Which alcoholic drink is flavoured with juniper?

5 What is the legal term for telling lies under oath?

6 In which town in 1914 was an archduke assassinated?

7 What was a Sopwith Camel?

8 In which London park would you find Birdcage Walk?

9 What was the trade of the famous Russian Fabergé?

10 Who composed "Finlandia"?

11 In which country did David Coulthard win his first F1 Grand Prix?

12 What is a dactylogram?

13 Which group of islands are you going to if you are sailing to Skye?

14 Whom did Edward VII marry?

15 Which striker John has played for Luton, Arsenal, West Ham, Wimbledon and Celtic?

16 From the fibres of which plant is linen made?

17 What does the letters I stand for in AIDS stand for?

18 Which king was responsible for building the Tower of London?

19 What instrument is Larry Adler famed for?

20 How many equal angles are there in an isosceles triangle?

21 What marine mammals include belugas, blues and sperms?

22 In which city is Sauchiehall Street?

23 On an American Monopoly board, what are B & O, Reading, Short Line and Pennsylvania?

24 For what are the letters OM an abbreviation?

25 What is shepherd's purse?

26 Which day of the week is the Jewish sabbath?

27 Whose official residence is the Mansion House in London?

28 Over which country did the Ptolemies once rule?

29 Which Shirley co starred with Cameron Diaz in "In Her Shoes"?

30 Which football manager modestly called his autobiography "Anatomy of a Winner"?

| **Answers** | Pop Groups (see Quiz 114) |

1 Paul Weller. 2 Dozy. 3 Busted. 4 I Believe in a Thing Called Love. 5 Pink Floyd. 6 Monday. 7 Pray. 8 U2. 9 Keith Moon. 10 UB40. 11 The Osmonds. 12 Supertramp. 13 Waterloo Sunset. 14 Thin Lizzy. 15 Manfred Mann. 16 The Moody Blues. 17 Status Quo. 18 Scotland. 19 Electric Light Orchestra. 20 Jackson Five. 21 Jam. 22 Leeds. 23 Stars. 24 T. Rex. 25 The Eagles. 26 The Troggs. 27 10cc. 28 Spandau Ballet. 29 Culture Club. 30 Seven Seas of Rye.

1 Which Ashley was named best Comedy Actress in the 2005 British Comedy Awards?

2 Who created the series "Extras" with Ricky Gervais?

3 Which show had the Enid Blyton spoof "Five Go Mad in Dorset"?

4 Name the first two regular team captains in "Have I Got News for You?".

5 Who created Algernon the Rasta and the Reverend Nat West?

6 Which writer hosts the ITV predecessor of "Auntie's Bloomers"?

7 Who created Lauren, the schoolgirl from hell?

8 What was Peter Cook and Dudley Moore's revue show called?

9 What is the surname of the family in "My Family"?

10 Who was the resident vocalist on "That Was the Week That was"?

11 Who impersonated Angela Rippon in "Not the Nine O'Clock News"?

12 Who closed his show with the phrase "May your god go with you"?

13 Who came to fame in "The Comedians" before heading for Walford?

14 Which "Only Fools and Horses" characters were the chief couple in the spinoff "The Green Green Grass"?

15 Which sitcom featured Jean and Lionel?

16 Who joined French and Saunders in the writing of "Girls on Top"?

17 In "The Frost Report" John Cleese was upper class and Ronnie Barker middle class: who was working class?

18 In which show would you find "The Argument Clinic" and the game show "Blackmail"?

19 Which 90s show featured "Jessie's Diets"?

20 In which comedy show did Sanjeev ask various celebrities into his home to be quizzed by his family?

21 Which Chris features in "Hello" and "The Thick of It"?

22 Who was Captain Fantastic in "Do Not Adjust Your Set"?

23 Who created the "Spitting Image" puppets?

24 Who is sports commentator Alan Partridge's true alter ego?

25 In "My Family" what is father Ben's profession?

26 Who has his own series "...Who Else"?

27 Who created Stavros, the kebab shop owner?

28 Who was the dumb, giggly blonde on "Rowan and Martin's Laugh In"?

29 Who is Jennifer Saunders' "alternative" comedian husband?

30 Who plays the character of Lou in "Little Britain"?

Answers Pot-Luck 51 (see Quiz 115)

1 Fullers. 2 Athos, Porthos and Aramis. 3 Gary Trudeau. 4 Harold Wilson. 5 Amstel. 6 Jarvis Cocker. 7 NW6. 8 Basque. 9 Oakham. 10 Charles Clarke. 11 The Rand. 12 The Bay of Bengal. 13 World War I. 14 Moonlight Serenade. 15 William Wordsworth. 16 Pluto. 17 Akala. 18 Peter Schmeichel. 19 Alfred Lord Tennyson. 20 Resource. 21 Central. 22 Matthew MacFadyen. 23 The Bahamas. 24 Rocky Marciano. 25 Elizabeth Bennet. 26 The Mountains of Mourne. 27 France. 28 Colin Baker. 29 The Italian Job. 30 Jerry Garcia.

1 What does GATT stand for?
2 Where would you see the Dow Jones index?
3 What is a group of producers acting together to fix prices called?
4 Why is Yemen unique in terms of currencies?
5 Which body assesses whether a takeover is in the public interest?
6 The Channel Islands, Gibraltar and the Isle of Man use British currency but, economically, what else do they have in common?
7 What is the chancellor of the exchequer's official London address?
8 Other than in Denmark where is the Danish krone used?
9 What name is given to economic activities which are unrecorded?
10 In which continent is the CFA franc a widespread currency?
11 In which country is the multinational Samsung based?
12 What is a country's GNP?
13 In which country was OPEC founded?
14 Which common market area does CARICOM deal with?
15 The European Union came into being in 1993 after which treaty?
16 In which country is the multinational Nestlé based?
17 Which area of the economy is the CAP concerned with?
18 What is the Japanese share index called?
19 What does ERM stand for?
20 Which states are referred to as the Visegrad Group or CEFTA states?
21 Who were the first two countries to withdraw from the ERM?
22 Which country is the world's largest coffee exporter?
23 Where is the headquarters of the International Monetary Fund ?
24 What name is given to the leading Western economic powers?
25 APEC encourages trade between countries bordering which ocean?
26 Where would you see the FT-SE share index?
27 What position did John Major hold immediately before becoming prime minister in 1990?
28 What does ECU stand for in terms of European Monetary Union?
29 What is the OFT?
30 Where is the headquarters of the Organization for Economic Cooperation and Development?

Answers | **Pot-Luck 49** (see Quiz 110)

1 Fish/eggs/rice. 2 Plucking the strings. 3 Its abbey. 4 Gin. 5 Perjury. 6 Sarajevo.
7 Aeroplane. 8 St James's Park. 9 Goldsmith. 10 Sibelius. 11 Portugal. 12 A fingerprint. 13 Inner Hebrides. 14 Princess Alexandra of Denmark. 15 Hartson. 16 Flax. 17 Immune (Acquired Immune Deficiency Syndrome). 18 William the Conqueror. 19 Harmonica. 20 Two. 21 Whales. 22 Glasgow. 23 Stations. 24 Order of Merit. 25 A wild flower. 26 Saturday. 27 Lord Mayor of London. 28 Egypt. 29 Shirley MacLaine. 30 Jose Mourinho.

Quiz 113 | Pot-Luck 50

Answers – page 239

1 Which 2005 TV series saw celebrities trying to discover their family tree?
2 Tsar Kolokol is the biggest what in the world?
3 In which fictitious Hampshire town does Chief Inspector Wexford work?
4 Which politician's memoirs appeared in the book "Upwardly Mobile"?
5 In the Victorian age what did Mary Ann Cotton gain notoriety as?
6 What instrument did Nat King Cole play?
7 Cleopatra supposedly bathed in the milk of which animal?
8 Who was the first Eliza Doolittle in the stage version of "My Fair Lady"?
9 What was tested at Bikini Atoll in 1954?
10 The Boat Race course is situated between Putney and where?
11 Charles II gives his name to which type of animal?
12 Who played the monster in the 1931 movie "Frankenstein"?
13 Who sang about Mr Woo?
14 Who had a flagship called "Victory"?
15 What toy is named after US president Theodore Roosevelt?
16 David Beckham scored his first senior goal for which club?
17 Which famous person did John Wilkes Booth shoot?
18 What is the pigment inside red blood cells?
19 In which London art gallery did an exhibition of Henri Rousseau's paintings open in 2005?
20 Who is the patron saint of mountaineers?
21 Who played Ma Larkin to David Jason's Pa?
22 Which ocean is the world's deepest?
23 Who was the author of the best-selling "Country Diary of an Edwardian Lady"?
24 Which bandleader shared his name with a British prime minister?
25 Which star from "Friends" appeared in London's West End in "Some Girls"?
26 In geography what is a shoal?
27 What is a ban on international trade with a country called?
28 In broadcasting what does CNN stand for?
29 Which Irish singer recorded the album "Day without Rain"?
30 What is Rumpole's first name in the character created by John Mortimer?

Answers | TV: Comedy (see Quiz 111)

1 Ashley Jensen. 2 Stephen Merchant. 3 The Comic Strip Presents. 4 Paul Merton, Ian Hislop. 5 Lenny Henry. 6 Denis Norden. 7 Catherine Tate. 8 Not Only ... But Also. 9 Harper. 10 Millicent Martin. 11 Pamela Stephenson. 12 Dave Allen. 13 Mike Reid. 14 Boycie and Marlene. 15 As Time Goes By. 16 Ruby Wax. 17 Ronnie Corbett. 18 Monty Python's Flying Circus. 19 The Fast Show. 20 The Kumars at No 42. 21 Chris Langham. 22 David Jason. 23 Fluck and Law. 24 Steve Coogan. 25 Dentist. 26 Rory Bremner. 27 Harry Enfield. 28 Goldie Hawn. 29 Adrian Edmondson. 30 David Walliams.

Quiz 114 | Pop Groups

Answers – page 234

1 Who was lead singer with Style Council?
2 Who sang with Dave Dee, Beaky, Mick and Tich?
3 Who brought out the album "A Present for Everyone" in 2003?
4 What was the first top ten hit single for the Darkness?
5 Which group featured Dave Gilmour and Roger Waters?
6 Which day did the Boomtown Rats not like?
7 What was Take That's first No 1?
8 Which Irish supergroup started life known as Feedback?
9 Who was the Who's original drummer?
10 Which group formed their own label Dep International?
11 Merrill, Jay, Wayne, Jimmy and Donny made up which group?
12 Which group made the album "Crisis? What Crisis"?
13 Which Kinks hit starts, "Dirty old river, must you keep rolling..."?
14 Which group was led by Phil Lynott?
15 Paul Jones and Mike D'Abo both sang lead with which group?
16 Justin Hayward and Denny Laine were members of which group?
17 Which group opened the Wembley Stadium section of Live Aid?
18 Wet, Wet, Wet come from which country?
19 Which group sang about Horace Wimp?
20 How were the Jacksons credited on their early hits?
21 Whose first top ten single was "The Eton Rifles" in 1979?
22 Which city do the Kaiser Chiefs come from?
23 Which Simply Red album contained "For Your Babies"?
24 Which glam group asked "Metal guru, is it you?"?
25 Which group wanted to "Take It to the Limit"?
26 Which group had the original hit with "Love is All Around"?
27 Who thought that "Life is a Minestrone"?
28 Gary and Martin Kemp were members of which group?
29 Which group had seven consecutive top four hits until the release of "The Medal Song"?
30 What was Queen's first hit?

Answers	Modern History: Boom and Bust *(see Quiz 112)*

1 General Agreement on Tariffs and Trade. 2 Wall Street. 3 Cartel. 4 Two. 5 Monopolies & Mergers Commission. 6 Issue their own bank notes. 7 11 Downing Street. 8 Greenland, Faeroe Islands. 9 Black economy. 10 Africa. 11 South Korea. 12 Gross national product. 13 Iraq. 14 Caribbean. 15 Maastricht. 16 Switzerland. 17 Agriculture. 18 Nikkei. 19 Exchange Rate Mechanism. 20 Czech Republic, Hungary, Poland, Slovakia. 21 UK, Italy. 22 Brazil. 23 Washington. 24 G7. 25 Pacific. 26 London. 27 Chancellor of the exchequer. 28 European Currency Unit. 29 Office of Fair Trading. 30 Paris.

Quiz 115 | Pot-Luck 51

Answers – page 235

1 Who brews London Pride?
2 Name the three Musketeers?
3 Which cartoonist draws the Doonesbury strip?
4 Which premier was Huddersfield's most famous son?
5 Which Dutch river is also the name of a beer?
6 Who executed a one-man stage invasion to disrupt Michael Jackson's appearance at the 1996 Brit Awards?
7 What is the postal code for Kilburn?
8 Which item of lingerie is also the language of the inhabitants of the Western Pyrenees?
9 What was the county town of Rutland?
10 Who took over from David Blunkett as Home Secretary?
11 What is the currency of South Africa?
12 What is the largest bay in the world?
13 The play "Journey's End" is set against the background of which conflict?
14 What was Glenn Miller's signature tune?
15 Which famous poet lived in Dove Cottage?
16 Which is the most distant planet in the solar system?
17 Who was the leader of the wolfpack in "The Jungle Book"?
18 Who was Man Utd's captain in the 1999 European Champions' Cup Final?
19 Who wrote the poem "The Lady of Shallot"?
20 What does the letter R stand for in URL?
21 Which Underground line is Marble Arch station on?
22 Who played the role made famous by Colin Firth in the 2005 remake of "Pride and Prejudice"?
23 Where did Edward VIII spend most of WWII?
24 Who retired as undefeated heavyweight boxing champion of the world?
25 What is the name of the heroine of Jane Austen's novel "Pride and Prejudice"?
26 Which Irish mountains sweep down to the sea?
27 Which country was selected to host the Rugby World Cup of 2007?
28 Who was the sixth TV Doctor Who?
29 Which 1969 film featured cockney ram-raiders in Turin?
30 Which member of the Grateful Dead died in 1995?

Answers | Pot-Luck 50 (see Quiz 113)

1 Who Do You Think You are?. 2 Bell. 3 Kingsmarkham. 4 Norman Tebbit. 5 A mass murderer. 6 Piano. 7 Ass. 8 Julie Andrews. 9 Hydrogen bomb. 10 Mortlake. 11 Dog. King Charles Spaniel. 12 Boris Karloff. 13 George Formby. 14 Lord Nelson. 15 Teddy bear. 16 Preston North End. 17 Abraham Lincoln. 18 Haemoglobin. 19 Tate Modern. 20 Saint Bernard. 21 Pam Ferris. 22 Pacific. 23 Edith Holden. 24 Ted Heath. 25 David Schwimmer. 26 An area of sandbanks. 27 Embargo. 28 Cable News Network. 29 Enya. 30 Horace.

The Hard Questions

If you thought that this section of this book would prove to be little or no problem, or that the majority of the questions could be answered and a scant few would test you then you are sorely mistaken. These questions are the *hardest* questions *ever*! So difficult are they that any attempt to answer them all in one sitting will addle your mind and mess with your senses. You'll end up leaving the pub via the window while ordering a pint from the horse brasses on the wall. Don't do it! For a kick off there are 3,000 of them, so at 20 seconds a question it will take you over 16 hours and that's just the time it takes to read them. What you should do instead is set them for others – addle your friends' minds.

Note the dangerous nature of these questions though. These are you secret weapons use them accordingly unless, of course, someone or some team is getting your back up. In which case you should hit them hard and only let up when you have them cowering under the bench whimpering "Uncle".

These questions work best against league teams, they are genuinely tough and should be used against those people who take their pub quizzes seriously. NEVER use these questions against your inlaws.

1 Which school had a No 1 with "There's No One Quite Like Grandma"?

2 Which American answer to Band Aid sang "We are the World"?

3 Which musical did Lee Marvin's sole hit, "Wandrin' Star", come from?

4 According to 1950s star Kitty Kalen what do "Little Things Mean"?

5 Which pop duo recorded "In the Year 2525"?

6 Which member of the cast of "Dad's Army" sang "Grandad"?

7 Who recorded "Let It Be" in 1987 for a disaster fund?

8 Where had Charlene never been to in 1982?

9 Who said "Move Closer" in 1985?

10 What is Marie Osmond's only solo hit?

11 Which Beatles song did the Overlanders take to No 1?

12 With the theme song for which sporting event did Kiri Te Kanawa have her only chart hit in 1991?

13 Which music accompanied Des Lynam's top 50 hit?

14 Who had a No 1 hit in 1999 with "Everybody's Free (to Wear Sunscreen)"?

15 What colour were the spots on Mr Blobby?

16 Who were the first two one-hit wonders to reach the top with the same song?

17 Two members of which group sang on both of them?

18 Which Twins sang "When" in 1958?

19 Whom did Ricky Valance tell he loved her in 1960?

20 Which airways featured on Typically Tropical's only No 1?

21 What is John Denver's only solo UK single hit?

22 Who joined New Order on England New Order's "World in Motion"?

23 Which travel terminal provided a hit for Cats UK?

24 With which TV theme did Geoffrey Burgon have his only hit in 1981?

25 What was the Johnny Mann Singers' only hit?

26 Who got to No 3 in 1968 with "Judy in Disguise (With Glasses)"?

27 What did the Pipkins say "Gimme" in 1970?

28 Which qualification sang "I won't let you down" in 1982?

29 Which TV character gave Ken Barrie his only chart hit?

30 How many performers made up Las Ketchup who served up "The Ketchup Song"?

Answers	**Performance Arts** *(see Quiz 3)*

1 Vocal with no instrumental accompaniment. 2 The man. 3 Christopher Bruce. 4 Break dancing. 5 Piccolo. 6 Berlin. 7 Diaghilev. 8 Trombones and tubas. 9 Comedy. 10 Philip Pullman. 11 Mark Morris. 12 Saturday Night Fever. 13 Keyboard. 14 Cakes given as competition prizes. 15 Festival Ballet. 16 Boston, Charleston. 17 Three. 18 Paul Jones. 19 Samba. 20 Egypt. 21 Kazoo. 22 Lyre. 23 Festivities associated with the building of a new barn. 24 World War II. 25 Balanchine. 26 Ukulele. 27 Bullfighter's cloak. 28 Cannes. 29 Not touching partner. 30 Harriet Walter.

1 Who shot the Archduke Franz Ferdinand?

2 In fiction, what were Milly Molly Mandy's proper names?

3 Which monarchs sat on the Peacock Throne?

4 Of what is a lux a unit?

5 In the early 19th century what did George Shillibeer bring to London?

6 Who first claimed that the world was not flat but a sphere?

7 Who was the first woman to fly the Atlantic single-handed?

8 Which animals communicate by touch, smell and dance?

9 Around which French town is the champagne industry centred?

10 A track by which female artist was used as the theme to ITV's "Celebrity Love Island"?

11 At what speed in mph does a wind become a hurricane?

12 Who officially opened the 1936 Olympiad?

13 What was the name of the first talking cartoon?

14 Which competition was organized by Mecca Ltd to coincide with the 1951 Festival of Britain?

15 Who invented the coordinate system to compare relationships on a graph?

16 What colour is the ribbon of the Victoria Cross?

17 Who or what lived in Honalee?

18 Which profession would use the terms occlusion, isohyet and adiabatic?

19 What name is used to describe a baby salmon?

20 In which building did Charles and Camilla hold their civil wedding ceremony?

21 Who is the husband of Meera Syal?

22 Who anonymously entered a contest in Monaco to find his lookalike and came third?

23 Where in Spain was Pablo Picasso born?

24 Who was Edward VI's mother?

25 Which sea has no coast?

26 Who was the first Briton to organize a continental holiday tour?

27 What was the first US No 1 for Destiny's Child?

28 Who discovered oxygen in 1774?

29 Which bird can fly the fastest?

30 Which is the largest human organ?

Answers Pot-Luck 2 *(see Quiz 4)*

1 Dublin. 2 Prostitute. 3 Pope John Paul II. 4 The Tories. 5 The Scottish red deer. 6 Frank Richards. 7 Number 13. 8 Yellow. 9 Scotland's largest cave. 10 The sixpence. 11 Chewing gum. 12 St Cecilia. 13 Nepal. 14 Sunny Afternoon. 15 Solomon. 16 Tom Cruise. 17 The White Tower. 18 Tetley. 19 The Huguenots. 20 The Anglican Church. 21 Greenland. 22 Burley. 23 Rosa Mota. 24 Jesus to a Child. 25 Baronet. 26 Aluminium. 27 Michael Caine. 28 A palindrome. 29 John Adams. 30 Lucy Davis.

1 How is a cappella music performed?
2 Which dancer performs a variation in a pas de deux?
3 Who stepped down as Artistic Director of the Rambert Dance Company in 2002?
4 Which dancing from the 1980s has dancers performing acrobatic feats?
5 Which instrument is also called the octave flute?
6 At which film festival is the Golden Bear awarded for best film?
7 Which impresario founded the Ballets Russes?
8 In a standard modern symphony orchestra which two brass instruments would be on the back row?
9 In 2005 Kim Cattrall made her West End debut at which theatre?
10 In 2003 the National Theatre premièred a stage version of a trilogy of books by which author?
11 Which US choreographer reworked "The Nutcracker" as "The Hard Nut"?
12 Which 1970s film is seen as greatly popularizing disco dancing?
13 What type of instrument is a celestea?
14 Why is a cakewalk so called?
15 What did the English National Ballet used to be called?
16 Which two dances take their names from US towns?
17 What is the minimum number of voices for performing a glee?
18 Which singer/radio DJ's name is also the name of a 19th-century dance?
19 Which dance is the bossa nova a type of?
20 Where are castanets thought to originate?
21 What is a mirliton another name for?
22 Which instrument are violins and violas descended from?
23 Why were barn-dances so called?
24 During which period did the jitterbug gain popularity?
25 Who founded the New York City Ballet?
26 Which instrument's name is the Hawaiian word for jumping flea?
27 In the paso doble what is the female dancer supposed to be?
28 At which film festival is the Palme d'Or awarded for best film?
29 What sort of dancing trend did the twist set?
30 Who won the 2005 Evening Standard Best Actress award for her performance in "Mary Stuart"?

| **Answers** | Pop: One-Hit Wonders *(see Quiz 1)* |

1 St Winifred's. 2 USA for Africa. 3 Paint Your Wagon. 4 A lot. 5 Zager and Evans. 6 Clive Dunn. 7 Ferry Aid. 8 Me. 9 Phyllis Nelson. 10 Paper Roses. 11 Michelle. 12 Rugby World Cup. 13 Fauré's Pavane. 14 Baz Luhrmanne. 15 Yellow. 16 Band Aid, Band Aid II, Do They Know It's Christmas. 17 Bananarama. 18 Kalin Twins. 19 Laura. 20 Coconut Airways. 21 Annie's Song. 22 England World Cup Squad. 23 Luton Airport. 24 Brideshead Revisited. 25 Up, Up and Away. 26 John Fred and the Playboy Band. 27 Dat Ding. 28 PhD. 29 Postman Pat. 30 Three.

Quiz 4   Pot-Luck 2

Answers – page 242

1 Which city is known in its own language as Baile Atha Cliath?
2 Kitty Fisher was 18th-century London's most highly paid what?
3 Which pope was shot by Mehmet Ali Agca on May 13th, 1981?
4 Which political party takes its name from a band of Irish outlaws?
5 Which is the largest wild animal in the British Isles?
6 Who created Billy Bunter?
7 People who are terdekaphobic are afraid of what?
8 What colour is worn for funerals in Egypt?
9 What is the Great Smoo?
10 Which British coin ceased to be legal tender on June 30th, 1980?
11 What is manufactured from the sapodilla tree?
12 Who is the patron saint of music?
13 Which country is ruled by King Gyanendra?
14 Which song starts, "The taxman's taken all my dough..."?
15 Who was David's son in the Bible?
16 Whose first box office film was called "Risky Business"?
17 Which is the oldest part of the Tower of London?
18 Which company first introduced tea bags in Great Britain in 1952?
19 What were the French Protestants led by Henry of Navarre known as?
20 Which Church's doctrine is set out in the Thirty-Nine Articles?
21 Which country left the EC in 1985?
22 Which George led Ipswich Town into the Premiership in 2000?
23 Which marathon runner won Olympic gold in 1988, making her the first Portuguese woman to do so?
24 Which George Michael No 1 begins "Kindness in your eyes"?
25 What does the abbreviation Bt signify after a name?
26 In the Earth's crust which metal is the most abundant?
27 Which English actor played the disillusioned journalist in "The Quiet American"?
28 What type of word reads the same forwards and backwards?
29 Who was the second president of the United States?
30 Which actress played Dawn Tinsley in "The Office"?

Answers   Pot-Luck 1 *(see Quiz 2)*

1 Gavrilo Princip. 2 Millicent Margaret Amanda. 3 The shahs of Persia. 4 Illumination. 5 A bus service (using horses). 6 Pythagoras. 7 Amelia Earhart. 8 Bees. 9 Epernay. 10 Jem. 11 73 mph. 12 Adolf Hitler. 13 Steamboat Willie. 14 Miss World. 15 René Descartes. 16 Purple. 17 Puff the Magic Dragon. 18 Meteorology. 19 Parr. 20 Guildhall, Windsor. 21 Sanjeev Bhaskar. 22 Charlie Chaplin. 23 Málaga. 24 Jane Seymour. 25 The Sargasso Sea. 26 Thomas Cook. 27 Bills, Bills, Bills. 28 Joseph Priestley. 29 The homing pigeon. 30 The liver.

1 Nanninga was the first sub to score in a World Cup Final ... for whom?

2 Which team are known as the Cherries?

3 What was strange about the tackle that ended the career of keeper Chic Brodie of Brentford back in 1970?

4 How many countries played in World Cup 2002 in Japan and South Korea?

5 Which club did Glenn Hoddle leave to become England manager?

6 Which country won the first World Cup held in 1930?

7 Which German club did Kevin Keegan play for?

8 Mike Walker and Martin O'Neill walked out on which chairman?

9 Who was the first uncapped player sold for over £1,000,000 in Britain?

10 What name is shared by Scunthorpe, Southend and Rotherham?

11 Fabien Barthez began his career with which French club?

12 Who was England's final substitute in the 2002 quarter-final defeat by Brazil?

13 Which country did Emlyn Hughes play for?

14 Emmanuel Petit joined Arsenal from which soccer club?

15 Which 4th Division team reached the first League Cup Final in 1962?

16 Who played in the first FA Cup Final ever to end 3–3?

17 Which team paid a record £1,000 for Alf Common in 1905?

18 Newcastle play at St James' Park but who plays at St James Park?

19 Who captained the Man Utd team that won the 1968 European Cup?

20 Who scored Scotland's only goal in the 1986 World Cup Finals in Mexico?

21 Where in England do you go to shout "Come on, you greens"?

22 An Italian boss replacing a Dutchman was a first at which English club?

23 Stokoe (Sunderland) and Revie (Leeds) were rival managers in the 1973 FA Cup Final. For which teams were they rivals as Cup Final players?

24 If you are at Turf Moor who is playing at home?

25 Which keeper played three games for Man Utd in the early 1990s and 23 games in 1999–2000?

26 Which club has been managed by Brian Clough and Jimmy Armfield?

27 Which player went from Juventus to Real Madrid for £46.5m in 2001?

28 Which team is known as "The Bairns"?

29 Which non-League team held Man Utd to a 0–0 draw in the third round of the 2005/6 FA Cup?

30 At which Lane did Wimbledon play when they entered the League?

Answers	**Great Buildings** *(see Quiz 7)*

1 Canterbury. 2 Winning an international competition. 3 Marble. 4 Etoile. 5 St Paul's. 6 Eiffel Tower. 7 Ivan the Terrible. 8 San Marco. 9 Cardinal Wolsey. 10 Devonshire. 11 Castle Howard. 12 It has sunk. 13 Castle Howard. 14 Mexico. 15 Versailles. 16 Chicago. 17 Cologne. 18 F. W. Woolworth. 19 Venus de Milo. 20 1894. 21 Extension to the National Gallery. 22 York Minster. 23 Montmartre. 24 Vatican, Rome. 25 Michelangelo. 26 Rangoon, Myanmar (Burma). 27 St Petersburg. 28 Coventry. 29 Amritsar. 30 To cover smoke stains. (It was set on fire by the British in 1814.)

Quiz 6 | Pot-Luck 3

Answers – page 248

1 Which organ in the body is affected by otitis?
2 Which was the first country, in 1824, to legalize trade unions?
3 Who replaced Christopher Eccleston as Dr Who?
4 Which is the smallest state of Australia?
5 In which castle was Edward II murdered?
6 In which year was North Sea oil discovered?
7 Californian and Stellar's are types of what?
8 What is a group of cats called?
9 Which former James Bond actor became a goodwill ambassador for UNICEF?
10 What is measured by an interferometer?
11 Which famous cliffs in Acapulco are used by daring divers?
12 Who broke Muhammad Ali's jaw in 1973?
13 Who was the voice of Shrek in "Shrek 2"?
14 Which airline's identification code is VS?
15 Which country decided by referendum against joining the European Union in 1994?
16 Who was the only English pope?
17 The kingdom of Navarre was divided between which two countries?
18 Which river does the water in real Irish Guinness come from?
19 In which Gilbert and Sullivan opera is eating a sausage roll a secret sign?
20 On which river is the Kariba Dam?
21 What is studied in the science of somatology?
22 Which football club was the first to use artificial turf?
23 Who succeeded Nelson Mandela as President of South Africa and leader of the ANC?
24 From which district in France do the majority of fine clarets come?
25 Who set up the first printing press in England in 1476?
26 In the film "Carry On Columbus" who played the title role?
27 If the image in the mirror shows the time as five past two, what time is it?
28 In heraldry what is meant by "couchant"?
29 Who was the leader of the first black band to play at Carnegie Hall?
30 Who was the Greek goddess of retribution?

Answers | Pot-Luck 4 *(see Quiz 8)*

1 252. 2 Strictly Come Dancing. 3 Mid Glamorgan. 4 Russ Abbot. 5. Gone with the Wind. 6 A monkey. 7 Corazón Aquino. 8 Borneo stick insect. 9 William Friese Green. 10 World War I. 11 Oldham, Lancs. 12 The issue of rum. 13 Richard II. 14 Edwin Land. 15 The weather forecast. 16 Bali. 17 Morgiana. 18 One vertebra fewer. 19 Telstar. 20 The monkfish. 21 From head to foot. 22 Nero. 23 West Point. 24 Egypt. 25 Organization of Petroleum Exporting Countries. 26 Mortimer. 27 The Princess Royal. 28 Millennium Bridge. 29 Bleak House. 30 A hoofed mammal.

Quiz 7 | Great Buildings

Answers – page 245

1 Which is Britain's oldest cathedral?
2 Jørn Utzon designed the Sydney Opera House as a result of what?
3 What is the Taj Mahal made from?
4 In which Parisian square is the Arc de Triomphe?
5 What is the cathedral of the diocese of London?
6 What was the highest building in the world until 1930?
7 Who ordered the building of St Basil's Cathedral in Moscow?
8 Which library in Venice was described as "the richest and most ornate building since antiquity"?
9 Who had Hampton Court Palace built?
10 Which dukes does Chatsworth House in Derbyshire belong to?
11 Which stately home was used in the film "Brideshead Revisited"?
12 Why is the Washington Memorial smaller now than when it was built?
13 Which building did James Martin's cookery series "Castle in the Country" come from?
14 Other than in Egypt, where were pyramids built?
15 Which French château has a Hall of Mirrors?
16 In which US city is the Sears Tower?
17 Where was Europe's largest Gothic cathedral rebuilt after World War II?
18 Which chain store proprietor commissioned the then tallest inhabitable building in the world in 1913?
19 Which famous statue, brought back as war loot by Napoleon, is still housed in the Louvre?
20 When was Blackpool Tower built?
21 Which plan did Prince Charles describe as "a monstrous carbuncle"?
22 The memorial service for former "Countdown" presenter Richard Whiteley took place in which famous building?
23 In which area of Paris is the Basilica of Sacré Coeur?
24 Where is the largest church in the world?
25 Who designed it?
26 Where is the Shwa Dagon Pagoda?
27 In which city is Rastrelli's Winter Palace?
28 Which cathedral, opened in 1962, contains the ruins of the old cathedral?
29 Where in India is the Golden Temple, centre of the Sikh religion?
30 Why is the White House white?

Answers | Sport: Football (see Quiz 5)

1 Netherlands (in 1978). 2 Bournemouth. 3 It was against a dog that ran on to the field. 4 32. 5 Chelsea. 6 Uruguay. 7 Hamburg. 8 Robert Chase. 9 Steve Daley (in 1979). 10 United. 11 Toulouse. 12 Teddy Sheringham. 13 England. 14 Monaco. 15 Rochdale. 16 Crystal Palace v Man Utd (1990). 17 Middlesbrough. 18 Exeter. 19 Bobby Charlton. 20 Gordon Strachan. 21 Plymouth. 22 Chelsea (Vialli replacing Gullit). 23 Stokoe, Birmingham and Revie, Manchester City in 1956. 24 Burnley. 25 Mark Bosnich. 26 Leeds United. 27 Zinedine Zidane. 28 Falkirk. 29 Burton Albion. 30 Plough.

1 How many old pennies were there in a guinea?
2 "Dancing with the Stars" was the US spinoff of which UK TV series?
3 Which is the most densely populated Welsh county?
4 How is Russ Roberts better known?
5 What was Margaret Mitchell's only book?
6 What is a Mexican "black howler"?
7 Who was elected president of the Philippines in 1986?
8 Which is the world's longest insect?
9 Who invented the first motion picture camera?
10 The play "The Accrington Pals" deals with which conflict?
11 In which town was the first test tube baby born in 1978?
12 Which naval tradition ceased in 1970?
13 Which English king had to pawn his crown to raise money?
14 Who invented the Polaroid camera in 1947?
15 Which TV programme began broadcasting daily on July 29th, 1949?
16 Kuta Beach on which holiday island was the scene of a bomb in a nightclub in 2002?
17 What was Ali Baba's female slave called?
18 What does an Arab horse have fewer of than any other?
19 Which satellite sent the first live TV transmission between America and Europe?
20 By what other name is the angel shark known?
21 What does "cap-a-pie" mean?
22 Which Roman emperor ordered St Peter to be crucified?
23 The British Military Academy is at Sandhurst; where is the American?
24 In which country did the study of geometry originate?
25 What is OPEC an acronym of?
26 What was Mickey Mouse's original name?
27 Which amateur jockey's first winner was Gulfland at Redcar in 1986?
28 Opened in 2000, what was the name of London's first new river crossing for 100 years?
29 In which novel does the character Quebec Bagnet appear?
30 What is an ungulate?

Answers   Pot-Luck 3 *(see Quiz 6)*

1 The ear. 2 Britain. 3 David Tennant. 4 Tasmania. 5 Berkeley Castle. 6 1966. 7 Sea-lions. 8 A clowder. 9 Roger Moore. 10 The wavelength of light. 11 La Quebrada. 12 Ken Norton. 13 Mike Myers. 14 Virgin Atlantic. 15 Norway. 16 Nicolas Breakspear. 17 France and Spain. 18 The Liffey. 19 The Grand Duke. 20 Zambezi. 21 The body. 22 Queen's Park Rangers. 23 Thabo Mbeki. 24 Médoc. 25 William Caxton. 26 Jim Dale. 27 9.55 – five to ten. 28 Lying down. 29 Count Basie. 30 Nemesis.

1 Who was the first royal bride to include her family's motto on her marital coat of arms?

2 Who said "We live above the shop"?

3 Which club was Prince Charles not allowed to join at Cambridge?

4 Princess Anne was the only female competitor at the Montreal Olympics not to be given which test?

5 On which occasion did Elizabeth II make her last curtsey?

6 Where did Princess Diana's mother have a farm at the time of the royal engagement?

7 Who designed the feathered headdress the Duchess of Cornwall wore to her wedding to Prince Charles?

8 Whose autobiography was called "The Heart Has Its Reasons"?

9 Who said "She's more royal than the rest of us" about whom?

10 In which year this century were there three kings of Britain?

11 What are the first names of Princess Diana's sisters and brother?

12 What was tied in a Windsor knot and who introduced the fashion?

13 What did George V refer to as "a mixed grill"?

14 What was Princess Margaret's luxury on "Desert Island Discs"?

15 Which member of the Royal family became an Honorary Captain in the Royal Navy in July 2005?

16 How is the heir to the throne known in Scotland?

17 What name links Earl Spencer and the Duchess of Windsor's first husband?

18 What was Prince Charles' nickname for Mark Phillips?

19 Which army regiment did Prince Harry join after Sandhurst?

20 What are Prince Edward's first names?

21 What is the birthdate of Lady Louise Windsor?

22 Which close relative does Prince Charles share his birthday with?

23 Why is Prince Michael's middle name Franklin?

24 Who is the father of the Earl of St Andrews?

25 Who or what were Susan, Sugar, Honey, Whisky and Sherry?

26 Of the Queen's children who was the heaviest at birth?

27 Last century, how many second sons succeeded to the throne?

28 How many royals had held the title the "Princess Royal" before Princess Anne?

29 Who is the fifth grandchild of the Queen and Prince Philip?

30 Which monarch last century was left-handed?

Answers Pot-Luck 5 *(see Quiz 11)*

1 Arsenal. 2 Bending the knee. 3 Harry S Truman. 4 Chromosomes. 5 Alistair Cooke. 6 Jupiter. 7 Kevin Spacey. 8 Salmon. 9 Hungary. 10 Longleat. 11 1947. 12 A lucifer. 13 Neptune. 14 Whooping cough. 15 IBM. 16 Neil Kinnock. 17 1965. 18 Fish. 19 The Royal College of Physicians. 20 Lord Protector. 21 Myanmar. 22 John Constable. 23 Italy. 24 1973. 25 Charles Lindbergh. 26 The leaves. 27 The Birdman of Alcatraz. 28 300. 29 Etymology. 30 Lake Titicaca.

Quiz 10 | 21st C British Politics | Answers – page 252

1 Which minister resigned over findings in the Budd Report?
2 Which ex-Tory politician left prison in 2000, his possessions in a bin bag?
3 Jack Straw was appointed to which post after Labour's victory in 2001?
4 What was Mo Mowlam's real first name?
5 Over which Bill did Tony Blair's Labour government lose their first Commons vote?
6 Who resigned as Leader of the House of Commons in 2003 over Iraq?
7 Who was Tony Blair's youngest Secretary of State for Education?
8 Who replaced the MP for Sheffield Brightside as Secretary of State for Work and Pensions?
9 After the 2005 election Deputy PM John Prescott held which other post?
10 Which politician wrote a novel called "The Devil's Tune"?
11 Which leader of the SNP left the post in 2000 only to return later?
12 George Galloway was elected MP for which constituency in 2005?
13 Who was Shadow Home Secretary at the start of the new millennium?
14 Following the 2001 General Election who became Father of the House?
15 Who was the only woman in the final stages of the election for London Mayor in 2000?
16 In what year was London's congestion charge introduced.
17 Who replaced David Davis as Tory Party Chairman in 2002?
18 How old was John Major's successor when he became Tory Party leader?
19 Who became Home Secretary a few months before 9/11?
20 Who was Minister for the Civil Service at the time of David Cameron's election as Tory leader?
21 Who became Tory leader the day after the World Trade Center attack?
22 Which Tory MP has the first names Michael Andrew Foster Jude Kerr?
23 Which female was appointed Solicitor General in Tony Blair's government in 2001?
24 Helen Carey chaired which group that heckled Tony Blair?
25 Which Tory David was a former managing director of Tate & Lyle?
26 Which Transport Secretary resigned after Railtrack's collapse?
27 What did Ken Livingstone say was his top priority when he became Mayor of London?
28 Who replaced Blunkett as Secretary of State for Education?
29 Which post did Clare Short resign from over the Iraq war in 2003?
30 What was the title of Labour's 2001 election manifesto?

Answers | The Beatles *(see Quiz 12)*

1 Three. 2 Winston. 3 Pete Best. 4 Day Tripper. 5 Lucy in the Sky with Diamonds. 6 A record store. 7 Julian and Sean. 8 The White Album. 9 Thank Your Lucky Stars. 10 The Quarrymen. 11 Helen Shapiro. 12 Penny Lane/Strawberry Fields Forever. 13 Rattle their jewellery. 14 Stuart Sutcliffe. 15 Harmonica. 16 All four. 17 My Sweet Lord. 18 The Ed Sullivan Show. 19 Fred Lennon (John's long-absent father). 20 Parlophone. 21 Paul McCartney. 22 Evening Standard. 23 Yellow Submarine. 24 In His Own Write. 25 Four (John). 26 San Francisco (1966). 27 Silver Beetles. 28 Yesterday. 29 George Harrison. 30 MBE.

Quiz 11 | Pot-Luck 5 | Answers – page 249

1 Which soccer team did England cricketer Denis Compton play for?
2 What are you doing if you are genuflecting?
3 Who was president of the United States at the end of World War II?
4 What are there 46 of in a normal human body cell?
5 Who died in 2004 just weeks after presenting his final "Letter from America"?
6 Which planet has at least 13 moons?
7 Which Hollywood movie star played Richard II at the Old Vic Theatre in London in 2005?
8 Parr, smolt and grilse are all stages in the growth of what?
9 Where does "Bull's Blood" originate?
10 What is the Marquis of Bath's Wiltshire home called?
11 In which year did India gain independence from Britain?
12 In the war song "Pack Up Your Troubles" what do you need to light a fag?
13 Which planet was discovered by Johann Galle in 1846?
14 What is pertussis more commonly known as?
15 Which company introduced its first commercial computer in 1953?
16 Which politician's books include "Making Our Way" and "Thorns and Roses"?
17 When was hanging abolished in Britain?
18 What do ichthyologists study?
19 Which body founded the anti-smoking organization, ASH, in 1971?
20 What title was Oliver Cromwell given in 1653?
21 To what did Burma change its name in 1989?
22 Which painter was born at East Bergholt?
23 In which country was King Juan Carlos of Spain born?
24 In which year did Ireland join the EC?
25 Who was the first solo aviator to fly the Atlantic non-stop?
26 Which part of a rhubarb plant is poisonous?
27 Convict Robert Stroud was better known as who?
28 What is the maximum score possible in a game of ten-pin bowling?
29 What name is given to the study of the origins of words?
30 What is the highest large lake in the world?

Answers	Royals (see Quiz 9)

1 Princess Diana. 2 Prince Philip. 3 Labour Club. 4 Sex test. 5 Her father's funeral. 6 Australia. 7 Philip Treacy. 8 Duchess of Windsor's. 9 The Queen about Princess Michael. 10 1936. 11 Jane, Sarah and Charles. 12 Tie, Edward VIII when Prince of Wales. 13 His ancestors. 14 Piano. 15 Prince Andrew. 16 Duke of Rothesay. 17 Earl Spencer. 18 Fog (thick and wet). 19 Blues and Royals (Household Cavalry). 20 Edward Antony Richard Louis. 21 8 November 2003. 22 Peter Phillips, his nephew. 23 Franklin Roosevelt was his godfather. 24 Duke of Kent. 25 Corgis. 26 Charles (7lb 6oz). 27 Two, George V and VI. 28 Six. 29 Princess Beatrice of York. 30 George VI.

Quiz 12 | The Beatles

Answers – page 250

1 How many Beatles were still alive when the album "1" first became No 1?

2 What was John Lennon's middle name?

3 Which original Beatle did Ringo Starr replace?

4 What was on the other side of the single "We Can Work It Out"?

5 Which Beatles song was banned by the BBC because its initials were said to be drug-related?

6 What did Brian Epstein manage before the Beatles?

7 What are John Lennon's two sons called?

8 How was the double album, "The Beatles", better known?

9 On which show did they make their first national TV appearance?

10 Which group did John Lennon form and name after his school in 1956?

11 Whom did the Beatles support on their first nationwide tour?

12 Which double-sided hit titles were Liverpool placenames?

13 On the Royal Variety Show John Lennon invited those in the cheaper seats to clap. What did he tell those in the more expensive seats to do?

14 Which Beatle died in Hamburg in 1962?

15 Which solo instrument did John Lennon play on "Love Me Do"?

16 How many Beatles appeared on one "Juke Box Jury" in 1963?

17 What was George Harrison's first solo hit?

18 On which show were the Beatles watched by 73 million in the US?

19 Who made a record called "That's My Life" in 1965?

20 What was the first label the Beatles recorded on with George Martin?

21 Who was the last Beatle to marry twice?

22 In which paper was John Lennon's remark that the Beatles were more popular than Jesus?

23 Which cartoon film did the Beatles make in 1969?

24 What was John Lennon's book published in 1964 called?

25 How many letters were in the title of Cynthia Lennon's biography of her first husband?

26 Where was the last live Beatles' performance?

27 What were the group known as immediately before being known as the Beatles?

28 Which Beatles song is the most recorded song of all time?

29 Who was the first Beatle to have a solo No 1 single this century?

30 What were the Beatles awarded by the Queen in 1965?

Answers | 21st C British Politics *(see Quiz 10)*

1 David Blunkett. 2 Jonathan Aitken. 3 Foreign Secretary. 4 Marjorie. 5 Terrorism Bill. 6 Robin Cook. 7 Ruth Kelly. 8 John Hutton. 9 First Secretary of State. 10 Iain Duncan Smith. 11 Alex Salmond. 12 Bethnal Green. 13 Ann Widdecombe. 14 Tam Dalyell. 15 Susan Kramer. 16 2003. 17 Theresa May. 18 36. 19 David Blunkett. 20 Tony Blair. 21 Iain Duncan Smith. 22 Michael Ancram. 23 Harriet Harman. 24 WI. 25 David Davis. 26 Stephen Byers. 27 Transport. 28 Estelle Morris. 29 International Development Secretary. 30 Ambitions for Britain.

Quiz 13 | Pot-Luck 6

1 Australia's Barossa Valley is noted for which industry?
2 Who succeeded Ted Hughes as Poet Laureate?
3 Which French building did architects Nervi, Breuer and Zehrfuss create?
4 Which programme did the late John Peel present on Saturday mornings on Radio 4?
5 Who was the voice of Stuart Little in the 1999 movie?
6 After which mythological Greek character was the drug morphine named?
7 In which year did Britain go decimal?
8 What is the world's fastest-moving insect?
9 What was the capital of the Roman province of Britain before Londinium (London)?
10 How many minutes approximately does it take for one revolution of the London Eye?
11 At what height does a pony become a horse?
12 Which bird was selected in 1961 as the British national bird?
13 Who invented neon lights in 1911?
14 Which country was the first to insist upon car registration plates?
15 What was the original name of the flagship the "Golden Hind"?
16 Who was the first sovereign to be addressed as "Your Majesty"?
17 Which painting was stolen and kept for two years by V. Peruggio?
18 When did the first televised debate of the House of Lords take place?
19 What is the capital of Samoa?
20 In which country did the first Christmas stamp appear in 1898?
21 Which volcano erupted to give the greatest explosion in recorded history?
22 For what did the Swede Jenny Lind achieve fame?
23 How many legs has a lobster?
24 Who won the last FA Cup Final of the 20th century?
25 Which is the largest of the anthropoid apes?
26 Who is the magical spirit of the air in Shakespeare's "The Tempest"?
27 Who wrote the lyrics to "A Whiter Shade of Pale"?
28 How many Oscars for best director did Alfred Hitchcock win?
29 Which paper was first published as the "Daily Universal Register"?
30 Which grain is used to make malt whisky?

Answers | Pot-Luck 7 *(see Quiz 15)*

1 Two Little Boys. 2 The Iceni. 3 The Babylonians. 4 Michael Grandage. 5 Whoopi Goldberg. 6 Thierry Vigneron. 7 Edward II. 8 The Po. 9 Venus. 10 Leprosy. 11 Foot and mouth. 12 Tallahassee. 13 10,080. 14 Bangladesh. 15 Andrei Sakharov. 16 Eric Morecambe. 17 Goalkeeper. 18 2000. 19 Patricia. 20 Grapes. 21 Knock. 22 The Colour of Magic. 23 Manchester United. 24 Margaret Thatcher. 25 Stella Rimington. 26 Robbie Coltrane. 27 Dick Turpin. 28 The meaning of words. 29 Salisbury. 30 Lady Jane Grey.

1 What do you add to béchamel to make an aurore sauce?
2 What three main ingredients are added to mayonnaise to make a Waldorf salad?
3 What is a Kugelhupf?
4 In which country do red onions originate?
5 What is added to cheddar cheese to make Ilchester cheese?
6 What is laver?
7 What type of fish are Arbroath smokies?
8 What size eggs are between 60 and 65 grams?
9 What type of milk was mozzarella cheese originally made from?
10 What sort of meat is used in a guard of honour?
11 What is something cooked in if cooked "en papillote"?
12 What do you add to vegetables to make a salmagundi?
13 What are Pershore eggs and Marjorie's seedlings?
14 What are the two main ingredients of a Hollandaise sauce?
15 What colour top do bottles of unpasteurized milk have?
16 What is the chief ingredient of boxty bread?
17 In which English county is Brie made?
18 What is the main meat ingredient of faggots?
19 Which has most fat: double cream, crème fraîche or whipping cream?
20 What is Cornish yarg cheese coated with?
21 Which country does skordalia come from?
22 What shape is the pasta called farfalle?
23 What is the main ingredient of dal?
24 In Indian cuisine what is ghee?
25 Where does coulibiac originate and what is it?
26 Which term in Italian cooking means "soft but firm"?
27 What is a carbonade cooked in?
28 How is steak cooked if cooked blue?
29 How does paella get its name?
30 What is the main vegetable ingredient of moussaka?

Answers   Marilyn Monroe (see Quiz 16)

1 Mortensen. 2 Niagara. 3 Jane Russell. 4 Paris. 5 Joe DiMaggio. 6 Baseball player. 7 Nine months. 8 Bus Stop. 9 All About Eve. 10 Lauren Bacall and Betty Grable. 11 In the fridge. 12 Arthur Miller. 13 Billy Wilder. 14 Laurence Olivier. 15 Clark Gable. 16 Birthday cake. 17 Photographer's model. 18 Lee Strasberg's. 19 London. 20 16. 21 Four. 22 Jack Lemmon, Tony Curtis (they were in drag). 23 Sugar Cane. 24 Persistent absence. 25 On time. 26 Red satin sheet. 27 Frankie Vaughan. 28 Los Angeles. 29 Sleeping pill overdose. 30 Monkey Business.

1 Which song contains the line, "Each had a wooden horse"?
2 Which tribe rose in revolt against the Romans and was led by Boadicea?
3 Who were the first people to measure the year?
4 Who replaced Sam Mendes as Artistic Director of the Donmar Warehouse?
5 Who was the voice of the female hyena in "The Lion King"?
6 Who was the first pole-vaulter to clear 19 feet?
7 Who was the first Prince of Wales?
8 Which is the longest river in Italy?
9 Which is the brightest planet visible to the naked eye?
10 What is Hansen's Disease more commonly called?
11 In January 2002 it was announced that Britain was declared to be free of which disease?
12 What is the state capital of Florida?
13 How many minutes are there in a week?
14 What is the most densely populated country in the world?
15 Which scientist was known as the "father of the Soviet H-bomb"?
16 Which comedian died of a heart attack in May 1984 at the age of 58?
17 Which position did Pope John Paul II play in the Polish amateur soccer team?
18 In what year did the first British women reach the South Pole?
19 Alfred Hitchcock's daughter appeared in "Psycho". What is her name?
20 What does a viticulturist cultivate?
21 Which Irish village is famous for its shrine to the Virgin Mary?
22 Which book was the first in Terry Pratchett's series of Discworld novels?
23 Which football team was formerly known as Newton Heath?
24 Who signed the Single Act Treaty for Britain in 1986?
25 Who became the first director general of MI5 whose identity was not kept a secret?
26 How is Anthony McMillan better known?
27 Who, in 1948, was the first black boxer to win a British title?
28 Of what is semantics the study?
29 What was Harare called before 1982?
30 Who was the shortest-reigning British monarch?

Answers	Pot-Luck 6 (see Quiz 13)

1 Wine production. 2 Andrew Motion. 3 The Unesco headquarters. 4 Home Truths. 5 Michael J. Fox. 6 Morpheus. 7 1971. 8 Tropical cockroach. 9 Camulodunum (Colchester). 10 30 minutes. 11 14.2 hands and over. 12 The robin. 13 Georges Claude. 14 France. 15 The Pelican. 16 Henry VIII. 17 The Mona Lisa. 18 1985. 19 Apia. 20 Canada. 21 Krakatoa. 22 Soprano singer. 23 Eight. 24 Man Utd. 25 The gorilla. 26 Ariel. 27 Keith Reid. 28 None. 29 The Times. 30 Barley.

Quiz 16   **Marilyn Monroe**   Answers – page 254

1 Which surname other than Baker did Norma Jean use?
2 Which 1952 film gave Monroe her first big role?
3 Which actress co-starred with Monroe in "Gentlemen Prefer Blondes"?
4 To which city do the girls go to look for rich husbands?
5 Who was Monroe's second husband?
6 What type of sportsman was he?
7 How long had they been married before Monroe filed for divorce?
8 Which film had the title "The Wrong Kind of Girl" on TV?
9 Which 1950 film with Monroe in a minor role is famous for the line, "Fasten your seatbelts – it's going to be a bumpy night"?
10 Who were Monroe's two flatmates in "How to Marry a Millionaire"?
11 In "The Seven Year Itch" where does Monroe keep her underwear?
12 Whom did Monroe marry in June 1956?
13 Who directed Monroe in "The Seven Year Itch" and "Some Like It Hot"?
14 Who played the Prince to Monroe's Showgirl in the film?
15 Who died shortly after making "The Misfits" with Monroe?
16 Where did Monroe appear from when she sang "Happy Birthday" to President Kennedy?
17 What career did Marilyn Monroe embark on in 1946?
18 At which Actors' Studio did she study?
19 In which city was "The Prince and the Showgirl" made?
20 How old was Norma Jean when she first married?
21 How many times does Monroe sing "you" in one chorus of "I Wanna be Loved by You"?
22 Who played Monroe's friends Daphne and Geraldine in "Some Like It Hot"?
23 What was the name of the Monroe character?
24 Why was she fired from "Something's Got to Give"?
25 Monroe said "I have been on a calendar but never ..." what?
26 What did Monroe pose on, on that notorious calendar?
27 Which English singer appeared with Monroe in "Let's Make Love"?
28 In which city did Monroe die?
29 What was the official cause of death?
30 In which film did she co-star with Cary Grant and Ginger Rogers?

Answers   Food and Drink *(see Quiz 14)*

1 Tomato purée. 2 Apple, celery and walnuts. 3 Cake. 4 Italy. 5 Beer and garlic. 6 Seaweed. 7 Haddock. 8 Three. 9 Buffalo. 10 Neck of lamb. 11 Paper. 12 Duck and chicken. 13 Plums. 14 Egg yolks and butter. 15 Green. 16 Potatoes. 17 Somerset. 18 Liver. 19 Double cream. 20 Nettle leaves. 21 Greece. 22 Bows or butterflies. 23 Lentils. 24 Clarified butter. 25 Russia, fish pie. 26 Al dente. 27 Beer. 28 Very rare. 29 From the pan it's cooked in. 30 Aubergines.

1 Condoleezza Rice became the first female provost at which American university?
2 Which was the first British daily paper to sell a million copies a day?
3 Which movie gave Jane Austen's story of Elizabeth Bennet and Mr Darcy a Bollywood twist?
4 In 1993 which film star bought himself a £12 million Gulfstream G-3 jet?
5 Swiss architect Charles-Edouard Jeanneret is better known as who?
6 What are also known as "The Decalogue"?
7 Who composed the tune to "Twinkle, Twinkle, Little Star"?
8 Which Arsenal manager completed the signing of Denis Bergkamp?
9 In Arthurian legend, what is the Holy Grail?
10 Why was income tax first levied in Britain?
11 Which herb is called milfoil?
12 How is the settlement the Town of Our Lady, the Queen of the Angels, by the Little-Portion River known today?
13 Which leading Nazi was born in Egypt?
14 What is psychometry?
15 In which novel does the land of Glubbdubdrib appear?
16 Which poet sold his home, Newstead Abbey, to pay his debts?
17 Who is the dictatorial father figure in Dickens' "Hard Times"?
18 What type of animal is a vmi-vmi?
19 Which animal was once called a foul marten?
20 In which year did women gain the vote in Switzerland?
21 The Strand Theatre in London was renamed after which writer and performer?
22 Where is Charles Darwin buried?
23 Where in the world can the largest cannon be seen?
24 Which bird is said to eat live sheep?
25 Who replaced Chris Woodhead as Chief Inspector of Schools?
26 Which British car was the first to sell over a million models?
27 In which city was the first underground railway?
28 What are the pointed pieces called on a ship's anchor?
29 Which detective lived in Cabot Cove, Maine?
30 What is a polyptych?

Answers	Charles Dickens (see Quiz 19)

1 Barrister. 2 Newman Noggs. 3 David Copperfield. 4 Gunshot wound. 5 Gordon riots. 6 Steerforth and Traddles. 7 Jarndyce v Jarndyce. 8 Mrs Sparsit. 9 Fanny and Tip. 10 Philip Pirrip. 11 Lizzy Hexam. 12 Jerry Cruncher. 13 Aunt. 14 Mr Dick. 15 Trent. 16 Miss Twinkleton's. 17 Ipswich and Bury St Edmunds. 18 Drowned attempting to rescue Steerforth. 19 Blacksmith. 20 Dogs. 21 Accidentally hangs himself. 22 Esther Summerson. 23 James Hawthorne. 24 They were debtors. 25 Transportation. 26 Barkis. 27 Mrs Bardell. 28 Mr Brownlow. 29 Sally. 30 Bentley Drummle.

Quiz 18 Elvis Presley

Answers – page 260

1 What was Elvis Presley's middle name?
2 Which song did he sing to win a talent contest at the age of ten?
3 Which country guitarist produced Elvis's early RCA records?
4 What was his wife Priscilla's maiden name?
5 Which white gospel group provided vocal backings on Elvis's recordings in the 1950s and 1960s?
6 Which label signed Presley before selling his contract to RCA a year later?
7 What were Elvis's parents called?
8 What was Elvis's first film?
9 Where was he posted when he joined the army in 1958?
10 Which was his first ever recording, made at Sam Phillips' studio?
11 What was his first US No 1?
12 Who were vs Elvis in the 2002 remix that topped the singles charts?
13 Who took charge of Presley's career when he moved to RCA?
14 What was the fourth of four consecutive No 1s between November 1960 and May 1961?
15 What was Elvis Presley's music publishing company called?
16 Which Elvis hit owes a debt to the Italian song "O Sole Mio"?
17 In what year was Elvis's last No 1 single of the 20th century?
18 What was his first UK No 1?
19 Which city was the focus of Presley's work in the 1970s?
20 Which record went to No 1 after his death in 1977?
21 Which dancer co-starred with Presley in "GI Blues"?
22 Which is the only part of Britain Presley set foot on?
23 Which Elvis film was a western?
24 Because his movements were so controversial, only which part of Elvis was it suggested should be shown on TV?
25 Which operation did James Peterson carry out on Presley in March 1958?
26 In 2005 which Elvis single replaced an Elvis single as a UK No 1 single?
27 What was the name of Elvis's famous mansion and where was it?
28 Which double-sided single was the top seller of the 1950s in the US?
29 Which Elvis hit was a No 1 for Dusty Springfield?
30 What was Elvis's last No 1 record in the UK in his lifetime?

Answers	Pot-Luck 9 (see Quiz 20)

1 Oscar Wilde. 2 The Case of the Terrified Typist. 3 Hercules. 4 Aled Jones. 5 Hutton. 6 £3.60 per hour. 7 Ambulance driver. 8 Nano. 9 King Faisal. 10 Pinocchio. 11 Wembley Stadium, London. 12 The wettest place in Great Britain. 13 1922. 14 Scatterbrook. 15 Inchworm. 16 Teflon. 17 A flight. 18 Phobos. They are moons of Mars. 19 Ben Jonson. 20 Power station. 21 In autumn. Name for a colchinium. 22 Noel Coward. 23 Riche Havens. 24 A couple. 25 Anya Jenkins. 26 Smell. 27 Lou Reed. 28 The help the American Indians gave to the first white settlers. 29 Harry Allen. 30 An expert on China.

1 In "A Tale of Two Cities" what is the occupation of Sydney Carton?

2 In "Nicholas Nickleby" who is Ralph Nickleby's clerk?

3 Which of his novels did Dickens say he liked the best?

4 In Oliver Twist's burgling expedition with Bill Sikes what sort of injury does Oliver receive?

5 Which historical events are the background to "Barnaby Rudge"?

6 Who are David Copperfield's two vastly different schoolfriends?

7 Which court case is at the heart of "Bleak House"?

8 In "Hard Times" who is Mr Bounderby's housekeeper?

9 In "Little Dorrit" who are Amy's brother and sister?

10 In "Great Expectations" what is Pip's full name?

11 In "Our Mutual Friend" whom does Eugene Wrayburn marry?

12 In "A Tale of Two Cities" what is the name of the grave robber?

13 In "Oliver Twist" what is Rose's relation to Oliver discovered to be?

14 In "David Copperfield" whom does David's aunt Betsey Trotwood live with?

15 In "The Old Curiosity Shop" what is Little Nell's surname?

16 In "Edwin Drood" at whose school at Cloisterham was Rosa brought up?

17 Which two Suffolk towns are the background for scenes in "Pickwick Papers"?

18 In "David Copperfield" how did Ham die?

19 In "Great Expectations" what is the profession of Joe Gargery?

20 What are Nip and Bullseye?

21 In "Oliver Twist" how does Bill Sikes perish?

22 In "Bleak House" who is Lady Dedlock's daughter, at first assumed dead?

23 In "Hard Times" who tries to seduce Louisa Bounderby, née Gradgrind?

24 What offence had inhabitants of the Marshalsea prison committed?

25 In "Nicholas Nickleby" what is the final fate of Squeers?

26 In "David Copperfield" who was "willin'"?

27 In "Pickwick Papers" who is Mr Pickwick's landlady?

28 In "Oliver Twist" who adopts Oliver?

29 In "The Old Curiosity Shop" who is Samson Brass's sister?

30 In "Great Expectations" whom did Estella first marry?

Answers	Pot-Luck 8 *(see Quiz 17)*

1 Stanford University. **2** Daily Mail. **3** Bride & Prejudice. **4** Arnold Schwarzenegger. **5** Le Corbusier. **6** The Ten Commandments. **7** Mozart. **8** Bruce Rioch. **9** The cup used at the Last Supper. **10** To pay for the Napoleonic Wars. **11** Yarrow. **12** Los Angeles. **13** Rudolf Hess. **14** Measurement of mental qualities. **15** Gulliver's Travels. **16** Byron. **17** Thomas Gradgrind. **18** A pig. **19** Polecat. **20** 1971. **21** (Ivor) Novello. **22** Westminster Abbey. **23** The Kremlin. **24** The kea parrot in New Zealand. **25** Mike Tomlinson. **26** Morris Minor. **27** London. **28** Flukes. **29** Jessica Fletcher. **30** Altarpiece with more than one panel.

1 Who said, "Philosophy teaches us to bear with equanimity the misfortunes of others"?

2 Which was the only case that Perry Mason ever lost in court?

3 Name the horse that pulled Steptoe and Son's rag-and-bone cart?

4 Which singer released the 2005 album "New Horizons"?

5 Who was the head of the inquiry investigating the death of Dr David Kelly?

6 In the UK, how much was the first minimum wage for those over 22?

7 What type of work did Ernest Hemingway do during World War I?

8 Which prefix denotes a one thousand millionth part?

9 Which Saudi Arabian king was assassinated in 1975?

10 In 1940 which classic Disney cartoon was made?

11 Where was the main arena for the 1948 Olympic Games?

12 Achnashellach is usually credited with what unfortunate title?

13 In which year did Mussolini seize power in Italy?

14 Where did Worzel Gummidge live?

15 What is a looper caterpillar called in the United States?

16 Polytetrafluoroethylene is usually known as what?

17 What name is given to swallows in the air?

18 What is the partner of Deimos?

19 Who was the first poet laureate?

20 What was the building that now houses the Tate Modern?

21 When would you see a naked lady in the garden?

22 Who wrote a song called the "The Stately Homes of England"?

23 Who opened the original Woodstock rock festival?

24 In "I Belong to Glasgow", how many drinks do I get on a Saturday?

25 "Buffy the Vampire Slayer" actress Emma Caulfield played which character?

26 If a person is anosmic, they have no sense of what?

27 How is Louis Firbank better known?

28 The Americans celebrate Thanksgiving in remembrance of what?

29 Who was Britain's last chief hangman?

30 What is a Sinologist?

Answers | Elvis Presley *(see Quiz 18)*

1 Aaron. 2 Old Shep. 3 Chet Atkins. 4 Beaulieu. 5 The Jordanaires. 6 Sun Records. 7 Vernon and Gladys. 8 Love Me Tender. 9 West Germany. 10 My Happiness. 11 Heartbreak Hotel. 12 JXL. 13 Colonel Tom Parker. 14 Surrender. 15 Elvis Presley Music. 16 It's Now or Never. 17 1977 (Way Down). 18 All Shook Up. 19 Las Vegas. 20 Way Down. 21 Juliet Prowse. 22 Scotland. 23 Charro. 24 Waist up. 25 Cut his hair for the army. 26 One Night/I Got Stung. 27 Graceland, Memphis. 28 Hound Dog/Don't be Cruel. 29 You Don't Have to Say You Love Me. 30 The Wonder of You.

1 In 2005 who became the biggest boxer to be WBA heavyweight champion?
2 Who after Ronnie O'Sullivan won two ranking snooker titles before his 19th birthday?
3 What two differences are there between the position and paddle of someone in a canoe and someone in a kayak?
4 In which two countries is curling most popular?
5 What is the longest-lasting, non-motorized sporting event in the world?
6 What is the biathlon a combination of?
7 What is Brian Gamlin of Bury credited with devising?
8 Which French rugby player (d. 2005) was called "The Little Corporal"?
9 What two types of bowling green are there?
10 In which part of London was the first equestrian jumping competition?
11 What are the three types of sword used in fencing?
12 Billiards probably gets its name from the French word "billiard". What is a billiard?
13 Who was first world champion at darts and which country did he represent?
14 What does karate mean, describing this kind of fighting?
15 What did the sport, baggataway, become?
16 Which country produced most winners of the World Rally Championship?
17 Which sport does the Fédération Internationale des Quilleurs control?
18 In which sport do you use a chistera?
19 Which sport is played on the largest pitch of any game?
20 Where is the world's oldest tobogganing club?
21 In Rugby League, who was the first person to be voted Man Of Steel in two consecutive seasons?
22 Which sport developed from a game called gossima?
23 Which sport has three lifts, squat, bench press and dead lift?
24 What is the object of sumo wrestling?
25 In judo which dan is the highest in the grading of black belts?
26 How does a hurl differ from a hockey stick?
27 How do you luge?
28 Aside from asymmetric bars, what are the three events for women gymnasts in the Olympics?
29 In which country was greyhound racing's first regular track?
30 How many players are there in a Gaelic football team?

Answers	TV Gold (see Quiz 23)

1 Boys from the Blackstuff. 2 Helen Flynn. 3 Simon Dee. 4 Fortunes of War. 5 A Premium Bond win. 6 Vanessa Redgrave. 7 Paul McCartney. 8 Wicksy. 9 Catering. 10 Trevor. 11 Eamonn Andrews. 12 The hairdressing salon. 13 As Time Goes By. 14 Richard Briers. 15 Man About the House. 16 Peter Duncan. 17 The Likely Lads. 18 The Last One: Part 2. 19 The Newcomers. 20 Our Man at St Mark's. 21 A Bit of a Do. 22 Frasier. 23 Shelley. 24 Terry Duckworth. 25 Fawlty Towers. 26 Strictly Come Dancing. 27 Denis Norden. 28 Neighbours. 29 Corky. 30 The Liver Birds.

Quiz 22 — Pot-Luck 10

Answers – page 264

LEVEL 3

1 In which year did Concorde make its last commercial flight?
2 Which prince was the first to have a Royal baby born in an NHS hospital?
3 What gas propels the cork from a champagne bottle?
4 What is the smallest Test Match-winning margin by England over Australia?
5 When did Celtic first have numbers on the back of their shirts?
6 What colour cap is worn by an English cricketer capped for his country?
7 Which player went from Barcelona to Real Madrid for £35.7m in 2000?
8 By what name was the outlaw Harry Longbaugh better known?
9 What was Richard Burton's original name?
10 What is the name of the RAF free-fall parachute team?
11 In what year did Spain and Portugal join the EC?
12 Which Country and Western singer joined Bob Dylan on the latter's album, "Nashville Skyline"?
13 Who became Secretary of State for Health in 1999?
14 Which fruit contains the most calories?
15 What is the minimum age for a three-star cognac?
16 What publication was launched in 1920 by American bank clerk DeWitt Wallace?
17 In which Scottish castle did Madonna marry Guy Ritchie?
18 Which two French sides did Zinedine Zidane play for before moving to Italy in 1996?
19 Which king converted Leeds Castle, in Kent, into a royal palace?
20 Who in the Old Testament is eaten by dogs?
21 What tune is Liechtenstein's national anthem sung to?
22 Who wrote the words of the hymn "Jerusalem"?
23 Who was Priapus in Greek mythology?
24 Which charge card was launched in Britain in September 1963?
25 What is the name of the world's largest flower?
26 What opened in 1894 and closed in London's Strand in 1988?
27 Where did Indian ink originally come from?
28 Who said, "Make love in the afternoon ... It's the only time for it"?
29 Which romantic poet wrote "The Bride of Abydos"?
30 How is Thomas Derbyshire better known?

Answers | Pot-Luck 11 *(see Quiz 24)*

1 Mo Mowlam. 2 Eltham, London. 3 Pickles. 4 Fishing. 5 Wren. 6 Benjamin Franklin in September 1752. 7 Traffic islands. 8 1852 in London. 9 Case for a ship's compass. 10 William the Conqueror. 11 One. 12 Sicily and parts of mainland Italy. 13 Saccharine. It's an anagram. 14 James Purefoy. 15 Colin Baker. 16 Pam Shriver. 17 Halibut. 18 Texas. 19 Juno. 20 Admiral of the Fleet. 21 In India. 22 1945. 23 J. J. Thomson. 24 Long jump, high jump, triple jump and pole vault. 25 Sting. 26 Mega City 1. 27 168. 28 The Globe theatre. 29 A host. 30 President Mitterrand.

1 Which Alan Bleasdale offering won the BAFTA Drama award in 1982?
2 Which character was killed in episode two of spy drama "Spooks"?
3 Which 1960s TV personality ended his show in a white E-type Jaguar?
4 Which Alan Plater TV adaptation starred Kenneth Branagh as Guy Pringle?
5 Where did Ken Barlow's father get the money that enabled him to move out of Coronation Street?
6 Who played Josephine opposite Ernie Wise's Napoleon?
7 Who is the richest person to have accepted a bit-part on "Bread"?
8 Which Eastender thought his father was Pete Beale when it was Kenny?
9 What was Robin Tripp studying when he lived upstairs from the Ropers?
10 Who was Sid's next-door neighbour in "Bless This House"?
11 Which quiz and chat show host devised "Whose Baby"?
12 Which department at Crossroads Motel was run by Vera Downend?
13 Lionel Hardcastle and Jean Pargetter are characters in which long-running comedy?
14 Which "Good Life" star played the lodger in "Goodbye Mr Kent"?
15 Which series about two girls and a guy was "Three's Company" in the US?
16 Which "Blue Peter" presenter was in "Space 1999" and "Fallen Hero"?
17 Which comedy featured characters called Terry Collier and Bob Ferris?
18 What was the last episode of "Friends" called?
19 Which 1960s soap cast Haverhill in Suffolk as Angleton new town?
20 Which TV series starred Leslie Phillips and Donald Sinden as vicars?
21 Which comedy series married David Jason to Gwen Taylor?
22 "Freudian Sleep" and "The Placeholder" are episodes of which comedy?
23 Which Hywel Bennett series had the same title as a drama about a poet?
24 Who ran away to stay with Susan Barlow?
25 Where does Polly Sherman work?
26 David Dickinson, Esther Rantzen and Dennis Taylor have all featured on which popular entertainment show?
27 Who was Frank Muir's most regular writing partner?
28 Which television series, which celebrated its twentieth anniversary in 2005, was originally called "People Like Us"?
29 Who was always trying to borrow food in "Sykes"?
30 Which series linked Polly James and "District Nurse" Nerys Hughes?

Answers   Sports Bag (see Quiz 21)

1 Nicolay Valuev. 2 Ding Jun Hui. 3 Kayak, seated, double paddle; canoe, kneeling, single paddle. 4 Scotland, Canada. 5 Tour de France. 6 Cross-country skiing, shooting. 7 Dartboard numbering. 8 Jacques Fouroux. 9 Crown, level. 10 Islington. 11 Foil, épée, sabre. 12 Stick with a curved end. 13 Leighton Rees, Wales. 14 Empty hand. 15 Lacrosse. 16 Finland. 17 Ten pin bowling. 18 Pelota. 19 Polo. 20 St Moritz. 21 Paul Sculthorpe. 22 Table tennis. 23 Powerlifting. 24 Force opponent out of ring. 25 Tenth. 26 Flat on both sides. 27 Lie on your back;. 28 Floor, beam, vault. 29 US. 30 15.

1 Which Labour politician was appointed Chancellor of the Duchy of Lancaster in 1999 and died in 2005?

2 Where was Bob Hope born?

3 Which dog found the World Cup when it went missing in 1966?

4 Which British sport has the most participants?

5 What is the commonest bird in the British Isles?

6 Who designed the first lightning-conductor?

7 What road safety measure was introduced in the streets of Liverpool in 1860?

8 When and where was the first public lavatory opened in Britain?

9 What is a binnacle?

10 Which king built Windsor Castle?

11 How many lungs do snakes have?

12 Where can you find porcupines in Europe?

13 How can cane chairs be rearranged to produce something sweet?

14 Which actor played Mark Antony in the BBC drama production "Rome"?

15 Who played the sixth Dr Who?

16 Which ex-tennis player married actor George Lazenby, an ex-James Bond?

17 What is the common name for the fish Hippoglossus hippoglossus?

18 Destiny's Child formed in which US state?

19 Who was the Roman goddess of marriage?

20 What is the top rank in the Royal Navy?

21 Where was the decimal system developed?

22 When was the International Monetary Fund established?

23 Who discovered the electron?

24 In athletics, what are the four jumping events?

25 Who recorded the album "The Dream of the Blue Turtles"?

26 In which city does Judge Dredd work?

27 How many spots are there on a full set of 28 dominoes?

28 Which London landmark theatre was burnt down in 1613?

29 What is a group or flock of sparrows called?

30 Which President of France opened the Channel Tunnel along with Queen Elizabeth II?

Answers | Pot-Luck 10 (see Quiz 22)

1 2003. 2 Prince Edward. 3 Carbon dioxide. 4 Two runs. 5 1994. 6 Blue. 7 Luis Figo. 8 The Sundance Kid. 9 Richard Jenkins. 10 The Falcons. 11 1986. 12 Johnny Cash. 13 Alan Milburn. 14 The avocado pear. 15 Five years. 16 Reader's Digest. 17 Skibo Castle. 18 Cannes & Bordeaux. 19 Henry VIII. 20 Jezebel. 21 God Save the Queen. 22 William Blake. 23 A fertility god. 24 American Express. 25 Rafflesia, which grows up to one metre across. 26 Lyons teashops. 27 China. 28 Arnold Wesker. 29 Lord Byron. 30 Tommy Cannon.

1 What was the capital of Russia before Moscow?
2 What is the capital of Andorra?
3 What lies to the north of Algiers?
4 Which country has the last capital alphabetically?
5 What was Harare's former name?
6 Which Asian capital is at the head of the Mekong Delta?
7 Which capital is known as Leukosia or Lefkosa by its inhabitants?
8 Tashkent is the capital of which former Soviet republic?
9 Which capital is on the slopes of the volcano Pichincha?
10 Which is further north, Pakistan's new capital, Islamabad, or the former one, Karachi?
11 St John's is the capital of Antigua and Barbuda but on which island does it stand?
12 Which capital's former name was Christiania?
13 In Berlin which avenue runs east from the Brandenburg Gate?
14 Which capital is the largest city in Africa?
15 Where was Botswana's seat of government prior to 1965, after which it moved to Gaborone?
16 What was the capital of Italian East Africa between 1936 and 1941?
17 Which capital lies on the river Helmand?
18 In Paris what links the Arc de Triomphe and the Place de la Concorde?
19 Which new capital's main architect was Oscar Niemeyer?
20 Which capital's main industrial area is Piraeus?
21 In which capital is the Teatro Colón opera house?
22 What is the full name of the capital of Colombia?
23 Which capital's heating comes from natural hot springs?
24 What did New Delhi replace as the capital of British India in 1912?
25 On which sea is the Azerbaijani capital Baku?
26 Which capital is known as the Eternal City?
27 What is the capital of Bahrain?
28 Which capital began as the village of Edo?
29 Which capital in the West Indies is to be found on New Providence Island?
30 Which capital houses the Great Mosque and the Gate of God?

Answers | Pop: MOR *(see Quiz 27)*

1 Mike Batt. 2 Burt Bacharach and Hal David. 3 Barbra Streisand. 4 None. 5 Andy Williams. 6 Eva Casssidy. 7 Des O'Connor. 8 Jambalaya. 9 Roger Whittaker. 10 Herb Alpert. 11 James Last. 12 Mantovani. 13 Peter Skellern. 14 Mary Hopkin. 15 Jack Jones. 16 Charles Aznavour. 17 Barber. 18 Tony Christie. 19 Johnny Mathis. 20 Shirley Bassey. 21 Leo Sayer. 22 Bert Kaempfert. 23 Henry Mancini. 24 Syd Lawrence. 25 Stranger in Paradise. 26 Al Martino. 27 Nat King Cole. 28 Helen Reddy. 29 Shirley Bassey. 30 Gerry Goffin.

1 Whom did Paris select as the most beautiful goddess?
2 Who sails "The Black Pig"?
3 In which year did Hitler come to power in Germany?
4 Who formulated the periodic table of elements commonly used today?
5 Which Pope succeeded John Paul II?
6 Who discovered the three basic laws of planetary motion?
7 Who was the first secretary-general of the United Nations?
8 Which of Kelly Holmes' 2004 Olympic golds did she win first?
9 Which country's wine may be labelled DOCG?
10 Who designed Blenheim Palace?
11 Who is the only British prime minister to have been assassinated?
12 Who gave Henry II the right to invade and conquer Ireland?
13 What is the name of the nearest star, other than the Sun, to Earth?
14 When was the first appendix operation performed?
15 For what line of business was model manufacturer Airfix originally known?
16 Which gift did the Americans receive from the French in 1886?
17 Which other John challenged John Major for the Tory leadership in the 1990s?
18 What is a crapulous person full of?
19 What is sophistry?
20 Andrew Flintoff played which indoor game for Lancashire schools?
21 Which subatomic particle is named after the Greek word for "first"?
22 What was the name of the first feature-length animated film?
23 Which ex wife of a Rolling Stone starred in "High Society" in London's West End?
24 What is the colour of the bull on an archery target?
25 In which sport are Doggetts Coat and Badge awarded?
26 Who founded the first public library in the City of London?
27 By what name was Asa Yoelson better known?
28 The RAF motto is "Per Ardua Ad Astra". What does it mean?
29 The TV series "Jamie's Kitchen" featured which restaurant?
30 Which of the Seven Wonders of the Ancient World survives today?

Answers | Sport: Cricket *(see Quiz 28)*

1 Andy Caddick. 2 The Oval. 3 Shane Warne (in 1994). 4 Durham. 5 Kevin Pietersen. 6 Bob Woolmer. 7 Philip Eric. 8 Essex. 9 Kepler Wessels. 10 West Germany. 11 Shane Warne. 12 Darren Gough. 13 Matthew Hoggard. 14 Mark Burgess. 15 355. 16 Yorkshire and Leicestershire. 17 Brian McMillan. 18 Wally Hammond. 19 New Zealand. 20 1968. 21 Somerset. 22 Hubert. 23 Phil Neale. 24 Surrey. 25 Leicestershire. 26 "Jimmy" Binks. 27 Derbyshire. 28 Malcolm Nash (Sobers batting, in 1968). 29 Viv Richards. 30 Darren Gough.

1 Who wrote Katie Melua's hit "The Closest Thing to Crazy"?

2 Which partnership wrote "Walk On By" for Dionne Warwick?

3 Who has recorded with Neil Diamond, Barry Gibb and Don Johnson?

4 How many No 1 singles has Neil Diamond had?

5 Who recorded film themes "Moon River" and "Love Story"?

6 Who was the first artist to score three posthumous No 1 albums in the UK?

7 Who had a Top Twenty hit in 1969 with "Dick-A-Dum-Dum"?

8 Which Carpenters hit was the name of a food dish?

9 Whose hits mention Durham, Skye and the New World?

10 Which trumpeter was a co-founder of A & M Records?

11 Who in 1993 became second only to Elvis Presley with his number of album chart entries?

12 Which hugely successful orchestra leader was born Annunzio Paolo?

13 Who has recorded with northern brass bands and sung the songs of Fred Astaire and Hoagy Carmichael?

14 Who won "Opportunity Knocks" and was signed by the Apple label?

15 Which MOR singer's father was famous for his "Donkey Serenade"?

16 Which French singer's autobiography was called "Yesterday When I was Young"?

17 What was Perry Como's job before becoming a singer?

18 Who enquired about the whereabouts of Amarillo again in 2005?

19 Who has recorded with Deniece Williams and Gladys Knight?

20 Who was known as "The Tigress of Tiger Bay"?

21 Who had a transatlantic hit with "When I Need Love"?

22 Which German bandleader was the first to record the Beatles?

23 Who wrote film themes "Days of Wine and Roses" and the Pink Panther?

24 Which British orchestra emulated the sound of Glenn Miller?

25 What was Tony Bennett's first chart entry and only UK No 1?

26 Who was chosen for the role of Johnny Fontane (reputedly based on Frank Sinatra) in "The Godfather"?

27 Whose many hits included "When I Fall in Love" and "Too Young"?

28 Whose first US No 1 was the self-penned "I am a Woman"?

29 Who topped the bill in the first Royal Variety Show to be held in Wales?

30 Who was Carole King's songwriting partner in the 1960s?

Answers   Geography: Capitals *(see Quiz 25)*

1 St Petersburg. 2 Andorra la Vella. 3 Mediterranean. 4 Croatia (Zagreb). 5 Salisbury. 6 Phnom Penh. 7 Nicosia (Cyprus). 8 Uzbekistan. 9 Quito (Ecuador). 10 Islamabad. 11 Antigua. 12 Oslo. 13 Unter den Linden. 14 Cairo. 15 Mafeking. 16 Addis Ababa. 17 Kabul. 18 Champs Elysées. 19 Brasilia. 20 Athens. 21 Buenos Aires. 22 Santa Fé de Bogotà. 23 Reykjavik (Iceland). 24 Calcutta. 25 Caspian. 26 Rome. 27 Manama. 28 Tokyo. 29 Nassau. 30 Damascus (Syria).

1 Which bowler ended Brian Lara's record-breaking Test innings of 375?
2 At which ground did Malcolm take nine wickets in a 1994 Test innings?
3 After Hugh Trumble's Ashes hat-trick in 1904, who was the next Australian to repeat the feat?
4 With which county did Ian Botham end his playing career?
5 Which England player reached a century with a six in Faisalabad in 2005?
6 Who left Warwickshire in 1994 to become coach to South Africa?
7 What are Alan Knott's two middle names?
8 The Benson & Hedges Cup in 1979 was the first trophy for which county?
9 Who was skipper of South Africa in their 1994 return to England?
10 In which country was England batsman Paul Terry born ?
11 H. P. Tillakaratne was the 500th Test victim of which bowler?
12 In 1994 who gave his son the middle names David and Michael after the Australian batsman whom he dismissed the day after the baby's birth?
13 Which English player took a hat-trick against the West Indies in 2004?
14 Who led New Zealand to their first-ever victory against England in 1978?
15 To ten either way, how many Test wickets did Dennis Lillee take?
16 Which two counties did Dickie Bird play for?
17 Who topped the South African batting and bowling averages in the 1994 Test series against England?
18 Which England captain was the first Test outfielder to take 100 catches?
19 For which country did Peter Petherick take a Test hat-trick in 1976?
20 To three years, when was Yorkshire's last Championship win pre-2001?
21 Which English county did New Zealander Martin Crowe play for?
22 What is Clive Lloyd's middle name?
23 Who skippered both Lincoln at football and Worcester at cricket in 1993?
24 Which county did Jack Hobbs play for?
25 Which English county did the late Hanse Cronje play for?
26 Which Yorkshire wicket-keeper had the first names James Graham?
27 Which English county did Michael Holding play for?
28 Which bowler was the first to be hit for six sixes in an over?
29 Which West Indian player turned out for Antigua in the 1978 World Cup?
30 Who was the only Englishman to take a hat-trick against the Aussies last century?

Answers | **Pot-Luck 12** *(see Quiz 26)*

1 Aphrodite. 2 Captain Pugwash. 3 1933. 4 Mendeleyev. 5 Benedict XVI. 6 Kepler. 7 Trygve Lie. 8 800 metres. 9 Italy (Denominazione di Origine Controllata e Garantita). 10 Sir John Vanburgh. 11 Spencer Perceval. 12 The English pope, Adrian IV. 13 Proxima Centauri. 14 1885. 15 Making combs. 16 Statue of Liberty. 17 John Redwood. 18 Alcohol. 19 False reasoning, meant to deceive. 20 Chess. 21 Proton. 22 Snow White and the Seven Dwarfs. 23 Jerry Hall. 24 Gold or yellow. 25 Rowing. 26 Robert Ford. 27 Al Jolson. 28 Through difficulties to the the stars. 29 Fifteen. 30 Pyramids.

1 In which decade was flogging abolished in Britain?
2 What sort of word is made up from initial letters of other words?
3 What is a necropolis?
4 Where did the Vikings originally come from?
5 What is the coldest substance?
6 Who wrote the book "Chitty Chitty Bang Bang"?
7 In which sport is there a york round?
8 Who wrote the song "If"?
9 In cricket how many runs is a Nelson?
10 Which British prime minister once said, "Is a man an ape or an angel? Now I am on the side of the angels"?
11 By what name is Jim Moir better known?
12 When was the first free vertical flight of a twin-rotor helicopter?
13 What does an aphyllous plant not have?
14 For how long did Alexander the Great rule?
15 What is the central administrative body of the Catholic Church?
16 Which decade saw the introduction of instant coffee?
17 In which city was Ray Davies of the Kinks shot in the leg in 2004?
18 Who launched the "Daily Mail"?
19 Which co founder of "The Guinness Book Of Records" passed away in 2004?
20 Which film did newspaper magnate William Randolph Hearst inspire?
21 Which city is built on the site of the Aztec capital Tenochtitlan?
22 To which king in the Bible was Jezebel married?
23 Which famous American singer was described in "Life" magazine in 1974 as having a "half-melted vanilla face"?
24 What do you do in music when you play a piece "con brio"?
25 What punishment did the Vestal Virgins of Rome suffer if they betrayed their vows of chastity?
26 Which movie actress has twins Phinnaeus and Hazel?
27 Which is the largest seed in the world?
28 To 20 years each way, when was Hyde Park opened to the public?
29 Which country built the Mars probe known as Beagle 2?
30 Gilberto Silva joined Arsenal from which club side?

Answers | Pot-Luck 14 *(see Quiz 31)*

1 The Spectator. 2 His cousin, Celeste. 3 George II (Dettingen, 1743). 4 Hydrogen. 5 The Sea. 6 The Milky Way. 7 1963. 8 Chelonia. 9 72. 10 Blenheim. 11 The Third World. 12 Poppies. 13 About eight minutes. 14 Carl Koller. 15 Betty Boothroyd. 16 Richard Branson. 17 Jack the Ripper. 18 An instrument for enlarging or reducing drawings. 19 Jeffrey Archer. 20 Shanghai. 21 Electric current. 22 Long sight. 23 106. 24 Lord Palmerston. 25 Goodbye, Mr Chips. 26 Milk. 27 Paul Neal. 28 The 1920s. 29 Wanderly Luxemburgo. 30 The Picts.

1 What was the name of the first commercial atomic-powered ship?
2 Who devised the prototype for the "Beetle"?
3 What was the first car to be powered by a gas turbine?
4 Who first patented the seat belt in 1903?
5 Which rail line, opened in 1830, was the world's first inter-city service?
6 To three miles, how long is the M25?
7 In 1775 who invented the tram drawn by two horses?
8 What was the first hot-air balloon, called the Montgolfier, made of?
9 In air flight, what is the characteristic of aerodynes?
10 Where did the Wright brothers fly their first glider in 1900?
11 What was the first airliner, which was put into service in 1933?
12 Who invented the preselector gearbox for battle tanks in 1917?
13 Who founded the Great Western Railway using a seven-foot wide track?
14 Which famous ocean liner made its maiden voyage in May 1936?
15 Who invented the "air bag" anti-shock air cushion?
16 Who made the first airship flight in 1852 in a hydrogen-filled craft powered by a steam engine?
17 What does the "U" in U-Boat stand for?
18 What did French engineer Georges Messier invent in 1924?
19 Who in 1878 invented the electric staff which prevents trains on single-track lines colliding?
20 Who built the first submarine which was tested in the River Thames?
21 Who invented laminated windscreens in 1909?
22 What was the name of the first successful flying boat built in 1912?
23 Which brothers built the first American petrol-driven motor cars in 1892?
24 On which railway was the first buffet car created in 1899?
25 Which airline company first made a commercial flight in a Boeing 747 from New York to London?
26 Which German company created the electronically variable shock-absorber in 1987?
27 What first left Gare de l'Est in Paris on October 4th, 1883?
28 Who was Secretary of State for Transport when the first 12-lane section of the M25 was opened?
29 Which British doctor invented the disc brake in 1902?
30 Where was the first take-off by a manned helicopter in 1907?

Answers	**European Community** *(see Quiz 32)*

1 Six. 2 European Coal and Steel Community. 3 Euratom. 4 Ireland, Denmark. 5 Foreign secretaries. 6 Ten. 7 Italy. 8 Luxembourg. 9 Brussels. 10 European Council. 11 May. 12 Luxembourg. 13 Economic and Monetary Union. 14 Poland. 15 EU citizenship. 16 Pillars. 17 Subsidiarity. 18 Germany (99). 19 European Investment Bank. 20 Jacques Delors. 21 Butter. 22 De Gaulle. 23 Treaty of Brussels. 24 Roy Jenkins. 25 VAT payments. 26 Greenland. 27 Corporal punishment of children if parents disapproved. 28 EFTA. 29 Deputy foreign secretary. 30 Five years.

1 Which journal did Addison and Steele found?

2 Whom did Babar the Elephant marry?

3 Who was the last British king to lead an army into battle?

4 Of which element is tritium an isotope?

5 What was the title of the book that won the 2005 Man Booker Prize?

6 In which galaxy is the Earth?

7 In what year did Valentina Tereshkova become the first woman in space?

8 To which order of reptiles do turtles and tortoises belong?

9 At what age did Des O'Connor became dad of a new baby in 2004?

10 In which palace was Winston Churchill born?

11 Which expression was coined by Alfred Sauvy in the early 1950s to describe countries with underdeveloped economic structures?

12 In "Penny Lane" what is a nurse selling from a tray?

13 How long does the light of the Sun take to reach the Earth?

14 Who discovered the pain-killing properties of cocaine?

15 In 1994, which female politician became Chancellor of the Open University?

16 Whose first business enterprise on leaving school was a magazine called "Student"?

17 Who murdered Catherine Eddowes on September 30th, 1888?

18 What is an eidograph?

19 Which former MP became Baron of Weston Super Mare?

20 Which city has the largest population in the world?

21 What is controlled by a rheostat?

22 What would you have if you were hypermetropic?

23 How many times was Bobby Charlton capped for England?

24 Whose last words were, "Die, my dear doctor! That's the last thing I shall do!"?

25 Which James Hilton novel was turned into a film classic about school life?

26 What does a galactophagist like to drink?

27 What is the real name of Red Adair, the American fire-fighter?

28 In which decade did the "par avion" airmail stickers appear in Britain?

29 Who was dismissed as Real Madrid's coach following Beckham's red card against Getafe in Dec 2005?

30 Kenneth I ruled which people in the 9th century?

Answers | Pot-Luck 13 (see Quiz 29)

1 1940s. 2 Acronym. 3 Cemetery. 4 Gotland. 5 Solid helium. 6 Ian Fleming. 7 Archery. 8 David Gates. 9 111. 10 Benjamin Disraeli. 11 Vic Reeves. 12 1907, by Paul Cornu. 13 Leaves. 14 12 years. 15 The Curia. 16 1938, Nescafé. 17 New Orleans. 18 Alfred Harmsworth, Viscount Northcliffe, in 1896. 19 Norris McWhirter. 20 Citizen Kane. 21 Mexico City. 22 Ahab. 23 Elvis Presley. 24 Play vigorously. 25 Live burial. 26 Julia Roberts. 27 Double coconut. 28 1637. 29 Britain. 30 Athletico Madrid.

Quiz 32 | European Community | Answers – page 270

1 How many countries were in the EEC at its beginning in 1957?
2 What did the Treaty of Paris set up in 1951?
3 What was the European Atomic Energy Commission known as?
4 Who joined the EC in 1973 with Britain?
5 Who are the members of the Council of Ministers?
6 How many countries joined the EU in May 2004?
7 Former EU president Romano Prodi came from which country?
8 Which country held the EU presidency from January to June 2005?
9 Where is the Commission's headquarters?
10 What are the meetings of the heads of government called?
11 In which month is Europe Day?
12 Where is the secretariat of the European Parliament based?
13 What does EMU stand for?
14 Which of the states that joined the EU in May 2004 was the largest in terms of population?
15 What qualification do you need to stand for the European Parliament?
16 What did the Maastricht Treaty call each of the three areas of the EU?
17 Which principle in the Maastricht Treaty says the Community will act on policies which member states would find difficult to deal with alone?
18 Which country has the most MEPs?
19 What is the EU bank called?
20 Who preceded Jacques Santer as Commission president?
21 In 1987 what did the EC sell to the USSR for 6p per pound?
22 Which statesman vetoed Britain's entry into the EEC in the 1960s?
23 Which treaty allowed Britain's entry into the EC?
24 Who was the first British president of the EC Commission?
25 What did Margaret Thatcher threaten to withhold if the EC did not cut Britain's budget contribution in 1980?
26 Who voted to withdraw from the EC in February 1982?
27 What did the European Court outlaw in the same month?
28 Of which trading association was Britain a member prior to joining the EEC?
29 Which post did Ted Heath hold when Britain first tried to join the EEC?
30 How long is an MEP elected for?

Answers | Transport (see Quiz 30)

1 The Savannah. 2 Ferdinand Porsche. 3 Rover. 4 Gustave Desiré Liebau. 5 Liverpool to Manchester. 6 117 miles. 7 John Outram. 8 Pack-cloth covered with paper. 9 They are heavier than air. 10 Kitty Hawk. 11 Boeing 247. 12 Major Wilson. 13 I. K. Brunel. 14 The Queen Mary. 15 Daimler-Benz. 16 Henri Giffard. 17 Unterseeboot. 18 First hydraulic suspension system. 19 Edward Tyer. 20 Cornelius Drebbel. 21 E. Benedictus. 22 The Flying Fish. 23 Charles and Frank Duryea. 24 Great Central Railway. 25 Pan Am. 26 Boge. 27 The Orient Express. 28 Alistair Darling. 29 Dr Lanchester. 30 Lisieux, France.

1 When was Prohibition introduced in the United States?
2 Which metal melts at 30 degrees centigrade?
3 Which animals congregate in musters?
4 How many "sisters" make up the Pleiades?
5 Which group of ships was known as the "The First Fleet"?
6 What is the influence of gravity on plants called?
7 What colour is the wine Tokay?
8 Who wrote the novel "Birds without Wings"?
9 In which decade did the Falkland Islands first become a British colony?
10 In which war did the Battle of Isandhlwana take place?
11 In miles, how far from the Earth do meteors usually burn out?
12 Who was the third husband of Jennifer Lopez?
13 When did Green Shield stamps come into use in Britain?
14 In 1803 what did the United States double?
15 Which prison closed on March 21st, 1963?
16 What is an eponym?
17 How is Marie Gresholtz better known today?
18 What is special about the words rose, oven, send, ends?
19 What is the heaviest element in the world?
20 Who founded Eton?
21 How many players were on the field at the end of the 1990 World Cup Final?
22 Which sport was banned in England in 1849?
23 Who scripted, directed and appeared in "The Plank"?
24 In 1997, Bobbi McCaughey of Iowa gave birth to how many children?
25 What is nostology?
26 To five years either way, in which year did London's first airport open?
27 Who is the patron saint of Germany?
28 What type of meat did Prince Charles champion to "get back in its rightful place?
29 On which country did the United States declare war in 1898?
30 Which British university was the first to offer a degree in brewing?

Answers	Pop: Novelty Songs *(see Quiz 35)*

1 A Beatle. 2 Chuck Berry. 3 Bryan Hyland and Bombalurina. 4 Tie Me Kangaroo Down. 5 Julian Clary. 6 It ain't 'Alf Hot Mum. 7 DLT, Paul Burnett. 8 Mike Reid. 9 Liverpool FC. 10 Smear Campaign. 11 Mouldy Old Dough. 12 Napoleon XIV. 13 The Singing Nun. 14 Magic Roundabout. 15 Geordie Boys. 16 The Goons. 17 Lord Rockingham's XI. 18 Peter Sellers, Sophia Loren. 19 Aintree Iron. 20 Ivor Biggun. 21 Roland Rat. 22 7 days. 23 Hale, Pace. 24 Pinky, Perky. 25 Loadsamoney. 26 Splodgenessabounds. 27 Corporal Jones. 28 The Matchroom Mob. 29 1st Atheist Tabernacle Choir. 30 Brand New Key.

Quiz 34 | Speed Kings

Answers – page 276

1 Michael Schumacher won the 2004 F1 title with second place in which race?

2 Which British driver had five British Grand Prix wins during the 1960s?

3 Whom did Barry Sheene ride for when he won his world championships?

4 Who was the second Briton to be World Rally Champion?

5 Who was the only Australian motor racing world champion in the 1960s?

6 Which motor cyclist won 122 world championships?

7 Which driver was runner-up in the world championship in '63, '64 and '65?

8 Which Brazilian was world champion driver in 1972 and 1974?

9 What was the nationality of Mario Andretti?

10 Which driver won the world championship posthumously in 1970?

11 David Jefferies won Isle of Man's Senior TT three out of four years – what stopped him the other year?

12 What is the nationality of Nelson Piquet?

13 How many times did Graham Hill win the Monaco Grand Prix?

14 Which Belgian won Le Mans six times between 1969 and 1982?

15 Who was driving for Ferrari when they became the first manufacturer to have 100 Grand Prix wins?

16 Who was the British driver with most Grand Prix wins before Nigel Mansell?

17 How many times was Ayrton Senna world champion?

18 At which sport did Ivan Maugher win six world titles?

19 Which British motorcyclist won 14 Isle of Man Tourist Trophy titles?

20 Which Briton broke the world land speed record in the US in 1983?

21 What is the nationality of Keke Rosberg?

22 Who was world championship driver in 1964 and motorcycling champion seven times?

23 Who was the first Briton to win the world motor racing championship?

24 What did Brazilian Helio Castroneves win in both 2001 and 2002?

25 Which Briton was world champion in 1976 and retired three years later?

26 Who moved to the Stewart team from Jordan and then to Ferrari in 2000?

27 Who drove the McLaren to its first Grand Prix win in 1968?

28 What was Gilles Villeneuve's home country?

29 Which driver apart from Senna lost his life in the 1994 Formula 1 season?

30 Which Grand Prix did Damon Hill win for the first time in 1994?

Answers | Pot-Luck 16 *(see Quiz 36)*

1 Lady Campanula Tottington. 2 Sir Christopher Meyer. 3 Noel Coward. 4 Six. 5 Gary Gilmore before his execution. 6 The sea horse. 7 The Phoenician. 8 Ten. 9 The Battle of Culloden in 1746. 10 Nine. 11 The International Red Cross. 12 Grumpy, Sleepy, Happy, Bashful, Sneezy, Dopey, Doc. 13 India. 14 Giant hailstones. 15 Baton Rouge. 16 A kiss. It is mistletoe 17 British Airways. 18 Charlie's Angels. 19 Roy Hattersley. 20 Orion. 21 Queen Victoria. 22 Beetles. 23 New Zealand. 24 Eaton Hall. 25 In 1812, during the Napoleonic Wars. 26 Silver. 27 Earth. 28 See in the dark. 29 Barbed wire. 30 Francis Scott Key.

Quiz 35 | Pop: Novelty Songs | Answers – page 273

1 What did Dora Bryan want for Christmas in 1963?
2 Who took his "Ding-a-ling" to No 1?
3 Which two versions of "Itsy Bitsy Teeny Weeny Yellow Polka Dot Bikini" have hit the charts 30 years apart?
4 On which of Rolf Harris's chart hits did we first hear a didgeridoo?
5 Which vocalist called himself the Joan Collins Fan Club?
6 Which TV series did the vocalists on "Whispering Grass" come from?
7 Which DJs were Laurie Lingo and the Dipsticks?
8 Which "EastEnders" star had a hit with "The Ugly Duckling"?
9 Who sang "Red Machine in Full Effect"?
10 Who was Mr Bean's backing group?
11 What are the only words on Lieutenant Pigeon's first No 1?
12 Who sang "They're Coming to Take Me Away Ha-Haaa" in 1966?
13 How was the Belgian Soeur Sourire known in Britain?
14 Which Jasper Carrott single was once banned by the BBC?
15 What was the title of Paul Gascoigne's Gazza Rap?
16 Who was "Walking Backwards for Christmas" in the 1950s?
17 Who got to No 1 in 1958 with "Hoots Mon"?
18 Who argued about "Bangers and Mash" in 1961?
19 What was the first thing Scaffold said "Thank U Very Much" for?
20 Who recorded with the Red Nosed Burglars and the D Cups?
21 Which Superstar recorded "Love Me Tender" nearly 30 years after Elvis Presley?
22 How long did it take Mr Blobby to reach No 1 in December 1993?
23 Who helped the Stonkers get a hit with "The Stonk"?
24 Which duo had a minor hit with "Reet Petite" in 1993?
25 What was the full title of Harry Enfield's 1988 hit?
26 "Two Pints of Lager and a Packet of Crisps Please" was a hit for which band?
27 Which "Dad's Army" character had a No 1 hit?
28 Who accompanied Chas and Dave on "Snooker Loopy"?
29 What was on the other side of Spitting Image's "Santa Claus is on the Dole"?
30 Which song did the Wurzels base their "Combine Harvester" on?

Answers | Pot-Luck 15 *(see Quiz 33)*

1 1920. 2 Gallium. 3 Peacocks. 4 Seven. 5 Ships transporting the first convicts to Australia in 1788. 6 Geotropism. 7 White. 8 Louis De Bernieres. 9 1830s. 10 The Zulu War of 1879. 11 About 50 miles. 12 Marc Anthony. 13 1958. 14 Its size. 15 Alcatraz. 16 A word formed from a name. 17 Mme Tussaud. 18 They form a word square so the words read the same across and down. 19 Osmium. 20 Henry VI. 21 20. Argentina had two players sent off. 22 Cockfighting. 23 Eric Sykes. 24 Seven. 25 Study of senility. 26 1919. 27 St Boniface. 28 Mutton. 29 Spain. 30 Heriot-Watt.

Quiz 36 | Pot-Luck 16 | Answers – page 274

1 Helena Bonham Carter was the voice of which character in "The Curse of the Were-Rabbit"?

2 Which former US ambassador's memoirs caused controversy in the autumn of 2005?

3 Which playwright told besuited actress Edna Furber that she looked like a man, and was given the reply "So do you"?

4 What was Patrick McGoohan's identity number in "The Prisoner"?

5 Whose last words were, "Let's do it"?

6 Which is the only fish able to hold objects in its tail?

7 From which alphabet did all the Western alphabets originate?

8 How many months were there in the old Roman year?

9 What is generally regarded as the last major battle on British soil?

10 How many sides has a nonagon?

11 Which medical body was set up at the Geneva Convention in 1864?

12 What are the names of all of Snow White's Seven Dwarfs?

13 In which country was "Release Me" singer Engelbert Humperdinck born?

14 In July 1923 what freak weather conditions killed 23 people in Rostov, USSR?

15 What is the state capital of Louisiana?

16 Viscum album provides an excuse for stealing what?

17 What did BOAC and BEA form on their merger?

18 What was the collective name of Sabrina, Jill and Kelly?

19 Who was Deputy Leader of the Labour Party under Neil Kinnock from 1983 to 1992?

20 In which constellation are the stars Bellatrix and Betelgeuse?

21 Who was the first British monarch to live in Buckingham Palace?

22 Which order in the classification of animals has most members?

23 Which country has a wine-producing area centred on Gisborne?

24 What is the Cheshire seat of the Duke of Westminster?

25 When did Britain last go to war against the United States?

26 With which metal is the Iron Cross edged?

27 Which planet lies between Venus and Mars?

28 What does scotopic vision allow you to do?

29 What did Lucien B. Smith first patent in 1867?

30 Who wrote the words of "The Star Spangled Banner"?

Answers | Speed Kings (see Quiz 34)

1 Belgian. 2 Jim Clark. 3 Suzuki. 4 Richard Burns 5 Jack Brabham. 6 Giacomo Agostini. 7 Graham Hill. 8 Emerson Fittipaldi. 9 American. 10 Jochen Rindt. 11 No race in 2001. 12 Brazilian. 13 Five. 14 Jacky Ickx. 15 Alain Prost. 16 Jackie Stewart. 17 Three. 18 Speedway. 19 Mike Hailwood. 20 Richard Noble. 21 Finnish. 22 John Surtees. 23 Mike Hawthorn. 24 Indianapolis. 25 James Hunt. 26 Rubens Barrichello. 27 Bruce McLaren himself. 28 Canada. 29 Roland Ratzenberger. 30 British.

1 In which part of London did Chaplin spend his early life?
2 What was his elder brother and fellow performer called?
3 What did the troupe, the Eight Lancashire Lads, do?
4 With which company did Chaplin travel to the United States in 1910?
5 For which company did Chaplin make his first films?
6 Who played the title role in "The Kid" in 1921?
7 Which film appeared in 1925 and had sound added in 1942?
8 Which wife of Chaplin co-starred in "Modern Times"?
9 How many times did Chaplin marry altogether?
10 Which was Chaplin's first sound film?
11 Whom did he choose to play the young ballerina in "Limelight"?
12 Which type of sound was heard in "City Lights" in 1931?
13 From which film, for which Chaplin wrote the music, did Petula Clark have a No 1 with "This is My Song"?
14 Which former silent movie star joined Chaplin in "Limelight"?
15 What is odd about Chaplin's comments on his ex-wife, Lita Grey, in his autobiography?
16 Who was Chaplin's last father-in-law?
17 What was his last wife called?
18 Which film distributing company did Chaplin found with D.W. Griffith, Douglas Fairbanks and Mary Pickford?
19 Who bought the company out in 1940?
20 Which of Chaplin's sons starred with him in "A King in New York"?
21 Which was the last film Chaplin made in the United States?
22 In which split-reel film did the Tramp first appear?
23 Which daughter of Chaplin starred in Doctor Zhivago?
24 How did Emil Jannings score over Chaplin in 1929?
25 Where did Chaplin live after being banned from the US in 1953?
26 Which award did Chaplin receive in 1975?
27 What did Chaplin win his Oscar for in "Limelight"?
28 On which day of the year did Chaplin die?
29 What happened on March 2nd the following year?
30 Who played the roles of Chaplin's parents in a 1989 TV series "The Young Chaplin"?

Answers	Classic Women Writers *(see Quiz 39)*

1 Clergyman. 2 Pride and Prejudice. 3 Harriet Smith. 4 Sense and Sensibility. 5 Jennifer Ehle. 6 Elizabeth, Anne, Mary. 7 Fanny Price. 8 Northanger Abbey. 9 Emma Thompson. 10 Charlotte. 11 Currer, Ellis and Acton Bell. 12 The Tenant of Wildfell Hall, Agnes Grey. 13 Brussels. 14 Their brother, Patrick Branwell. 15 Nicholls. 16 St John Rivers. 17 Lowood. 18 Villette. 19 Emily. 20 Mrs Gaskell. 21 Liverpool. 22 Isabella. 23 Edgar Linton. 24 George Eliot. 25 Eppie. 26 Middlemarch. 27 Dorlcote. 28 Carpenter. 29 Frankenstein. 30 Elizabeth Barrett Browning.

1 What is an encyclical?
2 Which famous TV cook died in 1994 at the age of 83?
3 What is the Latin name for the apple or fruit in general?
4 Which US city did Charles and Camilla first visit on their first overseas tour?
5 Which Hollywood film studio was founded in 1915 by Carl Laemmle?
6 Whom did the Walrus and the Carpenter invite to walk with them?
7 Where did the old London Bridge move to from the Thames?
8 In which language was the New Testament originally written?
9 Which famous dancer's legs were insured for $650,000?
10 Which Glenn Miller tune did Peter Sellers request for his own funeral?
11 In Roman mythology, who was the husband of Juno?
12 Where does the name Fray Bentos come from in connection with corned beef?
13 Who were the first group to have four consecutive double-sided hits?
14 In 2005 Tom Cruise announced his engagement to which actress?
15 Which Russian ruler imposed a beard tax?
16 What is blennophobia?
17 Which comic actor and writer co-wrote the book "Life and How to Survive It"?
18 Who wrote "The Napoleon of Notting Hill"?
19 Who played Hero in the 2005 BBC adaptation of "Much Ado About Nothing"?
20 What is the smallest breed of dog?
21 For how many months each year does a dormouse hibernate?
22 What were Franklin D. Roosevelt's four freedoms of democracy?
23 How was Alexander the Great's body preserved?
24 On the Chinese calendar which animal represents the year 2000?
25 How many "Monty Python" series were made?
26 The black swan is native to which country?
27 Who invented the game roulette?
28 Where was the wheel clamp first used in Europe?
29 To ten pence, what did the hourly minimum wage for over 21s rise to in 2005 in England?
30 What was the name of the captain of the "Titanic"?

Answers | Pot-Luck 18 *(see Quiz 40)*

1 Maria Friedman. 2 1950s. 3 Greece. 4 The giraffe. 5 A rodent. 6 "...and absolute power corrupts absolutely." 7 Mary Robinson. 8 Faraday. 9 The pigeon. 10 Ipswich players in 70s & 80s team. 11 Bakelite. 12 He designed the lions in Trafalgar Square. 13 The stethoscope. 14 L. S. Lowry. 15 Louis XIV of France (72 years, 110 days). 16 Speed of the film. 17 Shake hands. 18 First person on TV (at J. L. Baird's demonstration). 19 Seventy Two Virgins. 20 Archer fish of India. 21 Aramaic. 22 Richard Eyre. 23 1975. 24 Uncle Tom's Cabin. 25 Japan. 26 Dick Tracy. 27 Jesse Owens. 28 Bora. 29 Natal. 30 Viv Nicholson.

1 What was the occupation of Jane Austen's father?
2 Which Austen novel was originally called "First Impressions"?
3 Whom does Emma take under her wing in the novel of the same name?
4 Which Austen novel was first called "Elinor and Marianne"?
5 Who played Elizabeth Bennet in TV's "Pride and Prejudice" in 1995?
6 Who are Sir Walter Elliot's three daughters in "Persuasion"?
7 In "Mansfield Park" what is the name of the heroine?
8 In which Austen novel do we meet Catherine Morland?
9 Who wrote the screenplay for "Sense and Sensibility"?
10 Of the Brontë sisters that survived to adulthood who was the eldest?
11 Which pseudonyms did the Brontë sisters use when they published a collection of poems in 1846?
12 Which two novels did Anne Brontë write?
13 Where did Charlotte and Emily go to study languages in 1842?
14 Which member of the Brontë family died in the same year as Emily?
15 What was Charlotte's married name?
16 In "Jane Eyre" who cares for Jane after she flees Thornfield Hall?
17 In "Jane Eyre" what is the name of the asylum based on Cowan Bridge where Charlotte Brontë's sisters contracted the consumption from which they died?
18 Which novel by Charlotte reflects her life as a governess abroad?
19 Whom is the character of Shirley Keeldar based on in "Shirley"?
20 Which author of "Cranford" wrote the "Life of Charlotte Brontë" in 1857?
21 In which city does Mr Earnshaw first find Heathcliff?
22 Whom does Heathcliff marry?
23 Whom has Catherine Earnshaw married when Heathcliff returns from his three-year absence?
24 How is Mary Ann Cross better known?
25 Whom does Silas Marner adopt?
26 Which George Eliot novel is subtitled "A Study of Provincial Life"?
27 What is the name of the mill in "Mill on the Floss"?
28 What is the occupation of Adam Bede?
29 What is the title of Mary Wollstonecraft Shelley's "tale of terror"?
30 How is Elizabeth Moulton better known?

Answers | The Movies: Charlie Chaplin *(see Quiz 37)*

1 Lambeth. 2 Sydney. 3 Clog dancing. 4 Fred Karno. 5 Keystone. 6 Jackie Coogan. 7 The Gold Rush. 8 Paulette Goddard. 9 Four. 10 The Great Dictator. 11 Claire Bloom. 12 Music. 13 A Countess from Hong Kong. 14 Buster Keaton. 15 He never mentions her. 16 Eugene O'Neill. 17 Oona. 18 United Artists. 19 Sam Goldwyn. 20 Michael. 21 Limelight. 22 Kid Auto Races at Venice. 23 Geraldine. 24 Beat him to the first-ever Oscar. 25 Switzerland. 26 Knighthood. 27 Music score. 28 Christmas Day. 29 Coffin stolen. 30 Ian McShane and Twiggy.

1 Who originally took on the role of Marian Halcombe in "The Woman In White"?

2 In which decade did India go metric?

3 Which country held British plane-spotters on suspicion of spying in 2001?

4 The okapi is a relative of which animal?

5 What type of animal is the tucotucco?

6 Complete Lord Acton's phrase "Power tends to corrupt ... "?

7 Which former Irish President served as UN High Commissioner for Human Rights from 1997 to 2002?

8 Which famous scientist started out as a bookbinder's apprentice?

9 What is the fastest living creature regularly raced for sport?

10 In which trade did a Butcher, a Cooper and a Mariner work together?

11 What did Leo Baekeland invent in 1909?

12 Which animals in London are connected with Edwin Landseer?

13 What did 19th-century French physician René Laënnec develop?

14 Who said, "All the art in the world isn't worth a good potato pie"?

15 Who was the longest-reigning European monarch?

16 What does the DIN number denote in photographic film?

17 In polite society, what does a man do on two legs, a woman sitting down and a dog on three legs?

18 What famous first was achieved by William Tayton?

19 How many virgins feature in the title of a novel by Tory MP Boris Johnson?

20 Which fish "shoots" its food?

21 What language did Jesus speak?

22 Who was replaced as Director of the National Theatre by Trevor Nunn in 1997?

23 To ten years either way, until when were mules part of the British army?

24 In which American novel is there a character called Little Eva?

25 In which county is the Seikan tunnel?

26 Which comic-strip detective was created by Chester Gould?

27 Which athlete set six world records in less than an hour in 1935?

28 What is the name of the violent northwesterly wind that blows over the Adriatic?

29 Which land was first sighted by Vasco da Gama on a Christmas Day?

30 "Spend, spend, spend" was the cry of which winner of the football pools?

Answers Pot-Luck 17 (see Quiz 38)

1 A letter sent by the pope to all Catholic archbishops. 2 Fanny Cradock. 3 Malum. 4 New York. 5 Universal. 6 The oysters. 7 Lake Havasu City, Arizona, United States. 8 Greek. 9 Fred Astaire's. 10 In the Mood. 11 Jupiter. 12 A port on the River Uruguay. 13 UB40. 14 Katie Holmes. 15 Peter the Great. 16 Fear of slime. 17 John Cleese. 18 G. K. Chesterton. 19 Billie Piper. 20 The chihuahua. 21 Six. 22 Of speech, of worship, from want, from fear. 23 It was kept in a large jar of honey. 24 The Dragon. 25 Four. 26 Australia. 27 Blaise Pascal. 28 Paris. 29 £5.05. 30 Edward J. Smith.

1 Which cocktail would you find in a toolbox?
2 What is the best-known type of Hollands called?
3 What is the Russian drink kvass made from?
4 What is Drambuie made from?
5 What spice is used in a whisky sling?
6 What turns gin into a pink gin?
7 What are the traditional ingredients in a daiquiri?
8 What is added to brandy to make a sidecar?
9 What is the principal spirit in a Harvey Wallbanger?
10 What is a cocktail of rye whisky, vermouth and angostura called?
11 What is the brandy Birngeist made from?
12 Which drink was Prince Charles caught ordering while at Gordonstoun?
13 If a cocktail is served "in a mist", how is it served?
14 What is a dry Manhattan called?
15 What is the fruit in an old-fashioned?
16 What makes a whisky a whisky sour?
17 What are the two main ingredients of a cuba libre?
18 Which former prime minister do you get if you mix cinzano, apricot brandy and angostura bitters?
19 What savoury ingredient do you include in a Sputnik?
20 What does an Alexandra taste of?
21 Which card game is a mix of cinzano bianco, gin and maraschino?
22 What do you add to champagne to make a champagne flip?
23 What type of plant is tequila made from?
24 Which distillery was the first to conform to the licensing laws which made other stills illegal in 1823?
25 With which US state is bourbon most associated?
26 What is the apple brandy of Normandy called?
27 Where is the original home of bacardi?
28 What is slivovitz made from?
29 What sort of drink is Barbancourt?
30 Where is the Talisker whisky distillery?

Answers	Sport: Rugby (see Quiz 43)

1 Seddon drowned in Australia. 2 J. P .R. Williams. 3 20 teams. 4 Zimbabwe. 5 Lawrence Dallaglio. 6 Toulouse. 7 Cardiff. 8 80 points. 9 New Zealand. 10 England. 11 Leicester. 12 Gavin Hastings. 13 M. J. K. Smith. 14 21 times. 15 Bill Beaumont. 16 Currie Cup. 17 Peter Phillips (Princess Anne's son). 18 Australia. 19 Brisbane. 20 Auckland Warriors. 21 World Cup semi-final 2003. 22 Argentina. 23 Gareth Edwards. 24 Michael Dods. 25 Ranfurly Shield. 26 Devon. 27 England (1991). 28 Georgia. 29 1995 World Cup semi-final v England. 30 Small volcanic island.

1 What is the Duke of Argyll's stately home called?
2 In 2005 Max Egremont published a biography about which WWI poet?
3 Which spice comes from the crocus?
4 Who was the first person to sail single-handed non-stop around the world?
5 Which star is situated almost exactly above the North Pole?
6 What sort of creature is a tarantula hawk?
7 From which flower is digitalis obtained?
8 Whom did Harry Secombe play in the musical film "Oliver"?
9 Peter and Edmund were the boys, but which girls visited Narnia?
10 Which soccer club did Boris Becker have trials with?
11 Which single letter made the difference between two album titles of Robbie Williams?
12 Where was the world's first lighthouse, built of white marble?
13 Which politician shared the 1998 Nobel Peace Prize along with David Trimble?
14 In music what key is a piece written in if it has five flats?
15 Which tree has English, white and slippery varieties?
16 Which English county is known as the "county of sunsets"?
17 Which psychiatrist wrote "Bird of Paradise"?
18 Which artist includes "Away from the Flock" and "Mother and Child Divided" in his works?
19 Which politician had a dog called Pushinka?
20 Who in 1982 went topless at the England v Australia rugby game?
21 Which church leader had 27 wives?
22 Which opera star became Artistic Director of the Los Angeles Opera in 2000?
23 Who invented the first safety match?
24 What is the dog on "the Tweenies" called?
25 Which English queen banned mirrors as she grew old?
26 Which was the first stately home to open to the public?
27 When were driving tests first introduced in Britain?
28 Who was created by Mary Tourtel?
29 In Greek mythology which gift was given to Cassandra by Apollo?
30 Where would you find the vox humana and vox angelica together?

| **Answers** | **Modern History: Dictators** *(see Quiz 44)* |

1 Austria. 2 Art school. 3 Trying to overthrow the Bavarian government. 4 Night of the Long Knives. 5 Colonel Stauffenberg. 6 Axis. 7 Italian resistance. 8 Tonton Macoute. 9 First Consul. 10 Elba. 11 Generalissimo. 12 Man of steel. 13 National Movement. 14 1939. 15 Ferdinand Marcos. 16 Benigno Aquino. 17 Leopoldo Galtieri. 18 Very Mighty Ruler. 19 13. 20 Mao Tse Tung. 21 1979. 22 Born the same year. 23 General Zia. 24 Ceausescu. 25 Nicholas II. 26 Ho Chi Minh. 27 Pol Pot. 28 Tito. 29 Gaddafi. 30 Suharto.

1 Why did A. E. Stoddart take over from R. L. Seddon as captain on the Lions' first tour of Australia and New Zealand?
2 Which rugby international won junior Wimbledon in 1966?
3 How many teams took part in the 2003 World Cup?
4 Which African side was invited to the Rugby Union World Cup in 1987?
5 Who was the only player involved in every minute of his side's games in the 2003 World Cup?
6 Who were the first French side to win the Heineken/European Cup twice?
7 For which club did fly half turned broadcaster Cliff Morgan play?
8 England scored a record how many points in February 2001?
9 Where was the first Rugby Union World Cup held?
10 Whom did Russian Prince Obolensky play for in 1936?
11 Which Union club first won the John Player Cup three years in a row?
12 Who kicked six penalty goals for Scotland on his debut in 1986?
13 Which England cricket captain was capped for England at rugby?
14 To two each way, how many times did Clive Woodward play for England?
15 Who preceded Steve Sale as England captain?
16 What is South Africa's inter-provincial tournament called?
17 Which member of the royal family played in a rugby international?
18 In which country do Randwick play?
19 In which city did England play Wales in the 2003 World Cup quarter-final?
20 Which team did Andy Platt and Dean Bell join after leaving Wigan?
21 In which big game did Jason Leonard establish himself as the world's most capped player?
22 Which country did Hugo Porta play for?
23 Who won 53 caps without missing a single game?
24 Who scored all Scotland's 19 points against France in 1996?
25 What is New Zealand's inter-provincial championship called?
26 Which County Champions this century had to go back to 1957 for their last championship?
27 Before 2003, who were the last hosts to be World Cup runners up?
28 In 2003's World Cup Richard Hill was injured against which team?
29 Which match was Jonathan Davies' last game of League for Wales?
30 What did New Zealanders suggest should be named after Jonah Lomu following the Rugby World Cup?

Answers	Spirits and Cocktails (see Quiz 41)

1 Screwdriver. 2 Schnapps. 3 Rye. 4 Scotch whisky and heather honey. 5 Nutmeg. 6 Angostura bitters. 7 Bacardi and lime juice. 8 Cointreau. 9 Vodka. 10 Manhattan. 11 Pears. 12 Cherry brandy. 13 On crushed ice. 14 Bronx. 15 Cherries. 16 Orange and lemon. 17 Rum and coca cola. 18 Mr Callaghan. 19 Cocktail onion. 20 Chocolate. 21 Canasta. 22 Egg yolk. 23 Cactus. 24 Glenlivet. 25 Kentucky. 26 Calvados. 27 Cuba. 28 Plums. 29 Rum. 30 Isle of Skye.

Quiz 44

Modern History:
Dictators

Answers – page 282

LEVEL 3

1 In which country was Hitler born?
2 What type of school did he attend in Munich?
3 Why was Hitler imprisoned in 1923?
4 What name was given to the occasion in 1934 when Hitler had members of his own party murdered by the SS?
5 Who tried to assassinate Hitler in 1944?
6 What name was given to the link between Hitler's Germany and Mussolini's Italy?
7 Which organization executed Mussolini?
8 Which civilian militia was established under Papa Doc Duvalier?
9 Which title did Napoleon take in 1799, instituting a military dictatorship?
10 What was Napoleon given sovereignty over after his abdication in 1814?
11 What title did Stalin assume when he became war leader?
12 What does the word "Stalin" mean?
13 What was Spain's only legal party after the Civil War?
14 When did Franco become absolute leader of Spain?
15 Who declared martial law in 1972 in the Philippines?
16 Which opposition leader in the Philippines was murdered in 1983?
17 Who was the leader of Argentina at the beginning of the Falklands War?
18 What does the name Genghis Khan mean?
19 How old was Ghenghis Khan when he succeeded his father?
20 Which leader launched his "Great Leap Forward" in 1958?
21 When did Saddam Hussein become president of Iraq?
22 Chaplin played a Hitler-like figure in "The Great Dictator" but what else did they have in common?
23 Which leader sanctioned the execution of President Bhutto in 1979?
24 Which Romanian leader was shot with his wife at Christmas 1989?
25 Who was the last tsar of Russia?
26 Which Vietnamese leader had a city named after him?
27 Who was the leader of the Khmer Rouge?
28 Which Communist leader's real name was Josip Broz?
29 Who overthrew King Idris to gain power in 1971?
30 Which Indonesian president was responsible for the invasion of East Timor in 1975?

Answers	Pot-Luck 19 *(see Quiz 42)*

1 Inveraray Castle. 2 Siegfried Sassoon. 3 Saffron. 4 Robin Knox-Johnston. 5 Polaris or the Pole Star. 6 A wasp. (It hunts spiders.) 7 Foxglove. 8 Mr Bumble. 9 Susan and Lucy. 10 Bayern Munich. 11 W (Sing/Swing When You're Winning). 12 Pharos. 13 John Hume. 14 D flat. 15 Elm. 16 Lincolnshire. 17 R. D. Laing. 18 Damien Hirst. 19 John F. Kennedy. 20 Erica Roe. 21 Brigham Young of the Mormons. 22 Placido Domingo. 23 Johan Edvard Lundstrom. 24 Doodles. 25 Queen Elizabeth I. 26 Wilton House, near Salisbury. 27 1935. 28 Rupert Bear. 29 The gift of prophecy. 30 On an organ. They are stops.

1 In which cathedral were the first Anglican women in Britain ordained?
2 What is the name of Jewish New Year?
3 Which Cardinal, who later became Pope, led the opening prayer at John Paul II's funeral?
4 Who was Canada's first prime minister?
5 What were the first words spoken on a film soundtrack?
6 Which film won more Oscars than any other movie?
7 Who provided the voice for Woody Woodpecker?
8 W. C. T. Dobson is credited in the 1840s with sending the first what?
9 Which female politician wrote a novel titled "The Clematis Tree"?
10 Which conductor said, "The English may not like music but they absolutely love the noise it makes"?
11 Which creature lost its tail in the doors of Noah's ark?
12 "In Utmost Good Faith" is the motto of which organization?
13 What is the devil's coach horse?
14 Who succeeded Laurence Olivier as director of the National Theatre?
15 How old was Bill Gates when he co founded Microsoft?
16 Who was the voice of Princess Fiona in "Shrek 2"?
17 Which Beautiful South song begins, "He was just a social drinker..."
18 What was the first book printed from movable type in 1456?
19 What is the Pentateuch?
20 How many teeth does a mature male horse have?
21 By what name is the marsupial Sarcophilus harrisi better known?
22 What was produced by Henry D. Perky of Denver, Colorado, in 1893?
23 What is the colour of lobsters' blood?
24 The Greek for a "circle of animals" gave its name to what?
25 What is the largest and heaviest satellite in the solar system?
26 Which No 1 single included the bracketed words "In Perfect Harmony"?
27 Who invented the first replaceable razor blade?
28 What kind of lights were first used in 1868 near Parliament Square?
29 Where was the world's first cast-iron bridge built?
30 Horatio Nelson lost his right eye in 1794 at Calvi during the French Revolutionary War. When and where did he lose his right arm?

Answers Pot-Luck 21 *(see Quiz 47)*

1 Anne Boleyn. 2 Scout. 3 Albert Einstein. 4 £12. 5 Wales. 6 A ray. 7 1964. 8 Abdullah. 9 1856. 10 Winston Churchill (about Stafford Cripps). 11 24. 12 Elias. 13 All anagrams of animals. 14 The chinook. 15 Nick Hornby. 16 The Outlaws (in Richmal Crompton's books). 17 1965. 18 Tribophysics. 19 A labour. 20 Helium. 21 Francis II of France. 22 A reticulated python. 23 Gunner Parkin. 24 The Duke of Beaufort. 25 In 1842, after the First Opium War. 26 John Arbuthnot. 27 The Dog Star. 28 Tilda Swinton. 29 Richard Ingrams. 30 Tom Morris.

Quiz 46 | Pop: Instrumentals

Answers – page 288

1 The Shadows' first record went to No 1 – what was it?
2 Who left the Shadows and recorded "Diamonds" on their own?
3 Whose first hit was "Lonely Bull" and then went on to be one of the most successful instrumentalists of all time?
4 What was Perez Prado's 1994/5 hit?
5 Which new record label was "Tubular Bells" recorded on?
6 Whose album was "Oxygène"?
7 Who won an Oscar for the music from "Chariots of Fire"?
8 Where and at what time was Kenny Ball chartwise in 1961?
9 Which film theme was a chart No 1 for the Hugo Montenegro Orchestra?
10 In 1994 which group had a No 1 with a record with the same name as themselves ?
11 Which military band had a hit with "Amazing Grace"?
12 Which clarinettist had an early 1960s hit with the theme for a TV serial?
13 Who recorded "Walk – Don't Run"?
14 Which instrument does Sandy Nelson play?
15 Which guitarist's real name is Brian Robson Rankin?
16 Which pianist's reply to criticism was "I cried all the way to the bank."?
17 Who recorded "Let's Have a Party" and "Let's Have Another Party"?
18 The theme from which TV serial gave Juan Martin a Top Ten hit?
19 Who was the leader of Manuel and his Music of the Mountains?
20 Who had a hit with "The Hustle"?
21 Which Vivaldi concertos were popularized by Nigel Kennedy?
22 Who had No 1s with "Side Saddle" and "Roulette"?
23 What was the title of the pieces on a theme by Paganini recorded by Julian Lloyd Webber?
24 Which instrument is Horst Jankowski playing in his "Walk in the Black Forest"?
25 Which group included Tristan Fry, Herbie Flowers and Kevin Peek?
26 Whose "March" took Joe Loss into the charts in 1964?
27 Which 1950s star was known as Mr Piano?
28 Who joined James Last on the recording "Together at Last"?
29 From which TV series did Jan Hammer's "Crockett's Theme" come?
30 Which guitarist had a hit with the theme from "The Deer Hunter"?

Answers | Geography: The Weather *(see Quiz 48)*

1 Egypt. 2 Boscastle. 3 Solstice. 4 Cumbria. 5 Cold front. 6 Fastnet. 7 Rockies.
8 Katrina. 9 Cirrus. 10 Mirage, Strait of Messina, Italy. 11 Doldrums. 12 Dry, warm,
blowing down a mountain. 13 Alaska (wind). 14 Grey. 15 Russian wind. 16 Occluded
front. 17 Typhoon. 18 Spain. 19 German Bight. 20 South Africa. 21 12. 22 Iran
and Afghanistan. 23 Sirocco. 24 Rhône. 25 Australia. 26 Isobars. 27 Eye of the
storm. 28 Sandstorm. 29 Excessive dust, e.g. after a volcanic eruption. 30 Andes.

Quiz 47 | Pot-Luck 21

Answers – page 285

1 Which queen of England had 11 fingers?

2 In "The Lone Ranger" what was the name of Tonto's horse?

3 Which world-famous scientist said that any man who likes marching had been given a brain for nothing: just the spinal column would have done?

4 To £5 either way, how much did a colour TV licence cost in 1974?

5 Former Tory Party leader Michael Howard was born in which country?

6 What type of fish is a torpedo fish?

7 In which year was Nelson Mandela sentenced to life imprisonment?

8 Who followed Hussein as King of Jordan?

9 To ten years either way, when was the Victoria Cross instituted?

10 Who said, "There but for the Grace of God, goes God"?

11 Into how many international time zones is the world divided?

12 What was Walt Disney's middle name?

13 What is the link between the words act, flow, loin and shore?

14 In the Rocky Mountains what is the dry wind that is warm in winter and cool in summer?

15 Published in 2001, which male novelist writes as a first-person female narrator in "How to be Good"?

16 Which group were made up of Douglas, Ginger, Henry and William?

17 When did Rhodesia declare UDI?

18 What is the physics of friction properly called?

19 What is the collective noun for several moles?

20 What does hydrogen fuse into in the Sun's core?

21 Who was Mary Queen of Scots' first husband?

22 What is the longest snake in the world?

23 Which character gave the name to the series "It ain't Half Hot Mum"?

24 Which duke owns Badminton, setting for the well-known horse trials?

25 To ten years, when did Hong Kong become a British crown colony?

26 Who invented the caricature John Bull?

27 How else is the star Sirius known?

28 Who played the White Witch in the 2005 movie version of "The Lion, The Witch and the Wardrobe"?

29 Who became editor of "The Oldie" magazine in 1992?

30 Who won the first British Open Golf Championship?

Answers | Pot-Luck 20 (see Quiz 45)

1 Bristol. 2 Yom Kippur. 3 Cardinal Ratzinger. 4 Sir John MacDonald. 5 You ain't seen nothing yet. 6 Ben Hur (11). 7 Mel Blanc. 8 Christmas Card. 9 Ann Widdecombe. 10 Sir Thomas Beecham. 11 Manx cat. 12 Lloyd's of London . 13 A beetle. 14 Peter Hall. 15 19. 16 Cameron Diaz. 17 The Woman in the Wall. 18 The Mazarin Bible. 19 First five books of the Bible. 20 40. 21 Tasmanian devil. 22 Shredded wheat. 23 Pale blue. 24 Zodiac. 25 Ganymede. 26 I'd Like to Teach the World to Sing. 27 King Camp Gillette. 28 Traffic lights. 29 Coalbrookdale in England, 1779. 30 1797 at the Battle of Cape St Vincent.

1 Which country has the driest inhabited area in the world?
2 Which Cornish village suffered a freak flood in the summer of 2004?
3 What name is given to an occasion when the equator is furthest from the Sun?
4 Which county is England's wettest?
5 Which usually travels faster, a cold front or a warm front?
6 Which sea area is immediately to the south of Ireland?
7 Over which mountains does the chinook blow?
8 Which 1990s Eurovision Song Contest winner shares her name with a devastating hurricane?
9 The name of which type of cloud is Latin for a lock of hair?
10 What is Fata Morgana and where would you see it?
11 What is the belt of light variable winds near the equator called?
12 What sort of wind is föhn wind?
13 Where would you experience a williwaw?
14 What colour are altostratus clouds?
15 What is the buran?
16 What is the name of a front where a cold front has overtaken a warm front?
17 What is a hurricane called in the Pacific?
18 Where is the tramontana?
19 Which sea area lies due east of Dogger and Humber?
20 Where does the berg wind blow?
21 What number does the Beaufort scale go up to in international use?
22 In which two countries does the Seistan sand wind blow?
23 What is the hot, dry North African wind which blows from the Sahara called?
24 Down which valley does the mistral blow?
25 Where would you experience a southerly buster?
26 What are lines joining places of equal atmospheric pressure called?
27 What is the centre of a hurricane called?
28 What does a haboob create?
29 What causes a blue moon?
30 Over which mountains does the pampero blow?

Answers	Pop: Instrumentals *(see Quiz 46)*

1 Apache. 2 Jet Harris and Tony Meehan. 3 Herb Alpert. 4 Guaglione. 5 Virgin. 6 Jean-Michel Jarre. 7 Vangelis. 8 Midnight in Moscow. 9 The Good, the Bad and the Ugly. 10 Doop. 11 Royal Scots Dragoon Guards. 12 Acker Bilk (Stranger on the Shore). 13 The Ventures. 14 Drums. 15 Hank B. Marvin. 16 Liberace. 17 Winnifred Atwell. 18 The Thorn Birds. 19 Geoff Love. 20 Van McCoy. 21 The Four Seasons. 22 Russ Conway. 23 Variations. 24 Piano. 25 Sky. 26 March of the Mods. 27 Joe Henderson. 28 Richard Clayderman. 29 Miami Vice. 30 John Williams.

1 In the autumn of 2005 which major US civil rights activist died?
2 Under what name did William White find fame on TV?
3 Difford and Tilbrook were songwriters for which group?
4 Who was Mussolini's mistress, who was executed with him?
5 What are the four groups that make up the ape family?
6 According to Lord Birkenhead, who devoted the best years of his life to preparing impromptu speeches?
7 Which creature is involved in the French equivalent of an April Fool?
8 Who was the first musician to be made a life peer?
9 What is the deepest lake in the world?
10 What is a male swan called?
11 Who said, "Genius is 1 per cent inspiration and 99 per cent perspiration"?
12 Which was the first country to make seat belts compulsory?
13 Who created and provided the voice of Basil Brush?
14 To ten years either way, when did Britain launch its first submarine?
15 In which country was Princess Margaret born?
16 In which decade did Pablo Picasso die?
17 Who said, "For years politicians have promised the moon. I am the first one to be able to deliver it"?
18 Who was FIFA world player of the year in both 1998 and 2000?
19 Which former politician published a biography of Winston Churchill in 2001?
20 What does the whale shark feed on?
21 Who left a fortune in his will to develop a new phonetic alphabet?
22 Who became the first female to win five track and field medals at the same Olympics?
23 Who was the first king to award medals to his troops for bravery?
24 Who wrote "Bambi"?
25 Where in China is the Forbidden City?
26 Who drew the cartoon comic-strip character Andy Capp?
27 Whose autobiography was called "Black, White and Gold"?
28 Who said of his troops, "I don't know what effect these men will have upon the enemy but, by God, they terrify me"?
29 What is nephology?
30 Henry III put three barleycorns in a line to make which measurement?

Answers	Pot-Luck 23 *(see Quiz 51)*

1 The trapdoor failed to open. 2 Trinity College, Dublin. 3 Hilary Spurling. 4 Peru. 5 Edinburgh Festival. 6 Paul Merton. 7 David Blunkett. 8 Frankie Laine. 9 Ross Perot. 10 Robert Ford. 11 Dawn French. 12 L.A. Law. 13 They both begin with the word "midnight". 14 18. 15 Miss Saigon. 16 Putrid pot. 17 Orange. 18 Lord Northcliffe. 19 Captain Blood. 20 Ruth Ellis. 21 1950s. 22 Attempting to swim the rapids at Niagara Falls. 23 Reginald Perrin. 24 25th January. 25 Peace. 26 The Humblebums. 27 July 29th, 1981. 28 Claire Rayner. 29 Paolo Wanchope. 30 Netherlands.

1 Which country won the first Eurovision song contest in 1956?
2 Which Austrian sang "Rock Me Amadeus" in 1986?
3 Who sang the song called "Volver a Empezar" in his own language?
4 Who was runner-up to Ireland's Linda Martin in the 1992 Eurovision?
5 From which countries were Enigma, who had a No 1 with "Sadness"?
6 "Raindrops Keep Falling on My Head" is Sacha Distel's only chart entry, but how many times did it do so?
7 Who was the first person to win Eurovision for Britain?
8 Whose first UK chart hit was "Joe Le Taxi"?
9 Which two songs has Cliff Richard sung in Eurovision?
10 What are the first names of Russian duo t.A.T.u.?
11 Which country came last in the 2005 Eurovision Song Contest?
12 "Young Parisians" was a hit for which UK band?
13 Which country won Eurovision with "A-Ba-Ni-Bi" and "Hallelujah"?
14 Who were the only UK Eurovision winners in the 1980s?
15 What was Nicole's "Ein bisschen Frieden" in English?
16 What is A-Ha's home country?
17 When Abba won Eurovision with "Waterloo" who represented Britain?
18 Who had a No 1 in 1981 with "Computer Love"?
19 In which year were there four Eurovision winners tying for first place?
20 What was Gigliola Cinquetti's 1974 hit whose second line was "Before you break my heart"?
21 Where do Clubhouse hail from, who had hits with "Do It Again – Billie Jean" and "Light My Fire"?
22 Which artist was the first to win Eurovision twice?
23 What was the New Seekers' 1972 Eurovision entry?
24 Which "Opportunity Knocks" winner represented Britain on Eurovision?
25 What nationality were Nina and Frederick who had a 1960 hit with "Little Donkey"?
26 Who was the first person to win Eurovision for Ireland?
27 What was the title of DJ Jurgen's one and only top ten hit?
28 For which event did Helmut Zacharias have a Melody hit in 1964?
29 Who won Eurovision for Britain in 1976?
30 The duo who had a hit "Take Your Shoes Off" came from which country?

Answers | Sport: Tennis *(see Quiz 52)*

1 Olga Morozova. 2 The Queen. 3 Pancho Gonzales and Charlie Pasarell. 4 Eight games all. 5 Jean Borotra. 6 Elena Dementieva. 7 Peter Fleming. 8 Roger Taylor. 9 Five. 10 Australian. 11 Arnaud Clement. 12 Kevin Curren. 13 Seventh. 14 Andrea Jaeger. 15 Daniela Hantuchova and Leos Friedl. 16 It was televised. 17 Donald Budge. 18 Rod Laver. 19 Jaroslav Drobny. 20 Steffi Graf. 21 1968. 22 Margaret Court, Maureen Connolly. 23 Wear white flannels instead of shorts. 24 Boris Becker. 25 George VI (1926). 26 Twenty-five. 27 John and Tracy Austin. 28 MCC. 29 Manuel Santana. 30 Chuck McKinley.

1 In 1885, after being sentenced to death by hanging, how did John Lee survive three attempts by the hangman?
2 Where is the Book of Kells?
3 Who won the Whitbread Prize for her biography of Matisse.
4 Which country did Paddington bear come from?
5 Which festival was founded in 1947 and run by Rudolf Bing?
6 Which entertainer started life as Paul Martin?
7 In 2005 which high profile MP described the disability benefits system as "Crackers!"?
8 Who was the first performer to have British No 1 hits?
9 Which billionaire ran as an independent for the US Presidency in both 1992 and 1996?
10 Who shot Jesse James?
11 Which comedy actress founded the fashion label Sixteen47?
12 Which series featured the firm McKenzie, Brackman, Chaney and Kusak?
13 What is the lyrical link between "Memory" and "Green Door"?
14 How many French kings were named Louis?
15 Which musical on Broadway won Jonathan Pryce his first Tony award?
16 What is the exact translation of "potpourri"?
17 What flavour does the liqueur curaçao have?
18 Which legendary pressman said, "News is something that someone somewhere doesn't want to see printed"?
19 Which film first established Errol Flynn's fame as a swashbuckling actor?
20 Who was the last woman to be hanged in Britain?
21 In which decade did Disneyland open in California?
22 How did English Channel swimmer Matthew Webb die?
23 Joan Greengross was secretary to which fictional salesman?
24 When is Burns' Night?
25 In Greek mythology, what was Irene the goddess of?
26 Billy Connolly was a member of which group?
27 On what date was Prince Charles married to Lady Diana Spencer?
28 Which former nurse turned broadcaster writes in medical journals under the name of Ann Lynton?
29 Which all-time top scorer for Costa Rica has played club soccer in England?
30 In which country did the sport of speed skating originate?

Answers | Pot-Luck 22 *(see Quiz 49)*

1 Rosa Parks. 2 Larry Grayson. 3 Squeeze. 4 Claretta Petacci. 5 Chimpanzees, gorillas, gibbons and orang-utans. 6 Winston Churchill. 7 Fish. 8 Benjamin Britten. 9 Lake Baikal. 10 A cob. 11 Thomas Edison. 12 Czechoslovakia. 13 Ivan Owen. 14 1901. 15 Scotland. 16 1973. 17 Richard Nixon. 18 Zinedine Zidane. 19 Roy Jenkins. 20 Plankton. 21 George Bernard Shaw. 22 Marion Jones. 23 Charles I, in 1643. 24 Felix Salten. 25 Beijing. 26 Reg Smythe. 27 Kelly Holmes. 28 The Duke of Wellington. 29 Meteorological study of clouds. 30 Inch.

1 Whom did Chris Evert beat to win her first Wimbledon Singles title?
2 Who presented Virginia Wade with her Wimbledon trophy in 1977?
3 Who contested Wimbledon's longest-ever match?
4 At what score was the tie break used when it was first introduced at Wimbledon in 1971?
5 Which player was known as the "Bounding Basque"?
6 Who was runner-up in the 2004 Women's US Open Final?
7 With which doubles partner did John McEnroe have most success?
8 Which British man got to three Wimbledon semi-finals in the 60s and 70s?
9 Between 2000 and 2005 how many different players reached the women's final at Wimbledon?
10 What nationality did Hana Mandlikova take after leaving Czechoslovakia?
11 Whom did Andre Agassi beat to win the 2001 Australian Open final?
12 Whom did Becker beat to become the youngest Wimbledon champion?
13 What seed was 2005 Australian Open champion Serena Williams?
14 Who was the first player Martina Navratilova beat to win Wimbledon after her first three victories over Chris Evert ?
15 Which pair won the 2001 Mixed Doubles at Wimbledon?
16 What "first" happened at Wimbledon in 1937?
17 Who was the first player to win the Grand Slam?
18 Who was tennis's first millionaire?
19 Which exiled Czech beat Ken Rosewall at Wimbledon in 1954?
20 Who played her first professional match against Tracy Austin in 1982?
21 In which year did Wimbledon go open?
22 Who were the only two women to win Grand Slams before Steffi Graf?
23 What is Yvon Petra famous for being the last man to do?
24 Who said on losing his title in the second round at Wimbledon, "I lost a tennis match, not a war. Nobody got killed"?
25 Which future king played a doubles match at Wimbledon?
26 How many games did Rafael Nadal win in the 2005 French Open final?
27 Who were the first siblings to win the Wimbledon Mixed Doubles?
28 Whom did the LTA take over from in the management of tennis?
29 Which 1966 Wimbledon winner lost in 1967's first round?
30 Who was the only American to win the Men's Singles at Wimbledon in the 60s?

Answers | Pop: Euro Rockers *(see Quiz 50)*

1 Switzerland. 2 Falco. 3 Julio Iglesias (Begin the Beguine). 4 Michael Ball. 5 Germany and Romania. 6 Five. 7 Sandie Shaw. 8 Vanessa Paradis. 9 Congratulations, Power to All Our Friends. 10 Julia and Lena. 11 Germany. 12 Adam and the Ants. 13 Israel. 14 Bucks Fizz. 15 A Little Peace. 16 Norway. 17 Olivia Newton-John. 18 Kraftwerk. 19 1969. 20 Go. 21 Italy. 22 Johnny Logan. 23 Beg, Steal or Borrow. 24 Mary Hopkin. 25 Danish. 26 Dana. 27 Better Off Alone. 28 Tokyo Olympics. 29 Brotherhood of Man. 30 Romania.

1 Whom did Peeping Tom see naked?
2 Which author claimed the Man Booker Prize in 2005?
3 Who directed "The Seven Samurai"?
4 In which country was backpacker Peter Falconio murdered?
5 In Ancient Egypt what kind of bird is represented by Horus?
6 Which common water pollutant is believed to be harmful to babies?
7 What is the function of the Islets of Langerhans?
8 Which is the largest species of flatfish?
9 Where on the Pacific coast does the Trans-Siberian railway terminate?
10 Who designed the city of New Delhi?
11 Which new policy in 1958 was an attempt to achieve "true communism" in China?
12 Which element is the most toxic substance known?
13 Which philosopher invented "the Superman"?
14 Which singer is responsible for the Faenol Festival?
15 How did the suffragette Emily Davison meet her death in 1913?
16 What was the codename of the US development of the atom bomb?
17 Which planet has the Great Red Spot?
18 Lully was composer at the court of which king?
19 What do the French call the English Channel?
20 The classic text about which sport was written by Izaak Walton in 1653?
21 Brazilian Oscar Niemeyer followed which profession?
22 What is the link between saying "Madam, I'm Adam" and "Ma, I am"?
23 What did Thomas Blood try to steal in London in 1671?
24 What is the name of the southern lights?
25 What element gives amethyst its violet colour?
26 Which Bowie song includes the line: "The shrieking of nothing is killing me"?
27 Which former MP wrote "Charles and Camilla, Portrait of an Affair"?
28 Which technique developed by the painter Seurat uses small dabs of colour laid side by side?
29 At which fictional school is there a Ravenclaw House?
30 Which month is named after a two-faced god?

Answers | Pot-Luck 25 (see Quiz 55)

1 Marco Polo. 2 Once. 3 Ruth Kelly. 4 Robert Frost. 5 Ronnie Barker. 6 Auguste and Louis Lumière. 7 The Birth of a Nation. 8 Anther. 9 Four. 10 Jeremy Irons. 11 Telemetry. 12 Minoan. 13 1986. 14 IMF – The International Monetary Fund. 15 In a flying accident. 16 American Civil War. 17 Académie Française. 18 Jingles. 19 Jean Baptiste de Lamarck. 20 Madame Butterfly. 21 Lebanon. 22 The end of the watch. 23 Order of the Purple Heart. 24 Whitby. 25 None. 26 Unchained Melody. 27 Vienna. 28 Boulder Dam. 29 Karen Blixen. 30 Hendrik Verwoerd.

Quiz 54 | Pop: Frank Sinatra | Answers – page 296

1 What was Sinatra's middle name?
2 What are his children called?
3 What was Sinatra's own record label, founded in 1961, called?
4 Who was Sinatra's most frequent arranger in the 1940s?
5 For which film did Sinatra win an Oscar in 1953?
6 Which character in "The Godfather" is said to be based on Sinatra?
7 Which famous Sinatra song was the first to become a hit after being featured in a TV show?
8 Where was Sinatra born on 12 December 1915?
9 Which Sinatra hit was also a hit in Britain for Matt Monro?
10 What was Sinatra's big 1966 hit – a No 1 in 13 countries?
11 Who was Sinatra's second wife?
12 What was Sinatra's first No 1 in Britain?
13 What was the English version of "Comme d'Habitude"?
14 Which album did he release three years after announcing his retirement?
15 Which song did Sinatra sing in "Robin and the Seven Hoods"?
16 In which musical did he co-star with Gene Kelly?
17 From which musical does "The Lady is a Tramp" come and whom did Sinatra sing it to in the film?
18 With which French singer did Sinatra duet in "Duets" in 1993?
19 Who was his male co-star in "Guys and Dolls"?
20 In which film did Sinatra co-star with Laurence Harvey, Janet Leigh and Angela Lansbury ?
21 Who sang with Sinatra on "Me and My Shadow"?
22 Which No 1 did Sinatra have with his elder daughter?
23 Which song won Sinatra a Grammy in 1965?
24 Who was Sinatra's third wife?
25 Which US cities feature in two of Sinatra's hit singles titles?
26 In which film did Sinatra sing the song with the lines "Have you heard, it's in the stars, next July we collide with Mars"?
27 Who was Sinatra's fourth wife, Barbara, previously married to?
28 In which year did Frank face his final curtain?
29 In which year did "My Way" first hit the UK charts?
30 With whom did he duet on his final top ten single during his own life time?

Answers	American Literature (see Quiz 56)

1 Spanish Civil War. 2 Henry James. 3 Edward Albee. 4 Death of a Salesman. 5 Billy Budd. 6 China. 7 Isaac Asimov. 8 F. Scott Fitzgerald. 9 James Fenimore Cooper. 10 Ambulance driver. 11 England. 12 Philip Marlowe. 13 Dashiel Hammett. 14 Catcher in the Rye. 15 The Armies of the Night. 16 John Steinbeck. 17 Eugene O'Neill. 18 Cuba. 19 The Wonderful Wizard of Oz. 20 Sylvia Plath. 21 The Crucible. 22 The Misfits. 23 Lillian Hellman. 24 Ezra Pound. 25 Mark Twain. 26 Gertrude Stein. 27 Cat on a Hot Tin Roof. 28 Washington Irving. 29 Travel. 30 Harold Robbins.

1 Which explorer's last words were, "I have not told half of what I saw"?
2 How many times was David Beckham sent off when playing for Man Utd?
3 Who was Education Minister at the time of the 2005 Labour Party Conference?
4 Who read "The Gift Outright" at President Kennedy's inauguration?
5 The British Comedy Awards have a Writer of the Year award named after which comic?
6 Which French brothers patented their cinematograph in 1895?
7 What is Griffith's film about the aftermath of the Civil War called?
8 What is the name of the body at the tip of a stamen?
9 How many pecks are there in a bushel?
10 Which actor links the films "Being Julia", "The Lion King" and "Kingdom of Heaven"?
11 What is the name given to the technique of measuring at a distance?
12 The existence of which civilization was confirmed by Arthur Evans' excavations on Crete?
13 In which year did the space shuttle Challenger explode?
14 What was set up after the Bretton Woods Conference in 1944?
15 How did the car manufacturer, Charles Stewart Rolls, die?
16 In which war was the Battle of Shiloh?
17 Which body ensures the purity of the French language?
18 What is the name of the metal discs set in the rim of a tambourine?
19 Which French zoologist is associated with the concept that acquired characteristics can be inherited?
20 How is the character Cio-Cio-San more usually known?
21 The late Rafik Hariri was a former PM of which country?
22 What does the ringing of eight bells mean on board a ship?
23 What is the earliest US military award for service beyond the call of duty?
24 At which place does the ship bringing Dracula to England land?
25 How many humps does a newborn camel have?
26 What is the most successful song written by Alex North and Hy Zaret?
27 Where were the first European coffee houses opened?
28 From 1933 to 1947 how was the Hoover Dam on the Colorado known ?
29 Who wrote "Out of Africa"?
30 Which prime minister of South Africa was assassinated in 1966?

Answers	Pot-Luck 24 *(see Quiz 53)*

1 Lady Godiva. 2 John Banville. 3 Akira Kurosawa. 4 Australia. 5 Hawk. 6 Nitrate. 7 They secrete insulin. 8 Halibut. 9 Vladivostok. 10 Edwin Lutyens. 11 The Great Leap Forward. 12 Plutonium. 13 Friedrich Nietzsche. 14 Bryn Terfel. 15 She threw herself under the king's horse at the Derby. 16 Manhattan Project. 17 Jupiter. 18 Louis XIV. 19 La Manche. 20 Fishing. 21 Architect. 22 Both have the same letters reading forwards or backwards. 23 The crown jewels. 24 Aurora Australis. 25 Manganese. 26 Ashes to Ashes. 27 Gyles Brandreth. 28 Pointillism. 29 Hogwarts (Harry Potter). 30 January.

1 Against what is Hemingway's "For Whom the Bell Tolls" set?
2 Which US-born novelist lived much of his life in France and England and became a British citizen in 1915?
3 Who wrote, "Who's Afraid of Virginia Woolf?"?
4 In which Arthur Miller play do you meet Willy Loman?
5 What is a novel by Herman Melville and an opera by Benjamin Britten?
6 Where are most of Pearl S. Buck's novels set?
7 Who wrote the short story "I Robot" in 1950?
8 Who died at the age of 44 with his novel "The Last Tycoon" unfinished?
9 Who wrote the "Leatherstocking" tales of frontier life with their hero Natty Bumpo?
10 "A Farewell to Arms" is based on Hemingway's own experience as what in World War I?
11 Where were Robert Frost's poems first published?
12 Which character appears in all nine of Raymond Chandler's novels?
13 Who wrote "The Maltese Falcon"?
14 Holden Caulfield appears in which, once controversial, novel?
15 Which Norman Mailer novel is based on a protest march?
16 Whose novels are about social conditions in his native California?
17 Which dramatist wrote "Long Day's Journey into Night"?
18 What is the setting for Hemingway's "The Old Man and the Sea"?
19 What is L. Frank Baum's most famous story?
20 Which US poet married Ted Hughes, later poet laureate?
21 Which Arthur Miller play is a comment on McCarthyism?
22 Which screenplay did Miller write for his wife Marilyn Monroe?
23 Who wrote plays with a political theme such as "The Little Foxes"?
24 Which poet spent time in a US mental hospital after supporting Mussolini and the Fascists in World War II?
25 Whose real name was Samuel Langhorne Clemens?
26 Who coined the phrase "the lost generations"?
27 In which Tennessee Williams play do you meet Big Daddy?
28 Who wrote the story of Rip van Winkle?
29 What type of writing is Paul Theroux associated with other than novels?
30 Whose most famous novel is "The Carpetbaggers"?

Answers | Pop: Frank Sinatra *(see Quiz 54)*

1 Albert. 2 Nancy, Frank, Tina. 3 Reprise. 4 Axel Stordahl. 5 From Here to Eternity. 6 Johnny Fontane. 7 Love & Marriage. 8 Hoboken. 9 Softly as I Leave You. 10 Strangers in the Night. 11 Ava Gardner. 12 Three Coins in the Fountain. 13 My Way. 14 Ol' Blue Eyes is Back. 15 My Kind of Town. 16 On the Town. 17 Pal Joey, Rita Hayworth. 18 Charles Aznavour. 19 Marlon Brando. 20 Manchurian Candidate. 21 Sammy Davis Jr. 22 Somethin' Stupid. 23 It was a Very Good Year. 24 Mia Farrow. 25 Chicago, New York. 26 High Society. 27 Zeppo Marx. 28 1998. 29 1969. 30 Bono.

1 Who was the first person to successfully climb the Matterhorn?
2 What was the name of the eldest of the Railway Children?
3 Whom did David Steel succeed as leader of the Liberal Party?
4 NaOH is the chemical formula for what?
5 What is the term for a group of monkeys?
6 Which movie-making operation bought Spielberg's Dreamworks in December 2005?
7 The scene of much brutality this millennium, Dafur is in which country?
8 What pigment comes from the cuttlefish?
9 In which country is the Napa Valley?
10 Who narrated the Paddington cartoon series?
11 Whose victory over the Danes is celebrated in Wiltshire's White Horse?
12 Which is the largest lake in the United Kingdom?
13 Which planet other than Venus does not have moons?
14 Which two people created "EastEnders"?
15 Which two words does the word modem come from?
16 In films how is Betty Joan Perske better known?
17 Who became Archbishop of York in 2005?
18 Which dancer plays the 25-year-old Billy at the end of "Billy Elliot"?
19 Which element has the symbol P?
20 Who said, "I want to be the white man's brother, not his brother-in-law"?
21 In what year was the first soccer World Cup broadcast on British TV in colour?
22 What's the link between Maria von Trapp of "The Sound of Music" and Patrick Troughton of "Dr Who" fame?
23 Who designed the Spitfire?
24 When did the EEC become the EC?
25 Which pope occupied the Holy See for only two days?
26 Which veteran comedian wrote "If I Don't Write It, Nobody Will"?
27 The names of British racehorses are limited to how many letters?
28 What was S Club 7's biggest hit?'
29 Which river forms part of the frontier between Spain and Portugal?
30 Of which country did Leonid Kravchuk become President in 1991?

Answers | Pot-Luck 27 *(see Quiz 59)*

1 John Osborne. 2 Universal. 3 Sir Geoffrey Howe. 4 Dry ice. 5 A skulk. 6 Ellen MacArthur. 7 A seahorse. 8 Port. 9 Bedfordshire. 10 Adultery. 11 Stevie Wonder. 12 Horse. 13 1931. 14 Hazel. 15 Oxford Committee for Famine Relief. 16 Westminster Abbey. 17 Borstal, near Rochester, Kent. 18 Dame Kiri Te Kanawa. 19 Stalagmites. 20 Juventus. 21 The turkey. 22 Scarlett Johanssen. 23 Tony Hancock. 24 The Soviet Union. 25 1959. 26 Johnny Cash. 27 George II. 28 Silkworms. 29 Pope John Paul II. 30 Please Please Me.

1 Which comedian performed stunts in "Just Nuts" and "The Freshman"?
2 Who produced the "Keystone Kops" films?
3 Which actress starred in "Modern Times"?
4 About which actress did Kenneth Tynan say, "What one sees in other women drunk, one sees in her sober"?
5 Who was directed by D. W. Griffith in "Birth of a Nation" in 1916?
6 In which film does Rudolph Valentino play a father and his son?
7 Who directed the 1923 version of "The Ten Commandments"?
8 Which 1920 film with Douglas Fairbanks was based on the novel "The Curse of Capistrano"?
9 Who was the star of "The Paleface" in 1922?
10 In which year was the first version of "Ben Hur" made?
11 Which memorabilia were sold at Christie's in 1987 for £82,500?
12 Who was the "It" girl?
13 Who was the only woman in the quartet who founded United Artists?
14 What is Rudolph Valentino's job in "Blood and Sand"?
15 Which 1925 film starred John Gilbert as an American in the war in 1917?
16 Which 1926 film was remade in 1952 with James Cagney and Dan Dailey?
17 Although a silent movie, what did "Way Down East" contain?
18 Who played opposite Chaplin in "The Tramp"?
19 Which actress stars opposite Mack Sennett in "Mack and Mabel"?
20 Who asked D. W. Griffith to make the film "Hearts of the World"?
21 Who was Gaston de Tolignac, screenwriter of "Hearts of the World"?
22 Which English actor/playwright starred in "Hearts of the World"?
23 Who wrote and starred in the 1922 version of "Robin Hood"?
24 Which film about early aviation starred Clara Bow and Gary Cooper?
25 What nationality was the hero Valentino played in "The Four Horsemen of the Apocalypse"?
26 Which two roles did Mary Pickford play in "Little Lord Fauntleroy"?
27 What was Fatty Arbuckle's real first name?
28 Who played the title role in the 1928 version of "Sadie Thompson"?
29 Who won the first-ever Oscar for best actress for "Seventh Heaven"?
30 Where does the action of Buster Keaton's "The Navigator" take place?

Answers Sport: Golf *(see Quiz 60)*

1 Tom Watson. 2 Augusta, Georgia. 3 Bobby Locke. 4 Retief Goosen. 5 Gary Player (South Africa). 6 Ben Hogan. 7 Ian Baker-Finch. 8 Tony Jacklin. 9 Supermex. 10 15 strokes. 11 Byron Nelson. 12 Southport. 13 Wentworth. 14 Jack Nicklaus. 15 Portugal. 16 Newport, Rhode Island. 17 Muirfield. 18 Great Britain and Ireland. 19 Nick Faldo. 20 Curtis Cup. 21 British Open. 22 Ian Woosnam beat Padraig Harrington (2001). 23 Bobby Jones. 24 Amateurs. 25 Lee Trevino. 26 Vijay Singh. 27 Christy O'Connor. 28 Bernard Gallacher. 29 Todd Hamilton. 30 Dwight D. Eisenhower.

Quiz 59 Pot-Luck 27

Answers – page 297

LEVEL 3

1 Who wrote the play "Look Back in Anger"?
2 Which recording company did Prince sign with in 2005?
3 Who was Margaret Thatcher's first chancellor of the exchequer?
4 What is solid carbon dioxide commonly called?
5 What is the collective name for a group of foxes?
6 Which adventurer wrote "Race Against Time"?
7 What is the only male creature to carry and hatch eggs?
8 In polite circles, which drink should be passed to the left?
9 In which county is Woburn Abbey?
10 What shall you not commit according to the seventh commandment?
11 Who played every instrument on Cliff Richard's "She's So Beautiful"?
12 A centaur was a mythical creature halfway between a man and what?
13 When was the gold standard finally abandoned in Britain?
14 Which tree has the alternative name of "cob"?
15 What name was OXFAM originally registered as?
16 Where is the Jacobean playwright Ben Jonson buried?
17 Where was the first borstal in Britain?
18 Which female opera singer was appointed to the Order of Merit in 1995?
19 Which limestone formation found in caves grows upwards?
20 Which was the first Italian club side that Zinedine Zidane played for?
21 Which bird did Benjamin Franklin want to be the US emblem?
22 Which actress was the star of Woody Allen's Match Point?
23 Which comedian was known as "the lad himself"?
24 In 1920, which was the first country to legalize abortion?
25 In which year did the M1 motorway open?
26 Who started his career with the Tennessee Two?
27 Who was the last English monarch to be born abroad?
28 What do you breed if you are a sericulturist?
29 Who is the author of "Crossing the Threshold of Hope"?
30 What was the Beatles' first LP called in 1963?

Answers | Pot-Luck 26 *(see Quiz 57)*

1 Edward Whymper. 2 Roberta or Bobbie. 3 Jeremy Thorpe. 4 Caustic soda. 5 A troop. 6 Paramount Pictures. 7 Sudan. 8 Sepia. 9 United States. 10 Michael Hordern. 11 Alfred the Great. 12 Lough Neagh, Northern Ireland. 13 Mercury. 14 Julia Smith, Tony Holland. 15 Modulate, demodulate. 16 Lauren Bacall. 17 John Sentamu. 18 Adam Cooper. 19 Phosphorus. 20 Martin Luther King. 21 1970. 22 They died on the same day (March 30th, 1987). 23 Reginald Joseph Mitchell. 24 1965. 25 Stephen II. 26 Eric Sykes. 27 18 letters and spaces. 28 Don't Stop Movin'. 29 The Guadiana. 30 Ukraine.

1 Which American won five British Opens between 1975 and 1983?
2 Where is the US Masters held?
3 Which South African won the British Open in 1949, 1950, 1952 and 1957?
4 Who won his second US Open at Shinnecock Hills, New York, in 2004?
5 Who was the first non-American post-war winner of the US Masters?
6 Which American played in the British Open only once and won it?
7 Faldo won the British Open in 1990 and 1992. Who won in 1991?
8 Who was the first Englishman to win the US Open after World War II?
9 What is Lee Trevino's nickname?
10 Tiger Woods won the 2000 US Open by a record of how many strokes?
11 Which US golfer had 11 successive tournament wins in 1945?
12 In which town is Royal Birkdale golf course?
13 Over which course is the World Matchplay Championship played?
14 Who won the US Masters in 1986 for a record sixth time?
15 In which country is Penina golf course?
16 Where was the first-ever US Open played in 1895?
17 What name did Jack Nicklaus give to his own golf course in honour of his favourite British course?
18 Who opposed the US in the Ryder Cup between 1973 and 1977?
19 Who won the English Amateur Championship in 1975 aged 18?
20 Which trophy is played for by women golfers from the United States in competition with Britain and Ireland?
21 Which is the oldest open championship in the world?
22 Who played in the World Matchplay Championship Final when a Welshman beat an Irishman?
23 Which golfer was responsible for the the US Masters?
24 What is the status of competitors in the Walker Cup?
25 Who won the US Masters to stop Tiger Woods claiming all majors in a year?
26 Which actor shared his name with the winner of the 1939 British Open?
27 Which Irish golfer played in ten successive Ryder Cup teams?
28 Who captained the European team to victory in the 1995 Ryder Cup?
29 Who got his PGA Tour card in 2003 at his eighth attempt and a year later landed a Major?
30 Which US president's home was alongside the course on which the US Masters is played?

Answers | **The Movies: Silent Cinema** *(see Quiz 58)*

1 Harold Lloyd. 2 Mack Sennett. 3 Paulette Goddard. 4 Garbo. 5 Lillian Gish. 6 Son of the Sheikh. 7 Cecil B. de Mille. 8 The Mark of Zorro. 9 Buster Keaton. 10 1926. 11 Chaplin's hat and cane. 12 Clara Bow. 13 Mary Pickford. 14 Matador. 15 The Big Parade. 16 What Price Glory? 17 A colour sequence. 18 Edna Purviance. 19 Mabel Normand. 20 British government. 21 D. W. Griffith. 22 Noel Coward. 23 Douglas Fairbanks. 24 Wings. 25 Argentinian. 26 Young Cedric and his mother. 27 Roscoe. 28 Gloria Swanson. 29 Janet Gaynor. 30 Transatlantic liners.

1 In 2005, who released the album "Affirmation"?
2 What colour was Rupert Bear's face in early books and annuals?
3 Where did the world's first controlled nuclear reaction take place in 1942?
4 What is the collective name for a group of bears?
5 In our solar system which planet is farthest from the Sun?
6 What colour was the Queen's outfit for the blessing of Charles and Camilla after their wedding?
7 Which big cat has the proper name Acinonyx jubatus?
8 Who ordered the building of the Pavilion at Brighton ?
9 What is the side away from the wind called on a ship?
10 What was Robin's real name in the Batman TV series?
11 Which fish walks on land?
12 What does the musical term Vivace mean?
13 What was the real title of the painting called "The Laughing Cavalier"?
14 Which king was known as "Silly Billy"?
15 Who designed the first mechanical adding machine in 1641?
16 In which country did a cultural revolution take place during 1966–69?
17 Who drew the Katzenjammer Kids for the "New York Journal" in 1910?
18 Who was the first Irish athlete to win gold in the European Championships?
19 Which scale measures the effects of an earthquake at a particular place?
20 What is the vitamin riboflavin?
21 Which is the second largest island in the world after Australia?
22 Which actress starred in "Bend It Like Beckham" and "ER"?
23 What was the surname of soul musician Booker T.?
24 What would the Chuckle Brothers be called if they used their real surnames?
25 In which Alpine range is the Swiss mountain, Jungfrau?
26 What nationality was the first non-US, non-Soviet spaceman?
27 To two years in what year was the final episode of "Dad's Army" originally screened?
28 Where in Italy was Mussolini executed?
29 Which means of transport features on Darkness's album cover "One Way Ticket to Hell ... and Back"?
30 What was the surname of the Windsors before they changed it?

Answers | Pot-Luck 29 (see Quiz 63)

1 Train à Grande Vitesse. 2 Giant Squid. 3 Edgar Degas. 4 Glasgow. 5 Mount of Olives. 6 Lincoln. 7 32. 8 A fox. 9 Bull & Finch. 10 John Hinckley. 11 Happiness. 12 A knight in armour. 13 Rowland Hill. 14 Stanley Baldwin. 15 Bree Van De Kamp. 16 Cherries. 17 The nine of diamonds. 18 Tent stitch. 19 Barbados. 20 Robbie Fowler. 21 A tax to buy off the Danish invaders. 22 The typewriter. 23 Education. 24 The Pearl Fishers. 25 2005. 26 Nose bleed. 27 Dow Jones Index. 28 Henry Hall. 29 Somnus. 30 Boxer & Laura.

Quiz 62 | Pop: No 1s | Answers – page 304

1 How many number ones did Madonna have in the 1990s?
2 What was John Lennon's second No 1 hit, a month after his first?
3 Which was the first record to hit No 1 on two different occasions?
4 Who was the fourth artist to reach No 1 with the song "Unchained Melody"?
5 Which title was a No 1 for Kylie Minogue and Johnny Nash?
6 Elton John's first hit was in 1971. When was his first solo No 1?
7 How many singles were number one in 2003?
8 With which two groups did Gerry Marsden have the same No 1?
9 Which band had a No 1 with "Whatever People Say I am"?
10 What novelty record, by an Australian, was the first No 1 single of the 70s?
11 What were Art Garfunkel's first two hits at No 1?
12 Who took their first three hits to No 1 in 1984?
13 What was Christina Aguilera's fourth number one hit?
14 Who is the oldest person to have a No 1?
15 Who is runner-up to Madonna as female star with most weeks at No 1?
16 Who were the two different backing groups which accompanied Cliff Richard on two No 1 versions of "Livin' Doll"?
17 In 1954 "Oh Mein Papa" and "Oh! My Pa Pa" were recorded by different men with the same christian name, what is it?
18 Mother and son, Hilda and Rob Woodward, reached No 1 as what?
19 How many number ones did "Popstars" winners Hear'say have?
20 What were Rod Stewart's first two No 1 hits?
21 How many consecutive No 1s did the Beatles have between 1963 and 1966?
22 What were Abba's three consecutive No 1s in 1975–76?
23 Which song was Kylie Minogue's first hit to enter the chart at No 1?
24 "Ignition" was the second No 1 single for which male vocalist?
25 What were Adam Faith's two No 1s?
26 What was the Boomtown Rats' first No 1?
27 Who were the two acts who had No 1s with "Without You"?
28 Which No 1 links Elvis Presley and UB40?
29 Who sang with UB40 on their No 1 "I Got You Babe"?
30 Which song was a No 1 for Joe Cocker and Wet, Wet, Wet?

Answers	**Global Events** *(see Quiz 64)*

1 26th December. 2 Florida. 3 Madrid. 4 12. 5 Boscastle. 6 Paradise Square. 7 Saturn. 8 June. 9 Cuba. 10 Indian. 11 December. 12 Pacific. 13 Ukraine. 14 School. 15 202. 16 Paris. 17 Two. 18 Lebanon. 19 Columbia. 20 Saudi Arabia. 21 Afghanistan. 22 Slobodan Milosevic. 23 Libya. 24 Shoes. 25 Concorde. 26 March. 27 Space. 28 Vladimir Putin. 29 Sweden. 30 Isabel.

1 In France what do the initials TGV mean?
2 What is the largest living invertebrate?
3 Which French artist is known for his paintings of the ballet and dancers?
4 Which city comes from two Gaelic words and means "the place in the green hollow"?
5 Which hill marks the traditional site of the Ascension in the Bible?
6 Which is the third-largest cathedral in England?
7 How many pods or capsules does the London Eye have?
8 What type of animal was J. Worthington Foulfellow?
9 Exterior shots in "Cheers" featured a real bar. What was its name ?
10 Who shot Ronald Reagan in March 1981?
11 Of what is the bluebird a symbol?
12 Who would have worn a gorget, pauldron, beaver and greave?
13 Who instituted the penny post in England?
14 Who was the British prime minister when Edward VIII abdicated?
15 Steven Culp played the husband of which "Desperate Housewife"?
16 With what is the Belgian beer Kriek flavoured?
17 Which playing card is referred to as the "curse of Scotland"?
18 In needlework, which stitch may be described as "petit point"?
19 Which paradise holiday island is the most easterly of the West Indies?
20 Whose autobiography had the accurate, though not very original title "Robbie: My Autobiography"?
21 What, in English history, was the Danegeld?
22 With which invention of 1801 is the Italian, Pellegrine Tarri, credited?
23 Before he became party leader what was Neil Kinnock's shadow post?
24 In which work do Nadir and Zurga appear?
25 In what year did Placido Domingo make his proms debut?
26 What is epistaxis, a common complaint, the medical term for?
27 What is the US equivalent of the Financial Times Index?
28 Whose autobiography was entitled "Here's to the Next Time"?
29 What was the name of the Roman god of sleep?
30 In Rosemary & Thyme, what is Rosemary's surname and Thyme's first?

Answers	Pot-Luck 28 *(see Quiz 61)*

1 Beverley Knight. **2** Brown, although he was white-faced on inside colour pages. **3** Chicago. **4** A sleuth. **5** Pluto. **6** Cream. **7** Cheetah. **8** George IV, as Prince Regent. **9** The leeside. **10** Dick Grayson. **11** The climbing perch of India. **12** Lively. **13** Portrait of a Man. **14** William IV. **15** Blaise Pascal. **16** China. **17** Rudolph Dirks. **18** Sonia O'Sullivan. **19** Mercalli scale. **20** B2. **21** Greenland. **22** Parminder Nagra. **23** Jones. **24** The Elliot Brothers. **25** Bernese Alps. **26** Czech. **27** 1977. **28** Como. **29** Train. **30** House of Saxe-Coburg.

Quiz 64 | Global Events

Answers – page 302

LEVEL 3

1 On which date in 2004 was southeast Asia devastated by a tsunami?
2 In which US state was George W. Bush when the attacks began on 9/11?
3 Which European capital's railway station was attached in March 2004?
4 How many countries converted to the euro when it was first introduced?
5 Which Cornish town was a victim of freak flooding in August 2004?
6 What was the name of the Baghdad Square where Saddam Hussein's statue was toppled in 2003?
7 The space probe Cassini Hugens reached which planet in July 2004?
8 In which month in 2004 did the US hand power back to the Iraqis?
9 On which island was Camp X Ray?
10 An earthquake under which ocean caused Dec 2004's tsunami?
11 In which month of 2003 was Saddam Hussein captured after hiding in a cellar?
12 Islanders around which ocean were first to see the new millennium?
13 In 2004, which country had an election annulled and then rerun after accusations of fraud?
14 What type of building was besieged in Beslan in 2004 following the taking of hostages?
15 How many countries competed at the Athens Olympics in 2004?
16 In 2000, Concorde crashed near which European city?
17 How many hijacked civilian planes crashed into the World Trade Center on 9/11?
18 The militant movement Hezbollah was based in which country?
19 What was the name of the shuttle that broke up on returning to Earth in 2003 killing seven people on board?
20 Al Qaeda leader Osama Bin Laden was born in which country?
21 In which country was the Taleban based?
22 Which former Yugoslav president was charged with war crimes in 2001?
23 Which country vowed to give up its chemical weapons in a surprise move in December 2003?
24 Where did Richard Reid hide explosives on a 2001 Paris to Miami flight?
25 Which aircraft was taken out of service in October 2003?
26 In which month in 2003 did the US launch missiles against Iraq?
27 Yang Liwei was the first man from China to travel where?
28 Who was Russian President when the Iraq war began?
29 Which European country's Foreign Minister was stabbed to death in 2003?
30 Which hurricane hammered Washington DC in September 2003?

Answers | Pop: No 1s (see Quiz 62)

1 Two. 2 Woman 3 Bohemian Rhapsody. 4 Gareth Gates. 5 Tears on My Pillow. 6 1990. 7 Twenty-three. 8 The Pacemakers, the Crowd. 9 Arctic Monkeys. 10 Two Little Boys. 11 I Only Have Eyes for You, Bright Eyes. 12 Frankie Goes to Hollywood. 13 Beautiful. 14 Louis Armstrong. 15 Doris Day. 16 The Drifters, the Young Ones. 17 Eddie. 18 Lieutenant Pigeon. 19 Two. 20 Maggie May, You Wear It Well. 21 11. 22 Mamma Mia, Fernando, Dancing Queen. 23 Spinning Around. 24 R. Kelly. 25 What Do You Want, Poor Me. 26 Rat Trap. 27 Nilsson, Mariah Carey. 28 Can't Help Falling in Love. 29 Chrissie Hynde. 30 With a Little Help from My Friends.

304

1 On London's Shaftesbury Avenue which theatre is between the Lyric and the Gielgud?

2 What name is given to a young hawk taken from its nest for training?

3 Where in London would you find the sculpture of Prospero and Ariel?

4 Under which king was the Royal Observatory at Greenwich built?

5 Who, according to the Book of Samuel in the Bible, was born in Gath?

6 Which is the largest Gothic church in northern Europe?

7 What names are given to the old and new styles of calendar?

8 Musky Muskrat was the sidekick of which cartoon lawman?

9 What are Micmac, Cree and Ojibwa?

10 Which signal replaced the CQD signal in 1906?

11 What is the botanical emblem of Australia?

12 Who would wear an orphrey, morse and cope and carry a crozier?

13 What did the Polish oculist Dr L. Zamenhof invent?

14 Who was elected the first woman Lord Mayor of London in 1983?

15 In 1991 Jonathan Sacks took over which important post in Great Britain?

16 Which Scandinavian alcoholic spirit is made from potatoes?

17 In which country did the card game bridge originate?

18 Which Oscar-winning film features Colin Firth as Lord Wessex and Martin Clunes as Richard Burbage?

19 What are the Tonga Islands otherwise known as?

20 How many different albums reached number one in 2003?

21 Which English king invented a candle clock?

22 What Latin word is used to express the meaning "word for word"?

23 What did the American Hamilton Smith invent in 1858?

24 Where was the last battle between Britain and the United States?

25 In which London street is Hamley's toy shop?

26 What is the common name for the disease called trismus?

27 What is the French equivalent of the Stock Exchange?

28 Who composed the Symphony No 7, known as "the Leningrad"?

29 Who was the Greek goddess of victory?

30 Where are the birthplace and statue of King Alfred the Great?

Answers | Pot-Luck 31 *(see Quiz 67)*

1 Victoria Falls. 2 Chlorophyll. 3 Iolanthe. 4 The Vedas. 5 New Hampshire. 6 St Matthew. 7 Lactose. 8 Hong Kong harbour. 9 Lloyd George. 10 Morris Garages. 11 Lord Scarman. 12 A glider. 13 China. 14 Nil by Mouth. 15 1967. 16 Wedge. 17 Connecticut. 18 39 inquiries. 19 Countdown. 20 The Althing. 21 Jesuits. 22 Billy Elliot. 23 The kukri. 24 A dance. 25 Canada. 26 Touchstone. 27 Goering. 28 Caves. 29 The Atholl Highlanders. 30 Alpenstock.

1 Which hero is Beethoven's "Eroica" Symphony said to be named after?
2 Who were J. S. Bach's two sons?
3 What is the nationality of composer Isaac Albéniz?
4 On which instrument is Handel's "Harmonious Blacksmith" played?
5 What type of horns feature in Haydn's Symphony No 31 in D?
6 Whose ebony clarinet was Stravinsky's Clarinet Concerto written for, thus giving it the nickname "Ebony"?
7 In which country was Greek composer Iannis Xenakis actually born?
8 What was Vivaldi's profession aside from violinist and composer?
9 What type of works did John Wilbye compose?
10 To which composer is Bruckner's Symphony No 3 in D minor dedicated?
11 Who was Britten's Simple Symphony written for?
12 Which Gilbert and Sullivan opera has the subtitle "Flowers of Progress"?
13 Who wrote the tone poem "Tintagel"?
14 Which work provided Anthony Minghella with his operatic directorial debut?
15 Which American folk hero is the title of a ballet by Aaron Copland?
16 What is Debussy's dreamlike music often called?
17 What type of work is Elgar's "Dream of Gerontius"?
18 Which honorary degree was Haydn receiving when his Oxford Symphony was first performed?
19 Which modern English composer wrote the opera "Punch and Judy"?
20 Which two Russian revolutions does Shostakovich commemorate in his 11th and 12th symphonies?
21 What is the "joke" which gives Haydn's String Quartet in E flat its name?
22 Which Soviet republic did Khachaturian come from?
23 For which musical instrument were Liszt's "Liebesträume" written?
24 How many major symphonies did Mahler write?
25 What was Mussorgsky's first name?
26 Including interval time, how long does a performance of Richard Wagner's "Gotterdämmerung" last?
27 Which rival of Mozart has been accused, falsely, of poisoning him?
28 Who wrote "The Snow Maiden" and "The Golden Cockerel"?
29 What is the "Miracle" which gave Haydn's Symphony No 96 its name?
30 What were Johann Stamitz's "Mannheim rockets"?

Answers	**Geography: Natural Phenomena** *(see Quiz 68)*

1 Bam. 2 Cirrus. 3 Bogor, Java. 4 Snow. 5 Bracknell, north Wales. 6 Coriolis effect. 7 Krakatoa, near Java. 8 Sumatra. 9 St Elmo's fire. 10 Red, orange, yellow, green, blue, indigo, violet. 11 Tornado. 12 Aurora. 13 Tsunami (not tidal waves). 14 An annular eclipse. 15 Earthquake areas. 16 The International Ice Patrol. 17 Mauna Loa, Hawaii. 18 A waterspout. 19 Aurora Borealis. 20 Surtsey. 21 Empedocles. 22 Lebu, Chile. 23 Mount Erebus. 24 Geyser. 25 Pumice. 26 The Earth passes between the Sun and Moon. 27 Thermal. 28 Stalactites. 29 Fumarole. 30 The Mercalli scale.

1 What is the biggest tourist attraction in Zambia?
2 What name is given to the green colouring matter found in plants?
3 What was Reginald Perrin's middle name in the sit com with Leonard Rossiter?
4 What name is given to the four holy books of the Hindus?
5 Dan Brown was born in which American state?
6 Who is the patron saint of tax collectors?
7 What is the name of the sugar found in milk?
8 Where did the passenger liner "Queen Elizabeth" catch fire in 1972?
9 Who was the first prime minister to occupy Chequers?
10 What do the initials MG stand for on a sports car?
11 Who headed the inquiry into the Brixton Riots in 1981?
12 What kind of aircraft was the World War II Horsa?
13 Where did the Boxer Rising take place between 1898 and 1900?
14 Which movie was Gary Oldman's directorial debut?
15 In which year did the British breathalyzer law come into force?
16 In golf what is the traditional name for the number ten iron?
17 Which US state is called the Nutmeg state?
18 How many public inquiries were held before the go ahead was given for the M25?
19 On which TV programme does Susie Dent give her expert advice?
20 What is the Icelandic parliament called?
21 What were the names of the followers of Ignatius Loyola?
22 In which movie did the character in the title role say: "I don't want a childhood, I want to be a ballet dancer"?
23 What name is given to the knife which the Gurkha soldiers use?
24 What is a saraband?
25 In which country would you find the Laurentian Mountains?
26 What was the name of the jester in "As You Like It"?
27 Who created the German Luftwaffe?
28 What does a speleologist study?
29 What is the name of Britain's only private army?
30 What is the name of the long staff with an iron tip used in mountaineering?

Answers | Pot-Luck 30 *(see Quiz 65)*

1 Apollo. 2 Eyas. 3 BBC Broadcasting House. 4 Charles II. 5 Goliath. 6 Cologne cathedral. 7 Julian, Gregorian. 8 Deputy Dawg. 9 American Indian Tribes. 10 SOS. 11 Wattle blossom. 12 A bishop. 13 Esperanto. 14 Lady Donaldson. 15 Chief Rabbi (of Great Britain). 16 Aquavit. 17 Turkey. 18 Shakespeare in Love. 19 Friendly Islands. 20 Twenty-five. 21 Alfred the Great. 22 Verbatim. 23 Washing machine. 24 New Orleans. 25 Regent Street. 26 Lockjaw. 27 The Bourse. 28 Shostakovich. 29 Nike. 30 Winchester.

1 Which Iranian city was partially destroyed by a Dec 2003 earthquake?
2 What is the highest standard cloud formation called?
3 Where is the most thundery place on earth?
4 What occurred in the Kalahari Desert on September 1st, 1981?
5 Where did the longest-lasting rainbow glow for three hours?
6 What name is given to the bending of the winds caused by the Earth spinning on its axis?
7 Which volcanic eruption gave the loudest sound ever recorded?
8 Which Indonesian island was nearest the epicentre of the earthquake in December 2004?
9 What is the name given to the lightning which clings to ships' masts?
10 What are the seven colours of the rainbow in their correct order?
11 What is the name for a column of swiftly spinning air?
12 What name is given to the phenomenon of bright lights in the atmosphere caused by the solar wind entering the ionosphere?
13 What are caused by changes in the level of the ocean floor?
14 What occurs when the central zone of the Sun is covered?
15 What are the "Ring of Fire" and "Alpine Belt"?
16 Which patrol group keeps track of all icebergs?
17 Which is the largest active volcano on Earth?
18 What forms when a tornado runs over water?
19 What is the scientific name for the Northern Lights?
20 Which island emerged from the sea off the coast of Iceland in 1963?
21 Which Greek philosopher made 5th-century BC studies of vulcanology?
22 Where did the strongest earthquake ever recorded take place in 1960?
23 Which is the only active volcano in Antarctica?
24 What is a vent in the Earth's crust that spouts a fountain of boiling water?
25 Which volcanic rock is so strongly charged with gas that it appears frothy and floats on water?
26 What occurs when a lunar eclipse take place?
27 What is a rising air current caused by heating from below called?
28 What are Tugela and the Buyoma?
29 What name is given to a volcanic opening that gives out gas and steam?
30 What scale, other than the Richter, measures earthquakes?

Answers	**Classical Music** *(see Quiz 66)*

1 Napoleon I. 2 Carl Philip Emanuel, Johann Christian. 3 Spanish. 4 Harpsichord. 5 Hunting horns. 6 Woody Herman. 7 Romania. 8 Priest. 9 Madrigals. 10 Wagner. 11 Young people. 12 Utopia Limited. 13 Sir Arnold Bax. 14 Madame Butterfly. 15 Billy the Kid. 16 Musical impressionism. 17 Oratorio. 18 Doctorate. 19 Harrison Birtwhistle. 20 1905, 1917. 21 Several false endings. 22 Armenia. 23 Piano. 24 Nine. 25 Modest. 26 Six hours. 27 Antonio Salieri. 28 Rimsky-Korsakov. 29 Chandelier said to have fallen, but injured no one. 30 Brilliant scale passages.

Quiz 69 | Pot-Luck 32 | Answers – page 311

1 What, in computer terminology, do the initials COBOL stand for?
2 What are the two types of camel?
3 Which character announced "I'm not here" in times of crisis in "Drop the Dead Donkey"?
4 What name is given to the highest point of the heavens?
5 The September 11th USA attacks led to postponing news of the election of which new Tory leader?
6 In which city was the first boy scout troop registered?
7 On which date does International Labour Day fall?
8 Who created the popular 1920s cartoon character Felix the Cat?
9 Leap-Frog, the Gallant Hussar and Ampleforth are all types of what?
10 By what nickname was the criminal Albert De Salvo better known?
11 How many points has a Star of David?
12 What is the lace scarf worn over the head by Spanish women called?
13 Which Frenchman discovered the St Lawrence River?
14 Who was the BBC's principal TV commentator during the Queen's coronation?
15 What was Muse's first top ten hit?
16 Which drink do you associate with Holy Island in Northumberland?
17 Which English king reigned the longest?
18 In bridge, what jargon word describes "holding no trumps"?
19 What was the title of the first women's magazine ever published, in 1693?
20 What name is given to a whirling tornado-like cloud at sea?
21 Of which island republic is Antananarivo the capital?
22 Which movie, which began with the words "The hills are alive" celebrated its 40th anniversary in 2005?
23 With which invention is William Le Baron Jenny of the United States credited?
24 What was the title of John Wayne's final film?
25 Which stretch of water separates Sicily from Italy?
26 What is the Japanese word for goodbye?
27 Tom Naylor and Jacqueline King have both won what?
28 Which musical instrument do you associate with Dizzy Gillespie?
29 By what name is Portuguese West Africa now known?
30 Which photographer and cousin of the Queen died in November 2005?

Answers | Pot-Luck 33 (see Quiz 71)

1 Benjamin Britten's. 2 Helicon. 3 58. 4 Kestrel. 5 Dahlia. 6 Michael Buerk. 7 Sunday Times. 8 The Plymouth Brethren. 9 King Edward VII. 10 St Vincent. 11 Amalgam. 12 Clydebank. 13 Spoon. 14 Coco the Clown. 15 Sean O'Casey. 16 Susan Sarandon. 17 Ballistics. 18 Washington. 19 Hamilton. 20 All parts of a spinning wheel. 21 Belfast. 22 Fed Cup. 23 Kent. 24 Hindu. 25 Herbert Hoover. 26 Pistil. 27 The grouse family. 28 Two. 29 The Winchester. 30 Menelaus.

1 In which city was Yorkshire's Michael Vaughan born?
2 Which was the first English county that Anil Kumble played for?
3 Who was the last England captain to play South Africa before the ban?
4 Who won the county championships in every season from 1951 to 1958?
5 Where in the West Indies did Brian Lara score his record-breaking 375?
6 Who was the first player to make over 1,000 catches in first-class cricket?
7 What did ICC stand for before 1965?
8 Who were the first winners of the Women's World Cup in 1973?
9 What is Bob Willis's middle name?
10 Which England batsmen each scored double centuries against India in 1985 in the same innings?
11 Who was the first batsman to score 10,000 runs in Test cricket?
12 In which country are the first-class sides United Bank and National Bank?
13 Who were the first three members of the ICC?
14 What was the Nat West Trophy previously called?
15 Which New Zealander hit a double century in 153 balls vs England in 2002?
16 Who kept wicket for Yorkshire in 412 consecutive county championship games?
17 Who was England's most capped cricketer at the end of the 2002/03 Ashes series?
18 Who scored 322 runs against Warwickshire in less than a day in 1985?
19 In which country do first-class teams compete for the Plunkett Shield?
20 Who was Man of the Match in the 2003 World Cup Final?
21 What is the trophy played for by first-class inter-state sides in India?
22 Who captained England during the "bodyline" series?
23 Who was the first bowler to take 300 Test wickets?
24 Which bowler is nicknamed "The King of Spain"?
25 What was the title of Andrew Flintoff's autobiography?
26 Who said, "The bowler's Holding, the batsman's Willey"?
27 To three each way, how many Tests did it take Muttiah Muralitharan to reach the 400 wicket mark?
28 Michael Vaughan made his international debut against which country?
29 Which ex-England cricketer made his county debut in 1981 and retired on 22 June 2004?
30 Which cup succeeded the Shell Shield in the West Indies?

| **Answers** | Animals *(see Quiz 72)* |

1 Skomer vole. 2 Adder. 3 Sumatran tiger. 4 A small African antelope. 5 Ass. 6 Lizards. 7 Kangaroo hound. 8 Sea-cows. 9 Mongoose. 10 They act independently of each other. 11 South America. 12 Cockroaches. 13 Tiger. 14 Insects. 15 Fish, amphibians, reptiles, birds and mammals. 16 Animals which lay eggs. 17 Can precede "fly" to give the name of another creature. 18 Coypu. 19 Wombat. 20 Arthropods. 21 Types of beetle. 22 Desert fox. 23 Madagascar. 24 Leap. 25 China. 26 Viviparous. 27 Array. 28 Airedale terrier. 29 Worm. 30 Heavy horse.

1 Whose final opera was called "Death in Venice"?
2 Which Greek mountain is consecrated to the muses?
3 How old was John Paul II when he became Pope?
4 Which bird is sometimes called the windhover?
5 What is the national flower of Mexico?
6 Which newscaster's autobiography was called "The Road Taken"?
7 Which was the first British newspaper to issue a colour supplement?
8 Which religious sect was founded by J. N. Darby and E. Cronin?
9 Which British king was the first to own and drive a motor car?
10 Who is the patron saint of wine growers?
11 What name is given to an alloy of mercury?
12 In which shipyards were the "Queen Mary" and "QE2" built?
13 What is the traditional name for the number 3 wood in golf?
14 By what name is the Russian, Nicolai Poliakoff, better known?
15 Who wrote the classic Irish play "Cock-a-Doodle Dandy"?
16 Who won the '96 Oscar for Best Actress?
17 What name is given to the study of the paths taken by projectiles?
18 In which US city did Martin Luther King make his historic "I have a dream" speech?
19 Which city in Ontario is known as Steel City of Canada?
20 What do maiden, mother-of-all and footman have in common?
21 Which British city is served by Aldergrove airport?
22 In tennis, what name is given to the women's World Cup?
23 In which English county was Dame Kelly Holmes born?
24 Divali, or the Festival of Lights, is a celebration in which religion?
25 Who was president of the United States during the Wall Street crash of 1929?
26 What is the name given to the female reproductive organ of a flower?
27 To which group of birds does the capercaillie belong?
28 How many people (excluding the Queen's head) were on a 2005 Second Class Christmas stamp?
29 What was the name of the pub in "Minder"?
30 Who was the king of Sparta who was husband to Helen of Troy?

Answers | Pot-Luck 32 *(see Quiz 69)*

1 Common Business Oriented Language. 2 Dromedary and Bactrian. 3 Gus Hedges. 4 Zenith. 5 Iain Duncan Smith. 6 Glasgow. 7 May 1st. 8 Pat Sullivan. 9 Morris dances. 10 The Boston Strangler. 11 6. 12 Mantilla. 13 Jacques Cartier. 14 Richard Dimbleby. 15 Time is Running Out. 16 Lindisfarne Mead. 17 George III. 18 Chicane. 19 The Ladies' Mercury. 20 Waterspout. 21 Madagascar. 22 The Sound of Music. 23 The skyscraper. 24 The Shootist. 25 The Straits of Messina. 26 Sayonara. 27 National Lottery Jackpots. 28 Trumpet. 29 Angola. 30 Patrick Lichfield.

1 What creature is unique to Skomer Island, off the Pembrokeshire coast of Wales?
2 Which is the only snake to be found regularly north of the Arctic Circle?
3 What is the smallest tiger subspecies?
4 What is a dik-dik?
5 Which animal is the symbol of the US Republican Party?
6 What are goannas and anoles?
7 Which breed of dog is a cross between an Irish wolfhound and a greyhound?
8 What general name is given to manatees and dugongs?
9 Of which family is the linsang a member?
10 What is unusual about a chameleon's eyes?
11 What region is the arrow-poison frog a native of?
12 What group of insects include German, American and common?
13 Which animal might be Siberian or Caspian?
14 What do entomophagous animals eat?
15 What are the five groups of vertebrates?
16 What are oviparous animals?
17 What do horse, snake and scorpion have in common?
18 Which largest rodent became a serious pest in East Anglia?
19 What is the world's largest burrowing herbivorous mammal?
20 Which is the largest of all the animal phyla?
21 What are stag, rhinoceros and tiger other than animals in their own right?
22 What sort of animal is a fennec?
23 Where are the ayaye the remaining endangered animals?
24 What does an impala do when frightened?
25 What country are Père David's deer native to?
26 What name is given to a mammal which bears live young?
27 What is a group of hedgehogs called?
28 What is another name for an Old English terrier?
29 What is a sand mason?
30 What is a Clydesdale?

Answers	Sport: Cricket (see Quiz 70)

1 Manchester. 2 Northants. 3 M. J. K. Smith. 4 Surrey. 5 Antigua. 6 Frank Woolley. 7 Imperial Cricket Conference. 8 England. 9 Dylan. 10 Mike Gatting, Graeme Fowler. 11 Sunil Gavaskar. 12 Pakistan. 13 England, Australia, South Africa. 14 Gillette Cup. 15 Nathan Astle. 16 Jimmy Binks. 17 Alec Stewart. 18 Ian Botham. 19 New Zealand. 20 Ricky Ponting (Australia). 21 Ranji Trophy. 22 Douglas Jardine, Surrey. 23 Fred Trueman. 24 Ashley Giles. 25 Being Freddie. 26 Brian Johnston. 27 72 Tests. 28 South Africa. 29 Jack Russell. 30 Red Stripe Cup.

1 The Plains of Abraham overlook which city?
2 What were Vince's parents called in "Just Good Friends"?
3 Which French painter and sculptor created "The Pink Nude"?
4 By what other name is the constellation Pyxis known?
5 What is majolica?
6 The London Eye is located between Westminster Bridge and which mainline station?
7 To which family of flowers does the pimpernel belong?
8 In "Footballers' Wives" what was the name of Kyle Pascoe's stalker?
9 Whose final words were, "So little done, so much to do"?
10 Which is the smallest Canadian province?
11 What are the other three Christian names of Prince Charles?
12 The Three Stars is the national ice-hockey team of which country?
13 Which animated film features the voices of Timothy Spall, Julia Sawalha and Imelda Staunton?
14 Which is the only English city whose ancient walls are complete?
15 The Sam Maguire Trophy is the major competition in which sport?
16 What is the stage name of Carol Bongiovi's rock star son?
17 Mathurin Campbell is the real name of which female singer?
18 What is General Sherman in the Sequoia National Park?
19 Who along with Sitting Bull led the Native Americans at the Battle of Little Big Horn?
20 The Pindus are the principal mountain range of which country?
21 Who wrote the award-winning play "The History Boys"?
22 In yachting, what is a metal mike?
23 Who was the first Australian cricketer to be knighted?
24 What caused Prince Albert's death in 1861?
25 Who in 1989 said, "The Communist party has no God-given right to rule"?
26 What is a basenji?
27 Which planet did Mariner 9 photograph in 1971–72?
28 "Vision of a Knight" was the work of which Florentine painter?
29 What type of animal is a bariroussa?
30 By what other name do we know the Somers Islands?

Answers | Pot-Luck 35 (see Quiz 75)

1 Missile Defence Alarm System. 2 A wild goat. 3 Lesley Garrett. 4 They are meteorites. 5 Exodus. 6 A minaret. 7 Pickpocket. 8 A distress signal. 9 Prince Henry of Portugal. 10 Glenn Miller, Chattanooga Choo Choo. 11 Nelson Mandela and F. W. de Klerk. 12 Joan Crawford. 13 NW8. 14 The Sorbonne, Paris. 15 Mexico. 16 Perth. 17 Launching missiles or stones. 18 Fidel Castro. 19 All are types of wine glass. 20 India. 21 Jenny Pitman. 22 Paraguay. 23 Ludicrus Sextus. 24 The Weir of Hermiston. 25 Bent Sorensen. 26 Shoulder blade. 27 Hungarian. 28 A single horse hair. 29 Steps. 30 Bamboo.

1 Which "Coronation Street" character was murdered by his daughter in 2005?

2 Whom did Malcolm Ryder try to poison so as to claim insurance?

3 Which EastEnder received a marriage proposal from Benny Bloom?

4 Which "Neighbours" character was killed in the fire at Lassiter's?

5 Who appeared on TV in 1974 as she held up a bank in San Francisco?

6 What feature was dropped from "The Great Egg Race" in 1981?

7 Whom did Connie Hall stab in 1988 in Dallas?

8 Who sat on a protesting lesbian during the 6 o'clock news in 1988 and who continued to read the news?

9 Which series ended when Tara King sent the main character into space?

10 Which soap saw Jason Gioberti die in its first episode?

11 Who rescued Bet when the Rovers Return caught fire?

12 Who presented the first British TV programme of birds in their natural habitat?

13 In addition to the "Blue Peter" team, who took part in the 1971 safari?

14 Who was ditched by Dame Edna for being boring?

15 How many people died in the Crossroads motel fire?

16 Who admitted that her face erupted when she first used Camay soap?

17 Who was the first British politician to have a televised state funeral?

18 Which sporting event was the first programme to be in colour?

19 What did Brian Connell have that no other newsreader had?

20 Which soap's first death was May Hardman on December 31st, 1960?

21 In which year were subtitles first included in the Queen's speech?

22 Which newsreader's drugs for epilepsy made him appear to be drunk?

23 What TV first did Gareth Jones achieve during a live transmission?

24 Whose was the first televised royal funeral?

25 Which "Blue Peter" team member was knocked out by a flying marrow?

26 What did Stephanie Rahn do in the "Sun" in 1970 to find herself on TV?

27 Which news programme was first to enter the Top 10 ratings in 1967?

28 Who made his first appearance in Albert Square in November 2002?

29 In "EastEnders", who accidentally ran over Tiffany Mitchell on New Year's Eve 1998?

30 Who was the first British newsreader to lose an earring on television?

Answers	The Simpsons (see Quiz 76)

1 Kent Brockman. 2 Yeardley Smith. 3 Kelsey Grammer. 4 Daddy. 5 Barney Gumble. 6 Herb Powell. 7 Jebediah Springfield. 8 Ned Flanders' grill. 9 Malibu Stacy dolls. 10 A Streetcar Named Desire. 11 Leonard Nimoy. 12 Milhouse van Houten. 13 Second. 14 Lute. 15 Leonard. 16 Scratchy. 17 He's a rabbi. 18 Ralph Wiggum. 19 Cough syrup. 20 Danny Elfman. 21 Vietnam War. 22 Charles Montgomery. 23 Agnes. 24 The Little Barber Shop of Horrors. 25 Ganesha. 26 Pink. 27 Happy Sumo. 28 Dark grey. 29 The Android's Dungeon. 30 Woodrow.

Quiz 75 | Pot-Luck 35 | Answers – page 313

1 What is the meaning of the acronym MIDAS?
2 What type of animal is a markhor?
3 Which performer said, "Opera's an extreme sport, like jumping out of an aeroplane with a surfboard"?
4 What do Hoba, Baruberito and Williamette have in common?
5 In which Book of the Bible is found the story of the birth of Moses?
6 What is the high tower of a Muslim mosque called?
7 What type of person could have been referred to as a cutpurse?
8 What does it mean if the Union Jack is flown upside down from a ship?
9 Which European prince was known as "the Navigator"?
10 Who received the first gold disc and for which song?
11 Which two men were awarded the Nobel peace prize in 1993?
12 Which actress's story was portrayed in the 1983 film "Mommie Dearest"?
13 What is the postcode of the world famous studio at Abbey Road?
14 Which is the oldest of the European universities?
15 In which country is the volcanic mountain called Popocétapetl?
16 By what name is St Johnstown in Scotland now known?
17 In medieval times, what was a mangonel used for?
18 Who was the chief figure in the "26th of July" movement?
19 What do tulip, balloon and flute have in common?
20 Which country has the peacock as its national bird?
21 Which former trainer created the character Jan Hardy and her racing stable?
22 Of which country is Asunción the capital city?
23 Who was Frankie Howerd's master in "Up Pompeii"?
24 What was the name of Robert Louis Stevenson's last and unfinished novel?
25 Which composer created a new work based on Andersen's "The Little Mermaid" in 2005?
26 What is the other name for the scapula?
27 What nationality was the composer Bartók?
28 In Greek mythology what was the Sword of Damocles suspended by?
29 Which chart-topping quintet announced their split on Boxing Day 2001?
30 What is the world's tallest-growing grass?

Answers	Pot-Luck 34 *(see Quiz 73)*

1 Quebec. 2 Rita, Les. 3 Henri Matisse. 4 Mariner's Compass. 5 Enamelled pottery. 6 Waterloo. 7 Primrose. 8 Sheena Hamilton. 9 Cecil Rhodes. 10 Prince Edward Island. 11 Philip Arthur George. 12 Sweden. 13 Chicken Run. 14 Chester. 15 Gaelic football. 16 Jon Bon Jovi. 17 Shola Ama. 18 Tree. 19 Crazy Horse. 20 Greece. 21 Alan Bennett. 22 Automatic helmsman. 23 Sir Donald Bradman. 24 Typhoid fever. 25 Mikhail Gorbachev. 26 A small hunting dog. 27 Mars. 28 Raphael. 29 A pig. 30 Bermuda.

Quiz 76 | The Simpsons

Answers – page 314

1 What is the name of Springfield's newsreader?
2 Who is the voice of Lisa Simpson?
3 Which sitcom actor frequently guest starred as Sideshow Bob?
4 What was Maggie Simpson's first word?
5 Who was the Plow King?
6 What is the name of Homer's half brother?
7 Who founded the town of Springfield?
8 Who or what is Propane Elaine?
9 Waylon Smithers has the world's largest collection of what?
10 Marge Simpson once starred in a musical version of which play?
11 Which former "Star Trek" actor played himself in the episode "The Springfield Files"?
12 Kirk and Luann are the parents of which character?
13 In which season was the first Halloween special "Treehouse of Horror"?
14 Martin Prince plays which instrument?
15 What is the surname of Homer's colleague Lenny?
16 In the Itchy and Scratchy cartoons which character is the cat?
17 What does Krusty the Clown's father do?
18 Which character mistakenly thought Lisa was in love with him after she sent him a Valentine's card?
19 What was the secret ingredient in the cocktail the Flaming Homer?
20 Who composed the theme music to "The Simpsons"?
21 In which war did Principal Seymour Skinner fight?
22 What are Mr Burns' christian names?
23 What is the name of Groundskeeper Willie's shovel?
24 What was the title of the first Itchy and Scratchy episode Bart and Lisa wrote under Grampa's name?
25 There is a shrine to which Hindu god in the Kwik-E-Mart?
26 What colour is Otto's T-shirt?
27 What was the name of the sushi restaurant where Homer was poisoned by a piece of blowfish?
28 What colour is Snowball II?
29 What is the name of Springfield's comic book store?
30 What was the name of the man Bart made up to reply to Mrs Krabappel's personal ad?

Answers | TV: Memorable Memories *(see Quiz 74)*

1 Tommy Harris. 2 Meg Mortimer. 3 Ethel Skinner. 4 Gus Cleary. 5 Patty Hearst. 6 The actual egg race. 7 Ray Krebbs. 8 Nicholas Witchell and Sue Lawley. 9 The Avengers. 10 Falcon Crest. 11 Kevin Webster. 12 Sir Peter Scott. 13 Princess Anne. 14 Sir Cliff Richard. 15 One. 16 Katie Boyle. 17 Sir Winston Churchill. 18 Wimbledon. 19 A beard. 20 Coronation Street. 21 1981. 22 Reginald Bosanquet. 23 He died. 24 George VI's. 25 John Noakes. 26 Became the first topless page 3 girl. 27 News at Ten. 28 Alfie Moon. 29 Frank Butcher. 30 Angela Rippon.

1 What do the initials NASA stand for?

2 What is a palmiped?

3 In which city would you find the house of the painter Rubens?

4 What had Chloe and Jack become in Great Britain by the dawn of the new millennium?

5 Who was duped by a "Fake Sheikh" in January 2006?

6 Dodonpa, Goliath and Phantom's Revenge are all names of what?

7 What do Romney Marsh, Suffolk, Clun and Forest have in common?

8 Who was the singer on the radio classic "Take It from Here"?

9 Who succeeded Pope John Paul II?

10 In "Dad's Army" what was the occupation of Private Frazer?

11 What was Casanova's occupation at the time of his death?

12 Which Dutchman won the World Darts Championship in 2006?

13 Who wrote the forensic thriller "Predator"?

14 Which organization was founded in Ontario, Canada, by Mrs Hoodless in 1897?

15 What is the British equivalent to the US trademark Plexiglas?

16 Monte Marmolada is the highest peak of which mountain range?

17 Where in Britain would you find Roedean Girls' School?

18 Which Guy Ritchie film has the tagline "a disgrace to criminals everywhere"?

19 What was referred to as Black Forty-Seven?

20 2005 was which anniversary of the game of Monopoly?

21 What are Prince Andrew's three other first names?

22 Concord is the capital of which US state?

23 What is the opposite of oriental?

24 Which of Charles Dickens' novels was left unfinished in 1870?

25 Which Scottish mathematician invented logarithms?

26 What is the longest bone in the human body?

27 Who wrote "Anything Goes" and "Can Can"?

28 In Greek legend, which prophetess was the foreteller of doom?

29 Who was nicknamed "The Beard" by the US intelligence service?

30 The carnation is the national flower of which country?

Answers | Pot-Luck 37 (see Quiz 79)

1 Sidney Poitier. 2 The Reclining Figure. 3 1951. 4 The Royal Company of Archers. 5 Sweden. 6 A numismatist. 7 Friendship 7. 8 Harry Houdini. 9 Rifle shooting. 10 Beetles. 11 A mordant. 12 December 31st. 13 St James's Palace. 14 The Times. 15 Lawn Tennis. 16 C. T. Russell. 17 Rotary Club. 18 Paris and Brussels. 19 Goodbye, Farewell and Amen. 20 Christmas crackers. 21 Balalaika. 22 Wadi. 23 Whooping cough. 24 Northern Australia. 25 Trampolining. 26 Arundel Castle. 27 Antarctica. 28 Just Rewards. 29 Jo Grimond. 30 Britney Spears.

1 Which English county has the longest coastline?

2 Who is responsible for the blue plaques in London?

3 In which London borough are there the most blue plaques?

4 What was Marble Arch originally designed to be?

5 What is the stately home owned by the Spencer family in Northamptonshire called?

6 What are Grimes Graves and where are they?

7 Where is England's largest castle?

8 Which two English cathedrals have three spires each?

9 Which county used to be divided into Parts?

10 Which dukes are associated with Woburn Abbey?

11 Where would you go to watch a Furry dance?

12 Where are St Agnes, St Martin's and Bryher?

13 Which English county bordering the sea has the shortest coastline?

14 What is the eastern strait between the Isle of Wight and the English mainland called?

15 What is the main type of rock forming the North Downs?

16 Dunkery Beacon is the highest point where?

17 On which lake does Keswick stand?

18 Which part of England is associated with the novels of Arnold Bennett?

19 Under which London landmark are buried a razor, cigars and a portrait of Queen Victoria?

20 Where is there a Nelson's column other than the one in London ?

21 What is England's smallest mainland county?

22 Which stately home in Britain is the home of the Marquess of Bath?

23 In which city is Whip-ma-Whop-ma Gate?

24 How many parishes does Greater London have?

25 In which county is there a village called Middle Wallop?

26 Which Derbyshire village lost most of its population to plague in 1665 but prevented the spread of the disease?

27 Where would you find the Bell Harry tower?

28 Which English county has the smallest perimeter?

29 What are the chalk cliff headlands between Eastbourne and Seaford?

30 Where are trees laid out in the form of troops at a famous battle?

Answers	Food and Drink: Gourmets (see Quiz 80)

1 Egon Ronay. 2 Paul and Jeanne Rankin. 3 Heston Blumenthal. 4 Savoy, Carlton. 5 Michel Roux. 6 Alastair Little. 7 Italian. 8 Raymond Blanc. 9 Thailand. 10 Clement Freud. 11 Cork. 12 Simon Hopkinson. 13 Mireille Johnston. 14 Madhur Jaffrey. 15 Prue Leith. 16 The Greenhouse restaurant. 17 Darina Allen. 18 Michael Barry. 19 Terry Wogan. 20 John Tovey. 21 Evening Standard. 22 Vegetarian. 23 Caroline Conran. 24 Dorset. 25 Gareth Blackstock. 26 Jane. 27 Mr Beeton. 28 Ready Steady Cook. 29 Fanny and Johnny Cradock. 30 Philip Harben.

1 Who was the first black actor to win an Oscar?
2 Which sculpture by Henry Moore was stolen in December 2005?
3 In which year was the Festival of Britain?
4 What is the name of the Queen's bodyguard in Scotland?
5 Which country has had more monarchs – Norway or Sweden?
6 What is a person who collects coins called?
7 What was John Glenn's Mercury capsule called when he became the first American to orbit the Earth?
8 Under what name was Erich Weiss (1874–1926) better known?
9 With what sport is Bisley in Surrey associated?
10 If you were studying coleoptera what would you be examining?
11 In dyeing, what name is given to the substance used to fix the colour?
12 When is St Sylvester's night?
13 Where was the main residence of British sovereigns from 1698 to 1837?
14 What was the first newspaper to have a "Personal Column" on its front page?
15 Which game was patented under the name Sphairistike?
16 Which American founded the Jehovah's Witnesses?
17 Which club was founded by Paul Harris and others in Chicago in 1905?
18 Which two cities were the first two capitals to have a telephone link?
19 What was the final episode of M*A*S*H called?
20 Every year which invention by Tom Smith becomes a best seller?
21 What is the name of the Russian triangular guitar?
22 What name is given to a dry watercourse in a desert?
23 What is the common name for the illness pertussis?
24 Where is the Gulf of Carpentaria?
25 In which sport are the Triffus, Miller and Rudolf moves performed?
26 Which famous castle is the country seat of the Duke of Norfolk?
27 Adélie Land is a French territory on the coast of which continent?
28 What is the final novel in the series that began with "A Woman of Substance"?
29 Which British politician became leader of the Liberal Party in 1956?
30 Who was the first artist to release a single with Madonna?

Answers Pot-Luck 36 (see Quiz 77)

1 National Aeronautics and Space Administration. 2 A web-footed bird. 3 Antwerp. 4 Most popular first names for babies. 5 Sven-Goran Eriksson. 6 Roller coasters. 7 Breeds of sheep. 8 Alma Cogan. 9 Pope Benedict XVI. 10 Undertaker. 11 Librarian. 12 Jelle Klaasen. 13 Patricia Cornell. 14 Women's Institute. 15 Perspex. 16 Dolomites. 17 Brighton. 18 Lock, Stock and Two Smoking Barrels. 19 The potato famine in Ireland. 20 75th. 21 Albert Christian Edward. 22 New Hampshire. 23 Occidental. 24 The Mystery of Edwin Drood. 25 John Napier. 26 The femur (thigh bone). 27 Cole Porter. 28 Cassandra. 29 Fidel Castro. 30 Spain.

1 Who set up the Society of British Gastronomes?
2 Which couple had a TV show called "Gourmet Ireland"?
3 Whose restaurant was named Best Restaurant in The World by Restaurant magazine in 2005?
4 At which London hotels did Auguste Escoffier gain his reputation?
5 Which chef is associated with the world-class "Waterside Inn" at Bray?
6 Whose cookery book is called "Food of the Sun"?
7 What type of food does Valentina Harris specialize in?
8 Who is the chef/proprietor of "Le Manoir aux Quat' Saisons"?
9 Vatcharin Bhumichitr has written about the taste of which country?
10 Which writer, raconteur and food expert is a former Liberal MP for Ely?
11 In which city is Murphy's Irish stout brewed?
12 Which chef is the restaurant "Bibendum" associated with?
13 Which cook and writer produced a "Cook's Tour of France"?
14 Which expert on Indian cooking is also an accomplished actress?
15 Who founded a School of Food and Wine and was instrumental in improving British Rail sandwiches?
16 Where was Gary Rhodes chef when he shot to fame on TV?
17 Who founded the Ballymaloe Cook School in Ireland?
18 Which cook is a founder of Classic FM?
19 Who wrote the foreword to the collection of recipes in book form Delia Smith compiled as a response to Live Aid?
20 Who is chef/patron of the Miller Howe, Windermere?
21 Where did Delia Smith have a cookery column before achieving fame on TV?
22 What type of cuisine does Sarah Brown specialize in?
23 Which cook has been married to the founder of "Habitat"?
24 In which county is Hugh Fearnley-Whittingstall's River Cottage?
25 What was the name of the chef played by Lenny Henry?
26 What was the first name of Sophie Grigson's mother?
27 Who founded the magazine where Mrs Beeton's articles were printed?
28 Which TV programme consists of chefs producing a dish from a limited list of ingredients against the clock?
29 Which team wrote the Daily Telegraph's "Bon Viveur" column?
30 Who wrote "Man in the Kitchen" and was a TV cookery pioneer?

Answers	Around England (see Quiz 78)

1 Cornwall. 2 English Heritage. 3 Westminster. 4 Gateway to Buckingham Palace. 5 Althorp. 6 Flint mines, Norfolk. 7 Windsor. 8 Lichfield and Truro. 9 Lincolnshire. 10 Bedford. 11 Helston, Cornwall. 12 Scilly Isles. 13 Durham. 14 Spithead. 15 Chalk. 16 Exmoor. 17 Derwent Water. 18 The Potteries. 19 Cleopatra's Needle. 20 Great Yarmouth. 21 Tyne and Wear. 22 Longleat. 23 York. 24 None. 25 Hampshire. 26 Eyam. 27 Canterbury cathedral. 28 Isle of Wight. 29 Seven Sisters. 30 Blenheim.

1 Aluminium is extracted from which ore?
2 Which US statesman defined the "four freedoms"?
3 Which fairy story writer's bicentenary was celebrated in 2005?
4 Which word, meaning "I forbid" in Latin, means the right to prevent a law being enacted or an action being taken?
5 Who was the first golfer to win 15 career majors?
6 After Earth, which planet was orbited first by a man-made object?
7 Which instrument did Albert Schweitzer play?
8 Whom did Neil Kinnock describe as "the most courteous man in the western world"?
9 In cricket, who is the fielder who patrols the boundary behind the slips?
10 Who was the last emperor of the Incas?
11 Which gland in the body produces luteinizing hormone?
12 Who was the tightrope walker who repeatedly crossed Niagara Falls?
13 Which Australian cricketer needed to score only four in his final test innings to average 100, yet only got a duck?
14 Which theory compares the Earth to a living organism?
15 Which Italian opera composer said, "In the theatre the public will stand for anything except boredom"?
16 Which star of TV's "Lost" played the hobbit Merry in "The Lord of the Rings" trilogy?
17 Which painting medium uses egg yolk and water?
18 In the Sikh religion what is kesh?
19 Which twins are represented by the zodiacal sign Gemini?
20 Who said there are "lies, damned lies and statistics"?
21 Who is known as the founding father of eugenics?
22 What was the occupation of the "Wicked Lady" in the film?
23 Whose "guest" was six-year-old Stuart Lockwood in August 1990?
24 Which British actor played Magistrate Samuel Philips in "Sleepy Hollow"?
25 In how many films did James Dean appear?
26 What was the name of the landlord in "The Young Ones"?
27 What was Jim Hacker's wife called in "Yes Minister"?
28 What is the earliest known unit of length?
29 Who won "Strictly Come Dancing" the year after Jill Halfpenny won?
30 What is an astrolabe?

Answers | Pot-Luck 39 (see Quiz 83)

1 1922. 2 Tsunami. 3 Household management. 4 Chepstow. 5 1941. 6 Two. 7 Hammond organ. 8 Donna. 9 So that he could eat without leaving the gaming table. 10 Akihito. 11 T. S. Eliot. 12 White. 13 Insects. 14 Nitrogen oxides. 15 Medulla oblongata. 16 Turmeric. 17 DC Confidential. 18 Iron. 19 Chord. 20 Kemal Ataturk. 21 Crow. 22 Thornewill. 23 Sloane Square. 24 A violin bow. 25 Charlemagne. 26 He lost his sword arm. 27 Dakota Fanning. 28 Female. 29 P. T. Barnum's. 30 Lene Marlin.

Quiz 82 | Sport: Horse Racing | Answers – page 324

1 Which horse gave Lester Piggott his first Royal Ascot winner?

2 Kieren Fallon's third Derby win was on which horse?

3 When were women first elected to membership of the Jockey Club?

4 As the Knavesmire is to York, so the Carholme was to which course?

5 Which was the first horse to win two Grand Nationals?

6 Who owned triple Grand National winner Red Rum?

7 Which Grand National winner of the 80s was named after a lighthouse?

8 Who was the first woman to ride in the Cheltenham Gold Cup in 1984?

9 Over which racecourse is the Greenham Stakes run?

10 Which horse was the first to win both the Derby and the St Leger?

11 In Britain who was the first National Hunt rider of over 1,000 winners?

12 In which year was the Derby first run?

13 Where in Doncaster did the St Leger take place before it was transferred to Town Moor?

14 Who won the flat racing jockeys' championship 26 times?

15 Who was the first trainer to turn out winners of more than £1 million in one flat racing season in Britain in 1985?

16 Which jockey won the 1970 St Leger on Nijinsky?

17 Over which racecourse is the Ebor Handicap run?

18 Which European flat race is run annually on the first Sunday in October?

19 In which years did Red Rum win the Grand National?

20 Who was the first woman to ride in the Grand National in 1977?

21 Which trainer, who died in 1983 aged 95, saddled 13 Classic winners?

22 Who was the first jockey to win both the Epsom and Kentucky Derbies?

23 Over which flat racing course is the Welsh Derby run?

24 When is a racehorse's official birthday south of the equator?

25 Which horse was the second Derby winner for the jockey who first won on Commander in Chief in 1993?

26 Who was Champion Jockey on the Flat sandwiched between Kieren Fallon's string of victories?

27 The Hambleton Cup, first run in 1612, is still run at which course?

28 Where did Jonjo O'Neill break his leg so badly that amputation was considered?

29 Which trainer's autobiography was called "The Glorious Uncertainty"?

30 Whom is the St Leger named after?

Answers | **Modern History: US Politics** (see Quiz 84)

1 Jefferson. 2 Henry Kissinger. 3 Kansas. 4 John F. Kennedy. 5 Gerald Ford. 6 Ronald Reagan. 7 Richard Nixon. 8 Rosalyn Carter. 9 Lyndon Johnson. 10 Bobby Kennedy. 11 Pamela Harriman. 12 William McKinley. 13 Alexander Haig. 14 Tipper. 15 Harry Truman. 16 Teddy Roosevelt. 17 Eisenhower. 18 George Bush. 19 Jesse Jackson. 20 Strategic Defence Initiative. 21 Polio. 22 Carl Bernstein, Bob Woodward, Washington Post. 23 Sadat, Begin. 24 Texas Rangers. 25 Ambassador to Britain. 26 Mary Jo Kopechne. 27 Nancy Reagan. 28 Spiro Agnew. 29 Washington. 30 Donald Rumsfeld.

Quiz 83 — Pot-Luck 39

1 When did Howard Carter and Lord Carnarvon find Tut's tomb?
2 What is the proper name for a tidal wave?
3 What does the word "economy" mean in the original Greek?
4 At which racecourse is the Welsh Grand National held?
5 In which year did the Japanese attack Pearl Harbor?
6 How many people feature on the front cover of John Peel's autobiography?
7 What was the electric tone-wheel organ invented in 1934?
8 What was the name of Kathy Beale's long-lost daughter in "EastEnders"?
9 Why did Lord Sandwich invent the sandwich?
10 Who succeeded Hirohito as emperor of Japan?
11 Who wrote "The Four Quartets"?
12 What colour is the cross of the Greek flag?
13 In which animals would you find compound eyes?
14 Which emissions from cars are acidic?
15 Which part of the brain controls the heart rate?
16 Which member of the ginger family is used to colour curries?
17 What were Christopher Meyer's controversial memoirs called?
18 What metallic element is found in fool's gold?
19 What name is given to the line which joins any two points on a circle?
20 Who in 1934 took the name meaning "Father of the Turks"?
21 What can be a bird or a North American Indian tribe?
22 What was the surname of the first married couple to walk to both South and North poles?
23 London's Cadogan Hall is near which famous square?
24 What did the baton replace for conducting an orchestra?
25 Who was crowned the first Holy Roman emperor in AD 800?
26 What injury did Lord Raglan, after whom the Raglan sleeve is named, sustain in battle?
27 Which child star has appeared in "Upton Girls" and "Sweet Home Alabama"?
28 Which gender of earwig has straight rather than curved pincers?
29 Whose circus did General Tom Thumb join at the age of five in 1843?
30 "Sitting Down Here" was a hit in 2000 for which artist?

Answers | Pot-Luck 38 (see Quiz 81)

1 Bauxite. 2 Franklin D. Roosevelt. 3 Hans Christian Andersen. 4 Veto. 5 Jack Nicklaus. 6 Mars. 7 Organ. 8 George Bush. 9 Third man. 10 Atahualpa. 11 Pituitary. 12 Charles Blondin. 13 Donald Bradman. 14 Gaia hypothesis. 15 Verdi. 16 Dominic Monaghan. 17 Tempera. 18 Uncut hair or beard. 19 Castor and Pollux. 20 Mark Twain. 21 Francis Galton. 22 Highwaywoman. 23 Saddam Hussein's in a TV broadcast. 24 Richard Griffiths. 25 Three. 26 Jerzy Balowski. 27 Annie. 28 Cubit. 29 Darren Gough and Lilia Kopylova. 30 Device used before the sextant for navigation.

1 The name of which US president is Bill Clinton's middle name?
2 Which US statesman won the Nobel Peace Prize in 1973, although the man he shared it with declined his award?
3 Which state did Robert Dole become senator for in 1968?
4 Under whose presidency was racial discrimination made illegal?
5 Which US president was born Leslie Lynch King?
6 Who is the only US president to have been divorced?
7 Who was the first US president to resign office?
8 Which First Lady was nicknamed the "Steel Magnolia"?
9 Which president initiated his "Great Society" programme?
10 Who was John F. Kennedy's attorney general?
11 Which American ambassador is the mother of Winston Churchill MP?
12 Which president other than John F. Kennedy was killed this century?
13 Which secretary of state announced to the world that he was in charge after the assassination attempt on Ronald Reagan?
14 What is Al Gore's wife called?
15 Which president ordered the dropping of the atomic bombs on Hiroshima and Nagasaki?
16 Which president's foreign policy was to "speak softly with a big stick"?
17 Whose memoirs were called "Mandate for Change" and "Waging Peace"?
18 Which president was a former director of the CIA?
19 Which Democrat founded what he called his "Rainbow Coalition"?
20 What was the official name of the so-called "Star Wars" programme?
21 What was the cause of Franklin D. Roosevelt's paralysis?
22 Which two journalists broke the story of the Watergate burglary and which paper did they work for?
23 Which leaders did Carter bring to Camp David to sign a peace treaty?
24 George W. Bush was part of a consortium that bought which baseball team?
25 Which post did Joseph Kennedy hold at the outbreak of World War II?
26 Whose death at Chappaquiddick stopped Ted Kennedy's ambitions?
27 Which First Lady was nicknamed the "Iron Butterfly"?
28 Who was Richard Nixon's first vice-president?
29 Where did Martin Luther King make his "I have a dream" speech?
30 Which Secretary of Defence held the post in two separate centuries?

Answers | Sport: Horse Racing (see Quiz 82)

1 Malka's Boy. 2 North Light. 3 1977. 4 Lincoln. 5 Abd-el-Kader. 6 Noel Le Mare. 7 Corbière. 8 Linda Sheedy. 9 Newbury. 10 Champion. 11 Stan Mellor. 12 1780. 13 Cantley Common. 14 Sir Gordon Richards. 15 Henry Cecil. 16 Lester Piggott. 17 York. 18 The Prix de l'Arc de Triomphe. 19 1973, 1974 and 1977. 20 Charlotte Brew. 21 Cecil Boyd-Rochfort. 22 Steve Cauthen. 23 Chepstow. 24 August 1st. 25 Galileo (Michael Kinane). 26 Kevin Darley. 27 Thirsk. 28 Bangor. 29 Jenny Pitman. 30 Lt Col Anthony St Leger.

1 Marble is formed by the metamorphosis of which rock?
2 In which country was the playwright Tom Stoppard born?
3 Which constellation is named after the mother of Andromeda?
4 Where was Europe's first hard-paste porcelain made?
5 What kind of coolant is used in a fast reactor?
6 Who tells the tales of "The Thousand and One Nights"?
7 What was Queen Victoria first "not amused" by?
8 Who gave his name to the absolute scale of temperature?
9 At the end of 2005, what was Russia's only independent media corporation?
10 Who was Wyatt Earp's brother who, with Doc Holliday, fought the Clanton gang at the OK Corral?
11 What name is given to the technology of creating and reading codes?
12 Who replaced Geoffrey Howe as foreign secretary in 1989?
13 Who was the only US president whose terms of office were not consecutive?
14 Which children's author won the 2005 Blue Peter Book of the Year award?
15 Which radio presenter wrote "Melted into Air?"
16 Beriberi results from a lack of which vitamin?
17 Where does the Lhasa Apso dog originate?
18 What did Charles Dawson "discover" in the early 20th century that was proved a fake 40 years later?
19 In which year did the "Titanic" sink?
20 Who wrote "The Wealth of Nations"?
21 In which country did the first organized motor race take place?
22 How many time zones does mainland USA have?
23 Pidgin English originally evolved for trade between Britain and where?
24 How many reeds does an oboe have?
25 Which member of the "Gang of Four" was Mao Tse Tung's third wife?
26 Where was Celtic's first match after they signed Roy Keane?
27 In the international Code of Signals what does "Oscar" signify?
28 The biography "Three Act Life" was about which actor?
29 In which Wilkie Collins novel does the villain, Count Fosco, appear?
30 Where would you go to find a wild vampire bat?

Answers	Pot-Luck 41 (see Quiz 87)

1 Stratosphere. 2 Renal artery. 3 Sicily. 4 Dolly and Cissy. 5 Marcus Garvey. 6 Amritsar. 7 Lead. 8 Derek Roberts. 9 Iran. 10 Electoral college. 11 Sylvia and Christabel. 12 Neptune. 13 Sydney University. 14 Norway. 15 Wrestling. 16 A spore-producing body in a fern. 17 Jean Paul Gaultier. 18 Alice in Wonderland. 19 Cricket St Thomas. 20 Neil Simon. 21 Barbara Taylor Bradford. 22 Edward Hopper. 23 Ivana Trump. 24 78. 25 Mae West. 26 Christina Aguilera and Ricky Martin. 27 Belshazzar. 28 Red and yellow. 29 Hyperbole. 30 Gus Grissom.

1 What were the Supremes originally called?

2 What was the family relationship of the three Ronettes?

3 Which Ronettes hit was Phil Spector's only Grammy award?

4 What occupations did Martha Reeves, Rosalind Ashford and Annette Sterling have before they were Martha and the Vandellas?

5 Who sang "Stay" in 1993?

6 Which former Atomic Kitten took part in "Celebrity Love Island"?

7 The Girls Aloud hit "Jump" was taken from the soundtrack to which festive film?

8 Which quartet consisted of Susanna Hoffs, Annette Zilinskas and Debbi and Vicki Peterson?

9 Which group were "...in the Mood for Dancing" in 1979?

10 In 2001, which trio became the first US girl group to top the UK singles chart twice?

11 "Three" was the third album by which trio?

12 Which singer replaced Florence Ballard in the Supremes?

13 What was the Crystals first UK Top Ten hit?

14 BeBe Winans sang with which group on the No 1 hit "I Wanna be the Only One"?

15 Whose hit "We are Family" became an anthem for gay rights and the Pittsburgh Pirates baseball team?

16 Which of the Spice Girls' hits was the only one not to reach No 1?

17 Which band did Girls Aloud beat to win Popstar: The Rivals?

18 What was unusual about the Crystals' hit "He's a Rebel"?

19 Jessica, Melody, Kimberly, Nicole, Ashley and Carmit make up which group?

20 "Whole Again" was the first No 1 hit for which group?

21 Which girl group recorded the album "Saints and Sinners"?

22 Which duo were "Respectable" in 1987?

23 What was the real first name of Ronnie Spector, formerly Bennett?

24 The Sugababes' "Ugly" and "Push the Button" came from which album?

25 What was it raining according to the Weather Girls in 1984?

26 What was the first UK top ten hit for Destiny's Child?

27 Which actor is waiting in the title of the Bananarama hit?

28 Who married Dave Stewart and formed Shakespear's Sister?

29 Who backed Reparata on "Captain of Your Ship"?

30 Who had a 1960s hit with "Sweet Talkin' Guy"?

Answers | The Movies: Best of British *(see Quiz 88)*

1 Sir Ian McKellen. 2 Lion in Winter. 3 Rufus. 4 Brigitte Bardot. 5 Mike Newell.
6 Kind Hearts and Coronets. 7 Killing Fields. 8 Talbot Rothwell. 9 Prime of Miss Jean Brodie. 10 Don't Lose Your Head. 11 Lavender Hill Mob. 12 Room with a View. 13 I'm All Right Jack. 14 Oliver! 15 Lewis Gilbert. 16 Third Man. 17 Turin. 18 Harmonica. 19 Christy Brown. 20 Martita Hunt. 21 84 Charing Cross Road. 22 Gordon John Sinclair. 23 Italy, China. 24 Oh, Mr Porter! 25 Richard Briers. 26 Lauri Peters. 27 Peter Finch, Glenda Jackson, Murray Head. 28 How I Learned to Stop Worrying and Love the Bomb. 29 Albert Finney. 30 Gandhi.

1 In which part of the atmosphere is the ozone layer?
2 Which artery supplies the kidney with blood?
3 Which Italian region is the source of Marsala?
4 In "Dad's Army" what were Godfrey's two sisters called?
5 Who was the founder of the Back to Africa movement who largely inspired Rastafarianism?
6 In which Indian city did British troops open fire without warning on a crowd of 10,000 in 1919?
7 Which element gains its symbol from the Latin word "plumbum"?
8 Which Sun Hill Chief Inspector died in a car bomb in March 2002?
9 In which country did polo originate?
10 What is the name of the system by which the president of the US is elected?
11 What were Mrs Pankhurst's two suffragette daughters called?
12 Which planet has a Great Dark Spot?
13 Where was Enoch Powell a professor of Greek at the age of 25?
14 Which country's parliament is called the Storting?
15 Which sport has two main styles, called freestyle and Greco-Roman?
16 What is a "sorus"?
17 Which fashion designer created Madonna's famous conical bra?
18 Unsuk Chin's song cycle "Snag & Snarls" is based on which children's story?
19 In which village was Penelope Keith "To the Manor Born"?
20 Which playwright wrote "Barefoot in the Park" and "The Odd Couple"?
21 The biography "A Woman of Substance" was about which novelist?
22 Which painter caught the loneliness of city life in the 1930s and 1940s?
23 Who on the break-up of her marriage said "Gimme the Plaza, the jet and 150 million dollars"?
24 How many cards are there in a tarot pack?
25 Who said, "I used to be Snow White, but I drifted"?
26 Which vocalists released the single "Nobody Wants to be Lonely" in 2001?
27 In the Bible, which king of Babylon saw his own death prophesied?
28 What two colours are on a semaphore flag?
29 What is the deliberate use of exaggeration for emphasis called?
30 Who was the first man to go into space twice?

Answers | Pot-Luck 40 (see Quiz 85)

1 Limestone. 2 Czechoslovakia. 3 Cassiopeia. 4 Dresden. 5 Sodium. 6 Scheherazade. 7 An imitation of herself. 8 Kelvin. 9 Media Most. 10 Virgil. 11 Cryptography. 12 John Major. 13 Grover Cleveland. 14 Michael Morpurgo. 15 Sandi Toksvig. 16 Vitamin B1. 17 Tibet. 18 Piltdown Man. 19 1912. 20 Adam Smith. 21 France. 22 Four. 23 China. 24 Two. 25 Chiang Ch'ing. 26 Inverness (Caledonian Thistle). 27 Man overboard. 28 Anthony Hopkins. 29 The Woman in White. 30 South America.

1 Which actor from 2005's "The Magic Roundabout" was born in Burnley?

2 For which film did Katharine Hepburn win the first best actress BAFTA?

3 In "Love Actually" what is the name of Rowan Atkinson's jewellery salesman?

4 Who played opposite Dirk Bogarde in "Doctor at Sea"?

5 Who directed "Four Weddings and a Funeral"?

6 Which Ealing comedy was based on Roy Horniman's "Noblesse Oblige"?

7 Which 1984 film was based on "The Death and Life of Dith Pran"?

8 Who was the most prolific writer of "Carry On" scripts?

9 In which film did Maggie Smith call her girls "The crème de la crème"?

10 Which Carry On film was (very) loosely based on the Scarlet Pimpernel?

11 In which Alec Guinness film does a bank clerk carry out a bullion robbery?

12 Which 1986 film had "O Mio Babbino Caro" as its theme?

13 In which Boulting Brothers film did Ian Carmichael star as a graduate who starts work in a factory and causes a national strike?

14 Which musical was "the most non-U subject ever to be given a U certificate"?

15 Who directed "Educating Rita" and "Shirley Valentine"?

16 Which British film was the first non-French film to win the prestigious Palme d'Or at the Cannes Film Festival in 1949?

17 In which city does "The Italian Job" take place?

18 On what instrument is the music for the film "Genevieve" played?

19 Who was played by Daniel Day-Lewis in "My Left Foot"?

20 Who played Miss Haversham in David Lean's "Great Expectations"?

21 In which film was Anne Bancroft writing to a London bookseller?

22 What is John Gordon Sinclair called in the credits to "Gregory's Girl"?

23 "The Last Emperor" was a collaboration on film between Britain and which two other countries?

24 In which Will Hay movie does he play a haunted stationmaster?

25 Who plays Peter's father in Kenneth Branagh's "Peter's Friends"?

26 Who starred opposite Cliff Richard in "Summer Holiday"?

27 Which three actors made up the love triangle in "Sunday Bloody Sunday"?

28 What was the alternative title of "Dr Strangelove"?

29 Who turned down the role of T. E. Lawrence in "Lawrence of Arabia"?

30 Which film opens with the dedication "No man's life can be encompassed in one telling"?

| **Answers** | Pop: All-Girl Groups *(see Quiz 86)* |

1 The Primettes. 2 Two sisters, one cousin. 3 Walking in the Rain. 4 Motown secretaries. 5 Eternal. 6 Liz McClarnon. 7 Love Actually. 8 The Bangles. 9 The Nolans. 10 Destiny's Child. 11 Sugababes. 12 Cindy Birdsong. 13 Da Do Ron Ron. 14 Eternal. 15 Sister Sledge. 16 Stop. 17 One True Voice. 18 It wasn't the Crystals singing on the record. 19 The Pussycat Dolls. 20 Atomic Kitten. 21 All Saints. 22 Mel and Kim. 23 Veronica. 24 Taller in More Ways. 25 Men. 26 No, No, No. 27 Robert de Niro. 28 Siobhan Fahey. 29 The Delrons. 30 The Chiffons.

1 On the logo on an iPod which side of the apple is missing?
2 Which title did Bill Gates take on stepping down as Chief Executive Officer of Microsoft?
3 What do we call human-like robots?
4 What do the black bars and white spaces of bar codes represent?
5 What are optical fibres made from?
6 Who invented the mouse?
7 Which device converts chemical energy into electrical energy?
8 What was the name of the first communications satellite?
9 What does "laser" stand for?
10 Which separate companies invented and promoted the CD-ROM?
11 Which company developed the first electronic pocket calculator?
12 What device enables computers to send data down a telephone line?
13 Which software program was launched in 1982 by Lotus?
14 What name is given to a computer screen which responds to touch?
15 What does BASIC stand for?
16 What is the study of automated communication and control mechanisms in machines and humans called?
17 What do we call the wafer of silicon that carries miniaturized circuits?
18 What did the US company Diablo invent for use on typewriters?
19 How many bits or binary elements has a byte?
20 What is the largest bulletin board system (BBS) in the world?
21 What was the name of the first working electromechanical computer?
22 What is the name of the European Space Agency's satellite navigation system?
23 Who marketed the first dot matrix printers in 1957?
24 In digital communication terms what does MIME stand for?
25 What phrase applies to graphics programs which interact with people?
26 What was ARPANET a forerunner of?
27 What was launched in November 1985 by Microsoft?
28 Who invented the first calculating machine in 1642?
29 What term is given to part of a computer's memory that has its program permanently fixed?
30 Who developed the laser printer?

Answers	Foreign Literature *(see Quiz 91)*

1 Vaclav Havel. 2 Goethe. 3 Anton Chekhov. 4 Voltaire. 5 Dario Fo. 6 Pushkin. 7 Crimean War. 8 Actor. 9 Dostoyevski. 10 Czech. 11 Jakob, Wilhelm. 12 Rhinocéros. 13 The Blue Angel. 14 Honoré de Balzac. 15 Molière. 16 Omar Khayyam (Rubaiyat). 17 Aleksandr Solzhenitsyn. 18 Belgian. 19 Don Quixote. 20 Boris Pasternak (Doctor Zhivago). 21 Marcel Proust. 22 Aviator. 23 Les Fleurs du Mal. 24 Stendhal. 25 The Caucasian Chalk Circle. 26 Dreyfus. 27 Argentinian. 28 Simone de Beauvoir. 29 Jean-Paul Sartre. 30 George Sand.

1 Where was the Canadian goldrush which began in 1896?
2 Parsley belongs to which family?
3 Radioactivity is measured in which units?
4 What initials are used to describe chronic fatigue syndrome?
5 What device was originally used to explore the depths of an ocean?
6 What type of burial mounds date from the the early Bronze Age?
7 Which cricketer said about his autobiography, "I can honestly say that I've written one more book than I've read"?
8 In which year was the European Economic Community established?
9 Which "Casualty" character was played by an actor featured in "Strictly Come Dancing" 2005?
10 During which battle did the charge of the Light Brigade take place?
11 RP is the standard form of English accent – what do the letters stand for?
12 Which London bridge links St Paul's Cathedral to Tate Modern?
13 From which boat did Jacques Cousteau conduct his underwater research?
14 Which coin ceased to be legal tender from January 1st, 1991?
15 What is the feast of the Purification of the Virgin Mary?
16 From what colour rock is the Jordanian city of Petra carved?
17 In "Rising Damp" what is Rigsby's cat called?
18 What is the term for the energy obtained from hot underground rocks?
19 Where were the 2006 Winter Olympics held?
20 What does "lager" literally mean in German?
21 Who was appointed Chief Inspector of Schools in 1994?
22 What are crosses between bulldogs and terriers called?
23 Which element was used in the manufacture of the first florin?
24 To which Anglican movement did Newman, Pusey and Keble belong?
25 Which society was founded in London in 1884 to promote socialist ideas peacefully and to establish a socialist state in Britain?
26 Who was the French soldier whose constant drilling made his name a byword for strict discipline?
27 Which space probes failed to find life on Mars?
28 What was Beethoven's only opera?
29 What sort of creature was the best-selling robotic toy Teksta?
30 Where does the Australian Open Tennis Championship take place?

Answers | Pot-Luck 43 *(see Quiz 92)*

1 Spike Milligan. 2 Samuel Goldwyn. 3 Rolf Harris. 4 Saitama in Japan. 5 Mass. 6 Man Ray. 7 Brookfield. 8 Baron Munchhausen. 9 The Rubicon. 10 Carbolic acid. 11 Pluto. 12 Pink. 13 Steve Waugh. 14 24. 15 Meriwether Lewis and William Clark. 16 Orchid. 17 Korea. 18 Trevor McDonald. 19 Fleur. 20 Etruscan. 21 Hindenburg. 22 John Stuart Mill. 23 Citroën. 24 Holly. 25 Farsi. 26 Cremona. 27 Descent of Man. 28 Fred Quimby. 29 The pressure of fluids. 30 Harrison.

1 Which Czech dramatist became president after the fall of communism?
2 Which German poet was prime minister to the Duke of Saxe-Weimar?
3 Which Russian dramatist married one of the actresses in his company?
4 Which French philosopher and writer was imprisoned in the Bastille and also wrote the fable "Candide"?
5 Which Italian dramatist wrote "Can't Pay, Won't Pay" in 1974?
6 Who wrote the novel Eugene Onegin?
7 In which war was "War and Peace" author Tolstoy on active service?
8 Before success as a writer what did Hans Christian Andersen do?
9 Which Russian novelist was sentenced to hard labour in Siberia in 1849 for printing socialist propaganda?
10 Franz Kafka wrote in German but what nationality was he?
11 What were the first names of the brothers Grimm?
12 In which Eugène Ionescu play do the characters turn into animals?
13 Which famous film is Heinrich Mann's "Professor Unrat" based on?
14 Who wrote a sequence of 94 novels under the title "La Comédie Humaine"?
15 Which French playwright's real name was Jean Baptiste Poquelin?
16 Which Iranian poet's most famous translator was Edward Fitzgerald?
17 Which Russian dissident's memoirs were called "The Oak and the Calf"?
18 What was the nationality of "Maigret" creator Georges Simenon?
19 What is Cervantes' parody of chivalric literature called?
20 Which Russian declined the 1958 Nobel prize after his novel about his mother country was published in Italy?
21 Who wrote "A la Recherche du Temps Perdu"?
22 What was the occupation of the author of "Le Petit Prince"?
23 What is the French title of Baudelaire's "The Flowers of Evil"?
24 Which French novelist's real name was Marie Henri Beyle?
25 Which Brecht play presents a dilemma about motherhood?
26 Whom was Zola defending in his open letter "J'accuse"?
27 What is the nationality of short-story writer Jorge Luis Borges?
28 Which French feminist writer wrote "The Second Sex"?
29 Which World War II member of the French resistance wrote "Nausea"?
30 How is Amandine Aurore Lucie Dupin better known?

Answers | Hi-Tech (see Quiz 89)

1 Right. 2 Chief Software Architect. 3 Androids. 4 Binary numbers. 5 Pure glass. 6 Douglas Engelbart. 7 Battery. 8 Telstar. 9 Light amplification by stimulated emission of radiation. 10 Philips invented, Sony promoted. 11 Texas Instruments. 12 Modem. 13 1-2-3. 14 Tactile screen. 15 Beginners All-purpose Symbolic Instruction Code. 16 Cybernetics. 17 Silicon chip. 18 Daisy wheel printer. 19 8. 20 CompuServe. 21 Coloccus. 22 Galileo. 23 IBM. 24 Multipurpose Internet Mail Extension. 25 Virtual reality. 26 Internet. 27 Windows. 28 Pascal. 29 Read Only Memory. 30 Canon.

Quiz 92 | Pot-Luck 43

Answers – page 330

1 Who played the part of Eccles in "The Goon Show"?

2 Which film mogul said, "include me out"?

3 Whose portrait of the Queen was unveiled in December 2005?

4 Where was the John Lennon Museum opened on October 9th 2000?

5 In the general theory of relativity what causes space-time to be modified?

6 How was the Parisian photographer Emmanuel Rudnitsky better known?

7 In "The Archers", at which farm do Phil and Jill Archer live?

8 Which 18th-century German soldier was famous for his exaggerated accounts of his adventures?

9 On crossing which river did Julius Caesar say, "The die is cast"?

10 What did Lister use to improve the hygiene of surgical operations?

11 What did the astronomer Clyde Tombaugh discover in 1930?

12 "Try This" was the third album by which female artist?

13 Which former sporting captain called his autobiography "Out of My Comfort Zone"?

14 In a standard cine film how many frames are shown each second?

15 Which two explorers did Jefferson send to find a land route to the Pacific?

16 Which type of flower has pods which are a source of vanilla?

17 Where does the martial art taekwondo originate?

18 Which newscaster said "Goodnight and goodbye" in December 2005?

19 In "May to December" what was Alec and Zoe's baby called?

20 Excavating the tombs of which civilization revealed lively paintings showing feasting, dancing and swimming?

21 Which airship exploded in New Jersey in 1937?

22 Which English economist sat as a Radical in Parliament during 1865–68 and urged votes for women?

23 Who made history with the first front-wheel drive vehicle in 1934?

24 In "Red Dwarf" what was the spaceship's computer called?

25 What is the official language of Iran?

26 In which Italian city did Antonio Stradivari and Niccolò Amati make their violins?

27 Which book by Darwin discussed human evolution?

28 Who was the producer of the Tom and Jerry cartoons until 1956?

29 What does a manometer measure?

30 What surname did the 9th and 23rd presidents of the US share?

Answers | **Pot-Luck 42** (see Quiz 90)

1 Yukon. 2 Carrot family. 3 Becquerels. 4 ME. 5 A bathyscaph. 6 Round barrows. 7 Merv Hughes. 8 1957. 9 Woody. 10 Balaclava. 11 Received pronunciation. 12 Millennium Bridge. 13 Calypso. 14 5p pieces, which were the old shilling. 15 Candlemas. 16 Red. 17 Vienna. 18 Geothermal energy. 19 Turin. 20 Store. 21 Chris Woodhead. 22 Boston terriers. 23 Gold. 24 The Oxford Movement. 25 Fabian Society. 26 Jean Martinet. 27 Viking probes. 28 Fidelio. 29 Dog. 30 Flinders Park, Melbourne.

1 Which British dependent territory has a capital called the Valley?
2 The name of the capital of which country means "good air"?
3 Other than in Scotland, where is there a capital called Edinburgh?
4 What is the capital of Venezuela?
5 What is capital of Belarus?
6 What is the capital of the largest country in Europe after Russia?
7 Which US state's capital is the name of a lively 1920s' dance?
8 "One Night" in where is the name of a song from the musical "Chess"?
9 Oranjestad is the capital of Aruba but to whom does it belong?
10 Which fabric was originally made in Syria's capital?
11 In which US state's capital is the headquarters of the Mormon Church?
12 Which island's capital is Flying Fish Cove?
13 Which US state capital has the longest name?
14 In which capital was Gordon besieged for 10 months and then murdered?
15 Which African capital was sold to Italy in 1905?
16 What is the name of Greenland's capital, formerly Godthab?
17 Which country's capital is the end of a motor rally from Paris?
18 What shape is the Kremlin in Russia's capital, Moscow?
19 Which capital is linked to Almada by a bridge over the River Tagus?
20 Which US state capital is the name of the man credited with "discovering" America?
21 Which capital city has a state within it?
22 Which Arab capital's name is the name of a sweet dessert wine?
23 What did Abuja replace as Nigeria's capital?
24 Why is the Government Building in Wellington so notable?
25 Which Mexican state's name and state capital are also the name of a breed of small dog?
26 Which capital was founded in 1566 by the Knights of St John?
27 What is the capital of Malawi?
28 Which African capital's name was the name of a hit song by Tommy Steele in 1958?
29 "They Came to" which Middle Eastern capital in the title of a mystery by Agatha Christie?
30 Who sang about the capital of Catalonia in 1992?

Answers	Sports Bag *(see Quiz 95)*

1 Troon. 2 Geoff Howarth. 3 David Bryant. 4 Bradford. 5 Greyhound Racing Association. 6 Walter Swinburn. 7 1979. 8 Susan Brown. 9 Johnny Weissmuller. 10 Pat Smythe. 11 Curling. 12 Terry Griffiths. 13 Wimbledon. 14 Ayr. 15 Paavo Nurmi. 16 Four players. 17 100-metre breaststroke. 18 The Cresta Run. 19 Basketball. 20 Sonny Liston. 21 Parc des Princes. 22 Notts County. 23 Heather McKay. 24 Sandy Lyle. 25 Argentinian. 26 Doug Mountjoy. 27 Sampras and Agassi. 28 Hurst Park. 29 Multan. 30 Sydney, Australia.

Quiz 94 | Pot-Luck 44

Answers – page 336

1 What dye is named after a battle fought near Milan in 1859?
2 Which group of insects includes a hairstreak?
3 What component of CFCs causes destruction of ozone?
4 Which part of the gut absorbs water from the food?
5 Which pop star and pianist has a mother whose first name is Bong?
6 The mother and son of which king of England were both beheaded?
7 Which element is used in the preparation of light-sensitive film?
8 The Digambaras and the Swetambaras are sects of which religion?
9 What word for unthinking patriotism is derived from the name of one of Napoleon's admirers?
10 What metal is used for the filament in a light bulb?
11 Which planet has the lowest density?
12 Who was Millie, whose book was on the US bestsellers' list in 1990?
13 Margaret Thatcher and David Cameron share which star sign?
14 Which type of bond is most common in organic molecules?
15 How many wickets did Freddie Flintoff claim in the 2005 Ashes series?
16 Who was the first actress to turn up and accept a Razzie Award for Worst Actress?
17 Who converted the Louvre from a palace to an art gallery?
18 Which Marx brother was the piano player?
19 With which civilization did the legend of the phoenix begin?
20 Which veteran TV presenter called his autobiography "I Should Have been at Work"?
21 Whose theories of population growth helped Darwin form his theory?
22 What did social reformer George Williams found in 1844?
23 Whose plays include "Anna Christie" and "Mourning Becomes Elektra"?
24 In which battle were the British commander, Wolfe, and the French commander, Montcalm, both killed?
25 What is it called when the length of day controls the start of flowering?
26 Who wrote bad verse about the Tay Bridge disaster of 1879?
27 Who were the first to use tear gas in warfare and against whom?
28 Whose first film as a director was "Ordinary People"?
29 After a crash at Le Mans who stopped motor racing for over 30 years?
30 Which modern instrument was developed from the sackbut?

Answers | Pop: The Rolling Stones *(see Quiz 96)*

1 40 Licks. 2 Lennon and McCartney. 3 The Last Time. 4 Alexis Korner's. 5 Aftermath. 6 Sitar. 7 Drowned in pool. 8 Jean-Luc Godard. 9 Ned Kelly. 10 Jade. 11 Andy Warhol. 12 Jamaica. 13 Undercover. 14 Je suis un rock star. 15 David Bowie. 16 Willie and the Poor Boys. 17 Freejack. 18 Chuck Berry. 19 X-Pensive Winos. 20 Virgin. 21 Ian Stewart. 22 Muddy Waters. 23 Charlie Watts. 24 As Tears Go By. 25 Jeff Beck. 26 Have You Seen Your Mother Baby Standing in the Shadow? 27 Let's Spend the Night Together. 28 Brown Sugar. 29 Rolling Stones No 2. 30 2002.

Quiz 95 | Sports Bag

1 On which British golf course is the hole called the "postage stamp"?
2 Which New Zealand cricket captain also captained Surrey?
3 Who was the first world champion at bowls in 1966?
4 Which is the home town of Joe Johnson, the snooker player?
5 Which sport's governing body carries the initials GRA?
6 Which jockey rode Shergar when it won the 1981 Derby?
7 When did Seve Ballesteros win the first of his Open championships?
8 Who was the first woman to compete in the Boat Race?
9 Which Olympic swimmer played the film role of Tarzan?
10 Who won the British Show Jumping Association Ladies' championship eight times?
11 The Air Canada Silver Broom is won in which sport?
12 Which Welshman won the world snooker championship in his first season as a professional?
13 At which course is the greyhound racing classic, the Laurels, run?
14 Over which course is the Scottish Grand National run?
15 Whose statue is outside the Olympic Stadium in Helsinki?
16 How many golfers before Tiger Woods had won all four majors?
17 At which event did Duncan Goodhew win an individual gold at the 1980 Moscow Olympics?
18 The St Moritz Tobogganing Club stages which famous race?
19 What is the modern name of "Pok-ta-Pok", which originated in Mexico?
20 Whom did Muhammad Ali beat to win the World Heavyweight boxing championship in 1964?
21 On which ground does France play its home rugby union matches?
22 Which is the oldest club in the Football League, founded in 1862?
23 Which woman squash player was unbeaten for 16 years from 1962?
24 Who became the first British golfer to win the European Open in 1979?
25 What nationality is lawn tennis player Gabriela Sabatini?
26 Whom did Steve Davis defeat in his first world snooker title final in 1981?
27 Which two tennis stars contested both the 1990 US Open and 2002 Open?
28 Which racecourse used to be alongside the Thames near Hampton Court?
29 Where did England lose the first Test to Pakistan in 2005?
30 Where is Randwick racecourse situated?

Answers | Geography: Capitals II *(see Quiz 93)*

1 Anguilla. 2 Argentina. 3 Tristan da Cunha. 4 Caracas. 5 Minsk. 6 Kiev, Ukraine. 7 West Virginia. 8 Bangkok. 9 Netherlands. 10 Damask. 11 Utah. 12 Christmas Island. 13 Jefferson City. 14 Khartoum. 15 Mogadishu. 16 Nuuk. 17 Senegal. 18 Triangular. 19 Lisbon. 20 Ohio. 21 Rome. 22 Muscat. 23 Lagos. 24 It's made of wood. 25 Chihuahua. 26 Valletta. 27 Lilongwe. 28 Nairobi. 29 Baghdad. 30 Montserrat Caballé, Freddie Mercury.

1 What was the name of the 2003 world tour?
2 Who wrote their first Top Twenty hit?
3 Which was their first No 1 to be written by Jagger and Richard?
4 In which blues band did both Mick Jagger and Charlie Watts perform?
5 From which album was the US chart entry "Mother's Little Helper"?
6 Which instrument did Brian Jones play, other than guitar, on "Their Satanic Majesties Request"?
7 How did Brian Jones die?
8 Which French director made The Stones film "One Plus One"?
9 Which Australian outlaw did Mick Jagger play on film?
10 What is the name of Mick Jagger's daughter by his first wife, Bianca?
11 Who designed the sleeve and logo on "Sticky Fingers"?
12 Where did they record the album "Goat's Head Soup"?
13 Which 1983 video for the title track was banned?
14 Which record was a hit for Bill Wyman in 1983?
15 Whom did Mick Jagger sing "Dancing in the Street" with at Live Aid?
16 What was the name of Bill Wyman's group that performed charity gigs?
17 Which sci-fi thriller did Mick Jagger appear in in 1992?
18 Who was the subject of the film "Hail Hail Rock 'n' Roll", for which Keith Richards directed the music?
19 Who were Keith Richards' band on "At the Hollywood Palladium"?
20 For which record label did the Stones sign a deal in 1991?
21 Who was dropped from the group in its early days because "he looked too normal"?
22 Whose song were the Rolling Stones named after?
23 Which Stone described his career as "five years of playing and 20 of hanging about"?
24 Which Jagger-Richard song was Marianne Faithfull's first hit?
25 Which famous guitarist played on Jagger's album "She's the Boss"?
26 Which 1960s Stones' hit had the longest title?
27 What was on the other side of "Ruby Tuesday"?
28 What was their first hit on their own Rolling Stones record label?
29 What was the Rolling Stones' second album called?
30 To a year either way, when did Mick Jagger become Sir Mick?

| **Answers** | Pot-Luck 44 *(see Quiz 94)* |

1 Magenta. 2 The Lycaenidae, a family of butterflies. 3 Chlorine. 4 Colon. 5 Myleene Klass. 6 James I (Mary Queen of Scots and Charles I). 7 Silver. 8 Jainism. 9 Chauvinism. 10 Tungsten. 11 Saturn. 12 George and Barbara Bush's dog. 13 Libra. 14 Covalent. 15 24 wickets. 16 Halle Berry. 17 Napoleon. 18 Chico. 19 Egyptian. 20 Des Lynam. 21 Thomas Malthus. 22 YMCA. 23 Eugene O'Neill. 24 Quebec. 25 Photoperiodism. 26 William McGonagall. 27 Germans against Russians in World War I. 28 Robert Redford. 29 Mercedes Benz. 30 Trombone.

1 Huntingdon is the birthplace of which ruler of England?

2 To whom is the Dunmow Flitch awarded each year?

3 About whom did Otto Preminger say, "Directing her was like directing Lassie. You need 14 takes to get each one of them right"?

4 In "The Archers", which character "died" in the run-up to Christmas 2005?

5 Which "Professionals" were played by Lewis Collins and Martin Shaw?

6 Which married couple were Time magazine's People of the Year in 2005?

7 Besides Hadrian, which Roman emperor had a wall built across Britain?

8 How are train robbers Parker and Longbaugh better known?

9 What are the Christian names of the two brothers who formed Bros?

10 Which soap star released an exercise DVD called "Busy Life Workout"?

11 In which year did the ten-shilling note cease to be legal tender?

12 In "The Odyssey", into what did the witch Circe change the sailors?

13 In heraldry, what colour is gules?

14 Rolf Harris was once Australian Junior Champion at what?

15 Which country won the soccer World Cup in 1982?

16 In Scotland what is or was a tawse?

17 King Jigme Singwe Wangchuck is king of which country?

18 Holi is a spring religious festival. In which religion?

19 Who wrote the poems "Ozymandias" and "Ode to the West Wind"?

20 What does a psephologist study?

21 Which large island is said to have been discovered by Eric the Red?

22 Which comedy drama had the theme song "That's Living Alright"?

23 In mythology which riddle was solved by Oedipus?

24 Which novelist wrote the book "Westward Ho!"?

25 Who wrote "A Wayne in a Manger"?

26 What was the first Red Hot Chili Peppers album to reach number one?

27 Who directed Mia Farrow in "Rosemary's Baby"?

28 If someone is lachrymose, what do they do a lot?

29 Who appoints the BBC's board of governors?

30 Between which towns was the railway for Stephenson's first locomotive?

Answers | Pot-Luck 46 (see Quiz 99)

1 Their shorthand could not be deciphered. 2 All Gas and Gaiters. 3 Arlene Phillips. 4 Red and green. 5 London bombings. 6 Vostok 1. 7 Battle of Actium. 8 12. 9 James Hanratty. 10 Her surname (credited as Emma). 11 Bill of Rights. 12 Albania. 13 Saturn. 14 Michael Jackson. 15 Yalta. 16 Sonja Henie. 17 Paraguay. 18 Six. 19 Amelia Earhart. 20 Francis Maude. 21 Methane. 22 Sibneft. 23 Barbara Hepworth. 24 Romania. 25 Gertrude Stein. 26 Edward Teller. 27 Noriega. 28 Printing. 29 The Empire Strikes Back. 30 Bovine spongiform encephalopathy.

Quiz 98 | Hollywood Heyday | Answers – page 340

1 Which studio had a lion as its symbol?
2 Why didn't some of the cast of "Gone with the Wind" see its première?
3 Whose roles included characters called McLain, McLintock and McQ?
4 Which future politician was beaten by Elizabeth Taylor for the role of Velvet Brown in "National Velvet"?
5 Who starred with Bergman and Grant in "Notorious"?
6 In which film did Bette Davis play Margo Channingt?
7 How was Ronald Reagan overlooked for a cinematic "White House"?
8 For which film were live leeches imported to Africa?
9 Which artist devised the dream sequence in "Spellbound"?
10 Who was voted king of Hollywood in 1937?
11 Which Astaire-Rogers film had the Oscar-winner "Cheek to Cheek"?
12 What was the first film co-starring Humphrey Bogart and Lauren Bacall?
13 In 1933 who choreographed "42nd Street" in which Ginger Rogers had a lesser role as Anytime Annie?
14 In which film did James Cagney play vaudevillian George M. Cohan?
15 Who was "The Hunchback of Notre Dame" in 1923?
16 Which classic was based on "The Tin Star" by John W. Cunningham?
17 In which movie did Gary Cooper play a farmer who became a war hero?
18 Who played "Mildred Pierce"?
19 Which 1948 classic was described as "Greed, gold and gunplay on a Mexican mountain of malice"?
20 What was Citizen Kane's real first name?
21 What was shown at the beginning of Paramount pictures?
22 Which John Wayne western was described as "'Grand Hotel' on wheels"?
23 What was Cary Grant's real name?
24 Which musical was the first to pair Mickey Rooney and Judy Garland?
25 What were the names of the four Warner Brothers?
26 What is the name of the drunk played by James Stewart in "Harvey"?
27 What did Cary Grant donate his salary from "The Philadelphia Story" to?
28 Which film star's real name was Reginald Truscott-Jones?
29 Which western hero is the subject of "My Darling Clementine"?
30 Which film opens with an office memo including the words "I killed Dietrichson. Me. Walter Neff, insurance salesman, 35 years old..."?

Answers | Bestsellers *(see Quiz 100)*

1 Blue. 2 Agatha Christie. 3 Webster's Dictionary. 4 Harper Lee. 5 Frederick Warne. 6 Thirteen and three-quarters. 7 Catch 22. 8 Guinness Book of Records. 9 Mickey Spillane. 10 The Remains of the Day. 11 Hold the Dream. 12 Catherine Cookson. 13 Cranberries. 14 Joan Collins'. 15 Nelson Mandela. 16 Dan Brown. 17 Peter Benchley. 18 Jung Chang. 19 Joanne Harris. 20 Delia Smith. 21 Wales. 22 Lady Chatterley's Lover. 23 Riders. 24 Kate Hannigan. 25 Alistair MacLean. 26 Ruth Rendell. 27 Danielle Steel. 28 Robert. 29 Mary Wesley. 30 Dr Benjamin Spock.

1 Why were Samuel Pepys' diaries not published until after 1825?
2 Which sit com was set in and around St Ogg's Cathedral?
3 Which person with "Strictly Come Dancing" links was involved in adapting "Saturday Night Fever" for stage?
4 Which two colours are mixed in a television to produce yellow?
5 Which event caused Tony Blair to leave the 2005 Gleneagles G8 summit?
6 What was Yuri Gagarin's spacecraft called?
7 In which battle did Rome defeat the forces of Antony and Cleopatra?
8 What is the atomic number for magnesium?
9 Who was hanged for the A6 murder?
10 What did Emma Bunton drop when she charted with "Free Me"?
11 What name is given to the first ten amendments to the US constitution?
12 Zog was king of which country from 1928 to 1939?
13 Which planet has the largest number of moons?
14 Whose first solo hit was "Got to be There"?
15 Where did Roosevelt, Churchill and Stalin meet in 1945?
16 Which Norwegian Olympic skating champion featured in many Hollywood films in the 1930s and 1940s?
17 Which country's currency is the guaraní?
18 How many carbon atoms are there in the phenol molecule?
19 In 1937 which woman flyer vanished without trace over the Pacific?
20 Who was the Conservative Party Chairman at the time of the 2005 leadership election?
21 What is the main constituent of natural gas?
22 What was the name of Roman Abramovich's oil company which he sold in 2005?
23 Which English sculptress exhibited her "Mother and Child" in 1930?
24 Which country had a secret police called Securitate, banned in 1990?
25 Who said, "Rose is a rose is a rose is a rose"?
26 Who worked on the Manhattan Project and later testified against its director, Robert Oppenheimer?
27 Which Central American dictator had the nickname "Pineapple Face"?
28 Which industry uses the gravure method?
29 Which was the second of the Star Wars films?
30 Often known as mad cow disease, what do the initials BSE stand for?

Answers | Pot-Luck 45 *(see Quiz 97)*

1 Oliver Cromwell. 2 The year's happiest newlywed couple. 3 Marilyn Monroe. 4 Betty Tucker. 5 Bodie and Doyle. 6 Bill and Melinda Gates. 7 Antoninus. 8 Butch Cassidy and the Sundance Kid. 9 Matt and Luke. 10 Debra Stephenson. 11 1970. 12 Pigs. 13 Red. 14 Swimming (backstroke). 15 Italy. 16 Strap, leather belt. 17 Bhutan. 18 Hinduism. 19 Shelley. 20 Elections, how people vote. 21 Greenland. 22 Auf Wiedersehen Pet. 23 The Riddle of the Sphinx. 24 Charles Kingsley. 25 Gervase Phinn. 26 By the Way. 27 Roman Polanski. 28 Cry. 29 The Queen. 30 Stockton and Darlington.

1 What colour was the flying Ford Anglia in "Harry Potter and the Chamber of Secrets"?

2 Which author said, "An archaeologist is the best husband a woman can have; the older she gets, the more interested he becomes in her"?

3 According to the Bob Hope/Bing Crosby song, which bestseller is Morocco bound as they were they were in the Road film?

4 Who wrote "To Kill a Mockingbird"?

5 Who has published Beatrix Potter's "Tale of Peter Rabbit" since 1902?

6 How old was Adrian Mole when he started writing his autobiography?

7 Which Joseph Heller book describes a "no win" situation?

8 Which book is the bestselling contemporary book of recent years?

9 Who created the detective Mike Hammer?

10 Which prize-winning novel by Kazuo Ishiguro became a successful film?

11 What was the second in Barbara Taylor Bradford's Emma Harte series?

12 Who holds the record as the novelist most borrowed from libraries?

13 Which fruit appears on the cover of Delia Smith's "Winter Collection"?

14 Whose sister wrote "Hollywood Wives"?

15 Whose autobiography was called "Long Walk to Freedom"?

16 Which author wrote with his wife, "187 Men to Avoid: A Guide for the Romatically Frustrated Woman"?

17 Who wrote the book on which the film "Jaws" was based?

18 Who wrote "Wild Swans"?

19 Which author, apparently with a sweet tooth, wrote "Blackberry Wine"?

20 Who cooked through the four seasons?

21 In the books about Inspector Morse where does Lewis come from?

22 About which book did a judge once ask if it was the sort of thing you would want your wife or servant to read?

23 Which book's hero is Rupert Campbell-Black and Jake his main rival?

24 What was Catherine Cookson's first novel?

25 Who wrote 30 books, with 28 of them selling a million in Britain?

26 Who sets her detective novels in Kingsmarkham?

27 Whose novels include "Lightning", "Accident" and "The Gift"?

28 What is the first name of Dr Atkins, author of a "New Diet Revolution"?

29 Whose first novel, "Jumping the Queue", came out when she was 70?

30 Who wrote a multi-million bestseller about child care in 1946?

Answers	**Hollywood Heyday** *(see Quiz 98)*

1 MGM. 2 All-white cinema. 3 John Wayne. 4 Shirley Williams. 5 Claude Rains. 6 All About Eve. 7 Rejected for Rick in Casablanca (White House). 8 The African Queen. 9 Salvador Dali. 10 Clark Gable. 11 Top Hat. 12 To Have and to Have Not. 13 42nd Street. 14 Yankee Doodle Dandy. 15 Lon Chaney. 16 High Noon. 17 Sergeant York. 18 Joan Crawford. 19 Treasure of the Sierra Madre. 20 Charles (Foster). 21 Mountain. 22 Stagecoach. 23 Archie Leach. 24 Babes in Arms. 25 Jack, Harry, Samuel, Albert. 26 Elwood. 27 War relief. 28 Ray Milland. 29 Wyatt Earp. 30 Double Indemnity.

1 In which country did Eddie Cochrane die?
2 What does the South African secretary bird kill and eat?
3 In Venice, what links the Ducal Palace with the state prison?
4 The African and French marigolds are both natives of which country?
5 In which speech did President Lincoln state that American government: was "of the people, by the people, for the people"?
6 Stephen Tompkinson, Eddie Izzard and Richard Wilson all guest starred on which comedy programme?
7 Who stood against Margaret Thatcher for the Tory leadership in 1989?
8 Which Israeli Prime Minister suffered a stroke in January 2006?
9 Which monarch had as one of his titles "The Lion of Judah"?
10 "The Happy Campers" was the first band formed by which Scottish solo singer?
11 Which forbidden river can no pure Hindu pass?
12 What was Madonna's first UK No 1 single when she was a 40 something?
13 Who is the patron saint of grave diggers?
14 In which part of the body is pepsin produced?
15 Bell metal is an alloy of which two metals?
16 Who wrote "Guy Mannering"?
17 What descriptive term is applied to Force 11 on the Beaufort scale?
18 Which Sunday paper was launched in January 1990?
19 What does the letter A stand for in Quango?
20 Who was the second Pope?
21 In which year was the first Wembley FA Cup Final to need a replay?
22 What did Del Boy in have written on the side of his car?
23 Who was the founder in 1945 of the Theatre Workshop, which moved to Stratford in east London in 1953?
24 The term "veteran" refers to cars made up to the end of which year?
25 What did the Germans codename "Operation Barbarossa"?
26 Which English king was nicknamed "The Hammer of the Scots"?
27 The marimba is an African form of which instrument?
28 Whose book "Flanimals" was published in 2004?
29 In "The Archers" what is the name of the church in Ambridge?
30 Whom did Stephen Hendry beat to become the youngest-ever world snooker champion in 1990?

Answers	Eat and Drink: Pubs (see Quiz 104)

1 Isle of Man TT course. 2 The Nutshell. 3 X. 4 Grand Stand Bar. 5 Grace Neill's Bar. 6 The Fighting Cocks. 7 North Yorkshire. 8 The George Inn. 9 The Horse Shoe. 10 Crown Liquor Saloon. 11 Medieval farmhouse. 12 The Dove. 13 Stalybridge. 14 Brazen Head Inn. 15 Earl Grey. 16 Woolpack, Malt Shovel. 17 Southport. 18 Coach & Horses. 19 Chichester. 20 Downham Tavern. 21 Lovejoy. 22 Olde Trip to Jerusalem 23 The Dove, Hammersmith 24 Recruitment centre for the Napoleonic Wars. 25 Blue Peter. 26 Munich. 27 Lou's Place. 28 The B.B.C. 29 The Snowdon Summit Bar. 30 Red Lion.

Quiz 102 | Pop: Writers

Answers – page 346

1 Who wrote "Wichita Lineman" and "By the Time I Get to Phoenix"?

2 Who co-wrote Eurovision "Puppet on a String" with Bill Martin?

3 Which songwriting pair penned hits in the rock 'n' roll era such as "Teenager in Love" and "Save the Last Dance for Me"?

4 Who won an Oscar for their writing of the title song of "Born Free"?

5 Along with Chris Martin and Guy Berryman who wrote the Coldplay album "A Rush of Blood to the Head"?

6 Who helped Shania Twain pen the hit "Man! I Feel Like a Woman!"?

7 Who wrote "Sailing", recorded by Rod Stewart?

8 Who replaced Bernie Taupin as Elton John's lyricist in 1979?

9 Who wrote the satirical "Dedicated Follower of Fashion"?

10 Which Neil Diamond song was the Monkees' first No 1?

11 What product was advertised in the Cook & Greenaway hit of 1971?

12 Who wrote Chris Farlowe's No 1 hit "Out of Time"?

13 Which singer sold more than 15 million records of the songs of Bacharach and David between 1962 and 1970?

14 Who wrote "It's Not Unusual" for Tom Jones?

15 Which songwriting trio established the Invictus and Hot Wax labels?

16 Which classical pianist became a pop writer with Howard Greenfield?

17 Which songwriting pair wrote "The Locomotion" for Little Eva?

18 Which 10cc member wrote "For Your Love" for The Yardbirds?

19 Which Lennon and McCartney song was Cilla Black's first single?

20 Who was named "Officer of Arts and Letters" by France in 1993?

21 Which group was Stephen Stills with before Crosby, Stills, Nash and Young?

22 Which member of the Killers has a writing credit for all the tracks on their "Hot Fuss" album?

23 Who wrote Cliff Richard's first chart topper "Livin' Doll"?

24 Who wrote "Georgy Girl" and "I'll Never Find Another You"?

25 Who wrote the song which begins "I feel it in my fingers..."?

26 Who wrote the lyrics for Cliff Richard's "Heathcliff" musical?

27 Who wrote "If Not for You", a hit for Olivia Newton-John in 1971?

28 Who wrote the biggest-ever selling soundtrack album of its day in 1978?

29 How many tracks from David Gray's "White Ladder" album were written by him alone?

30 Which member of Fleetwood Mac wrote "Albatross"?

Answers Pot-Luck 49 (see Quiz 105)

1 Glandular fever. 2 Time. 3 Richard Pryor. 4 Brighton Rock. 5 Opera. 6 King of Britain. 7 Kensal Green Cemetery. 8 The kidneys. 9 The checkered tablecloth once used for accounting. 10 Ignace Jan Paderewski. 11 "Clock" symphony. 12 Edith Mary Coates. 13 The River Rhine. 14 Burke. 15 Daily Universal Register. 16 Paul Rudd. 17 365. 18 Songthrush. 19 Jacques Brel. 20 Japan. 21 Henri Rousseau. 22 Noel Coward. 23 The Island of Sodor. 24 The Poor Clares. 25 Edward Kennedy. 26 Brazil. 27 Wind. 28 1577. 29 Heinrich Himmler. 30 Marcus.

1 What is Muckle Flugga?

2 Which Flemish painter produced "Adoration of the Kings"?

3 Who was described by the "Radio Times" as "The scummiest toerag in the great laundry basket of English history"?

4 Which French engineer conceived the idea of the Suez Canal?

5 On which day is Canada's Dominion Day or Canada Day celebrated?

6 What was the "Gluckauf" the first of its kind?

7 Who was the criminal who used a violin case for carrying his tools?

8 Which pop star had Slave written on his cheek, as a protest about his dealing with Warner?

9 In which needlecraft is honeycomb stitch worked?

10 Which two surveyors drew a line to set the boundary of Pennsylvania and Maryland?

11 What was the occupation of Mary Read and Anne Bonny?

12 Italian dictator Benito Mussolini previously had which two jobs?

13 Which US film director's work includes "Taxi Driver" and "Raging Bull"?

14 Peter Stringfellow, Lionel Blair and Peter Andre made guest appearances playing themselves on which programme?

15 On whose novel was the film "Lassie Come Home" based?

16 Which film was considered to be the first of the spaghetti westerns?

17 How is Shalimar described in the title of Salman Rushdie's novel?

18 Which film of 1934 gained an Oscar for the song "The Continental"?

19 Who was the voice of Donkey in Shrek 2?

20 What is the German term printed on labels of a high-quality wine?

21 What type of soup is Dubarry?

22 Which football team play at Tannadice Park?

23 When was the radio-only licence fee abolished?

24 Who joined French and Saunders in the quartet of "Girls on Top"?

25 In canasta, how many playing cards are needed?

26 Where would you find Amsterdam Island, Kerguelen and Crozet Island?

27 What is the Australian name for a kind of long, narrow lake?

28 Where would you find a canal in a national park in Britain?

29 For what is Peter the Hermit particularly known historically?

30 Why was Aberdeen's win over Celtic in the 1990 Scottish Cup Final a famous first?

Answers   **Sport: Football** *(see Quiz 106)*

1 Mark Walters. 2 Wigan. 3 Queen's Park. 4 Frank McLintock. 5 Steve McManaman. 6 Stoke City. 7 Cardiff. 8 Stelios Giannakopoulos. 9 Back Home. 10 A C Milan. 11 Aldershot. 12 Kevin Keegan. 13 Kenny Dalglish. 14 Solskjaer. 15 Blackpool. 16 Ron Saunders. 17 Queen Alexandra, Edward VII's consort. 18 Leeds United. 19 Ray Wilkins. 20 Real Madrid. 21 Northampton. 22 Millwall. 23 Parma. 24 David Batty. 25 Jasper Carrott. 26 Tommy Docherty. 27 Wembley. 28 Liverpool. 29 Gordon Strachan. 30 Ronaldinho.

Quiz 104 Eat and Drink: Pubs

Answers – page 341

1 On which famous course is the Sulby Glen Hotel?
2 What is the name of the tiny pub in Bury St Edmunds?
3 What was the previous name of the "Merry Harrier" in Devon which gave it the shortest pub name in the country?
4 What's the bar Galway Racecourse which is 210 feet long called?
5 What is said to be the oldest pub in Northern Ireland?
6 Which pub in St Albans is an 11th-century building?
7 In which county is the elevated Tan Hill Inn?
8 Which pub in Southwark is mentioned by Dickens in "Little Dorrit"?
9 Which pub in Drury Street, Glasgow, has one of the longest bars in Britain?
10 Which Belfast pub in Great Victoria Street is owned by the National Trust?
11 What was the Fleece Inn in Evesham before it became a licensed house?
12 What is the name of the pub, with the smallest bar room, in Upper Mall Chiswick?
13 Where is "The Old Thirteenth Century Cheshire Astley Volunteer Rifleman Corps Inn"?
14 What is the name of the 17th-century pub in Lower Bridge Street, Dublin?
15 Which Gloucestershire pub with a small bar room shares its name with a type of tea?
16 Which two pubs feature in the soap "Emmerdale"?
17 Where will you find "The Lakeside Inn" reputed to be Britain's smallest?
18 Which Soho pub was Jeffrey Barnard's regular haunt?
19 Where is the Gribble Inn which makes its own Black Adder II?
20 Which pub in Bromley, built in 1930, is said to be the country's largest?
21 Which antique dealer might you have met at the Butt & Oyster in Suffolk?
22 Which East Midlands pub served soldiers prior to going to fight the Crusades?
23 In which Hammersmith pub was "Rule Britannia" written?
24 Why is "The Napoleon" in Boscastle, Cornwall, so called?
25 Which pub in Polperro, Cornwall, shares its name with a TV programme?
26 In which city is the largest beer-selling establishment in the world?
27 What was the name of the pub destroyed by fire in "Neighbours" in 2005?
28 The George in Great Portland Street, London is which Auntie's local?
29 Where is the highest place you can buy beer in Wales?
30 What is the commonest name for a pub?

Answers   Pot-Luck 50 (see Quiz 107)

1 As You Like It. 2 Stop Living the Lie. 3 Gold centre, then red, blue, black, white. 4 Tennis, anyone? 5 Margaret Beckett. 6 Victoria and Euston. 7 Admiral John Jellicoe. 8 Aeroflot. 9 Highest point of the city. 10 Silk screen painting. 11 Moldova. 12 3-tined fork. 13 A mollusc. 14 Apple. 15 Lizard. 16 American Indians in the United States. 17 Graham Sutherland. 18 The Coach. 19 Andromeda. 20 A mess of pottage. 21 Stained glass. 22 March 15th. 23 All are varieties of roses. 24 Clock face. 25 Dermot. 26 A large hat. 27 Wales. 28 Woodrow Wilson. 29 Grand National. 30 Tony Warren, creator of Coronation Street.

Quiz 105 Pot-Luck 49

Answers – page 342

1 What illness is caused by the Epstein-Barr virus?
2 What is the first word of Madonna's hit "Hung Up"?
3 Which comedian and co-writer of "Blazing Saddles" died in December 2005?
4 In which of Graham Greene's novels does Pinkie appear?
5 Ellen Kent specializes in which type of touring entertainment?
6 What title is held by Shakespeare's "Cymbeline"?
7 Which cemetery is the resting place of Thackeray and Trollope?
8 Which organ of the body is affected by Bright's Disease?
9 How did the word "exchequer" come into being?
10 In 1919 which pianist was elected prime minister of Poland?
11 What is the nickname of Haydn's Symphony No 101 in D major?
12 Which mezzo-soprano created the role of Auntie in "Peter Grimes"?
13 On which river is the rocky cliff of the Lorelei located?
14 What was Calamity Jane's married name?
15 What was "The Times" first known as, in 1785?
16 "Friends" character Mike Hannigan was played by which actor?
17 How many islands make up the Calendar Islands in Casco Bay?
18 By what name is the mavis better known?
19 Who wrote the song known in English as "If You Go Away"?
20 Of which country is the Easter lily a native?
21 Whose jungle paintings inspired the 2005 film "Madagascar"?
22 Which British playwright said, "Never trust a man with short legs – brains too near their bottoms"?
23 What is the imaginary setting for the Rev. W. Awdry's "Railway Series"?
24 Which sisterhood established at Assisi around 1212 adopted the Franciscan rule and habit?
25 Which US politician shares his name with with Duke Ellington?
26 Nossa Senhora da Aparecida is the patron saint of which country?
27 What would be measured with an anemometer?
28 To five years either way, in what year did Francis Drake begin his voyage around the world?
29 Whom did Hitler choose to head the SS in 1929?
30 In "Birds of a Feather" what is Dorien's husband called?

Answers | Pot-Luck 47 (see Quiz 101)

1 England. 2 Snakes. 3 The Bridge of Sighs. 4 Mexico. 5 Gettysburg Address. 6 Father Ted. 7 Sir Anthony Meyer. 8 Ariel Sharon. 9 The emperor of Ethiopia. 10 KT Tunstall. 11 Attock. 12 Music. 13 St Anthony. 14 Stomach. 15 Copper and tin. 16 Sir Walter Scott. 17 Storm. 18 The Independent on Sunday. 19 Autonomous. 20 Saint Linus. 21 1970. 22 Trotter's Independent Trading Company. 23 Joan Littlewood. 24 1918. 25 The invasion of the Soviet Union. 26 Edward I. 27 Xylophone. 28 Ricky Gervais. 29 St Stephen's. 30 Jimmy White.

Quiz 106 | Sport: Football

Answers – page 343

LEVEL 3

1 Which former Liverpool player's middle name was Everton?
2 After 19 games Peter Crouch managed his first Liverpool goal, but who were the opponents?
3 What is Scotland's oldest club?
4 Who captained Arsenal when they won the League and Cup in 1970–71?
5 Which English player featured in Real Madrid's 2002 Champions League Final triumph?
6 Which club, formed in 1863, won their first trophy 109 years later?
7 Which was the first Welsh side to win the FA Cup?
8 Which member of the Greek squad that won Euro 2004 played for Bolton?
9 What was the England World Cup Squad's No 1 hit in 1970?
10 Inzaghi, Rui Costa and Seedorf played together at which club?
11 Which football club folded in 1992 after 66 years in the League?
12 Which soccer player advertised "Brut" in the 1980s?
13 Who was the first Scot to make 100 appearances for his country?
14 Who hit Man Utd's late winner in the 1999 European Champions League Final?
15 With whom did Alan Ball begin his playing career?
16 Who was the first soccer manager to manage all three Birmingham clubs – Aston Villa, Birmingham and West Brom?
17 Who or what is Alexandra in Crewe Alexandra?
18 At which club were Robbie Fowler and Nigel Martyn team-mates?
19 Which England captain was sent off when captaining the side in 1986?
20 Who won the European Cup in the first five seasons from 1955 to 1960?
21 Which Football League club went from the fourth to the first division in five seasons in the 60s?
22 Which was the first 3rd division side to reach FA Cup semis?
23 Gianfranco Zola was a Chelsea player, but which club did he join them from?
24 Who missed the final penalty in England's 1998 World Cup campaign?
25 Who said on supporting Birmingham, "You lose some, you draw some"?
26 Which manager said he'd been in more courts than Bjorn Borg?
27 Which stadium hosted its first FA Cup semi-final in 1991?
28 Which team first won an FA Cup semi-final on a penalty shoot-out?
29 Who was the first Footballer of the Year in England and Scotland?
30 Who scored Brazil's winner in the 2002 World Cup game vs England?

| **Answers** | **Pop: Writers** *(see Quiz 102)* |

1 Jimmy Webb. 2 Phil Coulter. 3 Pomus and Shuman. 4 John Barry and Don Black. 5 Jonny Buckland and Will Champion. 6 Robert John "Mutt" Lange. 7 Gavin Sutherland. 8 Gary Osborne. 9 Ray Davies. 10 I'm a Believer. 11 Coca Cola (I'd Like to Teach the World to Sing). 12 Mick Jagger, Keith Richard. 13 Dionne Warwick. 14 Les Reed. 15 Holland Dozier Holland. 16 Neil Sedaka. 17 Gerry Goffin, Carole King. 18 Graham Gouldman. 19 Love of the Loved. 20 Elton John. 21 Buffalo Springfield. 22 Brandon Flowers. 23 Lionel Bart. 24 Tom Springfield. 25 Reg Presley. 26 Tim Rice. 27 Bob Dylan. 28 The Bee Gees. 29 Six. 30 Peter Green.

1 Sienna Miller was in which Shakespeare play, in the West End in 2005?
2 What was the first single by "Fame Academy" winner David Sneddon?
3 Starting at the centre, what are the five colours of an archery target?
4 What was the only line that Humphrey Bogart had in his first play?
5 In the 1990s, who was acting leader of the Labour Party after the sudden death of John Smith?
6 Name the first railway hotels opened in London in September 1839.
7 Who was the commander of the British fleet at the Battle of Jutland?
8 Which airline was originally called Dobrolet?
9 What is the literal meaning of acropolis ?
10 What is the common name for the craft known as serigraphy?
11 Who were the opponents when David Beckham made his first appearance for England?
12 What is a runcible spoon?
13 The shipworm is not a worm. What is it?
14 What is Gwyneth Paltrow's daughter called?
15 What is a chuckwalla?
16 Marlon Brando refused to accept his Oscar for "The Godfather" because of the oppression of which people?
17 Who painted the 80th-birthday portrait of Sir Winston Churchill?
18 In "Cheers" what was Ernie Pantouso's nickname?
19 Which constellation represents a princess in Greek mythology?
20 In the Book of Genesis, what did Esau get in return for his birthrigh?
21 Chartres cathedral in France is famed for what particular feature?
22 Julius Caesar was murdered on the Ides of March. What date was this?
23 What do Paddy McCready, Elizabeth of Glamis and Dorothy Perkins have in common?
24 In "Safety Last" where is stunt actor Harold Lloyd seen hanging from?
25 Whom did Harry Enfield play in "Men Behaving Badly"?
26 What kind of clothing is a dolly varden?
27 In which country was the explorer HM Stanley born?
28 Who was in office as president of the United States when the decision was taken to declare war on Germany during World War I?
29 Which major sporting event took place the same day as Charles and Camilla's wedding?
30 Whose autobiography was called "I was Ena Sharples' Father"?

Answers | Pot-Luck 48 (see Quiz 103)

1 The rock & lighthouse on Uist. 2 Brueghel. 3 Black Adder. 4 de Lesseps. 5 July 1st. 6 Custom-built oil tanker. 7 Charles Peace. 8 Prince. 9 Smocking. 10 Mason and Dixon. 11 Pirates. 12 Teaching, journalism. 13 Martin Scorsese. 14 Footballers' Wives. 15 Eric Knight's. 16 A Fistful of Dollars. 17 Shalimar the Clown. 18 The Gay Divorcée. 19 Eddie Murphy. 20 Kabinett. 21 Cream of cauliflower. 22 Dundee United. 23 1971. 24 Tracey Ullman, Ruby Wax. 25 108, two packs and four jokers. 26 Indian Ocean. 27 Billabong. 28 Brecon Beacons. 29 Led the First Crusade. 30 Decided on a penalty shoot-out.

How to Set Up Your Own
Pub Quiz

It isn't easy, get that right from the start. This isn't going to be easy. Think instead of words like "difficult", "taxing", "infuriating". Consider yourself with damp palms and a dry throat and then, when you have concentrated on that, put it out of your mind and think of the recognition you will receive down the local, imagine all the regulars lifting you high upon their shoulders dancing and weaving their way around the pub. It won't help but it's good to dream every once in a while.

What you will need:

- A good selection of Biros (never be tempted to give your own pen up, not even to family members)
- A copy of *The Best Pub Quiz Book Ever*
- A set of answer sheets photocopied from the back of the book
- A good speaking voice and possibly a microphone and an amp
- A pub
- At least one pint inside you
- At least one more on your table
- A table

What to do:

Choose your local to start with; there is no need to get halfway through your first quiz and decide you weren't cut out for all this and then find yourself in the roughest pub in Christendom 30 miles and a long run from home.

Chat it through with the landlord and agree on whether you will be charging or not; if you don't then there is little chance of a prize for the winners other than a free pint each and this is obviously at the landlord's discretion – if you pack his pub to bursting then five free pints won't worry him, but if it's only you and a couple of others then he may be less than unwilling, as publicans tend to be. If you decide on an entry payment keep it reasonable; you don't want to take the fun out of the quiz; some people will be well aware that they have very little hope of winning and will be reluctant to celebrate the fact by mortgaging their house.

Once location and prize are all sorted then advertising the event is paramount. Get people's attention, sell, sell, sell or, alternatively, stick up a gaudy-looking poster on the door of the bogs. Be sure to specify all the details, time, prize and so on – remember you are selling to people whose tiny attention span is being whittled down to nothing by alcohol.

After this it is time for the big night. If you are holding the event in the "snug" which seats ten or so you can rely on your voice, if not you should get hold of a good microphone and an amplifier so that you can boom out your questions and enunciate the length and breadth of the pub (once again, clear this with the landlord and don't let liquid anywhere near the electrical equipment). Make sure to practise, and get comfortable with the sound of your own voice and relax as much as possible, try not to rely on alcohol too much or "round one" will be followed by "rown' too" which will eventually give way to "runfree". Relax your voice so that you can handle any queries from the teams, and any venomous abuse from the "lively" bar area.

When you enter the pub make sure you take everything listed above. Also, make sure you have a set of tie-break questions and that you instruct everybody who is taking part as to the rules – and be firm. It will only upset people if you start handing out impromptu solutions, and let's face it the wisdom of Solomon is not needed when you are talking pub quiz rules; "no cheating" is a perfectly healthy stance to start with.

Finally, keep the teams to a maximum of five members, hand out your answer papers and pens and, when everybody is good and settled, start the quiz. It might not be easy and it might not propel you to international stardom or pay for a life of luxury but you will enjoy yourself. No, really.

ANSWERS

1 _____	**16** _____
2 _____	**17** _____
3 _____	**18** _____
4 _____	**19** _____
5 _____	**20** _____
6 _____	**21** _____
7 _____	**22** _____
8 _____	**23** _____
9 _____	**24** _____
10 _____	**25** _____
11 _____	**26** _____
12 _____	**27** _____
13 _____	**28** _____
14 _____	**29** _____
15 _____	**30** _____

ANSWERS

Part Two

1 _____

2 _____

3 _____

4 _____

5 _____

6 _____

7 _____

8 _____

9 _____

10 _____

11 _____

12 _____

13 _____

14 _____

15 _____

16 _____

17 _____

18 _____

19 _____

20 _____

21 _____

22 _____

23 _____

24 _____

25 _____

26 _____

27 _____

28 _____

29 _____

30 _____

ANSWERS

Part Three

1 _____

2 _____

3 _____

4 _____

5 _____

6 _____

7 _____

8 _____

9 _____

10 _____

11 _____

12 _____

13 _____

14 _____

15 _____

16 _____

17 _____

18 _____

19 _____

20 _____

21 _____

22 _____

23 _____

24 _____

25 _____

26 _____

27 _____

28 _____

29 _____

30 _____